HEBRIDEAN ISLAND HOPPING

A GUIDE FOR THE INDEPENDENT TRAVELLER

Martin Coventry

BIRLINN

Published by
Birlinn Limited
West Newington House
10 Newington Road, Edinburgh EH9 1QS
www.birlinn.co.uk

ISBN 13: 978 1 84158 440 9
ISBN 10: 1 84158 440 1

British Library Cataloguing-in-Publication Data
A catalogue record for this book is available from the British Library

Printed by Antony Rowe Ltd., Chippenham
Design, maps and typesetting by Martin Coventry
Goblinshead, 130B Inveresk Road, Musselburgh EH21 7AY, Scotland
goblinshead@sol.co.uk

DISCLAIMER
The information contained in this Hebridean Island Hopping
(the "Material") is believed to be accurate and complete at the time of
printing, but no representation or warranty is given (express or implied) as
to its accuracy, completeness or correctness. The author and publisher
do not accept any liability whatsoever for any direct, indirect or
consequential loss or damage arising in any way from any use of or
reliance on this Material for any purpose.

While every care has been taken to compile and check all the information
in this book, in a work of this complexity it is possible that mistakes and
omissions may have occurred. If you know of any corrections, alterations
or improvements, please contact the author (goblinshead@sol.co.uk) or
the publisher at the addresses above.

HEBRIDEAN ISLAND HOPPING

CONTENTS

Acknowledgments	vi
Preface	vii
How to Use the Book	x
Useful Information	xiii
Useful Contacts	xvii
Glossary	xix
Place-Name Elements	xxiii
Selected Further Reading	xxvi
List of Maps	xxix
Map of Islands	xxx
List of Islands (Alphabetical)	1
Skye	4
Raasay	38
Rona	42
Isle Martin	44
Summer Isles	45
Rum	48
Eigg	52
Muck	55
Canna and Sanday	57
Coll	60
Tiree	66
Mull	74
Iona	94
Erraid	100

Ulva   101
Staffa   103
Treshnish Isles   105

Lismore   108
Kerrera   113

Seil   116
Easdale   120
Luing   122
Shuna   126

Islay   128
Jura   142
Colonsay and Oronsay   148

Gigha   154

Bute   159
Cumbrae   168
Arran   173
Holy Island   187
Sanda   189
Ailsa Craig   191

Lewis   194
Great Bernera   213
Harris   217
Scalpay   228
Taransay   230
Shiant Isles   232
North Uist   234
Berneray   245

Baleshare   248
Benbecula   250
Grimsay   256
South Uist   258
Eriskay   266
Barra   270
Vatersay   277
Mingulay   280

St Kilda or Hirta   282

Index   286

ACKNOWLEDGMENTS

Thanks to everyone who checked or read over entries for the individual islands: these are listed at the end of the entry for each island – I apologise if I have forgotten anyone. Especial thanks to Joyce Miller who looked over the text, and Miss Ching-man Chan who also assisted in checking the information. It should be pointed out that, although every attempt has been made to provide accurate, up-to-date and relevant information, any mistakes, inaccuracies or flaws in the text are solely my responsibility and not those who kindly helped.

Photographs are by Martin Coventry or Joyce Miller (copyright © Martin Coventry/Joyce Miller 2006), except where stated in the acknowledgments section for each island and below.

I would like to thank for their kind permission to use illustrations (acknowledgments are in the section at the end of each entry):

COLIN PALMER (images courtesy Colin Palmer – www.buyimage.co.uk) Fine landscape prints together with digital images for publications taken throughout the Hebrides are available on-line at www.buyimage.co.uk

THE NATIONAL TRUST FOR SCOTLAND
Thanks to Isla Robertson

GEORGE LOGAN
Photography, web design, picture library and picture research (www.scottish-photography.co.uk)

ANDY GRAY
Andy Gray Digital (www.andygraydigital.com)

Also to thanks to **GEORGI COVENTRY, BILL** at Rona, **JEAN WILDER** (Summer Isles), **PETER MACKAY** (Coll), **JOHN KIRRIEMUIR** (Berneray) and **ALASDAIR MCKENZIE** (Benbecula)

PREFACE

I came to the Hebrides later in life than many, and I was rapidly approaching my twenty-eighth birthday before I had island-hopped my way onto any of the Hebrides.

Then my sister, who worked for a well-known wine retailer and had been involved in a whisky promotion, was given the chance to stay on Islay in cottages owned by the distillery at Bunnahabhain. It was a sufficiently large property to house two generations of the Coventry family, so we decided to go off en masse, packed the car, and departed for the west.

It was the end of March as we drove the long and roundabout route by Loch Fyne down to Kennacraig and the ferry to Islay. I was not looking forward to the trip as my last experience had been in something approaching a gale coming back across the Pentland Firth from Orkney. That had been two years before in April and the weather had been appalling: I had been sandblasted to the bone at Skara Brae, snowed on at Kirkwall and had shivered my timbers around all the sites. The ferry back rolled like a log in the mountainous seas: sky – sea – sky – sea – sky – sea – kerrang – sky – sea – sky – sea – kerrang, as waves broke against the hull. As we drove through Tarbert and approached Kennacraig my thoughts were along such dismal and queasy lines.

I need not have worried, of course. It was gloomy but the wind was light and apart from a slight swell mid-passage nothing to concern even the most anxious passenger (which I certainly was). We drove off the ferry at Port Askaig, covered the short distance to Bunnahabhain and were soon ensconced in Shore Cottages.

And I fell in love with the place, and then other islands, a love affair which has intensified over the years.

Undoubtedly some of this initial attraction was to do with the weather – we had a week of almost unbroken sunshine, although it was cold – but I was struck by the sheer beauty of the place, and the history, and the different feel to the grime and grind and bustle of everyday life. There was the magnificent Kildalton Cross, and the shattered ruin of Dunyvaig Castle, a tour of Bowmore distillery, going through the picturesque villages of Port Charlotte and Port Wemyss, visiting the fascinating Museum of Islay Life, searching for the elusive Cultoon stone circle, moving the stones sunwise at the cross at Kilchoman for good luck, discovering Finlaggan was closed (it was March and in those days you needed a boat to get out to the islands), walking on the sands at Traigh Gruinart and on to Kilnave where many MacLeods were burnt to death following the battle in 1598, and then a walk along the coastal path to the wreck of the *Wyre Majestic* in the Sound of Islay with the Paps of Jura in the background: impossibly sharp in the eldritch evening spring sun. Not only was it a beautiful island but the food was good, the people were friendly, and there were all those different whiskies from all the distilleries to sample.

It was a fantastic week, and we decided there and then to visit as many of the islands as we could, starting with Mull the next year, and then followed by Skye, Lewis and Harris, the Uists and Benbecula, Arran and then Bute. And from then on as many as time and holidays would allow.

I have many fantastic memories of the islands from down the years.

Reading the weather correctly when Scarba disappeared, and sheltering in the smallest cafe in the world outside the shop on Luing, eating ice cream, as the heavens opened and rain came down in buckets.

The most awe-inspiring sunrise with the sky lit up like the end of the world on our way to catch the ferry on our last day on North Uist.

My father putting glowing peat embers into a plastic waste bin even though it clearly said 'no hot ashes'.

The sausages on a roll on the CalMac ferry to Tiree and the fish and chips on the way back.

Climbing to the viewpoint over the flooded quarries and the Firth of Lorn on Easdale before sitting outside in the sun and consuming stovies and lager at the Puffer Bar.

Coming into close proximity with a family of Highland cattle (bull and all) on the track around Kerrera – undoubtedly the largest beasts with which I have ever come face to face, and luckily the most disinterested and docile. And seeing feral goats the same day. And Gylen Castle. And stunning scenery.

Negotiating the causeways out to Dun an Sticer and the slaister of mud to Teampuill na Trionaid on North Uist.

Watching the crashing waves at the Butt of Lewis on a calm day, and wondering what it would be like when it was windy.

Three local people stopping on the road to the ferry at Scarinish on Tiree and asking us if we would like a lift (I guess I looked a little hot), notwithstanding the traffic-calming measures at several points on the island, suggestive of the speeds some folk drive, even on single-track roads.

Not being able to open the car door at Kilmuir on Trotternish because it was so windy, and the Old Man of Storr appearing oh so briefly from the white mist like a ghost, before vanishing again in a blink of an eye.

The stubborn sheep on Lewis, who simply refuse to move off roads (locals nudge them off with their cars) and then follow visitors round fields in ever-growing flocks.

Fresh crabs and seafood on Gigha and the beauties of Achamore Gardens and buying plants from there for our own garden.

The scent of dog-roses and honeysuckle, and carpets of bluebells, and yellow flag irises, and wild flowers on the machair on many islands.

The peace and tranquillity and lovely scenery on Iona despite all the many people: you can see why Columba chose to found a monastery there.

The stones at Callanish in the snow ... the Cuillin hills looking like a location for *Lord of the Rings* as we drove down from Dunvegan ... Moy Castle and

Lochbuie and wondering if the headless horseman of the MacLaines might make an appearance ... once seeing Ben More on Mull without any cloud ... Uig sands on Lewis, so white that my eyes hurt, like snow blindness ... surviving the boat trip to Staffa, fine on the way there but on the way home it was into the waves and wind ...

There is a tendency to believe that when you leave a place where you have holidayed it somehow stays exactly the same as it was at the moment when you left. Perhaps there is even more of a tendency to believe this in the Hebrides. It is, of course, probably less true there than for many places. When I was in Lewis the Calanais Visitor Centre was not yet open and the Doune Broch Centre was a hole in the ground. We were some of the last passengers to go though the Sound of Scalpay on the Harris ferry to Skye before the bridge was built, and when we were on the Uists there was no causeway to Berneray or to Eriskay. It is good to see that you can now travel from Stornoway to Vatersay by ferry and road in the same day, and there is a general improvement in transport, with better ferries and flights, roads, amenities and visitor facilities.

It should also be said that I am not recommending which islands should be visited or which sites are just not to be missed. I do have my own favourites but I am one individual and I have individual opinions and preferences. A week of lovely weather can make any island look lovely. It is those that are beautiful and engrossing in terrible weather that are really worth visiting. I have spent more than fourteen years visiting the islands and eighteen months compiling and then checking the entries, but things do change, often without warning, mistakes are made, and misinterpretations occur. If you know of any corrections, omissions or improvements, please contact me at the email or postal address on the imprint page.

The book is intended is to give the independent traveller a good and useful starting point, a mine of information on the islands: how to get there; what there is to see and do; accommodation options and places to eat; activities from surfing to golf to climbing to boat trips to St Kilda or Rona or the Flannan Isles; arts and crafts and local produce; prehistoric monuments, castles, chapels, museums, some popular, others remote and little known; beaches and mountains; whales and dolphins; orchids and fairy foxgloves. In short, a beginning, an entry point for visiting the islands, with lists of books and websites to find more detailed information if that is what is desired.

It is then up to the readers to decide which islands are of interest, what it is they would like to do and see, and what opinions, memories and experiences they have on the myriad of unique islands that make up the Hebrides.

Would the independent traveller have it any other way?

Martin Coventry
May 2006

How To Use the Book

The books is organised as follows:

Contents

Acknowledgments

Preface

How to Use the Book

Useful Information

General information about the Hebrides, including travel, maps, booking accommodation, midges, single-track roads and access to the countryside

Useful Contacts

Contact details for travel to the islands, visitor attractions, tourist information, accommodation, and wildlife and nature. Please note that the entries for the islands in the main text have specific information on that island, which is in addition to this list

Glossary

Background information on many of the terms used or people mentioned in the book

Place–Name Elements

Common Gaelic and Norse elements found in place names

Selected Further Reading

A supplemental list to that given for each island in the main entry

List of Maps

List of the maps in the main text (with the main islands which are covered by each map) and page numbers

Map of the Islands

Map of all the islands, showing names, ferry routes, landing points, bridges and causeways between islands, tourist information centres, airports and railway stations

The Islands

Alphabetical list of the islands with page numbers

Island Entries

The main part of the text is arranged by island, beginning with Skye, then running through islands including Mull, Iona, Islay, Jura, Bute, Arran, Lewis, Harris, the Uists and Barra, and ending with St Kilda. There are photographs of the majority of the inhabited islands.

Each island or groups of islands begins with a map of the area, showing island names, villages or ferry landing points (black circles), townships or places of interest (grey circles), highest points (triangles), listed roads (thicker grey lines), unlisted roads (thinner grey lines), road numbers, and ferry routes (black lines). These maps are for general guidance only and locations and distances may be approximate.

Each entry for an island begins with the island's name, the derivation of the name, a list of websites providing more information on the island including the website for the local tourist authority, and a list of relevant tourist information centres (TICs). There then follows the Ordnance Survey Landranger map sheet numbers for that island, along with the page on which the relevant map (HIH map) for that island appears.

If a longer stay is planned, especially on one of the larger islands, the purchase of the Landranger Ordnance Survey maps may be desirable. There is also the Explorer series of maps, which is at a smaller scale, and is useful for climbing, hill-walking or mountain biking.

Following this are sections about the island:

TRAVEL
How to get to the island by sea, road or air with contact information

DESCRIPTION
Physical description of the island, including size, hills, beaches, climate, villages and roads, with a summary of facilities or amenities on the island

WILDLIFE
Flora and fauna that can be found on the island or in the nearby waters, and details of nature reserves

HISTORY
The history of the island from the past until the present day, linked to places which can be visited

TOURS
These follow the main roads or routes on the island, usually starting from the ferry landing place or the road going on to the island; or nearby or neighbouring islands which do not have a separate entry. These tours describe what can be seen along the way, both on and far from the route, including villages, historical monuments (National Grid References are provided in square brackets), visitor attractions, arts and crafts, and places to eat. Opening times and contact information are provided for many sites (in brackets).

There then follows further information about the island. This is arranged alphabetically within each section, and lists information such as telephone numbers, websites, location, opening and facilities.

This is arranged into:

Places to Stay
Such as hotels, guest houses, bed and breakfast (B&B), self-catering properties, hostels, retreats, camping and caravans

Places to Eat
Such as restaurants, cafes, hotels

Transport
Such as buses, car hire, taxis, cycle hire

Activities and Sports
Such as boat trips, yachting, sailing, kayaking, fishing, diving, swimming, sports, walking, climbing, riding, pony trekking, golf, outdoor activities

Local Produce
Such as sea food, smoked salmon, cheese, meat, whisky, beer, chocolate

Arts and Crafts
Such as exhibitions, oil paintings, watercolours, sculpture, design, photography, pottery, ceramics, jewellery, clothing, knitwear, and even weaponry

Visitor Attractions and Museums
Manned visitor attractions such as castles, museums, theatres, arts venues, wildlife reserves, distilleries

Additional Information
Such as petrol, banks

Events
Such as festivals, Highland games, agricultural shows with contact details, where known, and the month

Further Reading
A list of books concerning the island (books covering many islands or on a more general theme are list in the Selected Further Reading at the beginning of the book)

Acknowledgments
Those who helped in the preparation of the book or provided photographs of the islands

An index of all the islands (from largest to smallest) and villages mentioned in the text, along with places which can be visited and notable people (such as Flora MacDonald or Lord Leverhulme), clans and families, and events concludes the book.

USEFUL INFORMATION

Many islands are larger than it might seem from perusal of a map as travel by ferries and roads – particularly single-track roads – is slower (and more relaxed) than on most of the mainland. Allow enough time to explore thoroughly: a couple of days will not do justice to any of the larger islands, but arrive in plenty of time to get to ferries if taking a vehicle.

There are different travel options for getting to, and travelling between, the different islands: ferry, aeroplane, coach and rail – and car, motorcycle, bicycle and foot. Some fares can have a considerable discount, even combining different modes of travel, so check before booking: Caledonian MacBrayne (CalMac; www.calmac.co.uk), for example, which is the largest ferry operator, offers a range of packages, such as Island Rover tickets and Island Hopscotch. It is advisable to book all ferry journeys in advance for vehicles and make sure arrival at ferry ports is well before the loading time. Inter-island travel timetables can depend on tide and weather, so check with travel operators before setting out.

Although the weather on the islands is rarely as bad as some might have been led to think (Tiree is recorded as the sunniest place in the UK, and snow and frosts are rare in the islands and rarely last should they occur), many activities involve long periods out of doors and it can be wet and windy, even in the height of summer. It is wise to have sensible footwear, perhaps even walking boots, and waterproof and warm clothing. One good thing about wind in the summer is that it keeps the dreaded midge at bay (see below).

The Ordnance Survey (www.ordnancesurvey.co.uk/leisure) produce an excellent range of maps (Landranger and Explorer series), which are good for getting the most from visits as they, in addition to listing major routes, villages and settlements, show minor roads, tracks and many historical monuments and physical features.

Tourist Information Centres (TICs) provide a wide range of maps and guides as well as local information and accommodation booking; the local tourist authority is listed in the island entry and the Useful Contacts section. Books and guides are often produced on the island and are available from local shops. Most islands now have useful websites with a range of information about businesses, history, accommodation, wildlife, facilities (and much more) on their islands. Most are an excellent resource; others perhaps less so, although more are being built and improved all the time.

Accommodation can be booked through Visit Scotland, local tourist information centres or, of course, increasingly through the Internet. Websites for many places to stay are listed in the entries for the islands.

The midge is a biting insect and may be small in stature but it can en masse make a visit to the islands miserable, particularly from May onwards. People react differently to the bites, but they are at best irritating and itchy, at worst can cause inflammation; some people can get repeatedly bitten. Midges breed in damp areas, so islands which have high rainfall are particularly prone to clouds of the evil insects. The most likely times for being bitten are first thing in the morning and then at dusk and in the evening, and during still, overcast conditions, especially in woodland or under trees. There are many repellents available, and even machines which can capture millions of midges, but citronella (Avon Soft and Fresh is to be recommended) may be a more pleasant alternative to some.

In many areas in the islands it is not possible to get a signal for mobile phones. Although there are many native Gaelic speakers in the Hebrides, and especially in the outer isles, they can all speak English.

SINGLE TRACK ROADS

These roads are only wide enough for one vehicle to pass, but have passing places which are identified by posts, either with the legend 'Passing Place' attached or alternatively by poles, which are usually striped, or perhaps just by a widening of the road.

- Stop at a Passing Place on your left to allow approaching traffic to pass
- If the Passing Place is on your right, you must wait opposite to allow traffic to pass. You must stay on the left and do not cross to a Passing Place on your right
- Do not hold up following traffic: stop in a passing place on your left to allow them to overtake
- If you are overtaking a vehicle that has stopped in a Passing Place, look out for approaching traffic
- Be prepared to give way to traffic coming uphill
- Do not park in Passing Places
- Look out for pedestrians and cyclists
- Watch out for animals on all unfenced roads, particularly deer and sheep, the latter especially in the outer isles where they can be especially stubborn
- Some roads can narrow rather suddenly with dire consequences for those not paying attention
- Watch out for city dwellers who drive SUVs or four-by-fours as they are likely to force those with smaller or less expensive vehicles into ditches as these car owners do not appear to want to get their off-road monsters mucky

ACCESS TO THE COUNTRYSIDE

The Land Reform (Scotland) Act 2003 gave visitors to the countryside right of access to mountains, moorland and grassland, woodland and forests, rivers and lochs, coastal areas, fields (although not when growing crops), most parks and open spaces, golf courses (although only to cross them), both day and night. This includes use of areas for activities such as picnics, horse riding, walking, cycling, climbing and wild camping. Access is explicitly not given to houses, gardens or policies, commercial, industrial or non-residential buildings and associated land, sports or playing fields when in use, places like airfields, military bases and visitor attractions.

Some guidelines are suggested:

- Use (where possible) local transport, shops and garages (although check opening times – many outlets are open shorter hours than in cities and are closed on Sundays and sometimes during the week or non-boat days)
- Look out for local crafts and produce to buy, and support local events
- Park vehicles responsibly: do not block gateways, tracks, or park in passing places on single track roads
- When walking, use gates and stiles if possible and try not to damage fences or walls if crossing them
- Shut gates if found shut, and leave gates open if found open
- Keep dogs on leads and under control at all times and always away from ground-nesting birds and livestock, particularly from calves and lambs. Take especial care during lambing (March to May)
- Avoid disturbing farm animals, livestock and wildlife, including deer calves, which should not be approached even if they appear to have been abandoned
- All birds and nests are protected by law, and so are many mammals including otters
- Historic sites and scheduled monuments should not be damaged and are protected by law
- Use paths where possible, and try to avoid erosion by not making paths wider or taking short-cuts
- Walk around the edge of fields if possible
- Guard against all risk of fire
- Protect and do not damage trees, plants and wildlife
- Leave things as you find them: take nothing away and leave farm equipment alone even if it appears to have been abandoned

- Leave no litter or food
- Bury excrement well away from paths, streams, rivers, lochs or water courses

For the more adventurous:
- Do not attempt climbs, scrambles or strenuous walks unless you are experienced, skilled and well-equipped, and are sufficiently fit
- Check weather forecasts before setting out, and bear in mind that weather conditions in the hills and summits can be severe even when weather at sea level is good
- Make local enquiries to avoid areas (including woodland) used for shooting and stalking (most likely mid August to mid October)
- Wear good boots and have waterproof and warm clothing
- Take water and something to eat
- Take a good map and compass
- Tell someone where you are going and when you intend to return
- Take a mobile phone if you have one, although bear in mind there are parts of the islands where they do not work

In emergencies (police, fire service, ambulance, coastguard and mountain rescue) phone 999.

METRIC TO IMPERIAL CONVERSIONS
Although Britain has converted to the metric system, distances on road signs and most maps are still given in miles (while contours on Ordnance Survey maps are given in metres).

one mile = 1.61 kilometres
one mile = 1720 yards
one kilometre = 0.62 miles

one foot = 0.30 metres
one yard = three feet
one metre = 3.28 feet

Useful Contacts

Travel

Caledonian MacBrayne (CalMac)
08705 650000 www.calmac.co.uk
Ferries to many islands and other
routes

Traveline Scotland
0870 608 2 608
www.travelinescotland.com
Travel enquiries for Scotland

National Rail Enquiries
08457 484950
www.nationalrail.co.uk

First Scotrail
08457 484950
www.firstgroup.com/scotrail
Trains to many Scottish
destinations

Scottish Citylink
08705 505050 www.citylink.co.uk
Coaches to many Scottish
destinations

Highlands and Islands Airports
01667 464000 www.hial.co.uk
Airport authority for the Islands

British Airways/Loganair
0870 850 9850 www.ba.com/
www.loganair.co.uk
Flights to island locations

Local Travel Information

Argyll and Bute Council
01546 604360
www.argyll-bute.gov.uk/aboutargyll/
gettingabout/

Highland Council
01463 702457 www.highland.gov.uk

Western Isles Council
www.cne-siar.gov.uk/travel/

Visitor Information and Accommodation

Visit Scotland
0845 2255121
www.visitscotland.com

Western Isles Tourist Board
www.visithebrides.com
Includes Lewis, Harris, North Uist,
Benbecula, South Uist and Barra

Highlands Tourist Board
www.visithighlands.com
Includes Skye, Raasay, Rona, Rum,
Eigg, Canna and Muck

Argyll, the Isles, Loch Lomond, Stirling and the Trossachs Tourist Board (AILLST)
www.visitscottishheartlands.com
Includes Mull, Iona, Coll, Tiree,
Islay, Jura, Colonsay, Gigha and
Bute

Ayrshire and Arran Tourist Board
www.ayrshire-arran.com
Includes Arran and Cumbrae

Also see websites for local councils
listed in travel section

The National Trust for Scotland
0131 243 9300 www.nts.org.uk
Properties include St Kilda,
Mingulay, Staffa, part of Iona, Burg
on Mull, Goatfell and Brodick
Castle on Arran

Historic Scotland
0131 668 8800
www.historic-scotland.gov.uk
Sites such as Iona Abbey, Callanish,
Kissimul Castle, Rothesay Castle,
and the Blackhouse at Arnol

GARDENS OF ARGYLL
www.gardens-of-argyll.co.uk
Gardens include Achamore, An
Cala, Ardencraig, Ascog Hall
Fernery, Colonsay House, Jura
House, and Torosay Castle

SCOTLAND'S GARDENS SCHEME
0131 229 1870
www.gardensofscotland.org

SCOTTISH MUSEUMS COUNCIL
0131 229 7465
www.scottishmuseums.org.uk

Wildlife, Nature and Birding

THE NATIONAL TRUST FOR SCOTLAND
0131 243 9300   www.nts.org.uk
www.nts-seabirds.org.uk

SCOTTISH NATURAL HERITAGE
www.snh.org.uk

SCOTTISH WILDLIFE TRUST
www.swt.org.uk

**ROYAL SOCIETY FOR THE
PROTECTION OF BIRDS**
www.rspb.org.uk

NATIONAL NATURE RESERVES
www.nnr-scotland.org.uk

FORESTRY COMMISSION
www.forestry.gov.uk/scotland

**MOUNTAINEERING COUNCIL
OF SCOTLAND**
www.mountaineering-
scotland.org.uk

SCOTTISH OUTDOOR ACCESS CODE
www.outdooraccess-scotland.com

HIGHLAND 2007
www.highland2007.com
Scotland's year of Highland culture

GLOSSARY

barpa see chambered cairn.

Bonnie Prince Charlie Following the abdication of James VII in 1688, William and Mary came to the throne and eventually the House of Hanover. Those who wanted a return to the Stewart kings (Jacobites) made several abortive attempts to restore James, and then his son, to the British throne. The last of these was in 1745-6, led by Charles Edward Stewart (Bonnie Prince Charlie), grandson of James VII. His forces were defeated at the Battle of Culloden, included in which were many islanders, such as the MacQuarries from Ulva and the MacLeods from Raasay. The prince became a fugitive, and was sheltered on the Uists before being ferried over to Skye disguised as Flora MacDonald's Irish maid, Betty Burke. After a short period on Raasay and then Skye, he sailed back to the mainland and eventually fled to France, never to return. Many on Raasay and elsewhere were less lucky.

broch A tall round defensive structure or tower, characterised by a double-shelled wall with mural galleries and stair, dating from as early as 200 BC (Iron Age).

caisteal (castle in Gaelic) There are fewer castles in the isles than in Lowland areas of Scotland, due to land tenure, geography and tradition, although many duns (see below) were occupied into medieval and later times. Most castles have crumbled to ruin, but Dunvegan and Brodick withstood the ravages of time, while Duart, Rothesay, Kissimul, Gylen, Moy and Lochranza have been rebuilt, consolidated or are fine ruins.

chambered cairn Burial cairn with a central chamber or chambers, covered in a mound of pebbles or stones (although these may have been robbed): called barpa in the Outer Isles (eg Barpa Langass); date from as early as the Stone Age (4000 BC).

Christianity Although St Columba is often credited with converting Scotland to Christianity, he was by no means the first evangelist to come to Scotland: St Ninian predates him by more than 100 years, and St Brendan travelled up the western seaboard before Columba. Others were also prominent, such as Moluag, Molaise, Blane, Colmac and Maelrubha, but Columba benefited from having a devoted biographer. Iona became a great centre of Christianity in the west, also renowned for stone carving and manuscript illumination, but repeated Norse raids and settlement and then the shift of power to the east by the kings of Scots led to its ruin. The abbey was refounded in medieval times and became a popular place of pilgrimage, but was dissolved at the Reformation (see Iona). There are other notable Christian monuments in the Isles such as Oronsay Priory and Cross, the Kildalton and Kilchoman Crosses on Islay, Rodel Church on Harris, St Moluag's at Eoropie on Lewis, and early Christian cells on Rona and the Garvellachs.

cist A stone box for burial, inserted into burial cairns and dating from the Bronze Age; used for inhumation and cremation burials.

clearances A series of evictions and emigrations, some forced and some voluntary (from the point of view that life had become so tough that starting a new life abroad seemed preferable to failing harvests and repeated rounds of rent rises). Land was given over to sporting estates or sheep farms. By the second half of the nineteenth century, islanders began to take a stand, refused to pay rents and seized land. This ended in violence in many places, not least the battle of Braes on Skye in 1882, and imprisonment for protesters. Four years later the Crofter's Act was passed, which improved security of tenure, but depopulation continued. In recent years islanders have been given the chance to buy the land on which they live, and buy-outs have included Eigg, Gigha, North Harris and recently South Uist.

crannog A small artificial island in a loch on which was a dwelling, perhaps on stilts, believed to date mostly from the Iron Age.

dun A defended site usually on a small scale, protected by a wall or walls, some with many features associated with brochs (see above); duns date from the Iron Age but many were occupied into medieval and early modern times or used the sites of later castles; dun, doon or dum usually means a defended site in Gaelic.

fort (or hillfort) Shares many features with duns (above), but usually on a larger scale and utilising natural defensive features such as cliffs, promontories and ravines; dates from the Iron Age.

Gaelic Gaelic is still spoken in many parts of the Western Isles, especially on the north of Skye and in the Outer Hebrides. Today around 59,000 people speak the language according to the 2001 census, an apparent all-time low figure, although it is now taught in many primary schools. There is a Gaelic college on Skye, as well as Gaelic radio and television programmes and road signs on the outer isles. The language is closely related to Irish Gaelic, and all Gaelic speakers can also speak English.

Hebrides The name apparently comes from a misprint as the islands were called *Ebudae* by Ptolemy and then *Hebudes* by Pliny the Elder in 77 after the Romans had invaded southern Britain.

Iron Age Period dating from about 500 BC until Roman occupation of southern Britain, associated with the increased use of iron for weapons and tools and building of defensive settlements.

Lords of the Isles The title taken by the semi-autonomous lords, who held virtually all of the Western Isles, and large tracts of the mainland, including the Earldom of Ross. The lords were descended through Donald (hence

MacDonalds), a grandson of Somerled, and one of the most famous of the clan was Angus Og MacDonald, friend and supporter of Robert the Bruce. John of Islay married Amy MacRuari, who was heiress to considerable possessions, and he was the first to take the title 'Lord of the Isles'. He and his successors established a powerful, sophisticated and cultured domain, centred at Finlaggan on Islay, which came to rival the kings of Scots. The lords were head of a large court, and patrons of the arts, stone carving and medicine. They were buried on Iona. Their power and independence brought them into conflict with the kings of Scots, including the bloody Battle of Harlaw in 1411. James IV, King of Scots, raised an army in 1493 and the last Lord of the Isles surrendered and was imprisoned. The title was then given to the heir to the Scottish crown, and is currently held by Prince Charles. This branch of the MacDonalds tried to regain power, but to no avail and even Islay eventually passed to the Campbells with much of the rest of Argyll.

Mesolithic Middle Stone Age, 7000 BC to 4000 BC, period of hunter-gatherers with little evidence of permanent settlement.

Neolithic New Stone Age, 4000 BC to 2000 BC, beginning of permanent communities and building of communal monuments such as burial cairns and stone circles.

Norsemen Men from Scandinavia who raided Scotland before coming to settle: many place names throughout the isles are Norse in origin. They are accused of repeatedly raiding Christian monasteries, such as Iona, and slaying the monks. The islands remained under the lordship of the Norsemen, including Thorfinn the Mighty and Magnus Barelegs, until King Hakon of Norway lost the Battle of Largs in 1263, and three years later all the Western Isles came under the dominion of the kings of Scots. There is little evidence for the presence of the Norsemen except place names, Norse burials and some settlements which have been excavated.

Ogham An alphabet of straight and crossed lines, used for memorials and markers between about 300 to 800 AD.

Picts An Iron Age people, who occupied much of Scotland north of the Forth and Argyll, including Skye, Raasay and the Outer Isles; associated with souterrains, wheelhouses and possibly brochs; direct evidence is restricted to carved symbol stones such as at Clach Ard on Skye. The Picts and Scots were united under Kenneth MacAlpin in the ninth century, and the Picts were absorbed into the kingdom of Scots.

Somerled Somerled was of mixed Norse and Scottish descent, and in the twelfth century established himself in the western isles by driving out the Vikings. He became powerful and independent enough to confront the kings of Scots, but was slain (possibly assassinated) at Renfrew in 1158. His sons held on to the property, and it was through him that the MacDougalls and the MacDonalds were descended.

souterrain An underground passageway and/or chambers, associated with a house or settlement, perhaps used as a storeroom or refuge; also known sometimes as an earth house, although there is no evidence they were used as dwellings; date from the Iron Age.

standing stones Monoliths, erected as markers, memorials, grave stones or for reasons lost in antiquity; some are more than five metres in height; date from as early as the Stone Age.

stone circles and settings Circles, ellipses and grouping of standing stones, dating from as early as the Stone Age but used into the Bronze and Iron Age and perhaps into the historical period; their purpose remains unclear, although burials were inserted and some may have been used as lunar or astronomical observatories; the best examples are Callanish, Machrie Moor and Pobull Fhinn, but there are examples all over the Hebrides.

Vikings see Norsemen.

wheelhouse Dwellings with walls radiating from the centre like the spokes of a wheel; dates from the Iron Age and may have been associated with the Picts.

Place–Name Elements

Most of the names are from Gaelic (G), but those from Norse are marked (N); some common English equivalents are also listed.

–a island (N) i.e. Canna, Bernera
aber meeting of waters, mouth (of a river)
abhainn river
ach field
achadh field
aig bay
aird height, high
allt/ault stream, burn
am/an/a' the, to the
annat/annait church, mother church
ard height, high
ardan, arden point of land
auch field
ault stream, burn
avon river
–ay island (N) i.e. Berneray, Islay

baile/bal/balla/bally township, village
balloch pass
ban/bane white, fair
barr top, summit
beag small
bealoch pass
beg small
beinn/ben hill, mountain
bhan white, fair
–bie settlement, farm
–bister settlement, farm
bo/boc cattle
–boll settlement, farm (N)
–borg settlement, fort (N)
–bost/–bosta settlement, farm (N)
–broch settlement, fort (N); although now a dry-stone tower with galleries and double wall
beul mouth

buie yellow
bun foot, river mouth
–burgh settlement, fort (N)

cairn heap of stones
caisteal/chaisteil castle
cambus/camus (chamuis) bay
caol/caolas narrows or straits
carn cairn, heap of stones
carrick rock
ceann head
cille church, chapel, cell
clach stone
clachan village, township
cladach stony beach
cladh burial ground
coile a wood
coire/corrie hollow
coll/colly a wood
cool back, back of a hill
cnoc hill, rise
creag/craig rock, crag
cro/crodh/croe cattle
cros/cross cross
cull back, back of a hill

dail/dal field, dale (N); court, meeting place (G)
dearg red
deas south
donn brown, dun (colour)
drochit bridge
druim/drum fort, hill, ridge
dubh/duff black
duin/dum/dun fort, hill

eaglais church
ear east
eas waterfall
eccles/eglis church
eilean, ellen, ellan island
esk water
–ey island (N)

fada long
fell hill, mountain (N)
finn/fionn white, pale, blessed
firth sea inlet, estuary (S)
foss waterfall (N)
fraoch heather(y)

garbh rough, thick
gare/gearr/gair short
geal white
glac/glack hollow
glas, glass grey, green, grey-green
glen glen, valley
gorm blue, green

holm islet (N)
hop/hope bay (N)

–i, i island
iar west
inch/innis/insh island, often small
inver meeting of waters, mouth of river

ken head
kil (cille) church, chapel, cell
killie a wood
kin head
kirk church
knock hill, rise
kyle narrows or straits

lag/lagg hollow
laggan small hollow
lax salmon (N)
les garden
liath grey, grey-blue
linn/linne pool, waterfall
lios/lis garden
loch loch, lake
lui/luib bend

machar/machair sandy area by the sea
maddy dog, of the dog family
mams rounded hill
mara sea
maol bare
meall/mell/mellan rounded hill
mhor/mor/more big
mon/monadh hill, moor
muc/muck pig

ness/nes/nis headland (N)
nock hill

ob bay (N)
ord round hill

paps breasts
papa priest (N)
–pol/–poll/–pool settlement, farm (N)
poll, pool pool pit

rannach/rannoch fern, bracken
ruadh/roy red
ros/ross promontory, wood
rubha/ru point, headland

–set/–setter dwelling, house
sgeir/skerry reef, rocks uncovered at low tide
scur/sgor/sgurr rocky hill, peak
sean/shen ancient, old
shader settlement (N)
shee/sith fairy
shieling summer dwellings for tending beasts
siar west
slack hollow between hills
slew mountain, hill
sron nose, headland
–ster dwelling, house (N)
stob pointed hill

strath river or wide valley
strome/strone nose, headland
struth stream

taigh/tay house
tarbert/tarbet/tarbat isthmus
tay/tee/tigh house
teampull/teampuill church, religious
  site
tibber well
tir/tire land
tobar/tober well
torr conical hill
traigh sandy beach
tuath north
ty house
tyre land

uaine green
uamh cave
uig bay (N)
uisge water

–val hill, mountain (N)
vane fair
vig/vik village, inlet, bay (N)
voe bay (N)

–wall/–way bay (N)
wick village, inlet, bay (N)

SELECTED FURTHER READING

Further reading for individual islands is located at the end of the entry for each island.

The Ancient Monuments of the Western Isles (Fojut, Noel, Denys Pringle and Bruce Walker)
Historic Scotland, 1994

Archaeology of Skye and the Western Isles (Armit, Ian)
EUP, 1996

The Crofter and the Laird (MacPhee, John)
House of Lochar, 1998

Description of the Western Isles of Scotland circa 1695 and Voyage to St Kilda; Description of the Western Isles of Scotland by Sir Donald Munro, Dean of Lismore (1549) (Martin, Martin and Sir Donald Munro, Dean of Lismore)
Birlinn, 1999

Discovering Argyll, Mull and Iona (Orr, William)
John Donald, 1990

Discovery of the Western Isles: Voyages to the Western Isles 1745-1883 (Bray, Elizabeth)
Birlinn, 1996

Expedition to the Hebrides (Atkinson, George Clayton; David A. Quine (ed))
MacLean Press, 2001

An Eye on the Hebrides (Hedderwick, Mairi)
Canongate, 2000

From the Alleghenies to the Hebrides (Shaw, Margaret Fay)
Birlinn, 2000

The Furrow Behind Me: the Autobiography of a Hebridean Crofter (MacLellan, Angus)
Birlinn, 1997

Hebridean Journey (Sutherland, Halliday)
Geoffrey Bles, 1939

Hebridean Memories (Gordon, Paul Seton)
Neil Wilson, 1995

The Hebridean Traveller (Rixson, Denis)
Birlinn, 2004

The Hebrideans (Wylie, Gus)
Birlinn, 2005

The Hebrides at War (Hughes, Mike)
Birlinn, 2001

The Hebrides (Coventry, Martin)
Goblinshead, 1999

Inner Hebrides and their Legends (Swire, Otta F.)
Collins, 1964

Island Going (Atkinson, Robert)
Birlinn, 1995

An Island Odyssey (Haswell-Smith, Hamish)
Canongate, 2000

Island Quest: the Inner Hebrides (Stack, Pamela)
Collins and Harvell Press, 1979

Island Walks: The Southern Hebrides and Arran (Whitehorne, Steven)
Birlinn, 2002

Island Walks: The Western Isles, Skye and the Small Isles (Whitehorne, Steven)
Birlinn, 2002

The Island Whisky Trail (Wilson, Neil)
Angels' Share, 2003

Islands of Scotland, including Skye
(Fabian, D. J., Little, G. E. and
Williams, D. N.)
Scottish Mountaineering Trust,
1989

The Islands of Western Scotland (Murray,
William Hutchinson)
Methuen, 1973

The Islands (Pocket Mountains)
(Williams, Nick et al)
Pocket Mountains, 2004

Isles of the West (Mitchell, Ian)
Birlinn, 2004

The Lord of the Isles (Paterson,
Raymond Campbell)
Birlinn, 2000

*The Lord of the Isles: Clan Donald and
the Early Kingdom of the Scots*
(Williams, Ronald)
House of Lochar, 1997

The Lordship of the Isles (Grant, I. F.)
Moray Press, 1935

Oatmeal and the Catechism (Bennett,
Margaret)
Birlinn, 2002

The Outer Hebrides: Moor and Machair
(Angus, Stewart)
Whitehorse Press, 2001

*Scotch and Water: an Illustrated Guide to
the Hebridean Malt Whisky
Distilleries* (Wilson, Neil)
Neil Wilson, 1998

*Scottish Island Hopping: a Guide for the
Independent Traveller* (second
edition) (Andrew, Hubert et al)
Polygon, 1999

Scottish Islands (Grimble, Ian)
BBC Books, 1985

The Scottish Islands (Haswell-Smith,
Hamish)
Canongate, 2004

*Sea-Road of the Saints: Celtic Holymen in
the Hebrides* (Marsden, John)
Floris Books, 1996

Skye and the Western Isles (second
edition) (Penrith, James and
Deborah)
Vacation Work, 2004

*Somerled and the Emergence of Gaelic
Scotland* (Marsden, John)
Tuckwell, 2005

Summer in the Hebrides (Murray,
Frances)
1887 (repr 1994)

*To the Hebrides: Samuel Johnson's
Journey to the Western Isles and James
Boswell's Journal of a Tour* (Black,
Ronald (ed.))
Birlinn, 2006

*A Tour in Scotland and Voyage to the
Hebrides 1772* (Pennant, Thomas)
Birlinn, 1998

Travels in the Western Hebrides
(Buchanan, Revd John Lane)
MacLean Press, 1997

Twice Around the Bay (Hall, Christina)
Birlinn, 2001

The Unknown Hebrides (Macpherson,
John)
Birlinn, 2006

*A Very Civil People: Hebridean Folk,
History and Tradition* (Campbell,
John Lorne; Hugh Cheape (ed.))
Birlinn, 2000

Walking in the Hebrides (Redfern, Roger)
Cicerone Press, 2003

The West Highland Galley (Rixson, Dennis)
Birlinn, 1998

Western Isles Handbook (Perrott, David)
Kittiwake, 1998

The Western Isles: 25 Walks (Parker, June and Roger Smith (eds.))
Mercat Press, 1996

When I Was Young: the Islands – Voices from Lost Communities in Scotland (Neat, Timothy)
Birlinn, 2000

LIST OF MAPS

All maps by Martin Coventry (copyright © Martin Coventry 2006)

Map of the Islands	xxx
Skye and Neighbouring Islands (excluding Raasay and Rona)	2-3
Raasay and Rona	38
Isle Martin and the Summer Isles	44
Rum, Eigg, Muck, and Canna and Sanday (Small Isles)	47
Coll and Tiree	60
Mull, Iona, Erraid, Ulva, Staffa, Treshnish Isles and Neighbouring Islands	73
Lismore, Kerrera, and Seil, Easdale and Luing (Slate Isles), and Neighbouring Islands	107
Islay	127
Jura, and Colonsay and Oronsay	141
Gigha	154
Bute and Cumbrae	158
Arran, Holy Island, Sanda and Ailsa Craig	172
Lewis	192-193
Great Bernera	213
Harris, Scalpay, Taransay, Scarp, Shiant Isles and Nearby Islands	216
North Uist, Berneray, Baleshare and Heisker	233
Benbecula and Grimsay	249
South Uist and Eriskay	257
Barra, Vatersay, Mingulay and Neighbouring Islands	269
St Kilda or Hirta	282

MAP OF THE ISLANDS

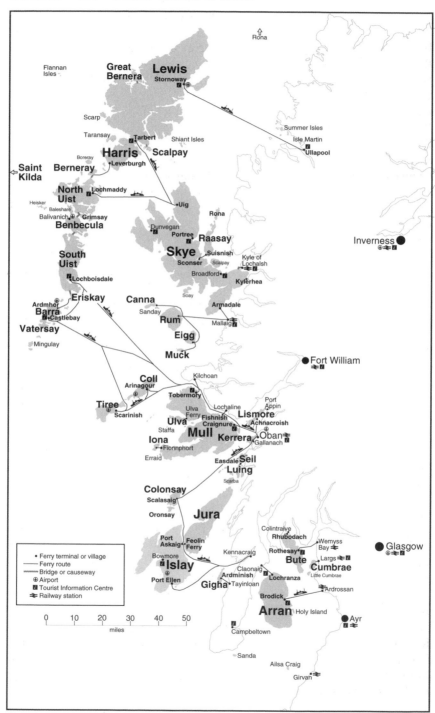

THE ISLANDS

Ailsa Craig	191	Longay *see* Skye	
Arran	173	Luing	122
Baleshare	248	Lunga *see* Luing	
Barra	270	Mingulay	280
Benbecula	250	Monach Isles *see* North Uist	
Bernera *see* Great Bernera		Muck	55
Berneray	245	Mull	74
Berneray *see* Mingulay		North Uist	234
Boreray *see* Harris		Oronsay *see* Colonsay	
Bute	159	Pabay *see* Skye	
Canna and Sanday	57	Pabbay *see* Harris	
Cara *see* Gigha		Pabbay *see* Vatersay	
Coll	60	Raasay	38
Colonsay and Oronsay	148	Rona	42
Crowlin Isles *see* Skye		Rona (North) *see* Lewis	
Cumbrae	168	Rum	48
Easdale	120	Sanda	189
Eigg	52	Sanday *see* Canna and Sanday	
Eilean More *see* Jura		Sandray *see* Vatersay	
Ensay *see* Harris		Scalpay	228
Eriskay	266	Scalpay *see* Skye	
Erraid	100	Scarba *see* Luing	
Flannan Isles *see* Lewis		Scarp *see* Harris	
Garvellach Isles *see* Luing		Seil	116
Gigha	154	Shiant Isles	232
Gometra *see* Ulva		Shuna	126
Great Bernera	213	Skye	4
Great Cumbrae *see* Cumbrae		Slate Isles *see* Seil, Easdale and	
Grimsay	256	Luing	
Harris	217	Small Isles *see* Rum, Eigg, Canna	
Heisker *see* North Uist		and Muck	
Hirta *see* St Kilda		Soay *see* Skye	
Holy Island	187	South Uist	258
Inch Kenneth *see* Mull		St Kilda or Hirta	282
Inchmarnock *see* Bute		Staffa	103
Iona	94	Summer Isles	45
Islay	128	Taransay	230
Isle Martin	44	Tiree	66
Jura	142	Torsa *see* Luing	
Kerrera	113	Treshnish Isles	105
Lewis	194	Ulva	101
Lismore	108	Vatersay	277
Little Cumbrae *see* Cumbrae			

Skye and Neighbouring Islands (excluding Raasay and Rona)

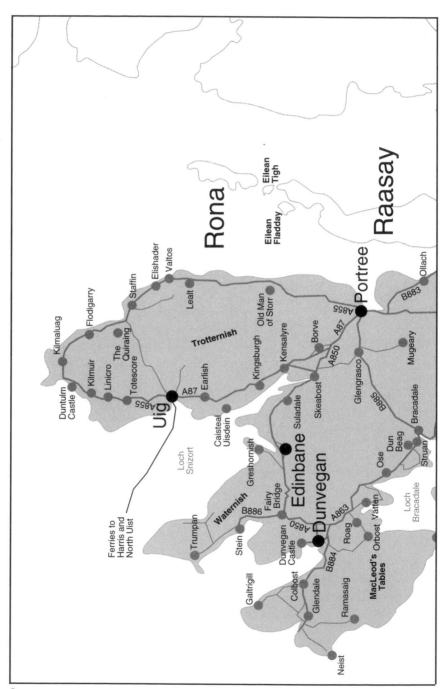

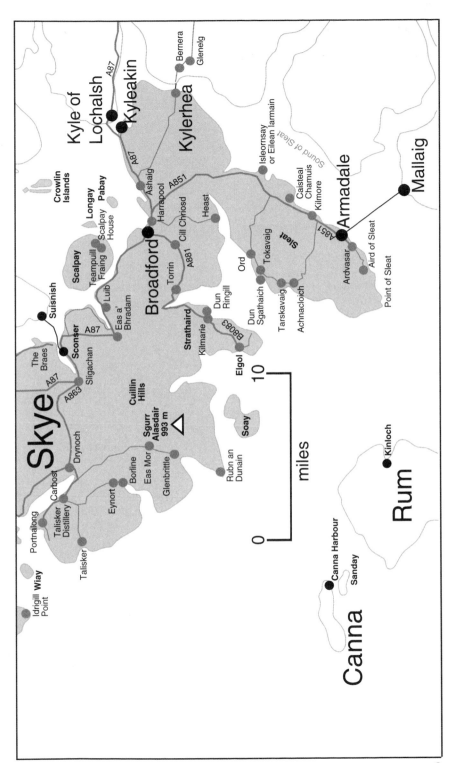

3

SKYE

('cloud' from Norse; An t-Eilean Sgitheanach from 'the winged isle' in Gaelic; also Eilean a' Cheo, 'island of mist' in Gaelic)

www.skye.co.uk
www.isleofskye.net
www.isleofskye.org.uk
www.isle-of-skye.org.uk
www.skye-hotels.co.uk
www.skye-birds.com
www.trotternish-skye.co.uk
www.gardenofskye.com (Sleat)
www.ealaghol.co.uk
www.elgolandtorrinhistoricalsociety.org.uk
www.kyleakin.com
www.glendale-skye.info
www.blaven.com
www.visit-waternish.co.uk
www.dive-and-sea-the-hebrides.co.uk
www.slaca.co.uk (artists/crafts) & www.handmadeinskye.co.uk
www.visithighlands.com (Highlands Tourist Board)

Tourist Information Centres
Portree (0845 2255121 (central no))
　Open Jan-Dec
Dunvegan (0845 2255121 (central no))
　Seasonal
Kyle of Lochalsh (mainland) (0845 2255121 (central no))
　Seasonal
Mallaig (mainland) (0845 2255121 (central no))
　Open Jan-Dec

Map Landranger
sheets: 23, 32, 33, 39
(HIH map page 2-3)

TRAVEL

The island lies off the mainland of Western Scotland, and can be reached by bridge (tolls have been discontinued since the bridge owner was bought out by the Scottish Executive) from Kyle of Lochalsh (A87) on the mainland. This is probably the quickest way and is a lovely route. The road passes Eilean

Caisteal Maol, Kyleakin, Skye

Donan Castle, one of the most atmospheric and photographed places in Scotland. The castle is open Apr-Oct (01599 555202; www.eileandonan.co.uk). Kyle of Lochalsh has a railway station (trains from Inverness; 0845 601 5929; www.firstgroup.com/scotrail), and the line from Fort William is one of the most picturesque in Britain, if not Europe. Scottish Citylink run bus services to (and around Skye) (0870 5 505050; www.citylink.co.uk) from major Scottish cities.

The island can also be reached by vehicle ferry (CalMac; 01687 462403/01471 844248; www.calmac.co.uk) from Mallaig (A830 from Fort William). There are eight crossings a day in the summer, the journey taking twenty-five minutes, with fewer crossings on a Sunday. The route to Mallaig is very scenic, and passes close to Glenfinnan, where Bonnie Prince Charlie raised a standard for his father and started the 1745-6 Jacobite Rising. The Glenfinnan Monument commemorates those who lost their lives in his cause (open summer; 01397 722270). Mallaig also has a railway station (trains from Fort William; 0845 601 5929; www.firstgroup.com/scotrail), and a heritage centre (01687 462085; www.mallaigheritage.org.uk).

A vehicle ferry also runs from Glenelg on the mainland to Kylerhea on Skye (runs Mar-Oct; 01599 511302; www.skyeferry.co.uk). This is reached from a turn-off at Shiel Bridge on the A87, and is a narrow road but very picturesque. It is in fact an old military road and there are the ruins of a barracks at Bernera, near the crossing point, as well as the remains of three brochs in Glenelg.

There is also a passenger service from Gairloch to Portree (0800 3286426; www.overtheseatoskye.com), running from April to September, and making two return journeys a day. The crossing takes one and a half hours.

There are also onward ferry services from Skye: from Uig to Harris and North Uist, and from Sconser to Raasay.

DESCRIPTION

Skye is the second biggest of the Western Isles (only Lewis and Harris is larger), being around sixty miles long and from three to twenty-five miles wide. It covers an area of 535 square miles. The island has many different landscapes in places, from the peaks of the Cuillin hills to the fertile 'garden' of Sleat. There are sandy beaches at Glen Brittle, Talisker and Fiskavaig on the west coast, and Achnacloich on the north coast of the Sleat peninsula.

The impressive sawtoothed Cuillin (pronounced Coolin) mountains dominate the island, and are especially beautiful from Elgol and the road south from Struan. The range is divided into the Red Cuillin to the east, which are more rounded, less high, and redder in colour. The Black Cuillin are jagged and sawtoothed, and massively impressive, beautiful and foreboding with peaks and ridges. There are fifteen Munros (peaks over 3000 feet or 910 metres) in the range, including Sgurr Alasdair ('Alasdair's peak') at 993 metres, Sgurr a' Ghreadaidh ('peak of torment') at 973 metres, Sgurr nan Gillean ('the lad's peak') at 965 metres, and Bruach na Frithe ('brae of the forest') at 958 metres. There are spectacular walks and climbs, but some of these are very difficult and should not be attempted by the inexperienced or unfit.

Trotternish is also very hilly, with a spine of land rearing up to daunting cliffs on the east side. Beinn Edra is 611 metres, while Creag a' Lain is 607 metres. This is another lovely part of the island. Many of the rock formations at the Quiraing, north of Staffin, are particularly notable – the Needle, the Prison and the Table – as are the pinnacles and crags at the Storr further to the south, and, of course, the Old Man of Storr, a pinnacle which rises to fifty metres. It can look especially memorable when the mist gets torn aside and it looms out of the pale clouds.

Sleat (pronounced 'Slate') is the peninsula in the south of Skye, and is renowned

The Cuillin Hills from Elgol

for its trees and fertile lands. It has been known as the garden of Skye. Glen Brittle, in the shadow of the Cuillin, is also particularly picturesque. The cliffs at Waterstein, to the far west, rise nearly 300 metres straight out of the sea; and the area is dominated by MacLeod's Tables, the flat-topped hills of Healabhal Mhor to the north and Healabhal Bheag to the south. The 'smaller' table is actually greater in height at 488 metres; Healabhal Mhor is 468 metres high.

The island has a relatively warm climate, and snow and frosts are unusual, although rainfall is high. About 1200 mm of rain falls by the coasts, although more than double this falls in the hills. The sunniest months to visit are June and September.

Portree, on the east coast, is the capital of Skye, and it has a full range of services, including places to eat, hotels, shops, craft outlets, banks, a post office, places to stay and a tourist information centre. The name, which means 'port of the king' in Gaelic, commemorates the visit of James V in 1540. To the north-west is Trotternish, with the Quiraing and the Storr, and on its west coast is Uig, a small village with a pottery and brewery. Uig is also the terminal for ferries across to Tarbert on Harris as well as Lochmaddy on North Uist.

Edinbane, on the north coast, has two hotels, a camp site, a sports centre, a restaurant, a pottery and a shop; to the north is the Waternish peninsula. Further west is Dunvegan, which has a full range of amenities – including the Giant MacAskill Museum – good places to eat, hotels and a filling station. To the north of the village is the very popular Dunvegan Castle, which is often bustling with tourists and coach parties.

To the west again are the hills known as MacLeod's Tables, and the townships of Glendale, Borreraig and Colbost. Further south, on the west coast, are Struan and Bracadale, which has a hotel, and Carbost, which has a distillery (Talisker). There is a picturesque route down to Glen Brittle, where there is a youth hostel, and beautiful scenery on the western side of the Cuillin hills.

On the east coast is Sconser, departing place for the ferry across to Raasay, and the village of Broadford which has shops, hotels, several craft shops, a filling station, and a seasonal tourist information centre. From here there is a fine journey down to Elgol on the south coast, which has boat trips to Loch Coruisk, a shop and a hotel. A road goes down the east coast to Isleornsay (also known as Eilean Iarmain), and Ardvasar and Armadale, and the ferry across to Mallaig on the mainland; another route travels to Kylerhea and a summer ferry across to Bernera and Glenelg on the mainland. The scenery on both sides of the narrow sound are especially lovely.

At Kyleakin on the east of Skye is a village with a range of services. This was for many years the main crossing point to Skye, until the bridge was built and the road bypassed the village. Kyle of Lochalsh on the mainland, a short (once expensive, before the tolls were abolished) journey from Kyleakin, has a leisure centre, railway station, and golf course, and many shops and places to stay and eat.

The roads on Skye are mostly good, although there are also stretches of single-track routes, such as down to Armadale and to Elgol. The main route between Kyleakin and Portree and Uig can be busy, especially in the height of summer.

WILDLIFE

Many different species of birds can be seen here, as many as 200, although some only visit for one part of the year or are small in number. These including corncrakes, warblers, finches, woodcock, spotted woodpeckers, grouse, sparrow hawks, golden eagles, white-tailed sea eagles, buzzards and owls. There are also ducks, geese, oystercatchers, sandpipers, terns, herons, dippers, cormorants, shags, guillemots, gannets, razorbills and kittiwakes, as well as bats. There is an office of the Royal Society for the Protection of Birds at Broadford (01471 822882; www.rspb.org.uk) and Scottish Natural Heritage at Portree (01478 613329; www.snh.org.uk).

There are both red and roe deer, and pine martens, as well as otters, which may be seen at Kylerhea Otter Haven (01320 366322; www.forestry.gov.uk) which has a viewing hide; in summer a warden can answer questions about the elusive wee rascals. There are also adders. Seals can be seen around the coasts, and there are dolphins, porpoises and whales in the waters around Skye.

HISTORY

Skye was occupied from the earliest times, and there are a range of prehistoric monuments, from standing stones and burial cairns to a fantastic collection of ruined Iron Age brochs and duns, the most notable of which is Dun Beag at Struan on the west coast. The island was apparently held by the Picts, and there is a carved symbol stone at Tote, known as Clach Ard. Another carved stone is now in the museum at Dunvegan Castle, while a third can be found on the nearby island of Raasay.

There are several early Christian sites, and the island has associations with the famous St Columba, as well as St Maelrubha and St Moluag. In 585 Columba is said to have settled three miles north of Uig at what is now known as Eilean Chaluim Chille and was formerly an island in a loch. Old churches and burial grounds can be found at Borline near Eynort, Cill Chriosd and Kilashik near Broadford, Kilmore on Sleat, Kilmuir on Trotternish, at Skeabost, and at Dunvegan.

For hundreds of years the island was held by the Norsemen, and many of the place names date from their occupation: Trotternish, Sleat, Waternish and Bracadale. The kings of Scots made efforts to recover the island in the thirteenth century, and Alexander III made a punitive raid on Skye, ravaging the island. Partly in response, King Hakon of Norway gathered his forces and sailed south in 1263. He is believed to have marshalled his longboats at Kyleakin: Kyleakin is named after him, being the 'kyles (narrows) of Hakon'. The Norsemen were defeated at Largs and three years later a treaty saw Skye and the Western Isles absorbed into the kingdom of Scots. Skye then fell under the dominion of the Lords of the Isles until the end of the fifteenth century.

Several of Scotland's most important clans held lands on Skye: the MacLeods, the MacDonalds and the MacKinnons. The MacLeods were (and are) based at Dunvegan Castle to the north of the island and held Harris and St Kilda, while the MacDonalds held Sleat and then Trotternish, and the MacKinnons were based at Dun Ringill and Caisteal Maol, holding the east of Skye, as well as the island of Scalpay. The MacDonalds and MacLeods fought long and hard over control of parts of the island of Skye, and there were fortresses at Caisteal Chamuis (Knock Castle) and Dun Sgathaich in Sleat, Caisteal Maol at Kyleakin, and

Dunvegan Castle

Caisteal Uisdein and Duntulm in Trotternish, and, of course, Dunvegan to the north. These fights, including a battle at Skeabost in 1539 and a massacre on Rum, led to the atrocity at Trumpan in 1578. A MacLeod congregation was at worship in the thatched church. The MacDonalds landed nearby and set fire to the building, killing all those inside barring one woman, who escaped and raised the alarm. The MacLeods hurried to Trumpan, bringing with them their famous Fairy Flag, and the MacDonalds were hunted down and slaughtered to a man.

Of these strongholds, only Dunvegan has survived the ravages of time. It is still owned by the chiefs of the MacLeods, and is now one of the premier visitor attractions on Skye, although the Victorians were probably a little less kind in altering and 'castellating' the old fortress than they might have been. The tattered remnant of the Fairy Flag is preserved within the walls, along with mementoes of Flora MacDonald and Bonnie Prince Charlie.

The last battle between the MacLeods and the MacDonalds took place at Coire na Creiche, at the head of Glen Brittle, in 1601. This fight is said to have been caused by Donald Gorm MacDonald of Sleat returning his betrothed, Margaret, the sister of Rory Mor MacLeod of Dunvegan, to her brother. The lady was unfortunate enough only to have one eye, and Donald Gorm sent her on her way with a one-eyed horse, a one-eyed groom and a one-eyed dog. Needless to say, Rory Mor was furious. The battle, however, was won by the MacDonalds and the MacLeods were routed. The poor lady, Margaret, is reputed to have been devastated, and her ghost is one of those that are said to haunt the ruins of Duntulm Castle.

Bonnie Prince Charlie sheltered on Skye and Raasay after the collapse of the Jacobite Rising and defeat at the Battle of Culloden. He had been on the Uists, but when the hunt became too close he was ferried over to Skye in the company of Flora MacDonald (also see South Uist – she was born at Milton), disguised as her Irish maid, Betty Burke. He arrived on Trotternish, and was to be taken to the

MacDonald seat at Monkstadt, but there were Hanoverian troops there and he was brought to Kingsburgh, then Portree. Flora and the prince parted in what is now the Royal Hotel in Portree and the prince was ferried across to Raasay.

Flora was soon accused of helping him, and was imprisoned briefly in Dunstaffnage Castle and then the Tower of London before being released in a general amnesty. She returned to Skye, where she married Allan MacDonald of Kingsburgh (an officer in the British army) at Armadale and had many children; her sons were also to go on to serve in the British Army. Late in life, she and her family emigrated to the Carolinas in America. Here she and her husband became embroiled in the American War of Independence, fighting for the Hanoverian government. They lost everything and returned to Skye in 1779. She stayed at Flodigarry (her house there now provides accommodation as part of the Flodigarry Hotel). She died at Peinduin in 1790 and was buried at Kilmuir (near the Skye Museum of Island Life), where there is a memorial to her.

The prince himself was ferried across to Raasay, but then returned to Skye and Broadford, again disguised as a servant. He was helped by the MacKinnons, and sheltered in Strathaird, hiding in a cave south of Elgol, now known as Prince Charles's Cave. From here, he was taken to Mallaig, and eventually fled Scotland in a French ship, never to return. The prince is believed to have given the chief of the MacKinnons the recipe for Drambuie, a whisky liqueur, although the original ingredients are said to have included cognac instead of whisky. MacKinnon may not have thought the gift sufficient recompense for the years he was to spend in jail. The prince had, indeed, found little support on Skye: both MacDonald of Sleat and MacLeod of Dunvegan supported (at least on paper) the Hanoverian government. However, of course, they were not to suffer as a consequence of the failure of the Rising, in contrast to the savage ravaging of the lands of the MacLeods of Raasay and the mistreatment of the folk of that island. Indeed, Flora MacDonald's husband, Allan MacDonald of Kingsburgh, was a government officer during the

Loch Bracadale

rebellion. All in all, Bonnie Prince Charlie only spent a week on Skye.

In 1773, when Dr Johnson and Boswell were on their famous tour, they had met and been impressed by Flora; but she was never to be very popular on Skye – some thinking that she had done well from her brief association with the bonnie prince. Her grave at Kilmuir was neglected (much of it is said to have been chipped away and removed by souvenir hunters) until a new memorial was placed there in the nineteenth century when a more romantic view of the Jacobites had become all pervasive.

Life on the island was to become extremely difficult in the eighteenth and nineteenth centuries as rent rises bit: one of the reasons, indeed, that Flora emigrated. The population was more than 23,000 in 1841 but declined due to both clearances and voluntary emigration to find a better life, following years of famine and failed harvests. There was a resurgence with the growth of the kelp industry, but this too then failed. There are deserted townships at Boreraig and Suisnish where some of the most infamous clearances took place.

In the 1880s there was a confrontation and then a stand-off between crofters and landowners; police were called in from Glasgow to control the situation. A fight erupted in 1882, known as the Battle of the Braes (Braes is an area south of Portree); marines and gunboats were called in by the government to quell the disturbances. Trouble also flared in Glendale. One of the results was the setting up of the Napier Commission, which in turn resulted in the 'Crofters' Act' of 1886. This established a fairer and more secure system of land tenure and rents, although things hardly improved. Some may see the process continuing to this day: tenants now have procedures which can be invoked to force landowners into selling their estates to their tenants – even against their will.

Many of the islanders speak Gaelic, especially on the north of the island; and there is a Gaelic college, Sabhal Mor Ostaig (01471 888000; www.smo.uhi.ac.uk), in Sleat. The *West Highland Free Press* (01471 822464; www.whfp.com) is the local newspaper, and is published in Broadford. The population of Skye is now around 9,000, although in the summer this is swollen by many tourists (estimated at as many as 400,000 visitors a year).

Along with agriculture and crofting, tourism is now one of the mainstays of island life, and Skye caters more for the tourist and visitors than most of the other islands: there are multitudes of places to stay and eat, arts and crafts outlets, souvenir shops and attractions catering for coach parties. It is, however, a large island and, although some of the tourist routes are a little over used, overly commercial and even tacky, wide swathes remain quiet, unspoiled and unquestionably lovely.

Tours
KYLEAKIN TO BROADFORD AND PORTREE (A87)
At Kyleakin, overlooking the old ferry crossing, is the shattered ruin of Caisteal Maol [NG 758264] ('bare castle'), dating from the fifteenth century or earlier and anciently held by the MacKinnons. Long before the present building was begun, a Norse princess, called 'Saucy Mary' and married to the then chief of the MacKinnons, is reputed to have built a stronghold here so she could extort money from ships using the sound. The story goes that when she died she was buried on the summit of Beinn na Caillich ('hill of the old woman') beneath a long cairn of stones. In 1951 a hoard of coins was found hidden in one of the crumbling walls of the castle.

The castle was also known as Dunakin, and both it and Kyleakin itself are named after King Hakon of Norway, whose longships were moored here on their way south. Kyleakin has shops, hotels, hostels, places to eat and many other amenities. This used to be a very busy place as the ferry from the mainland landed here, but it has since been bypassed by the bridge connecting Skye to the mainland.

The village is home to the Bright Water Visitor Centre (01599 530040; www.eileanban.org; open Apr-Oct; tel. to confirm opening times) which has wildlife trips to Eilean Ban and a museum on the author Gavin Maxwell, author of *Ring of Bright Water* and other books.

On the way into Broadford at Breakish is the Alba Restaurant (01471820000); while near Ashaig is Kilashaig [NG 687243], the scant remains of a chapel in a burial ground. The full name means the 'church of the ferry of St Maelrubha'. It was from here that Maelrubha would sail back over to his monastery at Applecross. The saint's bell, which was hung on a nearby tree, was said to ring of its own accord every Sunday. Tobar Ashik, near the shore, was a holy well and was also associated with Maelrubha.

At Broadford is the turn-off for Elgol (A881), and before that, at Harrapool, is the Skye Serpentarium (01471 822209; www.skyeserpentarium.org.uk; open Easter-Oct, Mon-Sat 10.00-17.00; also Jul-Aug, Sun 10.00-17.00; tel. to check outwith these dates) with snakes, lizards, frogs and tortoises in natural surroundings; there are snake-handling sessions and a gift shop. There is also the Harrapool Studio and Gallery (01471 820096; www.skyeart.co.uk); and Skyeline Ceramics (01471 822023; www.skyelineceramics.co.uk; open Mon-Sat 10.00-13.00 and 14.00-18.00, Tue/Thu 20.00) and Sandback Studio (01471 822064/011) with watercolours and mixed media works. Waterloo, to the east of Broadford, is so called because of the large number of Napoleonic War veterans who returned here following the victory in 1815. The small island to the north is Pabay.

Broadford is the second largest village on Skye and, as it is on the only route north (A87), it has a full range of services, including a 24-hour petrol station with groceries, cycle hire, and a Co-op supermarket. There are also hotels, a youth hostel, restaurants, notably Creelers of Skye Seafood Restaurant (01471 822281; www.skye-seafood-restaurant.co.uk; closed mid Dec-beg March; tel. to confirm; booking advised), and Claymore Restaurant (01471 822333), also specialising in local seafood, and shops, as well as a bank and cashline machines and a seasonal tourist information centre. The Broadford Hotel was one of the places visited by Bonnie Prince Charlie in 1746.

Arts and craft outlets and shops include Skye Jewellery (01471 820027; www.skyejewellery.co.uk), World of Wood (01471 822831; open Mar-Oct, Mon-Sat), Broadford Books (01471 822748; www.broadfordbooks.co.uk), Broadford Gallery (01471 822011; www.skye-arts.co.uk), Craft Encounters (01471 822754; www.craftencounters.co.uk), the Three Herons (01471 822152; www.isleofskye.net/threeherons/; open Mon-Sat), the Rupert Copping Gallery/Studio (01471 822669; www.rupertcopping.co.uk; open Apr-Nov, Mon-Sat 9.30-17.30; phone for hours in winter), and Woodrising Gallery (01471 820300; www.woodrising-photography.co.uk) at Old Corry.

There is also Family Pride Boat Trips, offering outings in a glass-bottomed boat to see marine wildlife (0800 7832175/07774 124125; www.glassbottomboat.co.uk); and Skye in Focus (01471 822531; www.steveterry.co.uk/www.skye-photos.com) illustrating Highlands and Islands landscape in colour and monochrome.

By the side of the road at Liveras, to the west of Broadford, is a chambered burial cairn [NG 642238], much robbed but with a cist visible. The cairn is more than twenty metres long and four high.

There is a forestry walk in the Cnoc na Cachaille plantation: the car park is about one and a half miles beyond Broadford. The mountain to the west is Beinn na Caillich, 732 metres, on top of which is said to be buried the 'Saucy Mary' mentioned under Castle Maol. The large hilly island to the north is Scalpay.

Further along the main road, on the east side of Loch Ainort, is the Luib Croft Museum, which features an atmospheric blackhouse, furnished from the early twentieth century (01478 822427; open Apr-Oct, daily 9.00-18.00). Two pistols were found here during renovation, believed to have been hidden in the roof during the Jacobite Rising of 1745-6. The main road skirts the impressive hill of Glamaig to the west. Further along the main road an unlisted route runs along the north side of Loch Ainort, and beyond the turn-off on the A87 is Eas a' Bhradain, a fine waterfall. The unlisted road rejoins the A87 further to the north, and is a scenic route.

At Sconser is the ferry to Raasay, the Isle of Skye Golf Club (01478 650414; www.isleofskyegolfclub.co.uk), and a hotel.

Sligachan is one of the gateways into the Cuillin hills, and there is a large hotel, a campsite, and fantastic views of both the Red and Black Cuillin. The road branches here: the A87 runs up to the east coast to Portree and Uig, while the A863 heads up the west side and eventually Dunvegan. If walking or climbing in the area, great care should be taken: many people have got into difficulties and others have died.

The A87 runs north through Glen Varragill for some miles, and there is a turn-off (B883), which runs south to the settlements of Conordan, Ollach, Gedintailor, Balmeanach and eventually the road ends at Peinchorran. The area at the south is known as the Braes, and this was the site of a confrontation between crofters and the authorities (including marines and a gunboat) in 1882 over land rights. There is a track which runs along the north of Loch Sligachan, and rejoins the A87 a little north of the Sligachan hotel.

Two miles beyond the B883 turn-off on the A87 is Portree ('port of the king'), a pleasant and attractive place with brightly painted houses, which developed around the excellent harbour. It was known as Kiltragleann before the name was changed in 1540 after the visit of James V. It was in MacNab's Inn (now the Royal Hotel)

The Cuillin Hills from Sligachan

that Bonnie Prince Charlie and Flora MacDonald parted ways, he to Raasay, she to Armadale. The village was developed as a fishing port in the eighteenth century, and there is still a thriving shellfish industry on the island.

There are a full range of amenities and services in Portree, including shops, banks, petrol and a tourist information centre, and many hotels, hostels, B&Bs, restaurants and places to eat. It can get very busy in high season. Aros (01478 613649; www.aros.co.uk; open all year) has a large restaurant and gift shop and is a venue for shows, concerts, music events and films; there is also a forest walk with a Gaelic alphabet trail. Portree is also home to the An Tuireann Arts Centre and Cafe (01478 613306; www.antuireann.org.uk; open Mon-Fri 10.00-17.00, Sat 9.00-17.00, Sun closed) which features local and national exhibitions, an art centre and cafe, and the village also has a swimming pool (01478 612655; open Mon-Sat) and cycle hire from Island Cycles (01478 613121). Near Portree at Garalapin are the Portree Riding Stables (01478 613124; www.portreeriding.co.uk).

Craft outlets in Portree include Skye Batiks (01478 613331; www.skyebatiks.com; open summer, Mon-Sat 9.00-18.00, Jul-Aug 9.00-21.00; winter, Mon-Sat 9.00-17.00) with wall hangings, clothing, batik shirts and other crafts; Over the Rainbow (01478 612555; www.skyeknitwear.com); and Mara (01478 612429; www.mara-direct.com). There is also Vanilla Skye Chocolates (01478 611295; www.vanillaskye.co.uk) and the Isle of Skye Soap Company (01478 611350; www.skye-soap.co.uk).

KYLERHEA TO ASHAIG (UNLISTED)

In the summer a vehicle ferry lands here from Glenelg on the mainland. It is a short crossing but especially picturesque, and there is a scattering of houses and the Kylerhea Otter Haven (01320 366322; www.forestry.gov.uk), which has a viewing hide for spotting otters, seals and other wildlife; there are also public toilets. The narrow single-track road goes up over the moor, and joins the main road (A850) at Ashaig, just before Broadford.

SLEAT: ARMADALE TO ISLEORNSAY AND SKULAMUS (BROADFORD) (A851)

The ferry from Mallaig lands at Armadale on the south-west of Sleat (pronounced 'Slate'); nearby is the pleasant village of Ardvasar. The villages have a garage and petrol, a hotel, cycle hire, a post office, craft shops, a general store, and places to eat and sleep, including a youth hostel. There are craft shops at the pier: Skye Batiks (01478 613331; www.skyebatiks.com), the Armadale Pottery (01471 844439; www.armadale-pottery.co.uk), the Bay Pottery (01471 844442; www.baypottery.co.uk) and Ragamuffin (01471 844217; www.ragamuffinonline.co.uk; open summer, daily 8.30-18.00 (Jul-Aug 19.00); winter, Mon-Sat 9.00-17.00, Sun 12.00-17.00; closed Jan-Mar – tel. to confirm). Local crafts are also for sale at the Old post office at Ardvasar (01471 844426; usually open Mon-Sat 9.00-17.00). There is a fine walk south to Point of Sleat, from where there are magnificent views.

Near here is West Highland Heavy Horses (01471844759/07769 588565; www.westhighlandheavyhorses.com), which has Clydesdale and Shire horse riding, trekking and trail riding for all abilities, and at Aird of Sleat is the Aird Old Church Gallery (01471 844291; www.skyewatercolours.co.uk; open Easter-Sep).

The lands were held by the MacDonalds (and the south part of Sleat is still held by the Clan Donald Lands Trust), and they built a grand mansion, Armadale Castle [NG 640047], designed by the Scottish architect James Gillespie Graham, which was later extended. Armadale has associations with Flora MacDonald: her mother's second husband was Hugh MacDonald of Armadale, and Flora came here after helping Bonnie Prince Charlie and was arrested not far from the castle. Flora was also married to Allan MacDonald of Kingsburgh at Armadale in 1750.

Armadale was to go the way of the other MacDonald seats, however, and is now ruinous, having been burned out (accidentally). In one of the outbuildings is the Clan Donald Centre and Museum of the Isles (01471 844305/227; www.clandonald.com; museum open Apr-Oct, grounds and shop open all year), with displays and a slide show charting 1,300 years of the MacDonald clan and the Lords of the Isles. The castle nestles in acres of gardens and grounds with nature trails, and there is a licensed restaurant, gift shop and facilities for genealogical research. Accommodation is available.

Off the A851 road is a narrow and twisting unlisted road leading north on a pretty route with great views to the townships of Achnacloich, with a sandy beach; Tarskavaig, home of Carol K. Kempt (01471 855368; www.handmadeinskye.co.uk; open Sun-Wed 10.00-14.00), who specialises in oils and small watercolours landscapes; Tokavaig; and Ord. It then sweeps back round to the main road beyond Teangue. At Tokavaig is Dun Sgathaich [NG 595121], which means the 'fortress of shadow'. This is now a fragmentary ruin, perched on a rock, but is very atmospheric. It was once held by the MacAskills, then the MacLeods and the MacDonalds. Several legends are attached to it. One has the warrior queen Sgathaich training warriors including Diarmid, companion to Finn MacCool. The castle is also said to have been built by a witch in a single night, although it has taken a lot

Caisteal Chamuis

longer to disintegrate to its current crumbling state, having probably been abandoned by around 1618. There is a hotel near here, by which are the slight ruins of a chapel, Teampuill Chaon [NG 618134], which was dedicated to St Congan, in an old burial ground. The views across to the peaks of the Cuillin hills are also fantastic on a good or clear day.

On the main A851 road is the township of Kilmore ('large church'), where there is the overgrown shell of the old parish church [NG 658070], with the new church nearby. The old church dates from the thirteenth century and was used until 1876. The MacDonalds of Sleat were interred here, and one legend has it that men who took shelter here after a battle in the seventeenth century were burned to death in the church. Nearby is the stone of St Columba, where he reputedly blessed the land on which the church was to be built.

Near Teangue on a headland by the sea is Caisteal Chamuis [NG 671087], which is also known as Knock Castle. This was originally held by the MacLeods, but passed with Sleat to the MacDonalds, and is now very fragmentary. The story goes that the old stronghold has a ghost, the Green Lady or gruagach, a phantom who was concerned with the welfare of the family that lived in the castle. Reputedly there was also a glaistig, a fairy woman who looked after the clan's cattle and beasts. The views from here are very fine, and the site has recently been put up for sale.

Just off the main road, with its lighthouse, is Isleornsay or Eilean Iarmain (from Eilean Dhiarmaid, 'Diarmid's Isle', named after the mythological hero, who reputedly whetted his fighting abilities at Dun Sgathaich). This a pretty white-washed village, although the small island is now joined to the mainland of Skye. It was from the compact harbour here that Flora MacDonald was transferred as a prisoner to a government ship; and this was later a centre of the herring fishing industry. There is the Isleornsay Hotel (where fishing or shooting can be arranged; www.eilean-iarmain.co.uk), a post office, and two galleries: Heaven's Ocean Art Studio (01471 833475; www.heavens-ocean.co.uk; open Easter-Oct, daily 10.00-18.00; winter tel. to confirm) and Laurence Broderick Sculptures (01767 650444; www.laurencebroderick.co.uk; open summer, Mon-Fri 9.00-17.00, Sat 9.00-13.00). Whiskies can be sampled and purchased at Praban na Linne (01471 833266).

There is also a good hotel at Duisdale and, off the main road, at Kinloch. The road turns inland and leads up across the moors to the main road (A87) a mile or so east of Broadford.

BROADFORD TO ELGOL (B8083)

The road travels south out of Broadford, passing a chambered cairn [NG 626221] and then Cill Chriosd [NG 617207]. This is the shell of a rectangular chapel and its graveyard, and is where the MacKinnons were buried. The name means 'Christ's church'. The road skirts the edge of the hill Beinn na Caillich, which is more than 730 metres high, and on the summit of which 'Saucy Mary' (see Kyleakin) is reputedly buried. This was the centre of the marble quarrying industry on Skye, but production ceased in 1912.

Kilbride is a small settlement before Torrin, and is home to Clach an h-Annait [NG 590203], which roughly translates as the 'stone of the mother church'. This is a standing stone, more than two metres in height, beneath which traditionally a bell and stoup were found. Near the stone is Tobar na h-Annait [NG 589202], a natural spring in a more modern well-house, which was revered as a healing well. A chapel may have also stood here, dedicated to St Bride, hence the name Kilbride.

There is a small settlement at Torrin, which has a shop selling groceries and crafts and a cafe, and the road scouts around the north of Loch Slapin, from where there are again fantastic views. To the north of the river at the north end of the loch is Clach Oscar [NG 564226], a boulder shaped like a bell which is said to ring when hit. The stone is said to have been thrown here from a nearby hill by a bellicose giant called Oscar.

Some miles further south is Kilmarie, the seat of the MacKinnons, and they had a 'castle' here, Dun Ringill [NG 562171], an ancient stronghold which was refortified in medieval times. It stands on cliffs above the sea, and the entrance passageway still has lintels in place. There are foundations of two rectangular buildings within the walls, but this was never a large or strong place.

The MacKinnons moved to Caisteal Maol at Kyleakin, before returning to a new house at Kilmarie. Also at Kilmarie is what appears to be a hillock, but is in fact a massive prehistoric chambered burial cairn called Cnoc nan Gobhar [NG 553173]. It is some twenty metres in diameter, and more than four metres to the top. Further north is Na Clachan Bhriege [NG 543177] ('the false stones'), a setting of four monoliths, one of which has fallen. At Strathaird is Duncan House Celtic Jewellery (01471 866366; www.duncan-house.com).

The scenery is stunning with the Cuillin hills rearing out of the sea, especially at

Elgol, where there are boat trips (Bella Jane Boat Trips 0800 7313089; www.bellajane.co.uk/www.aquaxplore.co.uk), a shop, Coruisk House, a restaurant specialising in squat lobster tails, and a hotel. The Elgol Shop and post office (www.isleofskye.net/elgolshop/; open all year except closed Sun; restricted opening winter) also provides refreshments. Also here is the Cuillin View Gallery and Coffee Shop (01471 866223; www.isleofskye.net/cuillinview; open daily, Apr-Oct).

At Glasnakille, east of Elgol, is Dun Grugaig [NG 535124], an ancient fort with an imposing wall defending the promontory behind it. The wall, rising four metres above the inside of the fort, has mural galleries and the treads of a staircase. The entrance passageway through the walls has a massive triangular lintel in situ and is roofed over for much of its length. Although the dun originated in the Iron Age, it may have still been in use in medieval times.

In a remote spot on the south coast is Prince Charles's Cave [NG 517124], where Bonnie Prince Charlie was sheltered before being shipped back to Mallaig and the mainland.

PORTREE TO TROTTERNISH AND UIG (A87)

The A87 runs north out of Portree and, after a few miles, is an unlisted road which runs through the township of Borve, and by this road is a setting of three standing stones [NG 452480], the tallest less than two metres high. This may have been part of a stone circle.

Just beyond this, back on the main road, is the turn-off (A850) to the west for Dunvegan and that side of the island.

Before Kensaleyre on the west side of the A87 is a large chambered burial cairn, twenty-five metres in diameter and five and a half metres high. Human bones were found in a cist at the cairn. Further north is the fort of Dun Cruinn [NG 411518], the defensive wall of which survives to a height of four metres in one place.

At Eyre are a pair of standing stones [NG 414524]; tradition has it that the hero Fingal, a giant in legend, used the stones to support a massive cauldron.

The peninsula is known as Trotternish, and the route skirts the west coast going through several townships.

To the east of the road are several places associated with Flora MacDonald and Bonnie Prince Charlie: Kingsburgh House (a private residence and not open to the public) where the prince was brought after landing on Skye (Flora married Allan MacDonald of Kingsburgh); Prince Charles's Well [NG 397565], from which he is reputed to have drunk; and Peinduin [NG 385575], north of the River Hinnisdal, where Flora died.

Some miles south of Uig, on the coast of Trotternish, is the gaunt ruin of Caisteal Uisdein [NG 381583] ('Hugh's castle'). This is called after Hugh MacDonald, a colourful character (if black can be thought of as a colour). Hugh had been

Duntulm Castle (see over)

16

outlawed for piracy, although he was subsequently pardoned and made Steward of Trotternish for his kinsman, the MacDonald chief Donald Gorm, who lived at Duntulm. Hugh then planned to make himself chief by slaughtering his fellow clansmen at Caisteal Uisdein, but letters got mixed up and the chief discovered the plot. Fleeing to North Uist, Hugh was besieged and then captured at Dun an Sticer, was brought back, and then imprisoned and starved to death at Duntulm after being given salted beef and no water. His skull and thigh bones were long preserved at the church of Kilmuir, but they (and indeed the church itself) are both long gone. Hugh's spirit is also said to be one of the several ghosts which haunts Duntulm.

Uig is the ferry port for services to Tarbert on Harris and Lochmaddy on North Uist; it was formerly a busy herring-fishing port and is still used for prawns, crabs and lobsters. There are shops, a filling station and places to eat, as well as two pubs, a hotel, a youth hostel, and a campsite. The round tower on the way into the village is a nineteenth-century folly, built by a Captain Fraser (it is on private land). At the pier is the Skye Brewery (01470 542477; www.skyebrewery.co.uk) with a shop selling its products, souvenirs and other Scottish bottled beers and country wines; and the Uig Pottery (01470 542421; www.uigpottery.co.uk), which makes functional and decorative pieces with decoration inspired by island landscapes. Also here is the Pub at the Pier (01470 542212), which is a bar-restaurant.

The A855 runs north around the coast of Trotternish.

TROTTERNISH: UIG TO PORTREE (A855)

The road north (A855) from Uig climbs up the side of a hill, and most of the route is single track with passing places. An unlisted road goes east and climbs over the moors of the middle of Trotternish to emerge at the Quiraing, where it rejoins the A855 near Brogaig. This is another scenic route.

On a headland to the west of the main road is Dun Skudiburgh [NG 374647], a large hillfort with impressive ramparts. Vitrified material has been found among the scatter of stones which were the walls. At Linicro is the Whitewave Outdoor Activity Centre (01470 542414; www.white-wave.co.uk) which has a cafe.

West of Balgown and three miles north of Uig is Carn Liath [NG 372688], the mutilated remains of a chambered cairn. The kerb can be traced in places, and it still has a height of more than four metres. Further east, in what was a loch, is Eilean Chaluim Chille [NG 377689], a former island on which there was an early monastery. The name means the island of St Columba, and he is supposed to have stayed here in the sixth century.

At Kilmuir is the excellent Skye Museum of Island Life (01470 552206; www.skyemuseum.co.uk; open Apr-Oct approximately, daily 9.00-17.30; tel. to confirm opening in winter), which is housed in seven atmospheric thatched dry-stone buildings, including a blackhouse and smithy.

Skye Museum of Island Life

It illustrates life on Skye in times gone by with a wide range of agricultural implements, old photographs and postcards, and a house furnished with period furniture. Kilmuir means the 'church of St Mary' and, although the original church itself has been reduced to footings, and its successor is also ruinous, the burial ground has a Celtic-cross memorial to Flora MacDonald, who was buried here in 1790, wrapped in the sheet in which Bonnie Prince Charlie had slept in 1746. Other memorials include a carved slab for Charles MacArthur, a celebrated seventeenth-century piper. Many of the MacDonalds were also buried here.

In a beautiful spot clinging to a cliff above the sea is the sadly reduced ruin of Duntulm Castle [NG 410743], once the seat of the MacDonalds and even visited by James V in 1540. Little now survives, although substantial walls were still upright 100 years ago. This was once a Norse stronghold, but later was held by the MacLeods then the MacDonalds of Sleat. Stories also make this one of the most haunted places in Scotland: the ghost of Hugh MacDonald, starved to death in the dungeon, manifested itself here; as did that of one of the chiefs, Donald Gorm, drinking and brawling with ghostly companions; then there was a maid who dropped a baby from one of the windows; then Margaret MacLeod, the one-eyed wife of Donald Gorm, abandoned and scorned by her husband, which slight led to the last battle between the MacLeods and the MacDonalds in 1602. There are fantastic views from here. The MacLeans, hereditary physicians to the MacDonalds, lived at Shulista, while their pipers the MacArthurs from Ulva lived at Hungladder.

Whether or not the ghosts were to blame, the MacDonalds moved to Monkstadt House [NG 380675], further south at Linicro, although it too is now unroofed and ruinous. This is where Bonnie Prince Charlie was brought by Flora MacDonald, but, finding Hanoverian troops there, they then went on to Kingsburgh, then Portree. At Kilmaluag is a hotel and the Trotternish Artist Studio and Gallery (01470 552302; open all year, daily) with landscape originals of Skye and the Highlands and Islands. There are some remains of a church [NG 445749] and burial ground near Port Gobhlaig.

Flodigarry is where Flora MacDonald lived in the 1750s with her husband Allan MacDonald of Kingsburgh, and five of her children were probably born here. Her cottage is now part of the Flodigarry Country House Hotel (01470 552203; www.flodigarry.co.uk), and it is possible to stay at the cottage.

To the west is the Quiraing and the impressive rock formations of the Table, the Prison (said to have been used to hide stolen cattle in medieval times) and the Needle, which is a pinnacle some thirty-seven metres high. There is a car park, but the popularity of the

The Quiraing

rocks has led to a considerable amount of erosion and access may be restricted. A minor unlisted road crosses the peninsula from Brogaig, climbing up over the ridge and moors and then going down to Uig on the west coast of Trotternish.

Down the coast near Digg was the Loch Siant Well [NG 471699]. This was once one of the most popular healing wells on Skye, and rags, pins and coloured threads were left here after walking three times around it sunwise.

At Elishader is the Staffin Museum (01470 562321; www.emory.edu/OXFORD/ Academics/International/Scotland/staffinmuseum/home.htm; open Easter-Oct, Mon-Sat 9.30-18.00), which has a collection of fossils collected from the area, found in Jurassic sediments. The collection is of international importance, and there are also displays of Bronze Age finds and crofting implements; at Staffin is Columba 1400 (01478 611400; www.columba1400.com), a community and international leadership centre. There are excellent views and a waterfall, Mealt Falls, which tumble nearly 100 metres. Further north, and up the coast, is the Kilt Rock.

There is a hotel at Culnaknock, a few miles south of Staffin, and a mile or so beyond on the main road is a fine waterfall and viewpoint near Lealt, where there is parking.

Further south, and to the west of road, is the spectacular Old Man of Storr, a tall rock pinnacle around forty-nine metres high, set against the daunting cliffs and crags of the Storr. There is a forest walk and parking by the road.

In a remote spot on the east coast, some miles from any road, is Prince Charles's Cave [NG 518482]. This is where the prince sheltered before being ferried over to Raasay in 1746.

The road goes on to Portree, passing Dun Gerashader [NG 489453] to the east of the road, the remains of an Iron Age fort, which was built on the summit of a ridge and had defensive outworks.

CARBOST TO DUNVEGAN (A850)

The A87 branches at Borve, and runs west (A850) to Carbost, while the B8036 leaves the A856 further north and runs down to Carbost.

North of the township of Carbost, on a minor road off the B8036, is one of the few Pictish symbol stones in the Western Isles. It is called Clach Ard [NG 421491], and is protected by railings. The stone, less than two metres in height, is carved with a crescent and v-rod, double disc and z-rod, and a mirror and comb. It was not always here: it was used as a door lintel before being retrieved and erected at its present site.

Skeabost [NG 418485] was once an important ecclesiastical centre, the seat of the bishops of the Isles in the fifteenth century, although their cathedral was never large. A burial ground is located on St Columba's Isle in the River Snizort, and there are some remains of two churches, one dedicated to St Columba. A grave slab is carved in relief with the figure of a warrior, and the chiefs of the MacNicols (or Nicolsons) were buried here. A path and bridge lead across to the island.

Skeabost is also home to the Skeabost Golf Club (01470 532202; www.skeabostcountryhouse.com), in the grounds of the country house hotel; fishing can also be arranged.

The Skye Riding Centre (01470 582419; www.skyeridingcentre.co.uk/www.skye-riding.co.uk; open all year) is at Suladale and has the Stables Cafe and a post office. Dun Suladale [NG 374526], south-west of Suladale township, is an interesting ruinous broch and defensive outwork, with the entrance, a small chamber and a cell or gallery all discernible.

Edinbane, which is bypassed by the main road, has a sports centre, two hotels (one of which is the sixteenth-century, haunted The Lodge (01470 582217; www.the-lodge-at-edinbane.co.uk/www.edinbane-hotel.co.uk), a campsite and a shop; there is also a music festival. It is also home to the Edinbane Pottery (01470 582234; www.edinbane-pottery.co.uk; open daily, Easter-Oct 9.00-18.00) which has wood-fired and salt-glazed hand-made functional pottery.

On the road between Edinbane and Dunvegan is a branch (B886) which leads north to Stein, Lusta and Trumpan. Near the junction is the famous Fairy Bridge [NG 278512], a meeting point. According to one version of the tale about the origins of the Fairy Flag, this is where the chief of the MacLeods was parted from his fairy wife, she having to return to her own enchanted land. She then gave him the flag.

Dunvegan is a pleasant place and has petrol, a garage, a grocers, other shops, restaurants (including the Old School Restaurant: 01470 521421; open Mar-Nov), a post office and two excellent hotels. On the way into the village from the east is the ruin of St Mary's Church [NG 256478], which stands in a burial ground. There is a memorial to the MacCrimmons, hereditary pipers to the MacLeods of Dunvegan; and the MacLeods were themselves buried here. Three carved grave slabs are in the cemetery, as well as other old markers.

Across the road from the burial ground is the Croft Studio (01470 521383; www.croft-studio.com; open all year, daily). In the village is the Giant Angus MacAskill Museum (01470 521296; open Apr-Oct, daily 9.30-18.00), with displays and information on the tallest Scotsman, who was 2.3 metres in height. He was born on the island of Berneray in the Sound of Harris in 1825, and died in Canada.

North of the village is the famous Dunvegan Castle (01470 521206; www.dunvegancastle.com; open all year: mid Mar-Oct, daily 10.00-17.00; Nov-mid Mar, daily 11.00-16.00), ancestral home of the chiefs of the MacLeods from the thirteenth century or earlier. It is in the probably unique position of being the only castle in the Western Isles to have never fallen ruinous, although alterations and extensions down the centuries have obscured much of the ancient core. Beneath the battlements and harling is the sixteenth-century Fairy Tower, which was built

Dunvegan Castle

by Alasdair Crotach MacLeod, whose fabulous tomb is in St Clement's Church at Rodel on Harris: the MacLeods of Dunvegan also held Harris and St Kilda.

Preserved in the castle is the famous, if tattered, Fairy Flag, protected behind glass. The flag is said to have many powers, not least ensuring victory in battle (and used at Trumpan) when it was unfurled; it could also make marriages fruitful (presumably to ensure successful procreation) when brushed across the nuptial bed, and even charm the fish from the sea.

The castle has many other interesting items, including Rory Mor's Horn (a horn which holds several pints and which the heir of the MacLeod's must empty in one attempt), mementoes of Bonnie Prince Charlie and Flora MacDonald, an exhibition about St Kilda, and a carved Pictish stone with a crescent and v-rod and disc. There are also boat trips to see seals, and two shops, two craft shops and a large restaurant.

The MacCrimmons were the hereditary pipers to the MacLeods, and they had a college at Borreraig to the west.

On the east side of Loch Dunvegan, north of the castle, are the ruins of Dun Fiadhairt [NG 231504], a relatively well-preserved broch with two entrances, the main one defended by two guard cells.

FAIRY BRIDGE TO TRUMPAN (B886 AND UNLISTED ROAD)

North of the Fairy Bridge, at Annait [NG 272527], is a triangular defensive site, between the meeting of Bay River and a burn; a wall cut off the other side. The footings of a chapel and indications of huts or cells may be the remains of an early Christian monastery: Annait means something like 'mother church'. One legend about the site is that unbaptised children were buried here, although this has not been confirmed by excavation.

At Stein is the eighteenth-century Stein Inn (01470 592362; www.steininn.co.uk) and Dandelion Designs and Images Gallery (01470 592218; www.dandelion-designs.co.uk; open Easter-Oct, daily 11.00-17.00; winter, tel. to confirm) which features pyrography, paintings, photographs, and cards; nearby is Brae Fasach Studio (01470 592732; www.isleofskye.net/braefasach; open all year except Jan), Dunhallin Crafts (01470 592271); Three Camuslusta Workshop and Gallery (01470 592264/201; open Easter-Oct, Mon-Fri 10.00-18.00, Sat-Sun, tel. to confirm) and Halistra Pottery (01470 592347; www.halistra-pottery.co.uk). Skyeskyns (01470 592237; www.skyeskyns.co.uk; open all year, daily 10.00-18.00) is an exhibition tannery, featuring traditional leather-making skills, sheepskin products, and lambskin fleeces. Also notable is the Lochbay Seafood Restaurant (01470 592235; www.lochbay-seafood-restaurant.co.uk).

There are ruinous brochs on the Waternish peninsula which warrant a visit. To the east of Hallin is Dun Hallin [NG 256592] which, although choked with debris, has impressive walls, an entrance and guard cells, and a gallery in a wall. Dun Borrafiach [NG 235637] and Dun Gearymore [NG 236649] are to the east of a track running north from Trumpan. Dun Borrafiach, on a rock on a slope, has three-metre-high walls, and the entrance and gallery can be seen. At Dun Gearymore the walls are lower, but two cells within the wall are entered from the broch.

The ruins of Trumpan Church [NG 225613] are located in a pretty and tranquil spot surrounded by a burial ground. This was the scene, however, of a massacre in 1578. The congregation were at church one Sunday when the building was attacked by a party of MacDonalds intent on avenging their kin who been murdered on Eigg. The thatch of the roof was set on fire, and all within were killed, except one girl who escaped and raised the alarm. The MacLeods came in force, bringing with them the Fairy Flag, and then it was the MacDonalds who were slaughtered.

This is probably an ancient Christian site, and was dedicated to St Conan. In the graveyard is the Truth Stone, a small monolith, with a hole in one side. To determine if someone was telling the truth, they were blindfolded – if they could then put their finger in the hole this proved they were not lying. Rachel, Lady Grange, imprisoned so that she could not tell of her husband's Jacobite plotting, was held in the Hebrides, and she is believed to be buried at Trumpan.

Trumpan Church and the Truth Stone

DUNVEGAN TO SLIGACHAN (A863)

The road runs south out of Dunvegan village, and to the west are the impressive hills known as MacLeod's Tables. Just south of the village is a road (B884) going to Colbost and Glendale.

South of Dunvegan, and on an unlisted road to the west, is the Phil Gorton Studio (01470 521842; 07876 072329; open all year: tel. to confirm) at Roag featuring photographic landscapes and colourful abstracts; and the Orbost Gallery (01470 521207/288; www.orbostgallery.co.uk; open Apr-Oct, daily 10.00-18.00), which has paintings, prints and calligraphy celebrating the landscape of Skye and the Highlands. A long walk from here goes south to Idrigill Point. There are cliffs with caves along the coast, and at the point are three stacks known as MacLeod's Maidens. The tallest rises to more than 200 metres high. The story goes that the wife and two daughters of one of the chiefs of the MacLeods were drowned. There are also fine views over Loch Bracadale and to the south and west.

To the west of the main road at Glen Heysdal [NG 298441] near Vatten are two large chambered cairns, one thirty metres round and five metres in height, the other slightly larger but not so high. Both cairns have kerb stones in situ. There is a legend that beneath the cairns are buried the remains of many MacLeods and MacDonalds who slew each other in battle, but they are much older.

Dun Beag [NG 339386] ('small dun') is located on a rocky crag, and is the well-preserved remains of a broch, which has an entrance passage, cell, and the first twenty steps of a stair. The broch may have been occupied into medieval times, and finds from here include pottery, a glass armlet, a gold ring, bronze objects, glass beads, and coins from the reigns of Henry II, Edward I, James VI, George II and George III.

Across the road at Knock Ullinish [NG 333384] is a souterrain, consisting of an underground passageway which runs for some five metres; there is a hotel at Ullinish.

To the south-west is Ullinish Point and the tidal island of Oronsay in Loch Bracadale. A mile or so west is the island of Wiay (probably 'yellow' from Gaelic) which is about a mile long and rises to sixty metres. There are cliffs around the coasts, and a large sea cave [NG 302370]. The island has been uninhabited since the 1890s and there are the remains of a settlement on the west side of the island.

South and west of Struanmore are the remains of a chambered burial cairn, known as Carn Liath [NG 337376]. It has been reduced in height and many of the stones taken; but it is still more than three metres tall. The entrance passage and some of the kerb can be identified, as well as possibly the remains of the chamber. At Struan are shops, a filling station, and a restaurant; Aurora Crafts (01470 572208) specialises in hand-made lace, knitwear, spinning and other craft work.

From Bracadale the B885 crosses the island back to Portree, and the views from here are excellent on a good day. In a very remote spot in a forestry plantation in Glen Tungadal [NG 408401] is a souterrain, consisting of a long underground passageway.

The A863 continues south above Loch Harport until it descends into Drynoch. Just beyond the hamlet is the B8009, which goes west to Talisker, Carbost and Portnalong, and south to Eynort and to Glen Brittle. The main road cuts across Skye through Glen Drynoch and to Sligachan and the east side of the island. The road through Glen Drynoch is said to be haunted by a phantom car, seen both during the night and in daylight hours.

DUNVEGAN TO COLBOST AND GLENDALE (B884)

From Lonmore, to the south of Dunvegan, a turn-off (B884, a single-track road) travels west and then north towards Colbost.

At the township is the Colbost Croft Museum (01470 521296; open Apr-Oct), a restored nineteenth-century thatched blackhouse with contemporary tools and furniture. A peat fire burns throughout the day, and there is also a replica of an illicit whisky still. Also here is the Raven Press Gallery (01470 511748; www.kathleen lindsley.co.uk; open Mon-Sat 10.00-17.00); and Skye Silver (01470 511263; www.skye

silver.com). This is also home of the renowned Three Chimneys Restaurant (01470 511258; w w w . t h r e e chimneys.co.uk).

At Borreraig is Dun Borreraig [NG 194531], a ruinous broch and outwork on a rocky crag by the sea. The Mac-Crimmons were the hereditary pipers to the MacLeods, and they had a college at Borreraig.

Colbost Croft Museum

The Glendale Toy Museum (01470 511240; www.toy-museum.co.uk; open Mon-Sat 10.00-18.00) is an award-winning attraction, for adult and child alike. There are unique displays of toys and playthings and, although the museum was destroyed by fire in 2002, it has now been rebuilt and reopened.

On the shore is a water mill [NG 168498], with its wheel in place, by the edge of Loch Pooltiel. Also at the village is a post office, cycle hire, and a general store, craft shop and small restaurant called An Strupag (01470 511204; open all year).

Further along the road is the unlisted turn-off for Waterstein, and beyond this is a rough track to Neist Point and the lighthouse there. There are fine views to the south and west, and holiday accommodation is available.

DRYNOCH TO GLEN BRITTLE, TALISKER, CARBOST, PORTNALONG (B8009)

A lovely route with fantastic views down to Glen Brittle, another way into the Cuillin hills, from Merkadale, runs south from a mile or so south-east of Carbost. There are waterfalls at several points near the road, as well as Eas Mor waterfall [NG 412226] on the east side of Glen Brittle. It falls some forty-five metres. There is a youth hostel and campsite near the waterfall, as well as public toilets by the beach.

In a remote but beautiful spot at Rubh' an Dunain, along a track on the east shore of Loch Brittle, are two impressive prehistoric monuments. One is a Neolithic burial cairn [NG 393163] with a round mound and a forecourt. The entrance passage to the chamber is still roofed over, but the burial chamber itself is open. During excavations the remains of six individuals were found. The ruins of a dun [NG 396160] has walls about three metres high along with an entrance and intramural galleries.

A turn-off onto an unlisted road from the B8009 before Carbost runs west to Talisker Bay, which has a fine sandy beach, and south to Eynort, which is a pleasant place with waterfalls to the east in the Glen Brittle forest. Just south, at Borline, [NG 375259] is a burial ground with the remains of two churches, one of which was dedicated to St Maelrubha. Outside the west end of the larger building are several carved grave slabs and part of a cross shaft.

At Carbost on the B8009 is the Talisker Distillery, which was built in 1830: the whisky is full bodied with peaty and smoky flavours. There are tours and a well-stocked distillery shop (01478 640203/614308; open Apr-Jun and Oct, Mon-Fri 9.00-16.30; Jul-Sep, Mon-Sat 9.00-16.30; Nov-Mar, Mon-Fri 14.00-16.30). Also at Carbost is an inn and hostel, a shop, a post office and petrol.

At Portnalong there is a hotel, a hostel, the Skywalker Cafe (01478 640250; www.skyewalkerhostel.com), a post office and shop, and the Little Gallery (01478 640254; www.the-little-gallery.co.uk; open all year, daily 10.00-18.00) featuring etchings, watercolours and prints, notelets and cards.

On the west side of Ardtreck Point with its lighthouse, north and west of Portnalong, is Dun Ardtreck [NG 335358], an Iron Age dun, which stands on a small peninsula above the sea. A wall on the landward side defends the dun. The wall is an impressive barrier, and the entrance in the middle has a guard chamber in the thickness of the wall.

SCALPAY, LONGAY AND THE CROWLIN ISLANDS

Scalpay ('isle shaped like a boat' or perhaps 'scallop') is a small island which lies off the north coast of Skye, a few miles north-west of Broadford and south of Raasay. It is oval in shape, and some four miles long at most. The land rises to about 396 metres at Mullach na Carn, and the island is hilly and has several forestry plantations on the south side.

The island was a property of the MacKinnons, and there are ruins of an old chapel, Teampuill Fraing [NG 629282], which was dedicated to St Francis. Ninety people lived on the island in 1841, and the island is still inhabited.

Oysters are widely found in the Sound of Scalpay, there is a herd of red deer on the island, and diving is available. The island is home to the Scalpay Woodturner (01471 822526; 07884 280816; www.scalpay.plus.com). Camping and fishing are available, although Scalpay House should be contacted first.

To the east is the small and uninhabited island of Longay ('long island'), which rises to 67 metres and covers 124 acres. It was said to be the resort of pirates and thieves in the sixteenth century.

Beyond this are the Crowlin Islands, made up of Eilean Mor ('big island'), Eilean Meadhonach ('middle island') and Eilean Beag ('little island'). Seals can be seen around the coasts, and the highest point is 114 metres. The islands have been uninhabited since the 1930s, although they are grazed by sheep.

PABAY

Pabay ('priest's isle') is another small island off the north coast of Skye, about three miles north of Broadford and four miles east of Scalpay. It is about a mile wide at its boadest, and covers some 300 acres.

The island has many species of birds, as well as otters and seals. There are some remains of a thirteenth-century chapel [NG 674265], and the island was held by the MacKinnons. Pabay was described as a den of thieves and pirates in 1549. There were once more than twenty people on the island but it has been uninhabited since the 1980s.

Boat trips to Pabay can be made from Broadford (0800 7832175/01471 822037/ 07880 731747; www.glassbottomboat.co.uk).

Postage stamps from Pabay are also available (www.pabay.org; 07787 565401).

SOAY

Soay ('sheep – or possibly sow's – island') is located off the south coast of Skye, three miles west of Elgol. The island is some three miles long, about two wide, and is bisected by two bays. The highest point of the island is 141 metres. The population has dwindled from a height of more than 150 down to being abandoned in 1953, although there are now a couple of permanent residents.

The island was long held by the MacLeods of Dunvegan until sold in 1944 to Gavin Maxwell, later author of *Ring of Bright Water*. Maxwell started a whaling station here in the 1940s, bringing a steam locomotive to power machinery; its rusting hulk survives, while the station closed soon after opening. Maxwell has been accused of seriously damaging the population of basking sharks, the damage extending to the present. He wrote about his experiences is his book *Harpoon at a Venture*.

Boat trips to the island and Loch Coruisk can be made from Elgol (0800 731 089/ 01471 866244; www.aquaxplore.co.uk – trips to Canna, Sanday and Rum can also be taken).

The *Soay of Our Fathers*, by Laurence Reed, is an account of the island and is available from Birlinn.

Places to Stay

HOTELS AND GUEST HOUSES

An Airidh (01478 612250)
    Portree; guest house; open all year
Ard na Mara (01470 542281)
    Uig; guest house; open all year
Ardvasar Hotel (01471 844223;
    www.ardvasarhotel.com)
    Ardvasar, Sleat; hotel and restaurant; open all year
Atholl House Hotel (01470 521219;
    www.athollhotel.co.uk)
    Dunvegan; hotel and bar; open Mar-Dec

Bosville Hotel (01478 612846;
    www.bosvillehotel.co.uk)
    Portree; hotel, bar and restaurant
Broadford Hotel (01471 822253)
    Broadford; hotel and bar; open Feb-Dec
Cuillin Hills Hotel (01478 612003;
    www.cuillinhills-hotel-skye.co.uk)
    Portree; hotel and restaurant in fifteen acres of grounds; open all year
Duisdale Country House Hotel (01471 833202;
    www.duisdale.com)
    Duisdale, Sleat; hotel
Dunollie Hotel (08000 507711; www.british-trust-hotels.com)
    Broadford; hotel; open Mar-Oct

Dunorin House Hotel (01470 521488; www.dunorinhousehotel-skye.com) Herebost, Dunvegan; hotel, restaurant and bar

Duntulm Castle Hotel (01470 552213; www.duntulmcastle.co.uk) Duntulm; hotel with bar meals and dinner; self-catering properties; open all year

Dunvegan Hotel (01470 521497; www.dunveganhotel.co.uk) Dunvegan; hotel and bar

Eilean Iarmain Hotel (01471 833332; www.eilean-iarmain.co.uk) Isleornsay, Sleat; hotel and restaurant; open all year

The Ferry Inn (01470 542242; www.ferryinn.co.uk) Uig; hotel, restaurant and bar; open all year

Flodigarry Country House Hotel (01470 552203; www.flodigarry.co.uk) Staffin; hotel and Flora MacDonald's cottage; open all year

Glenview Hotel (01470 562248; www.glenview-skye.co.uk) Culnaknock, Staffin; hotel and restaurant; open all year

Greshornish House Hotel (01470 582266; www.greshornishhotel.co.uk) Greshornish, between Portree and Dunvegan; hotel in eighteenth-century house in ten acres of grounds; open all year

Harlosh House (01470 521367/512) Harlosh, Dunvegan; hotel and restaurant; open Easter-mid Oct

Isles Inn (01478 612129) Portree; inn and bar; open all year

King's Arms Hotel (01599 534109; www.british-trust-hotels.com) Kyleakin; hotel

Kings Haven (01478 612290) Portree; guest house; open all year

Kinloch Lodge (01471 833214; www.kinloch-lodge.co.uk) Kinloch, Sleat; hotel and renowned restaurant; open all year

Kyle Hotel (01599 534204; www.kylehotel.co.uk) Kyle of Lochalsh; hotel and restaurant

The Lodge, Edinbane (01470 582217; www.the-lodge-at-edinbane.co.uk/www.edinbane-hotel.co.uk) Edinbane; sixteenth-century hunting lodge and coaching inn, offering accommodation, restaurant, bar and ghosts!; open all year

MacKinnon Hotel (01599 534180; www.mackinnonhotel.co.uk) Kyleakin; hotel

Meadowbank Guest House (01478 612 059; www.meadowbankguesthouse.co.uk) Portree; guest house; open all year

Old Inn (01478 640205; www.carbost.f9.co.uk) Carbost; B&B and hostel accommodation; meals and drinks; open all year

Pink Guest House (01478 612262) Portree; guest house; open mid Mar-mid Dec

Portree Hotel (01478 612511; www.hendersonhotels.com) Portree; hotel, restaurant, bistro and bar; open all year

Portree House (01478 613713; www.portreehouse.co.uk) Portree; hotel, restaurant and bar; open all year; also self-catering accommodation

Quirang Guest House (01478 612870) Portree; guest house; open all year

Rosedale Hotel (01478 613131; www.rosedalehotelskye.co.uk) Portree; hotel and restaurant; open Apr-Nov

Roskhill House (01470 521317; www.roskhillhouse.co.uk) Roskhill near Dunvegan; guest house; open Mar-Nov

Royal Hotel (01478 612525; www.royal-hotel-skye.com) Portree; hotel, leisure club, restaurant and bar; open all year

Sconser Lodge Hotel (01478 650333; www.sconserlodge.co.uk) Sconser; hotel, restaurant and bar in nineteenth-century hunting lodge; open Mar-Dec

Shielings Guest House (01478 613024) Portree; guest house; open all year

Shorefield House (01470 582 444; www.shorefield.com) Edinbane; guest house

Skeabost Country House Hotel (01470 532202; www.skeabostcountryhouse.com) Skeabost; hotel set among golf course

Skye Picture House (01471 822531; www.skyepicturehouse.co.uk) Ard Dorch (7 miles north of Broadford); guest house; open all year

Sligachan Hotel (01478 650204; www.sligachan.co.uk) Sligachan; hotel, bar and restaurant; self-catering lodge, sleeps twelve; and self-catering cottage, sleeps eight

Stein Inn (01470 592362; www.steininn.co.uk) Stein, Waternish; eighteenth-century inn with B&B, bar and restaurant; self-catering apartment; open all year

Tables Hotel and Restaurant (01470 521404; www.tables-hotel.co.uk) Dunvegan; hotel and restaurant; open all year, except Christmas and New Year

Taigh Ailean Hotel (01478 640271; www.taigh-ailean-hotel.co.uk) Portnalong; hotel, bar and restaurant; open all year

Talisker House (01478 640245) Talisker; guest house; open Mar-Oct

Toravaig House Hotel (01471 833231/820200; www.skyehotel.co.uk) Knock Bay, Teangue, Sleat; hotel and restaurant; open Feb-end Dec

Uig Hotel (01470 542205; www.uig-hotel.co.uk) Uig; hotel, bar and restaurant; open all year

Ullinish Lodge Hotel (01470 572214; www.theisleofskye.co.uk) Ullinish, Struan; hotel and restaurant; open Easter-Oct

Viewfield House (01478 612217;
www.viewfieldhouse.com)
Portree; hotel in twenty acres of woodlands;
open mid-Apr-mid Oct
White Heather Hotel (01599 534577;
www.whiteheatherhotel.co.uk)
Kyleakin; hotel; open all year

BED AND BREAKFAST

Achtalean (01470 562723; www.isleofskye.net/
achtalean/)
Stenscholl, Staffin; B&B; open all year
Alderburn (01478 611264; www.alderburn.co.uk)
Portree; B&B; open all year; self-catering
annexe
Almondbank (01478 612696)
Portree; B&B; open all year
Ard Chuain (01478 613513; www.ard-chuain-
portree.co.uk)
Portree; B&B; open Mar-Nov
Ard na Mara (01470 542281;
www.bandbisleofskye.co.uk)
Idrigill, Uig; B&B; open all year
Ashaig (01470 582335; www.skye-bed-and-
breakfast.co.uk)
Kildonan, Edinbane; B&B; open Apr-Oct
Ashlea Guest House (01478 612996; www.ashlea-
guest-house.co.uk)
Portree; B&B; open all year
Balloch (01478 612093)
Portree; B&B; open Easter-Oct
Bay View House (01478 640244)
Talisker Bay; B&B; open all year
Beams (01470 592754; www.waternish-herbs.co.uk)
Waternish; B&B
Benview (01471 822445; www.isleofskye.net/
benview/)
Broadford; B&B; open Easter-Oct
Berabhaigh (01471 822372; www.isleofskye.net/
berabhaigh/)
Broadford; B&B; open Apr-Oct
Birnam (01471 822417; www.isleofskye.net/birnam)
Broadford; B&B; open all year
Blairdhu House (01599 534760;
www.blairdhuhouse.co.uk)
Kyleakin; B&B
The Blue Lobster (01478 640230)
Glen Eynort, near Carbost; B&B; open Apr-Jan
Brae Fasach (01470 592732; www.isleofskye.net/
braefasach/)
Waternish; B&B; open all year
Braigh Uige (01470 542228; www.uig-skye.co.uk)
Uig; B&B; open Mar-Oct
Ceol-na-Mara (01599 534443; www.isleofskye.net/
ceol-na-mara/)
Kyleakin; B&B; open all year
Ceol na Mara (01470 562242;
www.ceolnamara.co.uk)
Stenscholl, Staffin; B&B; open all year
Clar-Inis (01470 521511)
Harlosh, Dunvegan; B&B; open all year
Cnoc Ban (01471 866294; www.isleofskye.net/
cnocban/)
Elgol; B&B; open May-Sep

Coruisk House (01471 866330; www.seafood-
skye.co.uk)
Elgol; B&B; open Apr-Sep
Credo (01599 534629; www.kyleakin.com)
South Obbe, Kyleakin; B&B
Cruinn Bheinn (01470 532459;
www.cruinnbheinn.co.uk)
Kensaleyre, Isle of Skye, Scotland
Darnbrook Guest House (01470 592301;
www.darnbrook.com)
Waternish; guest house; open all year
Drumorell (01478 613058)
Portree; B&B; open all year
Drynoch Farmhouse (01478 640441;
www.isleofskye.net/drynochhouse/)
Drynoch, by Carbost; B&B; open all year
Dunsgarth (01478 612851; www.dunsgarth.com)
Portree; B&B; open all year
Earsary (01471 822697; www.isleofskye.net/earsary)
Broadford; B&B; open all year
Easandubh (01470 521424)
Dunvegan; B&B; open Jan-Nov
Fairwinds (01471 822270; www.isleofskye.net/
fairwinds/)
Broadford; B&B; open Mar-Oct
Fernlea (01471 822107; www.isleofskye.net/fernlea)
Breakish; B&B; open all year
Gairloch View (01470 562718;
www.gairlochview.co.uk)
Staffin; B&B, also self-catering
accommodation, sleeps four; open all year
Glenview Inn (01470 562248; www.glenview-
skye.co.uk)
Culnacnoc, Staffin; open Mar-Oct
Greenbank (01470 592369;
www.greenbankonskye.co.uk)
Waternish; B&B
Green Gables House (01470 562718;
www.greengableshouse.co.uk)
Harrapool, Broadford; B&B; open all year
Harbourview (01478 612069)
Portree; B&B
Harris Cottage (01470 542268; http://
website.lineone.net/-trotternish/harrisc.html)
Uig; B&B; open Apr-Oct
Hazelwood Cottage (01471 822294;
www.isleofskye.net/hazelwoodcottage/)
Heaste; B&B; open Apr-Nov
Hazelwood (01471 822431; www.isleofskye.net/
hazelwood/)
Lower Breakish; B&B; open Apr-Oct
The Hebridean Hotel (01471 822486;
www.hebrideanhotel.co.uk)
Broadford; B&B; open all year
Heronfield (01478 613050)
Portree; B&B; open Apr-Oct
Hillcrest (01471 822375)
Broadford; B&B; open Mar-Oct
Java Croft (01470 542361; www.javacroft.co.uk)
Earlish, Uig; B&B; open Mar-Oct
3 Kilmore (01471 844272; www.isleofskye.net/
3kilmore/)
Kilmore, near Armadale; B&B; open Easter-
September

Kilmuir House (01470 521644;
www.kilmuirhouse.co.uk)
Dunvegan; B&B; open Mar-Oct
Kilmuir House (01470 542262; www.kilmuir-
skye.co.uk)
Kilmuir, near Uig; B&B with walled garden;
open all year
Kilmuir Park (01470 521586;
www.kilmuirpark.co.uk)
Kilmuir, Dunvegan; B&B; open all year
15 Kyleside (01599 534468; www.kyleakin.com)
Kyleakin; B&B
17 Kyleside (01599 534197; www.kyleakin.com)
Kyleakin; B&B
Langal (01478 640409; www.isleofskye.net/langal)
Carbost; B&B; open all year
Limestone Cottage (01471 822142;
www.smoothhound.co.uk/hotels/
limestone.html)
Broadford; B&B; open all year
Loch Aluinn (01478 650288; www.isleofskye.net/
loch-aluinn/)
Sconser; B&B, also self-catering; open Apr-Oct
Lon Ruadh (01470 542408; www.lon-ruadh.co.uk)
Kingsburgh, Uig; B&B; open Mar-Nov
Lorgill (01470 592346)
Waternish; B&B
5 Luib (01471 822427; www.isleofskye.net/5luib/)
Luib; B&B; open all year
Luib House (01471 820334; www.luibhouse.co.uk)
Luib; B&B; open all year
Lyndale House (01470 582329; www.lyndale.net)
Edinbane; B&B and self-catering
accommodation; open all year
Meadowbank House (01478 612059;
www.isleofskye.net/meadowbankhouse/)
Portree; B&B; open Mar-Oct
Medina (01478 612821; www.medinaskye.co.uk)
Portree; B&B; open all year
Millbrae House (01471 822310)
Broadford; B&B
Mo Dhachaidh (01599 534724;
www.skyeguesthouse.co.uk)
Kyleakin; B&B and self-catering apartment;
open all year
Moorfield (01470 521416)
Dunvegan; B&B; open Apr-Oct
Obbe View (01599 534859; http://
members.aol.com/ObbeViewSkye/)
Kyleakin; guest house
1 Olaf Road (01599 534440; www.kyleakin.com)
Kyleakin; B&B; open all year
4 Olaf Road (01599 534483; www.kyleakin.com)
Kyleakin; B&B; open Apr-Oct
Orasay (01470 542316; www.orasay.freeserve.co.uk/
bandb.html)
Uig; B&B; open all year
The Pink Guest House (01478 612263; www.pink-
guest-house.co.uk)
Portree; guest house
Ptarmigan (01471 822744; www.ptarmigan-
cottage.com)
Broadford; B&B and self-catering cottage
sleeping two; open all year

Quiraing View (01470 562388; www.isleofskye.net/
quiraingview/bedandbreakfast)
Staffin; B&B and self-catering apartment
Rose Croft (01471 866377; www.isleofskye.net/
rosecroft/)
Elgol; B&B
Roskhill House (01470 521317;
www.roskhillhouse.co.uk)
Roskhill, by Dunvegan; B&B; open Mar-Nov
Rowan Cottage (01471 866287;
www.rowancottage-skye.co.uk)
Glasnakille, Elgol; B&B; open Mar-Nov
The Rowans (01478 640478; www.stemdp.co.uk/
bandb.html)
Portnalong; B&B; open all year
Ruisgarry (01471 822850; www.isleofskye.net/
ruisgarry/)
Breakish; B&B; open Mar-Nov
Seaview (01471 820308; www.isleofskye.net/
seaview/)
Broadford; B&B; open all year
The Shieling (01471 822533;
www.skyeserpentarium.org.uk)
Broadford; B&B
Shiloh (01471 822346; www.isleofskye.net/shiloh/
bedandbreakfast/)
Upper Breakish; B&B; open Easter-Sep
Shorefield House (01470 582444)
Edinbane; B&B; open all year
Silverdale Guesthouse (01470 521251;
www.silverdaleskye.com)
Skinidin, Dunvegan; guest house; open all year
Strathaird House (01471 866269)
Strathaird (ten miles south-west of Broadford);
B&B
Swordale House (01471 822272;
www.isleofskye.net/swordalehouse/)
Glen Suardal, by Broadford; B&B; open
Feb-Nov
Tarner (01478 640377; www.ardtreck.co.uk)
Ardtreck, by Carbost; B&B; open all year
Tern House (01470 592332; www.ternhouse.com)
Waternish; B&B
Three Chimneys Restaurant (01470 511258;
www.threechimneys.co.uk)
Colbost, near Dunvegan; renowned restaurant
and rooms
Tigh-a-Cladach (01599 534891;
skyelochalsh.topcities.com/bed.html)
Badicaul, Lochalsh; B&B; open all year
Tigh na Mara (01471 822475)
Lower Harrapool, Broadford; B&B; open
May-Sep
Tir Alainn (01471 822366; www.visitskye.com)
Breakish; B&B; open all year
Torwood (01470 532479; www.selma.co.uk)
Peinness, by Portree; B&B
Uig Bay Bed and Breakfast (01470 542714;
www.uig-camping-skye.co.uk/bed-and-
breakfast.htm)
Uig; B&B; open all year
Westside (01471 820243; www.isleofskye.net/
westside/)
Broadford; B&B; open Mar-Dec

West Haven (01599 534476; www.kyleakin.com)
Kyleakin; B&B
Woodbine House (01470 542243)
Uig; B&B; open all year

SELF-CATERING PROPERTIES

Alderburn (01478 611264; www.alderburn.co.uk)
Portree; self-catering studio apartment,
sleeps two
The Anchorage (07773 770319; www.skye-
anchorage.com)
Kyleakin; self-catering cottage, sleeps six
Ard Thurinish (01631 562239;
www.peaceofskye.co.uk)
Aird of Sleat; self-catering cottage, sleeps six
Armadale (01471 844305/227;
www.clandonald.com)
Armadale, Sleat; accommodation available:
seven cottages and Flora MacDonald suite;
open all year
Ardmore Holiday Cottage (01470 592305)
Waternish; self-catering cottage
Auld Alliance, The (01470 592363; www.the-auld-
alliance.co.uk)
Waternish; self-catering
Barabhaig (www.unique-cottages.co.uk/cottages/
westcoast/skye/barabhaig/)
Camus Croise; self-catering croft cottage,
sleeps six
Bayview (01478 612669; www.bayview-
portree.co.uk)
Portree; self-catering property
Beaton's Croft House (0131 243 9331;
www.nts.org.uk)
Bornesketaig (twenty or so miles north of
Portree); simple accommodation in a restored
eighteenth-century thatched house in a
crofting township, sleeps two; open all year
Ben Edra (01470 562419; www.isleofskye.net/ben-
edra/)
Staffin; self-catering, sleeps four
Ben View Cottage (01471 822210;
www.benviewcottage.com)
Harrapool, by Broadford; self-catering cottage,
sleeps four-six
Bergerie, La (01470 592282; www.la-bergerie-
skye.co.uk)
Waternish; self-catering
Braevalla Chalets (01470 582221; www.edinbane-
self-catering.co.uk)
Upper Edinbane; three chalets; open all year
3 Breckery (01159 730668; www.isleofskye.net/
3breckery/)
Breckery, by Staffin; self-catering traditional
cottage, sleeps four
Brook Cottage (01478 612980)
Portree; slef-catering bungalow, sleeping five;
open all year
Burnside (01470 562235)
Culnacnock, Staffin; self-catering property,
sleeps four; open all year
Burnside (0151 625 6137; www.isleofskye.net/
burnside/)
Elgol; self-catering trad. cottage, sleeps six

Cairn Ban (01471 822 296; www.isleofskye.net/
cairnban/)
Breakish; caravan, sleeps six
Cairn Ban Chalet (01471 822 296;
www.isleofskye.net/cairnban/chalet/)
Breakish; self-catering chalet, sleeps four
Calligary Cottages (01471 844205;
www.calligarycottages.co.uk)
Ardvasar, by Armadale; two self-catering
cottages, sleep four/five; open all year
Camus Edge (01470 592326;
www.holidaycottages.cc/detail.html?id=906)
Waternish; self-catering
The Captain's House (01470 592223/218; www.the-
captains-house.co.uk)
Waternish; self-catering
Carbost (01478 640218; www.glendrynoch.co.uk)
Glendrynoch Lodge, Carbost; two self-catering
cottages, sleep eight
Carn Ban (08708 704474; www.skye-holiday-
home.co.uk)
Staffin; self-catering traditional croft house,
sleeps six-eight
Clover Hill Holiday Cottage (01471 822763;
www.host.co.uk)
Rowanlea, Torrin; self-catering, sleeps six
Cnoc Mhairi (01478 613513; www.ard-chuain-
portree.co.uk)
Portree; self-catering house, sleeps six; open
all year
Coille Bhurich (01520 722992; www.kyleakin.com)
Kyleakin; self-catering
2 Connista (01470 552265; www.isleofskye.net/
2connista/)
Connista, Trotternish; residential caravan,
sleeps four; open Easter-Oct
Corrie Cottages (01478 640324;
www.corriecottages.co.uk)
Satran, Carbost; two cottages, both sleeping up
to four people
Dunmhor (01984 656348; www.isleofskye.net/
dunmhor/)
Torrin; self-catering croft cottage, sleeps
four-six
Duntulm Coastguard Cottages (01470 552213;
www.duntulmcastle.co.uk)
Duntulm; self-catering cottages, three sleeping
six-seven, one sleeping eight-ten; hotel with
bar meals and dinner; open all year
Dunvegan Cottages (01470 521206;
www.dunvegancastle.com)
Dunvegan; three self-catering cottages; open
all year
Edinbane Self-Catering Cottages (01470 582221;
www.edinbane-self-catering.co.uk)
Edinbane; two-self-catering cottage, each sleep
four; three chalets (near Dunvegan), sleep up
to four
Eilean Isay (0141 942 9295; www.eilean-isay.co.uk)
Waternish; self-catering croft house, sleeps
six-eight
Ellen Cottage (01470 521505)
Brunigill Farm, near Dunvegan; self-catering,
sleeps five; open all year

Gairloch View (01470 562718;
www.gairlochview.co.uk/cottage/)
Staffin; self-catering cottages, sleep four; open
all year

Gesto Cottage (01470 592281/767; www.gesto-
cottage.co.uk)
Waternish; self-catering cottage

Gramarye Cottage (01539 741042;
www.skyecottage.co.uk)
Peinachorran, by Portree; self-catering croft
cottage, sleeps four-six

Greshornish Cottages (01470 582318)
Edinbane; self-catering, sleeps four-five, on
working farm; open all year

2 Harrapool (01471 822498; mysite.freeserve.com/
SkyeAccommodation/)
Harrapool, by Broadford; self-catering
apartment, sleeps two-three

Henderson House (01470 592235; www.skye-
cottage.co.uk)
Waternish; self-catering house

Heron Cottage (01471 822840;
www.isleofskye.net/heroncottage/)
Luib; self-catering cottage, sleep two

Hillview (01471 822840; www.isleofskye.net/
hillview/)
Broadford; self-catering town-house, sleeps
four-eight

Inver Rose (0191 384 0151; www.isle-of-skye-self-
catering.co.uk/)
Kyleakin; self-catering bungalow, sleeps six

Isle of Skye Holiday Homes (01470 552279;
www.isle-of-skye-holiday-homes.co.uk
Kilmuir; two self-catering cottages, sleep up to
four; self-catering house, sleeps eight; open
all year

Kilbride House (01471 822245)
Kilbride near Broadford; one chalet, one flat,
sleeps two-four; open Apr-Oct

Loch Aluinn (01478 650288; www.skye-holiday-
home.co.uk)
Sconser; self-catering apartment, sleeps four

The Longhouse (01471 855326; www.isleofskye.net/
longhouse/)
Tokavaig, Sleat; self-catering house, sleeps
eight

5 Luib (01471 822427; www.isleofskye.net/5luib/
caravan/)
Luib; caravan

Lusta Cottage (01628 476149; www.isleofskye.net/
lustacottage/)
Waternish; self-catering bungalow

Lyndale (01470 582329; www.lyndale.net)
Edinbane; two self-catering cottages, each
sleep two; self-catering gate lodge, sleeps four;
B&B also available; open all year

MacGregor Cottage (www.unique-cottages.co.uk/
cottages/westcoast/skye/macgregor)
Ord; self-catering cottage, sleeps six

Mary's Cottages (01471 866275;
www.maryscottages.co.uk)
Elgol; self-catering thatched cottages,
sleep four

Merman Cottage (01470 582221; www.edinbane-
self-catering.co.uk)
Upper Edinbane; self-catering cottage, sleeps
six; open all year

New House (01687 460095; www.isleofskye.net/
new-house-old-corry/)

Neist Point Lighthouse (01470 511200;
www.sykelighthouse.com)
Glendale; three self-catering cottages, sleep up
to eight; open all year

Old Croft House (01494 776789;
www.beautifulskye.co.uk)
Aird, Sleat; self-catering traditional croft
house, sleeps six

Old Croft House (01471 822685;
www.oldcrofthouse.net)
Glen Suardal, by Torrin; self-catering
traditional stone-built cottage, sleeps two

The Old Mission Hall (01470 521655;
www.oldmissionhall.co.uk)
Waternish; self-catering

Orasay Caravans (01470 542316;
www.orasay.freeserve.co.uk)
Uig; caravans, sleep up to six

Ose Farm (01470 572296)
Struan; self-catering cottage, sleeps four; open
all year

The Pier House (01471 866259; www.gael.net/
pierhouse/)
Elgol; self-catering apartment, sleeps two-four;
open all year

Primrose Cottage Apartments (01470 542216;
www.primrosecottage-skye.co.uk)
Uig; self-catering apartments in traditional
cottage, sleep two-four

Ptarmigan (01471 822744; www.ptarmigan-
cottage.com)
Broadford; B&B and self-catering cottage
sleeping two; open all year

Quiraing View (01470 562388; www.isleofskye.net/
quiraingview/)
Staffin; self-catering flat, sleeps four

Sandaig Cottage (01471 833212;
www.sandaigonskye.co.uk)
Duisdalemhor, Isleornsay; self-catering cottage,
sleeps four

Scavaig View (01471 866 315; www.isleofskye.net/
scavaig-view/)
Elgol; self-catering crofthouse, sleeps six

Seaford Croft (01339 886023; www.isleofskye.net/
seafordcroft/)
Waterloo, by Broadford; self-catering
traditional crofthouse, sleeps six

Seaview (01229 716777; www.isleofskye.net/
sgoirebreac/)
Elgol; self-catering traditional crofthouse,
sleeps seven

Sgoirebreac (01478 650322;
www.silverdaleskye.com)
Sconser; self-catering bungalow, sleeps four

Silverdale Cottage (01470 521251
Skinidin, Dunvegan; traditional croft cottage,
sleeps two

Skylark Cottage (01502 502588;
www.isleofskye.net/skylarkcottage/)
Breakish; self-catering thatched cottage,
sleeps four

Staffin Bay Holiday Homes (01470 562217)
Staffin; three bungalows, each sleeps four; open
all year

Stein Inn (01470 592362; www.stein-inn.co.uk)
Waternish; self-catering accommodation
available

Talisker House (01638 674749;
www.statelyholidayhomes.co.uk/properties/
scotland/talisker/talisker.htm)
Near Carbost; self-catering Georgian house,
sleeps twelve

Taigh an Tuath (01471 844 350; www.southskye-
selfcatering.co.uk)
Isle Ornsay; self-catering house, sleeps eight

Taigh a' Choin (01471 866 366; www.duncan-
house.com/accommodation/)
Kirkibost, near Elgol; self-catering apartment,
sleeps four-six

Tides Reach (01835 870779; www.unique-
cottages.co.uk/cottages/westcoast/skye/
tidesreach/)
Isleornsay; self-catering croft cottage, sleeps
up to six

Tigh Dhomhnuill (01471 833365;
www.cottageguide.co.uk/tighdhomhnuill/)
Camus Cross, Isle Ornsay; self-catering croft
cottage, sleeps six

Tigh Holm Cottages (01471 822848;
www.isleofskye.net/tighholm/)
Broadford; self-catering cottages, sleep four

Tigh Mhartainn (01470 542279)
Hungladder, Kilmuir; self-catering house,
sleeps eight; open all year

Tigh na Keppoch (01471 866330;
www.isleofskye.net/coruiskhouse/
tighnakeppoch/)
Keppoch, by Elgol; self-catering cottage, sleeps
four-six

Tigh Phòil (01471 866330 ; www.isleofskye.net/
coruiskhouse/tighphoil/)
Elgol; self-catering traditional cottage,
sleeps two

Tigh Uilleand (01478 640424/427;
www.skyeholiday.co.uk)
Fiscavaig; self-catering cottage, sleeps six; open
all year

Taigh Ur (01471 822078; www.isleofskye.net/
9torrin/taighur/)
Torrin; self-catering upstairs flat, sleeps four

9 Torrin (01471 822078; www.isleofskye.net/
9torrin/)
Torrin; caravan, sleeps six

10 Torrin (01471 822669; www.isleof

HOSTELS AND RETREATS

Armadale Youth Hostel (0870 004 1103;
www.syha.org.uk)
Armadale; youth hostel, sleeps forty-two; open
Apr-Sep

Broadford Youth Hostel (0870 004 1106;
www.syha.org.uk)
Broadford; youth hostel, sleeps sixty-five; open
Mac-Oct

Croft Bunkhouse and Bothies (01478 640254)
Portnalong, near Carbost; four hostels, sleep
fourteen to two; open all year

Dun Caan Independent Backpackers (01599
534087; www.skyerover.co.uk)
Kyleakin; sleeps sixteen; open all year (although
check Nov-Mar)

Dun Flodigarry Hostel (01470 552212)
Staffin; hostel, sleeps forty; open Mar-Oct

Flora MacDonald Hostel (01471 844440/272)
Kilmore, Sleat; sleeps twenty-four; open
all year

Fossil Bothy Hostel (1471 822297)
13 Lower Breakish; hostel

Glenbrittle Youth Hostel (0870 004 1121;
www.syha.org.uk)
Glenbrittle; youth hostel, sleeps thirty-six;
open Apr-Sep

Glen Hinnisdal Bunkhouse (01470 542293)
Glen Hinnisdal, near Snizort; sleeps up to six;
open all year

Kyleakin Youth Hostel (0870 004 1134;
www.syha.org.uk)
Kyleakin; youth hostel, sleeps 125; open all year

Portree Backpackers Hostel (01478 613641)
Portree; hostel, sleeps sixty; open all year

Portree Independent Hostel (01478 613737)
Portree; hostel, sleeps sixty; open all year

Skye Backpackers Guest House (01599 534510;
www.kyleakin.com)
Kyleakin; hostel

Skyewalker Independent Hostel (01478 640250;
www.skyewalkerhostel.com)
Fiskavaig Road, Portnalong; hostel, sleeps
thirty-six; shop and post office; small campsite

Uig Youth Hostel (0870 004 1155;
www.syha.org.uk)
Uig; youth hostel, sleeps sixty-two; open
Apr-Sep

Waterfront Bunkhouse (01478 640205;
www.carbost.f9.co.uk)
Old Inn, Carbost; hostel and B&B, meals and
drinks; open all year

CAMPING AND CARAVANS

Glenbrittle Campsite (01478 640404/521206;
www.dunvegancastle.com)
Loch Brittle; campsite with shower and toilet
block, and shop; fishing permits; open mid
Apr-early Oct

Loch Greshornish Caravan and Campsite (01470
582230; www.skyecamp.com)
Loch Greshornish; 130 Touring pitches, 28
Electric hook-ups, licensed on-site shop,
showers and laundry; bike and canoe hire; open
Apr-mid Oct

Kinloch Camp Site (01470 521210; www.kinloch-
campsite.co.uk)
Kinloch, Dunvegan; campsite

Sligachan Camp Site (07786 435294)
Sligachan Carbost; camp site

Staffin Caravan and Camping Site (01470 562213)
Staffin; two-acre park accommodating fifty; open mid Apr-Sep

Torvaig Caravan And Camping Site (01478 612209)
Staffin; caravan and campsite, 90 touring pitches; open Mar-Oct

Uig Bay Caravan and Campsite (01470 542714; www.uig-camping-skye.co.uk)
10 Idrigill, Uig; caravan and campsite, cycle hire; B&B; open all year

PLACES TO EAT

Alba (01471820000)
Old School, Breakish; fish, seafood and meat restaurant; open Easter-early Oct

Bosville Hotel (01478 612846; www.bosvillehotel.co.uk)
Portree; hotel, bar and restaurant

Castle Moil Restaurant and Bar (01599 534164)
Kyleakin; local seafood

Chandlery Seafood and Game Restaurant (01478 612846)
Portree; restaurant; open all year

Claymore Restaurant (01471 822333)
Broadford; restaurant and bar meals; open all year

Coruisk House Restaurant (01471 866330; www.seafood-skye.co.uk)
Coruisk House, Elgol; restaurant (squat lobster tails a speciality): booking recommended; accommodation also available; open to mid-Oct

Creelers of Skye Seafood Restaurant (01471-822281; www.skye-seafood-restaurant.co.uk
Broadford; sea-food restaurant; closed mid Dec-beg. March: tel. to confirm and booking advised even in season

Cuillin Hills Hotel (01478 612003; www.cuillinhills-hotel-skye.co.uk)
Portree; hotel and restaurant in fifteen acres of grounds; open all year

Granary Restaurant (01478 612873)
Portree; licensed restaurant; open all year

Harbour View Seafood Restaurant (01478 612069; www.harbourviewskye.co.uk)
Portree; cottage restaurant and wine bar; open Mar-Oct

Kinloch Lodge (01471 833214; www.kinloch-lodge.co.uk)
Sleat; renowned restaurant, open to non-residents; accommodation available

Lochbay Seafood Restaurant (01470 592235; www.lochbay-seafood-restaurant.co.uk)
Stein, Waternish; sea-food restaurant; open Easter-Oct

The Lodge, Edinbane (01470 582217; www.the-lodge-at-edinbane.co.uk/www.edinbane-hotel.co.uk)
Edinbane; sixteenth-century hunting lodge and coaching inn, offering accommodation, restaurant, bar and ghosts!; open all year

Lower Deck Restaurant (01478 613611)
Portree; restaurant; open Mar-Oct

The Old School House (01470 521421)
Dunvegan; restaurant; open Mar-Nov, daily

Portree House (01478 613713; www.portreehouse.co.uk)
Portree; hotel, restaurant and bar; open all year

Pub at the Pier (01470 542212(
Uig; bar restaurant; open all year

Skywalker Cafe and Shop (01478 640250)
Portnalong; licensed cafe; open Easter-mid Oct

Sligachan Hotel (01478 650204; www.sligachan.co.uk)
Sligachan; hotel, bar and restaurant

Stables Restaurant (01471 844305)
Armadale Castle gardens; licensed restaurant

Stein Inn (01470 592362; www.steininn.co.uk)
Stein, Waternish; eighteenth-century inn with B&B, bar, restaurant and ghosts; and self-catering apartment; open all year

An Strupag (01470 511204)
Lephin, Glendale; local produce, restaurant; also grocers and craft shop; open all year

Tables Hotel and Restaurant (01470 521404; www.tables-hotel.co.uk)
Dunvegan; hotel and Scottish restaurant; open Mar-Oct

Three Chimneys Restaurant (01470 511258; www.threechimneys.co.uk)
Colbost, Dunvegan; renowned restaurant and rooms

Uig Hotel (01470 542205; www.uig-hotel.co.uk)
Uig; hotel, bar and restaurant; open all year

Many of the hotels listed in the earlier section on places to stay also have restaurants or serve bar meals.

Further Information

TRANSPORT

BUSES

Nicolsons of Borve (01478 640400)
Borve

Postbuses: Dunvegan - Glendale; Portree - Waternish - Dunvegan and (summer only) Portree - Glenbrittle; Elgol-Broadford; www.royalmail.com/postbus

Rapsons (01478 612622; www.rapsons.com)
Portree; timetable is posted on website but many routes around the island

CAR HIRE

PC Portree Coachworks (01478 612688)
Portree

West End Garage (01478 612554)
Portree

CYCLE HIRE

Fairwinds (01471 822270; www.isleofskye.net/fairwinds/cyclehire/)
Elgol Road, Broadford; touring, sports and mountain bikes

Sutherlands Garage (01471 822225)
Main road, Broadford

Island Cycles (01478 613121)
The Green, Portree; touring and off-road bikes; repairs, tools and range of tyres

Skye Ferry Filling Station (01471 844249)
Ardvasar, Sleat
Glendale Cycle Hire
Glendale; by the post office; closed Sun
Cycle hire is also available from Loch Greshornish
Caravan and Campsite and Uig Bay Caravan
and Camp Site

TAXIS

A1 Cabs (01478 611112)
A2B (01478 613456)
Ace Taxis (01478 613600)
Armadale and Ardvasar Taxis (01471 844361)
Clan MacDonald Taxis (01471 844272)
Donald Nicolson Taxis and Island Tours (01471
844338; www.nicolsonhire.co.uk)
Duncan MacLean Taxi and Private Hire (01471
822343)
Gus's Taxis (01478 613000)
Kyleakin Private Hire (01599 534452;
www.scotland-info.co.uk/skye-tours.htm)
Skye Hire (01599 534110)
Waterloo Private Taxis (01471 822630;
www.isleofskye.net/cairnban/waterloo/)

ACTIVITIES AND SPORTS

BOAT TRIPS

(also see Skye and Lochalsh Marine Tourism
Association 01471 866244; www.slmta.co.uk)
Aquaxplore/Bella Jane (0800 731 3089/01471
866244; www.aquaxplore.co.uk/
www.bellajane.co.uk)
Elgol; boat trips to Loch Coruisk, as well as
Soay, Canna and Rum
Brigadoon Boat Trips (01478 613718)
Fishing trips and tours
Coel na Mara Charters (01478 612461;
www.skyewaves.co.uk)
Portree; wildlife trips and charter (open Mar-
Oct)
Family Pride Boat Trips (0800 7832175/07774
124125; www.glassbottomboat.co.uk)
Broadford; boat trips in a glass-bottomed boat:
scenery and marine wildlife, above and below
the water; also trips in SkyeJet a rigid inflatable
boat (RIB)
Sea.fari (01471 833316; www.seafari.co.uk/skye)
Armadale or Isleornsay; trips to the south of
Skye in rigid inflatable boats
Staffin Bay Cruises (01470 562217;
www.trotternish.co.uk/boattrips.html)
Staffin; boat trips along the Trotternish coast
and charters

SAILING AND YACHTING

Fyne Leisure and Marine (01471 833470)
Isleornsay; classic yacht available for charter
Isle of Skye Yachts (01471 844216;
www.isleofskyeyachts.co.uk)
Ardvasar, Sleat; yacht charter, marine services
and repair, mooring and supplies
The Skye Boat Centre (01471 822070;
www.skyeboatcentre.co.uk)
Strollamus, near Broadford; boating, fishing,
ATV and diving resource centre
Skye Sailing Club (www.skyesc.org.uk)
Portree; dinghy sailing club

Skye Sail Yacht Charters (01471 613426; www.skye-
sail.co.uk)
Portree; cruises of varying lengths

KAYAKING

Whitewave Outdoor Activity Centre (01470
542414; www.white-wave.co.uk
Linicro, Kilmuir; activities, including archery,
kayaking, canoeing, rock climbing and
windsurfing; B&B accommodation and cafe
Skyak Adventures (01471 833428;
www.skyakadventures.com)
Camuscross, Isleornsay; kayaking for all ages,
novice or experienced including courses in
whitewater and the sea

DIVING

Dive and Sea the Hebrides (01470 592219;
www.dive-and-sea-the-hebrides.co.uk)
Lochbay, Waternish; diving holidays with
accommodation at the dive centre; boat
charter; suitable for qualified divers

SWIMMING AND SPORTS

Isle of Skye Swimming Pool (01478 612655)
Camanachd Square, Portree; swimming pool;
open Mon-Sat
There is also a leisure centre with a swimming
pool and fitness suite at Kyle of Lochalsh and
an indoor sports centre at Edinbane.

WALKING AND CLIMBING

There are many fine hill and ridge walks,
scrambles and climbs, ranging from easy
through moderate to the extremely difficult,
including fifteen Munros (hills over 3000 feet
or 900 or so metres). Many routes should only
be attempted by the fit, experienced and well
equipped. There are mountain huts at Glen
Brittle (01882 632240) and Coruisk (0141 577
9415). Coruisk can be reached by boat from
Elgol. Many local guides offer a variety of types
of trips from coastal walks to rock climbing.
Blaven Guiding (01478 613180;
www.blavenguiding.co.uk)
Cuillin Guides Mountain and Climbing Guides
(01478 640289; www.cuillin-guides.co.uk)
Experience Skye Mountain Guides (01478 822018;
www.experience-skye.co.uk)
Guiding on Skye and the Cuillin (01478 650380;
www.guidingonskye.co.uk)
Hebridean Pathways (01471 820179)
Mike Lates (01471 822116; www.skyeguides.so.uk)
Christopher Mitchell (01470 511265)
Mountain Guiding on Skye (01471 822964)
Pinnacle Ridge (01478 640330)
Scottish Youth Hostels Association (01786
891400; www.syha.org.uk)
Skyetrak Safari (01470 532436)
A free guide to forest walks and trails is available
from Forest Enterprise.
Mountain Rescue (01478 612888)

FISHING

Glenbrittle Campsite shop (01478 640404)
Glenbrittle; permits for River Brittle
Isle of Skye Sea Angling Club (01470 521724)
Dunvegan; sea angling
Isle Ornsay Hotel (01471 833332; www.eilean-
iarmain.co.uk
Isle Ornsay permits for estate

Jansport (01476 612559)
Portree; permits for Storr Lochs
Skeabost Country House Hotel (01470 532202;
www.skeabostcountryhouse.com)
Skeabost; fishing permits for River Snizort
Sligachan Hotel (01478 650204;
www.sligachan.co.uk)
Sligachan; permits for River Sligachan

RIDING AND PONY TREKKING—

Portree Riding Stables (01478 613124;
www.portreeriding.co.uk)
Garalapin, Portree; holiday riding centre
Skye Riding Centre (01470 582419;
www.skyeridingcentre.co.uk/www.skye-
riding.co.uk)
2 Suledale, Clachamish, by Portree; horse
riding, pony trekking and lessons for all ages;
accommodation available; cafe; open all year
West Highland Heavy Horses (01471844759/07769
588565; www.westhighlandheavyhorses.com
Ardvasar, Sleat; Clydesdale and Shire horses
riding, trekking and trail riding for all abilities

GOLF

Isle of Skye Golf Club (01478 650414;
www.isleofskyegolfclub.co.uk)
Sconser; nine-hole course with eighteen tees;
clubhouse with cafe and shop
Skeabost Golf Club (01470 532202;
www.skeabostcountryhouse.com)
Skeabost; nine-hole course with eighteen tees
in the grounds of Skeabost Hotel
There is also a course at Kyle of Lochalsh, just
over the bridge

OUTDOOR ACTIVITIES

Whitewave Outdoor Activity Centre (01470
542414; www.white-wave.co.uk
Linicro, Kilmuir; activities, including archery,
kayaking, canoeing, rock climbing and
windsurfing; B&B accommodation and cafe
Isle of Skye Falconry (01470 532489/07808 218999;
www.discoverituk.plus.com/isleofskye/)
Kensaleyre; flying demonstrations and displays,
courses, hawk walks and talks

LOCAL PRODUCE

Anchor Seafoods (01478 612414)
Portree; freshly caught local seafood; open
Tue-Fri
Borealis Products (01471 822669;
www.borealisskye.co.uk)
Old Pier Road, Broadford; natural skin-care
products, plus wholefoods, herbal remedies
Isle of Skye Soap Company (01478 611350;
www.skye-soap.co.uk)
Portree; hand-made aromatherapy soap, made
using pure essential oils and remedies and
essential oils
Isle of Skye Seafood (01471 822135; www.skye-
seafood.co.uk)
Broadford; shop selling local shellfish and
smoked fish, also on-line sales

Skye Brewery (www.skyebrewery.co.uk; 01470
542477)
Uig Pier; the island's brewery with shop selling
own brand beer, souvenirs and other Scottish,
bottle beers and country wines
Skyeskyns (01470 592237; www.skyeskyns.co.uk)
Waternish; exhibition tannery: traditional
leather-making skills, sheepskin products, and
lambskin fleeces; open all year, daily 10.00-
18.00
Talisker Distillery (01478 640203/614308)
Carbost; distillery in a fine location; tours and
a well-stocked distillery shop; open Apr-Jun
and Oct, Mon-Fri 9.00-16.30; Jul-Sep, Mon-Sat
9.00-16.30; Nov-Mar, Mon-Fri 14.00-16.30
Vanilla Skye Chocolates (01478 611295;
www.vanillaskye.co.uk)
Bayfield Road, Portree; hand-made chocolates
with high percentage cocoa solids and natural
ingredients
World of Wood (01471 822831)
Broadford; ecological importance of planting
trees, arboretum with native trees, and
woodcraft items for sale; open Mar-Oct, Mon-
Sat

ARTS AND CRAFTS

Aird Old Church Gallery (01471 844291;
www.skyewatercolours.co.uk)
Aird of Sleat; watercolours and prints; open
Easter-Sep, Mon-Sat 10.00-17.00
An Tuireann Arts Centre and Cafe (01478 613306;
www.antuireann.org.uk)
Portree; local and national exhibitions, art
centre and cafe; open Mon-Sat, Sun closed;
cafe open Tue-Sat
Aros Experience (01478 613649; www.aros.co.uk)
Portree; exhibitions, audio-visual show theatre,
cinema, shop and restaurant
Armadale Pottery (01471 844439; www.armadale-
pottery.co.uk)
Armadale; large variety of domestic and
ornamental pottery and jewellery
Aurora Crafts (01470 572208)
Ose, near Struan; hand-made lace, knitwear,
spinning and other craft work. Lace making
demonstrations; open Easter -mid Oct, daily
9.00-19.00
Bay Pottery (01471 844442; www.baypottery.co.uk)
Armadale; open Mon-Fri, Easter-Oct also Sat-
Sun, 9.00-17.30
Brae Fasach Studio (01470 592732;
www.isleofskye.net/braefasach)
Loch Bay, Waternish; decorative and functional
ceramics, paintings, hand-made cards, paint
your own pots; open all year, daily 10.00-17.00
Broadford Books (01471 822748;
www.broadfordbooks.co.uk)
Old post office Building, Broadford; wide range
of books and artists materials; open Mon-Sat
Broadford Gallery (01471 822011; www.skye-
arts.co.uk)
Old Pier Road, Broadford; original oil paintings
and watercolours of Skye

Carol K. Kempt (01471 855368;
www.handmadeinskye.co.uk)
Tarskavaig, Sleat, isle of skye; oils and small
watercolours landscapes; open Easter-Oct,
daily

Castle Keep (01471 866376; www.castlekeep.co.uk)
Strathaird; hand-forged claymores, swords,
basket-hilted broadswords, dirks, sgian dubhs
and custom pieces; mail order or on-line

Craft Encounters (01471 822754;
www.craftencounters.co.uk)
Broadford post office; Scottish crafts, many
locally produced; open Mon-Sat 9.00-17.30;
open Sun in high season

The Crafts Shop (01470 612585)
Hungladder, Kilmuir; large range of crafts;
open May-Oct

Croft Studio (01470 521383; www.croft-
studio.com)
Dunvegan; ranges of crafts inspired by the
beauty, nature, culture and history of Skye;
open all year, daily

Cuillin View Gallery and Coffee Shop (01471
866223; www.isleofskye.net/cuillinview)
Elgol; art gallery and coffee shop; open daily,
Apr-Oct

Dandelion Designs and Images Gallery (01470
592218; www.dandelion-designs.co.uk)
Stein, Waternish; workshop and gallery:
pyrography, paintings, photographs, cards, local
artists and craftmakers; open Easter-Oct, daily
11.00-17.00; winter, tel. to confirm

Diana Mackie Artist (01470 511795; www.diana-
mackie.co.uk)
Borreraig Park, by Dunvegan; oil landscape
artist, specialising in climatic changes; open all
year: tel. to confirm

Duncan House Celtic Jewellery (01471 866366;
www.duncan-house.com)
Strathaird, near Elgol; Celtic jewellery

Dunhallin Crafts (01470 592271)
Waternish; knitwear made in the workshop;
open spring/summer, daily; tel. in low season

Dun Studio (01470 521883)
Dunvegan; paintings based on north-west
landscape, prints and cards; open (normally) all
year, daily 10.00-18.00

Edinbane Pottery (01470 582234; www.edinbane-
pottery.co.uk)
Edinbane; workshop and gallery, wood-fired
and salt-glazed hand-made functional pottery;
open Easter-Oct, daily 9.00-18.00

Halistra Pottery (01470 592347; www.halistra-
pottery.co.uk)
Hallin; functional domestic earthenware
pottery with coloured glaze; open summer,
daily 10.00-17.00, winter Mon-Thu 10.00-17.00

Harrapool Studio and Gallery (01471 820096;
www.skyeart.co.uk)
Harrapool, by Broadford; small studio/gallery;
open Apr-Oct, Mon-Sat 10.00-18.00; closed
Sun

Heaven's Ocean Art Studio (01471 833475;
www.heavens-ocean.co.uk)
Camus Croise, Isle Ornsay; original
watercolours of Skye and the west coast,

driftwood pieces, collages and hand-made
cards; open Easter-Oct, daily 10.00-18.00;
winter tel. to confirm

Isle of Skye Bindery (01478 613123; www.laura-
west.com)
Portree; book binding: regular workshops

Laurence Broderick Sculptures (01767 650444;
www.laurencebroderick.co.uk)
Isle Ornsay; stone carvings and bronze
sculptures of wildlife including otters, turtles,
bears and elephants; open summer, Mon-Fri
9.00-17.00, Sat 9.00-13.00

The Little Gallery (01478 640254; www.the-little-
gallery.co.uk)
Portnalong; etchings, watercolours and prints,
notelets and cards; open all year, daily 10.00-
18.00

Mara (01478 612429; www.mara-direct.com)
Portree, isle of skye; interiors, accessories,
Harris Tweed, and hand-crafted jewellery; open
Mon-Sat 10.00-18.00

Octave (01471 844426)
Ardvasar, Sleat; local crafts; usually open Mon-
Sat 10.00-17.00

Orbost Gallery (01470 521207;
www.orbostgallery.co.uk)
Orbost, near Dunvegan; paintings, prints and
calligraphy, celebrating the landscape of Skye
and the Highlands; open Apr-Oct, daily 10.00-
18.00

Over the Rainbow (01478 612555;
www.skyeknitwear.com)
Portree; Scottish knitwear and textiles,
Hebridean crafts, Harris Tweed; open summer,
daily 9.00-19.00; winter 9.00-18.00 (six days)

Phil Gorton Studio (01470 521842; 07876 072329)
Roag, by Dunvegan; photographic landscapes
and colourful abstracts, limited editions, digital
inkjets, greeting cards and postcards; open all
year: tel. to confirm

Ragamuffin (01471 844 217;
www.ragamuffinonline.co.uk)
The Pier, Armadale (also Edinburgh); unique
collection of knitwear, original clothes and
accessories; open summer, daily 8.30 - 18.00
(Jul-Aug 19.00); winter, Mon-Sat 9.00-17.00,
Sun 12.00-17.00; closed Jan-Mar – tel. to
confirm

Raven Press Gallery (01470 511748;
www.kathleenlindsley.co.uk)
Colbost, by Dunvegan; monochrome wood
engravings, books, hand-knit design, resist
dyed silks; open Mon-Sat 10.00-17.00

Rupert Copping Gallery/Studio (01471 822669;
www.rupertcopping.co.uk)
Broadford; oil and watercolour paintings,
prints and cards; open Apr-Nov, Mon-Sat 9.30-
17.30; phone for hours in winter

Sandbank Studio (01471 822064/011)
Broadford; watercolours and mixed media;
open Mon-Sat

Shilasdair Yarns (01470 592297; www.shilasdair-
yarns.co.uk)
Waternish, isle of skye; natural-dyed yarns,
designer garments, knit kits, felted and resist-
dyed textiles; open Apr-end Oct or by appt

35

Skye Batiks (01478 613331; www.skyebatiks.com)
Portree and Armadale; Celtic wall hangings,
colourful shirts, funky clothing, jewellery;
open: summer, Mon-Sat 9.00-18.00, Jul-Aug
9.00-21.00; winter, Mon-Sat 9.00-17.00

Skye in Focus (01471 822264;
www.steveterry.co.uk/
www.skye-photos.com)
Ard Dorch, near Broadford; Highlands and
Islands landscape in colour and monochrome

Skye Jewellery (01471 820027;
www.skyejewellery.co.uk)
Broadford; Celtic rings and jewellery (mail
order available); open all year, daily

Skyeline Ceramics (01471 822023;
www.skyelineceramics.co.uk)
Grianach, Harrapool; studio (& shop) hand-
made ceramics; open Mon-Sat 10.00-13.00 and
140.00-18.00 (Tue and Thu 20.00), sometimes
closed on Mon or Sat

Skye Silver (01470 511263; www.skyesilver.com)
Colbost, near Dunvegan; jewellery to Celtic
and natural designs; open all year

Teo's Handspun (01471 822876)
Broadford; hand-spun sweaters, cashmere and
exotic yarns

Terry Williams Photographer (01471 820146;
www.terrywilliams-photographer.co.uk)
Broadford; available in local tourist outlets and
on-line

Three Camuslusta Workshop and Gallery (01470
592264/201)
Camuslusta, Waternish; gallery of
contemporary paintings, prints, artists' books,
the-dimensional work; open Easter-Oct, Mon-
Fri 10.00-18.00, Sat-Sun, tel. to confirm

Three Herons Studio/Gallery (01471 822152;
www.isleofskye.net/threeherons/kenbryan)
Broadford and Culnaknock, by Staffin;
photographic prints, paintings, hand-woven
scarves, felted scarves and cards; open Mon-Fri
10.00-17.30 (studio also Sat 9.00-13.30)

2 Fishes Designs (01599 534029;
www.2fishes.co.uk)
Elgol; Cross stitch designs; from local craft
shops and on-line

Trotternish Artist Studio and Gallery (01470
552302)
Kilmaluag; landscape originals of Skye & the
Highlands and Islands; open all year, daily

Uig Pottery (01470 542421; www.uigpottery.co.uk)
Uig; distinctive pottery with decorations
inspired by the local land and seascape, Celtic
range; open: May-Oct, Mon-Sat 8.30-18.00.
Nov-Apr 9.00-17.00

Woodrising Gallery (01471 820300;
www.woodrising-photography.co.uk)
Old Corry, Broadford; environmental images
by Alan Campbell

VISITOR ATTRACTIONS AND MUSEUMS

Armadale Castle and Clan Donald Centre (01471
844305/227; www.clandonald.com)
Armadale, Sleat; ruined mansion in acres of
grounds and gardens; museum of the Isles and
Clan Donald Centre; restaurant and shop;
accommodation is available; museum open
Apr-Oct, grounds and shop open all year

Aros Experience (01478 613649; www.aros.co.uk)
Portree; exhibitions, audio-visual show theatre,
cinema, shop and restaurant

Bright Water Visitor Centre (01599 530040;
www.eileanban.org)
Kyleakin Pier; trips to see wildlife on Eilean
Ban; Gavin Maxwell museum; accommodation
available in keepers cottages; confirm opening
times before visiting

Colbost Croft Museum (01470 521296)
Colbost; thatched blackhouse and whisky still;
open Apr-Oct

Dunvegan Castle (01470 521206;
www.dunvegancastle.com)
Dunvegan; ancestral castle of the MacLeods;
restaurant; two gift shops and two craft shops;
boat trips; open all year: mid Mar-Oct, daily
10.00-17.00; Nov-mid Mar, daily 11.00-16.00

Giant Angus MacAskill Museum (01470 521296)
Dunvegan; displays and information on the
tallest Scotsman, who was 2.3 metres in height;
open Apr-Oct, daily 9.30-18.0

Glendale Toy Museum (01470 511240; www.toy-
museum.co.uk)
Glendale; award-winning visitor attraction,
adult and child friendly; open Mon-Sat
10.00-18.00

Kylerhea Otter Haven (01320 366322;
www.forestry.gov.uk)
Kylerhea; viewing hide, in summer with
warden; public toilets

Luib Croft Museum (01478 822427)
Luib, near Broadford; atmospheric blackhouse
museum from the early twentieth century;
open Apr-Oct, daily 9.00-18.00

Praban na Linne (01471 833266; www.gaelic-
whiskies.com)
Eilean Iarmain; whisky can be sampled and
there is a display of artefacts concerning
whisky

Skye Museum of Island Life (01470 552206;
www.skyemuseum.co.uk)
Kilmuir; thatched croft houses show life on
Skye in times gone by; open Apr-Oct, daily
9.00-17.30: tel. to confirm outwith May-Sep

Skye Serpentarium (01471 822209;
www.skyeserpentarium.org.uk)
Old Mill, Harrapool, Broadford; Serpentarium
with snakes, lizards, frogs and tortoises in
natural surroundings: snake-handling sessions;
gift shop; open Easter-Oct, Mon-Sat 10.00-
17.00; also Jul-Aug, Sun 10.00-17.00; tel. to
check outwith these dates

Staffin Museum (01470 562321; www.emory.edu/
OXFORD/Academics/International/Scotland/
staffinmuseum/home.htm)
Elishader, Staffin; internationally important
collection of fossils, found in Jurassic
sediments, displays of Bronze Age finds, and
crofting implements (open Easter-Oct, Mon-
Sat 9.30-18.00)
Talisker Distillery (01478 640203/614308)
Carbost; distillery in a fine location; tours and
a well-stocked distillery shop; open Apr-Jun
and Oct, Mon-Fri 9.00-16.30; Jul-Sep, Mon-Sat
9.00-16.30; Nov-Mar, Mon-Fri 14.00-16.30

ADDITIONAL INFORMATION

There is petrol available at Kyleakin, Broadford
(twenty-four hours), Ardvasar on Sleat, Portree,
Uig, Dunvegan, Struan and Carbost.

There are banks in Portree, Broadford and Kyle of
Lochalsh, and libraries in Portree and
Broadford.

Mountain Rescue (01478 612888)

EVENTS

Garden and Craft Fair (Armadale)	May
Isle of Skye Story Telling Festival	May
Isle of Skye Half Marathon	June
Donald MacDonald Quaich Piping Recital Competition (Armadale)	June
Highland Festival (www.highlandfestival.org)	June
Celtic Festival (Dunvegan)	June
Glamaig Hill Race (01478 650204)	July
Feis an Eilean (www.skyefestival.com)	July
Dunvegan Show	July
Edinbane Music Festival (www.edinbane-festival.com)	July
Skye Agricultural Show (Portree)	August
Skye Highland Games (Portree; www.skye-highland-games.co.uk)	August
Silver Chanter Piping Competition (Dunvegan)	August
Talisker Sheep Dog Trials (Portree)	August
Celtic Chaos Festival (Talisker Distillery)	September
Fireworks at Dunvegan Castle	November

FURTHER READING

50 Best Routes on Skye and Raasay (Storer, Ralph)
  Time Warner, 1999
The Cuillin (Stainforth, Gordon)
  Constable and Robinson, 2002
Harpoon at a Venture (Maxwell, Gavin)
  House of Lochar, 1952 (repr 1998)
History of Skye (Nicolson, Alexander)
  MacLean Press, 1930 (repr 1994)
Isle of Skye (Townsend, Chris)
  Collins, 2001
The Isle of Skye (Newton, Norman)
  Pevensey, 1995
Isle of Skye: a Walkers Guide (Marsh, Terry)
  Cicerone Press, 2002
Last Ferry to Skye (Uncles, Christopher J.)
  Stenlake Publishing, 1995
A Long Walk on the Isle of Skye (Patterson, David)
  Peak Publishing, 1999
Medieval Castles of Skye and Lochalsh (Miket, Roger
  and David L. Roberts)
  MacLean Press, 1990
Old Skye Tales: Traditions, Reflections and Memories
  (MacKenzie, William)
  Birlinn, 2002
Ring of Bright Water (Maxwell, Gavin)
  Penguin, 1969
Skye (Sillar, Frederick Cameron, Ruth M. Meyer and
  Norman S. Newton (eds))
  David and Charles (Pevensey), 1995
Skye (Cooper, Derek)
  Birlinn, 1995
Skye (MacLean, Cailean)
  Birlinn, 2006
Skye 360: Walking the Coastline (Dempster, Andrew)
  Luath Press, 2002
Skye Scrambles (Williams, D. Noel)
  Scottish Mountaineering Club and Trust, 1998
Skye and Kintail: 25 Walks (Brown, Hamish)
  Mercat Press, 2002
Skye and North West Highland Walks (Brooks, John)
  Jarrold, 1996
Skye: the Island (Hunter, James)
  Mainstream, 1996
Skye: the Island and its Legends (Swire, Otta; edited by
  Ronald Black)
  Birlinn, 2006
The Soay of our Forefathers (Reed, Laurance)
  Birlinn, 2002
A Summer in Skye (Smith, Alexander)
  Birlinn, 2004

RAASAY

('roe deer island' or 'roe ridge island'
from Norse, or possibly 'horse island')

www.raasay.com
www.raasay-house.co.uk
www.angelfire.com/il2/
  raasayheritagetrust/index.html
www.skye.co.uk
www.visithighlands.com
  (Highlands Tourist Board)

Tourist Information Centre
Portree (0845 2255121 (central no))
  Open Jan-Dec

Map Landranger sheets: 24, 32

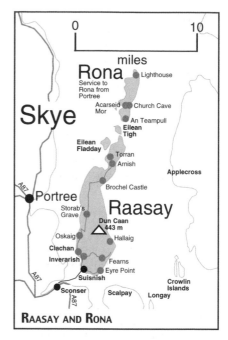

RAASAY AND RONA

TRAVEL

The vehicle ferry leaves from Sconser
on Skye (CalMac 01475 650100), which
is on the A87, the road between Broadford and Portree, eleven miles south of
Portree and thirteen miles from Broadford. The ferry runs up to ten times daily in
the summer, but there are only two crossings on Sundays. The crossing takes fifteen
minutes and lands at Suisnish on Raasay, one mile south of the village of Inverarish.

DESCRIPTION

Raasay lies off the north coast of Skye, about one mile east of the Trotternish coast
and six miles west of Applecross and Wester Ross on the mainland. The island is
fourteen miles long and between one and four miles wide, covering about sixty
square miles; it is very hilly, rising to 443 metres at the flat-topped peak of Dun
Caan, from where there are fantastic views. A third of the island is more than 150
metres high, while there is good fertile land on the west coast. Several woods and

forestry plantations are
dotted around Raasay,
and there are also
stretches of moorland.
  Clachan, Inverarish
and Oskaig are the
main settlements, and
the population is
around 200 people.
Many of the inhabi-
tants are devout
Presbyterians, and
Sundays are seen as
days of rest, hence
there is little activity,
other than church
going, on that day.

Raasay from Applecross

WILDLIFE

The island is home to red deer, hares, the unique Raasay vole (which is not found anywhere else) and otters, and more than sixty different species of birds, including golden eagles, sea eagles, kestrels and buzzards, and waders, oystercatchers, sandpipers and curlews. Seals can be seen on the shore, and porpoises and whales in the waters around the island.

HISTORY

The island was long held by the MacLeods of Raasay, who had a castle at Brochel, but later moved their seat to Kilmaluag, near the present Raasay House. The island was renowned for its pipers.

Bonnie Prince Charlie hid on the island in 1746 after his forces had been defeated at the Battle of Culloden. One hundred islanders fought for the Jacobites at the battle.

The island was raided in retaliation for the MacLeods' support of the Jacobites, and Brochel and Kilmaluag were both torched along with every other dwelling on Raasay: women were raped and men slain and the islanders' boats were holed and 280 cows and 700 sheep (and even chickens) were slaughtered.

The chiefs survived the onslaught, and Raasay House was built in 1747 near Kilmaluag by the MacLeods. It was here that Dr Johnson and Boswell visited and were generously entertained in 1773.

By 1841 the population was around 650 people, but two years later the last MacLeod chief, who was facing financial problems (following a legal a dispute about the purchase of two massive mermaid statues, which can still be seen near the house), sold the island and it was cleared of many of its people; the population was halved in only thirty years. MacLeod himself emigrated to Tasmania, where the present chief now lives.

Raasay was to have a succession of owners, most of whom appeared to care little for the islanders: one even forbad the islanders to marry unless they emigrated. Raasay was used as a sporting estate with pheasants, woodcock, grouse and deer all bred for shooting. Baird and Co. bought the island in 1912 and opened an iron ore mine, which was later worked by German prisoners of war, the remains of which survive, although it was closed by 1919. The island then changed hands again, and little or nothing was done to improve the lot of the islanders. Raasay House deteriorated until it was renovated as the Raasay Outdoor Centre in the 1980s after the estate had been taken over by the Highlands and Islands Development Board.

The poet Sorley MacLean was born on Raasay, and he wrote in a well-known spoem about the cleared township of Hallaig, which is on the east side of the island. A cairn commemorates the former inhabitants. Sorley MacLean retired to Raasay in his later years, and died in 1996.

Tours

SUISNISH TO ARNISH (UNLISTED ROAD)

The ferry lands at the pier at Suisnish. One unlisted road leads north, up the west coast, while another branch goes east along to the south coast to Eyre Point with its lighthouse.

The north branch leads to Inverarish, where there is a post office and shop, and public telephones. Part of the village was built to house German prisoners of war in the First World War. They had been brought here to work in the iron ore mine [NG 565365], the remains of the surface buildings, along with the course of a railway to the pier at Suisnish, can be visited on the Miner's Trail. The mine opened in 1913, and was a drift mine, but closed soon after the First World War.

Above Inverarish in the forest is Dun Borodale [NG 555364], the ruins of an Iron Age stronghold. The walls survive to a height of more than two metres. Also from the village a road leads to the youth hostel at Creachan Cottage [NG 553378], which stands in a superb location and is run by the Scottish Youth Hostels Association. A branch of the road leads across the island to the east coast, and a track from here goes to Dun Caan, the island's flat-topped peak. The unlisted road goes on to Fearns on the east coast, and the footpath goes on to the abandoned township of Hallaig.

The road north from Inverarish goes to Clachan, passing an Iron Age souterrain known as Uamh nan Ramh [NG 550364], the 'cave of oars'. It was also used for smuggling. At Clachan is the Raasay Outdoor Centre (01478 660266; www.raasay-house.co.uk), housed in the eighteenth-century Raasay House, which was (as mentioned earlier) the seat of the MacLeods of Raasay. A small museum is located in one of the wings, and there is a carved Pictish stone in the garden. At Clachan is also the Isle of Raasay Hotel (01478 660222; www.isleofraasayhotel.co.uk).

Nearby is St Moluag's chapel (Kilmaluag) [NG 548366], which dates from the thirteenth century. Moluag was a saint from Ireland, who died at the end of the sixth century, and is also associated with Lismore and Rosemarkie on the Black Isle, near Inverness. The MacLeods of Raasay were buried at Kilmaluag.

The road continues through Oskaig and three miles north of Clachan, west of the road, is Storab's Grave [NG 561417], a prehistoric burial cairn. Legends tell that this is the burial place of Storab, a king of Norway slain while raiding Raasay. The road eventually turns east across the island to the scant but picturesque remains of Brochel Castle [NG 585463] on its rock, more than six miles from Clachan. The castle was the seat of the MacLeods of Raasay before they moved to Clachan in the middle of the seventeenth century, and there are fine views across to Applecross. The MacLeods were accused of being involved in piracy, and often supported the MacDonalds of Sleat rather than the MacLeods of Dunvegan (they were descended

Brochel Castle, Raasay

from the MacLeods of Lewis, rather than Dunvegan and Harris). The road runs on to the townships at Arnish and Torran.

The road did not originally run all the way to Torran. One of its inhabitants, Calum MacLeod, believed that having no road would lead to his township being abandoned, so he set out to construct the road himself. He started work in 1966, and the two-mile stretch of road took him more than ten years to build. By the time it was finished, however, the last two occupants of Torran were Calum and his wife. He died in 1988.

There are several walks around the island, including one to the summit of Dun Caan, from where there are also wonderful views. James Boswell, companion to Dr Samuel Johnson, fortified with mutton, bread, cheese, punch and brandy, danced a Highland jig here in 1773.

PLACES TO STAY

Isle of Raasay Hotel (01478 660222; www.isleofraasayhotel.co.uk)
Clachan; family-run establishment open all year; Cuillin View Restaurant and Borodale bar are both open to non residents from 11.00, serving morning coffee, snacks and bar meals, afternoon teas and an evening menu.
Raasay House and Raasay Outdoor Centre (01478 660266; www.raasay-house.co.uk/ www.raasayoutdoorcentre.co.uk)
Open Mar-mid Oct; offers accommodation to guests (not only those taking courses) in the 250-year-old Raasay House; cafe and restaurant; small gift shop; camping is also available.

Anda Nicholson (01478 660237)
B&B
Raasay Cottage (01463 831333; www.raasaycottage.co.uk)
Inverarish; self-catering house, sleeps four-six; open all year
Raasay Youth Hostel (01478 660240/0870 0041146; www.syha.org.uk)
Creachan Cottage; youth hostel, sleeps thirty; open May-Oct

PLACES TO EAT

See Places to Stay

FURTHER INFORMATION

There is a post office and shop at Inverarish; but there is no petrol nor a bank on Raasay
Raasay Outdoor Centre (01478 660266; www.raasayoutdoorcentre.co.uk) offers courses on sailing, windsurfing, rock climbing, kayaking archery and outdoor sports, lead skills and development courses and run holidays and day activities
A free leaflet with details of walks around Raasay and information about the island can be obtained from Raasay House, the shop, the hotel or from TICs on Skye. Many of these walks start from the information point near the southern edge of the forest at Inverarish
Loch and sea fishing can be arranged

FURTHER READING

50 Best Routes on Skye and Raasay (Storer, Ralph)
Time Warner, 1999
Calum's Road: One Man's Journey (Hutchinson, Roger)
Birlinn, 2006
I Remember: Memories of Raasay (Nicolson, John)
Birlinn, 2002
Medieval Castles of Skye and Lochalsh (Miket, Roger and David L. Roberts)
MacLean Press, 1990
Raasay: a Study in Island History (Sharpe, Richard)
Grant and Cutler, 1982
Raasay: the Island and its People (MacLeod, Norma)
Birlinn, 2002

ACKNOWLEDGMENTS

Thanks to Katherine Raybole at the Isle of Raasay Hotel and Lyn and Kirstin Wilson at Raasay House for checking the entry; and Georgi Coventry for the photo of Brochel Castle

RONA

('rough island' from Norse or 'seal island' from Gaelic; also sometimes known as South Rona

www.isleofrona.com
www.visithighlands.com (Highlands Tourist Board)

Tourist Information Centre
Portree (0845 2255121 (central no))
   Open Jan-Dec

Map Landranger sheet: 24 (HIH map page 38)

TRAVEL

The passenger ferry (07798743858) runs from Portree on Skye to Acairseid Mhor ('big harbour') on Rona. It runs on Saturdays for accommodation arrivals and departures, and Wednesdays for day-trippers (summer service). The trip takes one hour, and three hours are allowed ashore on a Wednesday. Telephone to confirm sailings as services are subject to the weather. The ferry boat can be chartered to Rona, contact the operator.

DESCRIPTION

The island lies just to the north of Raasay, about half way between Trotternish on Skye and the Applecross peninsula of Wester Ross. The island is about five miles long, and about one mile wide, covering 2000 acres. Like its southern neighbour it is hilly, and rises to 125 metres above sea level at Meall Acairseid.

Rona

There are three ruined settlements, abandoned in the 1920s. Facilities now include a pontoon for safe landing, camping near the pier, a bothy, three cottages for holiday let and B&B at Rona Lodge.

WILDLIFE

Seals and otters can be seen around the island, and whales, porpoises and dolphins offshore. There are also red deer, Highland cattle and sheep, and many different species of birds, including fulmar, shag, black guillemot, gulls, ducks, herons and oystercatchers. Golden eagles, sea eagles and other raptors have also been seen.

HISTORY

The island was also owned by the MacLeods of Raasay, and for much of its history shared ownership with that island.

Before a church was built in 1878, the residents worshipped in the Church Cave [NG 627570], also known as Giants Cave, on the east coast across from Acairseid Mhor. This is an impressive structure and extends into the cliffs for some forty-five metres. Babies continued to be baptised in the cave, drips from the roof being collected in a font. A low stone pillar was used as a pulpit, and stone seats carved from the rock as pews. Worship still occasionally takes place in the cave.

There is an old burial ground at An Teampull [NG 616544], and many abandoned houses. A lighthouse, built in 1857, stands at the northern tip of the island.

The population was once more than 180, some of whom had been cleared from Raasay, although good land on Rona was always scarce and most of the population left following the First World War. The population had sought land on Raasay after it was bought by Baird and Co., but they were refused and some were jailed after they took matters into their own hands and seized land. This led to an outcry, and most of the island was later acquired by what became the Highlands and Islands Development Board. The 'Rona Raiders' were freed and given lands.

Since 1992 the island has been owned by Danish Ecologist and farmer Dorte Jensen, whose sensitive approach to the rebirth of Rona has made it accessible to visitors.

There are now only two full-time residents.

PLACES TO STAY

Rona Lodge
  B&B and dinner
Seascape and Skyescape
  Self-catering cottages
Bunkhouse (Acairseid Mhor)
Camping is available
Places are available on working parties
(For all enquiries contact: 07775593055;
  www.isleofrona.com)

FURTHER INFORMATION

There is a good and picturesque anchorage for yachts at Acairseid Mhor (showers and toilets as well as a washing machine and dryer are available at Rona Lodge; contact 07775593055; www.isleofrona.com)
Postage stamps and First Day Covers from Rona are available

ACKNOWLEDGMENTS

Thanks to Bill for checking over the text and providing the photograph

Isle Martin and the Summer Isles

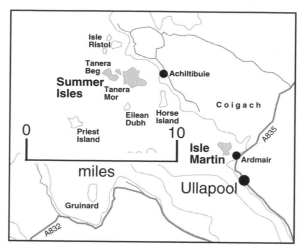

Isle Martin

('island of (St) Martin')

www.islemartin.co.uk
www.visithighlands.com (Highlands Tourist Board)

Tourist Information Centres
Ullapool (mainland) (0845 2255121 (central no))
    Open Jan-Dec
Inverness (mainland) (0845 2255121 (central no))
    Open Jan-Dec

Map Landranger sheet: 19

Travel
Boat trips (01854 612555/613228 for information) to Isle Martin are available from May to September, weather permitting, departing from the jetty at Ardmair (A835, north of Ullapool). The *Summer Queen* (01854 612472; www.summerqueen.co.uk) has tours of Loch Broom and the Summer Isles.

Description, Wildlife and History
Isle Martin is a small island at the mouth of Loch Broom, five miles north-west of Ullapool in Wester Ross. It is triangular in shape and one mile across, and covers about 400 acres. The island is hilly, rising to 120 metres, and the settlement on the island was at the south. The population was between forty and fifty for most of the nineteenth century.

Places to Stay
Contact Isle Martin Trust (01854 612555/613228)
The Croft House; sleeps 6
The Mill House; larger groups
Own sleeping bags required. No dogs.

Acknowledgments
Thanks to Sheila Didcock, Joint Secretary of the Isle Martin Trust, for checking the text

SUMMER ISLES

(the islands were used for summer grazing, hence the name)

www.summer-isles.com
www.visithighlands.com (Highlands Tourist Board)

Tourist Information Centres
Ullapool (mainland) (0845 2255121 (central no))
   Open Jan-Dec
Inverness (mainland) (0845 2255121 (central no))
   Open Jan-Dec

Map Landranger sheet: 15 (HIH Map page 44)

TRAVEL
Holiday accommodation, including the crossing, is available on the island. There are boat trips from Ullapool (A835) around the Summer Isles (with forty-five minutes on Tanera Mor) on the *Summer Queen* (01854 612472; www.summerqueen.co.uk), and also crossings from Achiltibuie (A835 and many miles by unlisted road; 01854 622200; www.summer-isles-cruises.co.uk).

DESCRIPTION
The Summer Isles lie at the mouth of Loch Broom, off the west coast of Scotland, two miles west of Achiltibuie in Wester Ross. The largest island, Tanera Mor ('big haven island'), is two miles long, and rises to 124 metres; while Tanera Beag ('small haven island') lies to the west and is about half a mile in length. There are several other smaller islands, including Isle Ristol, a nature reserve, managed by the Scottish Wildlife Trust (www.swt.org.uk), and has a mass of flowers on machair land from June to August. Excellent views are to be had from the top of Tanera Mor.

WILDLIFE
Seals, porpoises, dolphins and whales can be seen around the islands, and there are breeding colonies of birds, including shags, terns and cormorants. Other birds visiting the islands include herons, shelducks and buzzards.

Tanera Mor

HISTORY

The land is rough and rocky, but Tanera Mor supported a population of more than one hundred in 1881 (the school formerly had more than thirty students). There was a herring station at Tigh an Quay, but this was closed when the company that owned it became bankrupt. The island is said to have been used for illicit whisky production and smuggling.

It had been abandoned by the 1930s, but there are a few crofters on the island. Tanera Mor has a good anchorage for fishing boats and yachts, and there are the remains of a herring station. The island has a post office and cafe in the summer.

PLACES TO STAY

Murdo's Cottage
The School House
The Farmhouse
All self-catering (contact 01854 622272; www.summer-isles.com)

FURTHER INFORMATION

Courses catered for in shore-side studio
Dinghy sailing/power boat tuition – RYA recognised training centre
Cafe and post office, which sells exclusive stamps and First Day Covers from the Summer Isles. Groceries are available locally.
Telephone box at post office.
There is a hotel at Achiltibuie (01854 622282; www.summerisleshotel.co.uk)

ACKNOWLEDGMENTS

Thanks to Jean Wilder for checking the entry and providing the photograph

Rum, Eigg, Muck, and Canna and Sanday (Small Isles)

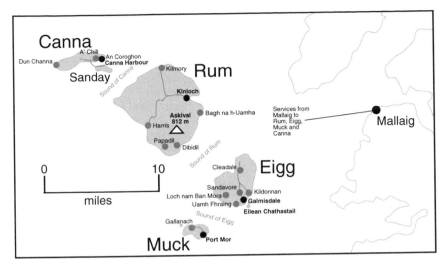

Canna

RUM

(possibly 'wide island' from Norse, but the name may be much older)

www.road-to-the-isles.org.uk/rum.html
www.nnr-scotland.org.uk/reserve.asp?NNRId=22
www.kcfa.org.uk (Kinloch Castle Friends Association)
www.isleofrum.com (being built)
www.kinlochcastle.com (being built)
www.visithighlands.com (Highlands Tourist Board)

Tourist Information Centres
Mallaig (mainland) (0845 2255121 (central no))
    Open Jan-Dec
Inverness (mainland) (0845 2255121 (central no))
    Open Jan-Dec

Map Landranger sheet: 39 (HIH map page 47)

TRAVEL

A passenger ferry (cars cannot be brought onto the island) runs from Mallaig on the mainland to Kinloch on Rum (CalMac 01687 462403; www.calmac.co.uk), Monday, Wednesday, Friday and Saturday. Times, crossing duration and time on the island vary from day to day. The ferry lands on Rum a mile or so from the main facilities. Mallaig is on the A830 and has a railway station (trains from Fort William; www.firstgroup.com/scotrail; 08457 484 950). Bruce Watt Sea Cruises (01687 462320; www.knoydart-ferry.co.uk) run trips from Mallaig harbour.

Arisaig Marine (01687 450224; www.arisaig.co.uk) also run trips to Rum from May-September on Tuesdays and Thursdays and from June to August also on Saturdays and Sundays. This allows two (three on Thurs-

Rum

day) hours on the island, although time on the island is not certain. Arisaig is on the A830 road between Fort William and Mallaig, and has a railway station (trains from Fort William).

Bella Jane boat trips (0800 7313089; www.bellajane.co.uk) are also available to Rum, Eigg and Loch Coruisk from Elgol (B8083) on Skye.

DESCRIPTION

Rum is one of the Small Isles, although far from 'small' itself, and lies some seven and a half miles west of Point of Sleat on Skye. Canna is to the northwest, while Eigg and Muck are to the south and east. Rum is the largest of the group, eight miles long by the same wide, and covering sixteen square miles.

The island is extremely hilly, particularly the south, and very impressive from both land and sea. The Cuillin of Rum have several peaks over 700 metres, while Askival rises to 812 metres, and the mountains have their origins in an ancient volcano. Much of the island was once wooded, and there are still many trees around Kinloch planted by the Bulloughs, while other woodland has been more recently replanted. The height of the mountains makes Rum one of the wettest places in Scotland; it is also haunted by clouds of midges.

The only inhabited settlement on the island is at Kinloch on the east coast. This is where the ferry lands, and the settlement has a well-stocked licensed shop and post office. The village hall serves teas some afternoons. Hours for both can be limited, and if the shop and village hall are closed there is nowhere to eat for day visitors.

WILDLIFE

The island is home to many unusual and rare plants and is recognised as a Special Site of Scientific Importance and a Biosphere Reserve. A large herd of deer live on the island, and there are also wild goats and Rum ponies. Some 150 species of birds have been recorded as visiting the island. A huge breeding colony of manx shearwaters numbering some 120,000 birds and visits the island from March, and there are also substantial numbers of puffins, guillemots, razorbills and kittiwakes. White-tailed sea eagles have been reintroduced, and there are seals and otters. Whales, porpoises and dolphins frequent the water around Rum and the Small Isles.

HISTORY

Rum was occupied from prehistoric times, and evidence from the Mesolithic period was found during excavations near Kinloch Castle. Few other sites have been noted, probably because the island has never been fully investigated.

There is evidence of early Christian sites at Kilmory [NG 361037], five miles north-west of Kinloch, and Bagh na h-Uamha [NM 421972], two miles south-east of Kinloch, both of which have stones carved with crosses dating from the seventh or eighth centuries (both are also weathered), the latter having been recently erected near where it was found. At Kilmory on the north coast, which was dedicated to St Mary, is an old burial ground near the substantial abandoned township and sandy beach, while there is another deserted settlement at Bagh na h-Uamha on the east coast, as well as a cave [NM 423974] where pottery dating from the Iron Age has been found. The island fell under Viking rule: most of the mountain names are Norse in origin.

Rum was later a property of the Clanranald branch of the MacDonalds. It was raided by the MacLeans of Duart in 1588, but passed to the MacLeans of Coll in

Kinloch Castle

1695. The island once supported a population of more than 400 people, but it was cleared of much of its population in 1826 by the MacLeans of Coll; many islanders went to Nova Scotia. The island was used as a sheep farm and a sporting estate. The population is now about twenty-five residents.

In 1886 Rum was sold for £35,000 to John Bullough, a successful machinery manufacturer. It was during this time that the (reputedly) teetotal Bulloughs are said to have changed the spelling of the island from Rum to 'Rhum', in an attempt to differentiate it from the spirit. The spelling, however, was used before their tenure, and it is unlikely they were teetotal as there is a large wine cellar at Kinloch Castle.

Bullough's son built the magnificent and luxurious Edwardian Kinloch Castle (which was recently a subject on BBC's *Restoration* programme), although its use declined in the 1930s and it is desperately in need of restoration. The building is perhaps a little impractical for the west coast of Scotland despite its splendour, although it was one of the first buildings in Scotland to have electricity, produced by its own generator. The gardens and glasshouses have gone to ruin. Tours of the castle can be taken (01687 462037), and hostel accommodation is available.

At Harris [NM 336956], eight miles south-west of Kinloch and by a rough and winding track, on the south coast is the Greek-style mausoleum of the Bulloughs (there are also the remains of an extensive township). There was also a hunting lodge at Papadil [NM 365922], which can be reached by a track from Kinloch, seven miles south of the village.

In 1957 Rum was sold to the Nature Conservancy Council and turned into a nature reserve, now managed by Scottish Natural Heritage as a National Nature Reserve of international importance. Access may be restricted to certain parts of the island at different times of year.

Places to Stay

Lea Cottage (01687 462036)
B&B
Hostel accommodation (sleeping forty-seven) and meals are available from Kinloch Castle (01687 462037; www.nnr-scotland.org.uk/ reserve.asp?NNRId=22)
Camping is available, ten minutes from the ferry (01687 462026)
Hostel or camping should be booked in advance, and there are mountain bothies at Guirdil and Dibidil.
Fishing and deer stalking can be arranged (contact Reserve Office).

Places to Eat

The Village Hall at Kinloch houses a cafe some afternoons during the summer (01687 462026 to confirm opening).
The Bistro at Kinloch Castle offers breakfasts and evening meals (01687 462037: booking is advisable)

Further Information

For any queries about the island contact the Reserve Manager (01687 462026)

There are many walks on the island, including two nature trails beginning from Kinloch. There are guided daily walks around Rum by Scottish Natural Heritage in the summer months (a booklet, published by Scottish National Heritage, is available). There are also more challenging walks and climbs. Kinloch Castle can also be toured.

Fishing permits are available.
Deer stalking (01687 462030) can be arranged.
There is a public phone at Kinloch Castle, and mobile phones have limited or no coverage on the island.

Midges can be truly fearsome on Rum, probably due to the high rainfall

Further Reading

Rum: Nature's Island (Magnusson, Magnus)
  Luath Press, 1997
Rum: a Landscape without Figures (Love, John A.)
  Birlinn, 2002
Small Isles, The: Canna, Rum, Eigg and Muck (Rixson, Dennis)
  Birlinn, 2001

Acknowledgments

Thanks to Kim Gleenie at Kinloch Castle and George W. Randall of Kinloch Castle Friends Association for checking over the text. Thanks also to George Logan for the photos (01250 883211; 07870 742219; www.scottish-photography.co.uk)

EIGG

('nick' or 'hollow': the 'notched island' from Gaelic; or 'edge' from Norse)

www.isleofeigg.org
www.road-to-the-isles.org.uk/eigg.html
www.visithighlands.com (Highlands Tourist Board)

Tourist Information Centres
Mallaig (mainland) (0845 2255121 (central no))
   Open Jan-Dec
Inverness (mainland) (0845 2255121 (central no))
   Open Jan-Dec

Map Landranger sheet: 39 (HIH map page 47)

TRAVEL

A passenger ferry (cars cannot be brought onto the island) runs from Mallaig on the mainland to Galmisdale on the east side of Eigg (CalMac 01687 462403; www.calmac.co.uk), Monday, Tuesday, Thursday, Friday and Saturday. Times, crossing duration and time on the island vary depending on day. Mallaig is on the A830 and has a railway station (trains from Fort William; www.firstgroup.com/scotrail; 08457 484 950). Bruce Watt Sea Cruises (01687; www.knoydart-ferry.co.uk) run trips from Mallaig harbour.

   Arisaig Marine (01687 450224; www.arisaig.co.uk) also run trips to Eigg from May-Sep on Monday, Tuesday, Wednesday, Friday, Saturday and Sunday (summer 2006). This allows from three to five hours on the island. Arisaig is on the A830 road between Fort William and Mallaig, and has a railway station (trains from Fort William).

Eigg, from Arisaig

DESCRIPTION

Eigg lies some five miles south-west of Point of Sleat on Skye, and four miles south-east of Rum. It is about six and a half miles long by up to four miles wide. It is divided in the middle by a glen, which divides the ridge of An Sgurr, which is some 393 metres above sea level, from the rest of the island: hence the name 'notched island'. There is good land on Eigg, which supported a substantial population; and there are several wooded areas including a large forestry plantation. There are sandy beaches on Eigg, most notably the fine beach at the Bay of Laig and, further north, the famous singing sands – the sands 'sing' when walked on, although only when dry. The bays at Galmisdale and Kildonnan are also sandy.

The ferry arrives at Galmisdale to the south-east of the island, and in the pier complex is a licensed tearoom/restaurant, shop, post office, well-stocked grocers and craft shop. There are also settlements at Sandavore just north of the village and Cleadale on the west side, three miles north of Galmisdale. The population now stands at around eighty people.

WILDLIFE

The island has much wildlife, including golden eagles and buzzards, as well as colonies of manx shearwaters and puffins; around the coasts are otters, seals, whales and dolphins. Five hundred varieties of plant have been identified, including many orchids and alpines. Three areas are designated as wildlife reserves (www.swt.org.uk).

HISTORY

Eigg was occupied from prehistoric times, and there are impressive forts at An Sgurr [NM 461847] and Rubha na Crannaig [NM 491848]. The fort on An Sgurr is two miles north-west of Galmisdale, and is located in a strong position on the ridge. It covered some nine acres, and a wall, surviving to height of six feet, defends the only accessible side. Nearby, there is a small crannog in the middle of Loch nam Ban More, built of Sgurr stones. The name means the 'loch of the large (or powerful) women'. Rubha na Crannaig, one mile north-east of Galmisdale, at Kildonnan is triangular in shape, and this has been suggested as the monastery of St Donan.

Eigg is associated with Saint Donan (or Donnan), who was from Ireland and is believed to have founded a monastery here in the seventh century. Unusually for Scotland, Donan was slain and martyred, along with his followers (said to number 52). Although the culprits have not been identified other than as pirates or perhaps the 'warrior women', led by their pagan queen, mentioned above, it was rather too early for Vikings. Eilean Donan Castle is named after him as he is believed to have lived at Loch Alsh for a time. Kildonnan [NM 489853], one mile north of Galmisdale, has a ruinous church, with a recessed tomb dating from the sixteenth century. In the associated burial ground is the shaft of a cross, dating from the period of the Lordship of the Isles two hundred years earlier, and there are other carved stones in the church and the porch of Eigg Lodge.

St Columba's Well (Tobar Chaluim Chille) [NM 478889] can be seen in Cleadale, where the water, which never runs dry, was used to baptise infants, the number of rivulets foretelling their future. The Well of the Holy Woman (Tobar Na Beanmha) [NM 457840] is situated on the other side of the island behind a huge erratic block in the midst of Clearance ruins at Grulin, on the south of the island.

Viking graves were found here in the nineteenth century, in one of which was an impressive Norse sword. Eigg was a property of the Clanranald branch of the MacDonalds, who were involved in fighting with the MacLeods. This resulted in a legendary atrocity on the island. In 1577 the islanders sheltered in a cave, Uamh

53

Fhraing ('cave of St Francis' but also known as the Massacre Cave) [NM 475835], half a mile south-west of Galmisdale, when the MacLeods of Duart barricaded the entrance with brushwood and then set it on fire. This suffocated all those within, some 200 (or 395) men, women and children. In the nineteenth century, the floor was said to have been littered with bones, which were then buried. The massacre is said to have led to the retaliatory slaughter at Trumpan on Skye. The island was raided in 1588 by the MacLeans. Nearby is the Cathedral Cave, which was used for Catholic worship following the proscription of Catholicism and the Reformation.

The islanders supported the Jacobites in the 1745 rising, and fought at Culloden under MacDonald of Laig. In reprisal a government ship captured some of the menfolk involved, most of whom were transported to Jamaica.

In 1826 the island was sold to Hugh MacPherson, a professor at Aberdeen University; and by 1841 the population had reached 550, although it had declined to around 300 only forty years later. It then passed through several hands, and in the 1930s the Runcimans built the present lodge, which has fine sub-tropical gardens. After several further owners, the island was bought in 1997 by its own inhabitants, the Isle of Eigg Heritage Trust.

PLACES TO STAY

(also see www.isleofeigg.org for further details of accommodation below)
Kildonan House (01687 482446)
    Kildonan; guest house, packed lunches and evening meals
Lageorna (01687 482405)
    Cleadale; B&B, packed lunches and evening meals; also two self-catering cottages, each sleeping six
Laig Farm (01687 482412)
    Guest house
Cnoc-Mor Bungalow (01369 701749/01687 482496)
    Cleadale; self catering
Sandavore Farmhouse and Cottage (01687 482438; www.piercottage.com)
    Sandavore; self-catering house and cottage, sleeps six-eight and sleeps two
The Glebe Barn (01687 482417; www.glebebarn.co.uk)
    Cleadale; self catering accommodation for individuals or groups of up to twenty-four people; open Apr-Oct, and all year for larger groups
Glebe Cottage (01687 482422)
    Cleadale; self-catering cottage
Top House (01362 668435)
    Cleadale; self-catering croft house
Shore Cottage (01687 482482)
    Self-catering mobile home
Cuagach Bothy (01687 482486)
Sandavore Bothy (01687 482480)
The Smiddy (Bothy) (01687 482438)
Camping is also available (01687 482480)

PLACES TO EAT

Licensed tearoom/restaurant in pier complex at Galmisdale, which does evening meals (01687 482487, advance booking necessary in the evening; open Apr-Oct: check other times)

FURTHER INFORMATION

Isle of Eigg Shop and post office (01687 482432)
    By jetty; well-stocked shop
Ceilidhs and other events are held in the pier complex or village hall
Bikes can be hired (01687 482405 or 482432)
There are fine walks and some challenging climbs, ranging from easy to severe
Isle of Eigg Heritage Trust (01687 482486; www.isleofeigg.org)
Scottish Wildlife Trust Warden (01687 482477)

EVENTS

Eigg Anniversary Ceilidh   June
Feis Eige (Eigg Festival)   July

FURTHER READING

Eigg: an Island Landscape (Martins, Susanna Wade)
    Available from Eigg Craftshop
Eigg: the Story of an Island (Dressler, Camille)
    Polygon, 1998
Geology of Eigg, The
    Available from Eigg Craftshop,
The Small Isles: Canna, Rum, Eigg and Muck (Rixson, Dennis)
    Birlinn, 2001

ACKNOWLEDGMENTS

Thanks to Maggie Fyfe, Camille Dressler and Simon Helliwell for checking over the entry. Thanks also to George Logan for the photo (01250 883211; 07870 742219; www.scottish-photography.co.uk)

Muck

('island of pigs' from Gaelic; possibly sea-pig or porpoise)

www.road-to-the-isles.org.uk/muck.html
www.islemuck.com (history of Muck)
www.visithighlands.com (Highlands Tourist Board)

Tourist Information Centres
Mallaig (mainland) (0845 2255121 (central no))
    Open Jan-Dec
Inverness (mainland) (0845 2255121 (central no))
    Open Jan-Dec

Map Landranger sheet: 39 (HIH map page 47)

Travel

A passenger ferry (cars cannot be brought onto the island, nor would there be any point in doing so) runs from Mallaig on the mainland to Port Mor on the east side of Muck (CalMac 01687 462403; www.calmac.co.uk), Tuesday, Thursday, Friday and Saturday. Times, crossing duration and time on the island vary. Mallaig is on the A830 and has a railway station (trains from Fort William; www.firstgroup.com/scotrail; 08457 484 950). Bruce Watt Sea Cruises (01687 462320; www.knoydart-ferry.co.uk) run trips from Mallaig harbour.

Arisaig Marine (01687 450224; www.arisaig.co.uk) also run trips to Muck from May-Sep on Monday, Wednesday and Friday. This allows two hours on the island. Arisaig is on the A830 road between Fort William and Mallaig, and has a railway station (trains from Fort William; www.firstgroup.com/scotrail; 08457 484 950).

Description

Muck is the smallest of the Small Isles, being three miles long by about two wide. It lies three miles north-west of the west coast of Scotland at Sanna Point and three miles south-west of Eigg. The island is relatively flat and fertile, although it rises to 137 metres at Beinn Airein, from where there are excellent views. There is a fine white sandy beach at Bagh a' Ghallanaich (Gallanach).

The main settlement is at Port Mor, where the ferry lands, and there is a shop and tearoom. There are also some houses at Gallanach to the north of the island.

Wildlife

The island has many species of birds, including sea eagles, puffins, kittiwakes, fulmars and shearwaters, greylag geese; eighty different species of bird nest here. Otters can occasionally been seen around the coasts, as can porpoises in Gallanach Bay, and there is a colony of seals. There are no rabbits.

History

Caisteal an Duin Bhain [NM 422787], half a mile south of Port Mor, is a very ruinous prehistoric fort, which was probably occupied into medieval times. There is also a ruinous chapel and burial ground [NM 421795] at Kiel just north of the village. This may have been dedicated to St Finian, and two stones carved with early Christian crosses were found here, which are now in the craft shop.

The island was held by the monks of Iona Abbey before passing to the MacLeans of Ardnamurchan, then to the MacDonalds of Clanranald. Dr Johnson reported that in 1773 the then laird was embarrassed to be known as the 'laird of Muck' or just 'Muck'. Much of the island was depopulated in the nineteenth century, from 300 people in 1821 to 155 inhabitants in 1831 to 51 in 1891; now around thirty people live here. Muck has been held by the MacEwens for more than one hundred years.

PLACES TO STAY

Godag House (01687 462371)
  0.5 miles north of Port Mor; full board or B&B
Port Mor House (01687 462365)
  Port Mor; guest house, packed lunches and evening meals
New House (01687 462362)
  Gallanach; self catering, sleeps nine
Seileachean (01687 462362)
  Gallanach; self catering, sleeps nine
Bunkhouse (01687 462042)
  Port Mor; open all year, sleeps four plus family room
Replica of a Mongolian Yurt or an Native American Tipi can also be hired (01687 462362)

Camping is available (free)

PLACES TO EAT

Craft Shop/Restaurant
  Port Mor; lunches, teas (and dinners by arrangement)

FURTHER INFORMATION

Ceilidhs and quiz nights are sometimes held in the Craft Shop, and a range of crafts are available
Craft courses are also available (01687 462362)
Tours of the island are offered in the summer, Wed at 13.30
There is a public telephone at Port Mor
Contact Lawrence MacEwen (01687 462362) for any queries about visiting and accommodation or for information about Muck

FURTHER READING

The Isle of Muck: A Short Guide (MacEwen, Lawrence)
  Published Privately, 2002
The Small Isles: Canna, Rum, Eigg and Muck (Rixson, Dennis)
  Birlinn, 2001

CANNA AND SANDAY

('porpoise', 'whale' or possibly 'rabbit' island; or 'can or pot-shaped' island; and 'sandy isle')

www.road-to-the-isles.org.uk/canna.html
www.hebrideantrust.org/canna.htm
www.nts.org.uk
www.visithighlands.com (Highlands Tourist Board)

Tourist Information Centres
Mallaig (mainland) (0845 2255121 (central no))
　Open Jan-Dec
Inverness (mainland) (0845 2255121 (central no))
　Open Jan-Dec

Map Landranger sheet: 39 (HIH map page 47)

TRAVEL

A passenger ferry (cars cannot be brought onto the island) runs from Mallaig on the mainland to Canna (CalMac 01687 462403; www.calmac.co.uk), Monday, Wednesday, Friday and Saturday. Times, crossing duration and time on the island vary. Mallaig is on the A830 and has a railway station (trains from Fort William; www.firstgroup.com/scotrail; 08457 484 950). Bruce Watt Sea Cruises (01687 463320; www.knoydart-ferry.co.uk) run trips from Mallaig harbour.

Bella Jane boat trips (0800 7313089; www.bellajane.co.uk) are also available to Canna, Rum and Loch Coruisk from Elgol (B8083) on Skye.

DESCRIPTION

Canna, and its adjacent island Sanday ('sandy isle'), lies across the Sound of Canna, two miles north-west of the coast of Rum, and nine miles south-west of Skye. Canna is four and a half miles long by one wide at its most, and covers about 3000 acres. It is connected to the island of Sanday by a bridge. That island is itself about two miles long.

Canna and Sanday have much good land, but the north of Canna is much rougher and rises to 210 metres at Carn a' Ghaill, and there are cliffs along the north coast. Compass Hill (140 metres), to the north-east of the island, is so called because of the effect the rocks (which have high quantities of magnetic metal) have on compasses. The weather is relatively sunny and dry because of the lack of high ground. The land is fertile, as mentioned above, and because of the climate early crops, vegetables and fruit were grown, giving the island the title 'Garden of the Hebrides'. This was before the people were replaced by sheep.

Most of the population of about thirteen people live on Sanday. The islanders were Roman Catholic, although the large prominent nineteenth-century church, dedicated to Saint Edward the Confessor, now houses a study centre for visitors, which has recently suffered water damage and is currently not open. The church was built at a time when the population was considerably larger, and many fisherman from Barra also used the excellent harbour. The names of many boats are carved into a large rock and can be seen when entering the harbour.

There is a post office and the Harbour View Tearoom and Craft Shop (01687 462465/460041; www.harbourview-canna.co.uk) on the island, and toilets are available at the pier. There are cliff-top walks around the islands.

Canna

WILDLIFE

The island is a bird reserve, and 157 species have been observed here. There are large colonies of puffins, manx shearwaters, razorbills and black guillemots, puffins and shags and different types of ducks, as well as corncrakes, golden eagles and peregrine falcons. The island is also home to rare butterflies (some 260 types of butterflies and moths have been identified). Dolphins, whales and basking sharks can be seen in the waters around Canna and Sanday, and common and grey seals by the harbour. Otters are also sometimes seen.

Bird numbers have plummeted over recent year due to rat predation. This winter a project to eradicate rats from the island was carried out. It seems to have been successful but it is too early to tell. Hopefully ground-nesting bird numbers will recover: see www.ntsseabirds.org.uk/properties/canna/canna.aspx.

HISTORY

St Columba is believed to have visited Canna, and at A' Chill [NG 269055], half a mile west of the pier, there is an old burial ground which had a chapel dedicated to the saint. In the kirkyard is a broken and weathered carved cross, dating from the eighth or ninth century. Nearby is a two-metre standing stone [NG 269055], known as the 'stone of punishment'. There are also the remains of a cashel [NG 223 044], or early monastery, on the south coast at Sgorr nam Ban-Naomha ('cliff of the holy women'), beneath the cliffs. Access is down a difficult path.

On a remote and largely inaccessible rock stack is Dun Channa [NG 206048] on the western tip of Canna, the ruined remains of a fort, while above the harbour is Coroghon Castle [NG 288055]. Little remains on the steep rock, a stronghold of the MacDonalds. One story is that it was used as a prison for the lovely wife of one of the Lords of the Isles, incarcerated to prevent her from seeing her MacLeod lover. Her ghost is reputed to haunt the rock.

The lands were held by Iona Abbey, then the MacDonalds of Clanranald. The island was plundered by the MacLeans of Duart in 1588. The MacDonalds sold Canna to Hector Munro in 1820, who then cleared much of the population. There were nearly 450 islanders then, but by 1871 this was reduced to just forty-eight. Canna and Sanday then changed hands several times before being gifted to the National Trust for Scotland in 1981 by John Lorne Campbell.

PLACES TO STAY

Lag nam Boitean (www.ntsholidays.com)
  Self-catering cottage, sleeps four
The Bothy (www.ntsholidays.com)
  By tearoom; self-catering cottage, sleeps four
Tighard (www.ntsholidays.com)
  Self-catering house, sleeping ten until Sep 2006; after that will be operated as a guest house
Sanday (01687462829)
  Self-catering cottage, sleeps four
Self-catering holidays can be booked through the National Trust for Scotland (01687 462466/0131 243 9331; www.ntsholidays.com)
Camping is also available, but there are no facilities, not even toilets

PLACES TO EAT

Harbour View Tearoom and Craft Shop (01687 462465/460041; www.harbourview-canna.co.uk)
Licensed tearoom serving lunches and dinner (booking essential by 17.00) with picnic tables; open Mar-Oct

FURTHER INFORMATION

The island has a good harbour which is used by many yachts. The new pier project has new toilet facilities and there is also a toilet and shower facility available at the main farm for the use of yachts people and also campers.
National Trust for Scotland (01687 463466; www.scotlandforyou.com/ www.ntsholidays.com)
The Canna Primary School website also has information about the island (www.canna.highland.sch.uk)
The Royal Commission on the Ancient and Historical Monuments produce an archaeological leaflet about the island.

FURTHER READING

Canna: The Story of a Hebridean Island (Campbell, John Lorne) Canongate, 1994
The Small Isles: Canna, Rum, Eigg and Muck (Rixson, Dennis) Birlinn, 2001

ACKNOWLEDGMENTS

Many thanks to Wendy Mackinnon and Pete McHugh for checking over the text; and to Isla Robertson and the National Trust for Scotland for the permission to use the photos

COLL AND TIREE

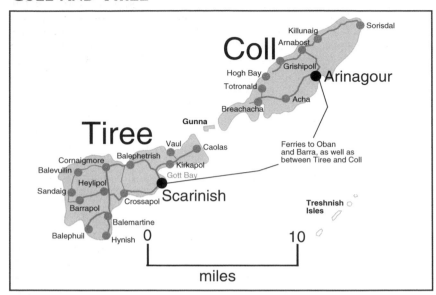

COLL

('hazel tree' from Gaelic, although the name may be older and the derivation lost)

www.visitcoll.co.uk
www.isleofcoll.org
www.isleofcoll.net
www.visithighlands.com (Highlands Tourist Board)

Tourist Information Centre
Oban (mainland) (08707 200630)
   Open Jan-Dec

Map Landranger sheet: 46

TRAVEL
The vehicle ferry (CalMac 01631 566688; www.calmac.co.uk) leaves from Oban on the mainland or Scarinish on Tiree, and arrives at Arinagour on Coll. There are services every day from Oban in the summer (three a week in winter), and the crossing takes two hours and forty-five minutes from Oban, and fifty-five minutes from Scarinish on Tiree. More ferries are planned for the winter.

   Day trips, with around two and a half hours on the island, are possible on Mondays, Saturdays and Sundays from Oban: check before setting out. There are whole day trips on Thursdays in the summer, leaving Oban at 08.30 and arriving back at 22.15, with around eight hours on the island.

   An air service is planned from Oban (North Connel with a regular bus service to Oban) to the island airstrip which is currently being reconstructed. There is a helicopter landing pad beside Arileod Farm, used by coastguard and medevacs.

   Private boat charter through Skipinnish Sea Tours (01879 220009/07843 250445; www.skipinnish-sea-tours.co.uk) is available on Tiree to Coll and back.

DESCRIPTION

Coll, along with its near neighbour Tiree, is a beautiful and scenic island and lies about eleven miles west of Mull at Treshnish, nineteen miles north-west of Iona and just two miles north-east of Tiree. The island is around twelve miles long and between one and three wide, covering about twenty-nine square miles. It is mostly flat, although the north end is much rougher, and the highest point is at Ben Hogh (106 metres), from where there are excellent views as far as South Uist and Jura on a good day, as well as the rocking stone.

Coll, along with Tiree, enjoys a very sunny and usually mild and relatively dry climate with more sunshine than anywhere else in Britain, although it can be extremely windy, especially in December and January. There are many excellent sandy beaches, such as those at Feall Bay and Crossapol Bay to the south and Hogh Bay on the west coast.

The main settlement is at Arinagour ('shieling of the goats') on the east side, from near where the ferry lands. This has most of the island's facilities, including a hotel and bar, shop, post office, crafts, petrol and a cafe.

WILDLIFE

The island has many different birds (up to 150 different species depending on the season), including corncrakes, barnacle and whitefronted geese, ducks, razorbills, many waders, Arctic skuas, gulls and terns, and herons. There are also many curlews, ringed plovers, lapwings, oystercatchers, sanderlings and dunlins. Seals and otters can be seen, and minke whales, basking sharks, porpoises, dolphins and even killer whales visit the waters around the island. There is an RSPB reserve at Totronald, and guided walks take place at 14.00 on a Wednesday. The island also had a huge population of rabbits (possibly around 100,000), which were once farmed here but caused much damage (neighbouring Tiree has no rabbits). The population has

Breachacha Castles, old and new, Coll

collapsed in recent years. The machair land near the coast has a wonderful variety of flowering plants, particularly in the summer months.

A large Fin whale, more than fifty feet long, was washed up on the island. There are plans to erect casts of the jaw bone at the pier behind the pottery shop.

HISTORY

Coll was occupied from prehistoric times, and there are Bronze and Iron Age sites around the island. Many of the place names are Viking in origin, from when the Norsemen held this part of Scotland. The island was later a property of the MacDougalls of Lorn, before being given to the MacDonalds (later Lords of the Isles) by Robert the Bruce. Coll passed to the MacLeans of Coll with the forfeiture of the Lords, although there was fighting between different branches of the clan, the MacNeils and the MacDonalds. The MacLeans held the island until 1856 from their base at Breachacha Castle (pronounced Breh-cha-cha: the 'ch' soft as in loch), both old and newer, then the property was sold to the Stewarts of Glenbuckie, who then cleared many of the inhabitants. The island had a population of more than 1400 in 1841, while now it is about 180: many of the inhabitants emigrated to Canada and Australia. As the land was good, islanders were replaced by sheep and cattle. One of the abandoned townships is at Sorisdale at the far northern tip of Coll, and there is another at Bousd.

Tours
ARINAGOUR TO HOGH BAY (B8071)

The ferry lands at the pier, about half a mile south of the main settlement of Arinagour. The village has a hotel and bar, cafe-restaurant, post office, shop and crafts, and petrol (see other information section for details); and there is a public toilet and telephone, as well as two churches and a primary school.

Cnoc a' Bhadain [NM 222581], half a mile north of the village, stands to the east of the road and is a prehistoric burial cairn, about thirteen metres in diameter and one in height. Two cists can be identified.

At Arnabost there is a junction and the B8071 leads south and west (the other route (B8072) goes north and east); and at Cliad is the island's nine-hole golf course. A souterrain [NM 209600], an underground passageway usually associated with the Picts, was found here, but there are no visible remains. Further west but to the north of the road is Grishipoll House [NM 190597], built in the eighteenth century although now ruinous. It was visited by Dr Johnson and Boswell in 1773, when it was described as 'an excellent slated house'.

There are fine beaches down the coast, and excellent views from Ben Hogh [NM 181581], the highest point of the island. Near the summit is the rocking stone, a huge boulder balanced on three much smaller stones. This is a natural feature, caused by glaciation.

There is another very ruinous prehistoric fort [NM 171581], known as 'the castle', near Ballyhaugh on the north side of Hogh Bay.

ARNABOST TO SORISDALE (B8072)

From the junction Arnabost the B8072 leads north. There are sandy beaches along this stretch of coast, and at Killunaig, three miles north of Arinagour, are the remains of an old church and burial ground, with markers from the seventeenth and eighteenth centuries. The site was dedicated to St Fynnoga of Coll. Many of the MacLeans of Coll were buried here, including Dr Johnson's and Boswell's host during their visit of 1773 (MacLean drowned off Mull the following year).

Two Bronze Age burial cists [NM 219617] can be seen 300 metres west of the church. Further north, by the sea, are the slight remains of another dun [NM 234634].

The road runs near the coast to the abandoned township of Sorisdale and more fine beaches.

ARINAGOUR TO BREACHACHA BAY (B8070)

The road runs south and east, passing near to Dun an Achaidh [NM 183545] by Acha, the ruins of a prehistoric fort on the top of a rocky ridge. The walls survive to about the height of one metre.

The road then goes west past Breachacha, where there is Breachacha Castle [NM 159539], and a later house known as the New Castle and dating from the eighteenth century. The old castle dates from some 400 years earlier, when Coll was given to Angus Og MacDonald by Robert the Bruce. It changed hands, and the new mansion was built nearby for the MacLeans of Coll, the old stronghold becoming ruinous. The chiefs of the clan did not support the Jacobites in the 1745 rising, and this new house was visited by Dr Johnson and Boswell in 1773.

The property was sold to the Stewarts of Glenbuchie in the 1850s, and the old castle was later purchased and restored as a home in 1965 by a descendant of the MacLeans. The newer house is also a private residence, and there are the remains of the MacLean mausoleum [NM 149524] nearby.

The island's airstrip is close by, and there is a fine beach by the old castle. The MacLeans of Coll are said to have beaten the MacLeans of Duart at a battle near here in 1593. There were so many slain that the burn was choked with severed heads, so that is was afterwards known as Sruthan nan Ceann ('stream of heads').

An unlisted road at Arileod branches north to Totronald, where there is the RSPB reserve. By this road are two impressive standing stones [NM 167560], known as Na Sgailaichen – 'the tellers of tales'. The taller of the stones is some two metres high.

There is a burial cairn [NM 198565] on the west side of Loch nan Cinneachan, some fifteen metres in diameter, but less than two metres high, and some of the

Coll

kerb stones can be seen. There is a standing stone, and good views can be had from here. A track leads from the end of the unlisted road at Totronald by the fine sands of Hogh Bay to the end of the B8071 at Ballyhaugh. The B8070 turns south and there is a car park near Crossapol Bay. Tracks go to the superb beaches at Crossapol and at Feall Bay.

Crannogs or duns, Iron Age defensive island settlements, have been identified in Loch Cliad, Loch an Duin, Loch nan Cinneachan and Loch Anlaimh.

GUNNA

The small island of Gunna ('Gunni's island', from a Norse personal name) lies between Coll and Tiree, and covers some 168 acres. The island has colonies of terns and gulls, and geese and shelducks also visit. Seals can be seen around the coast.

Places to Stay
HOTELS AND GUEST HOUSES

Coll Hotel (01879 230334; www.collhotel.com)
By the harbour, Arinagour; hotel with garden, Gannet Restaurant and bar; open all year except Christmas and New Year

BED AND BREAKFAST

Caolas (01879 230438; www.caolas.net)
South-west of island; B&B; organic food; fishing trips available
Cliad Farmhouse (01879 230208; www.isleofcoll.net)
Cliad; B&B
Talla Lan (01879 230440)
Arinagour; B&B
Tigh na Mara (01879 230354; www.sturgeon.dircon.co.uk)
Arinagour Bay; B&B plus self-catering chalet

SELF-CATERING PROPERTIES

Arinagour Farmhouse (01260 291970; www.collholidays.co.uk)
Above Arinagour; farm steading
Benmeanach (01879 230342)
North side of island; self-catering cottage, sleeps five; open all year
Caolas (01879 230438; www.caolas.net)
Accommodation in bothy
First Port of Coll: Malin and Hebrides (01879 230262; www.firstportofcoll.com)
Arinagour; two flats above cafe, sleep six and five
Gallanach Farmhouse (01879 230348; www.gallanach.co.uk)
Gallanach; self-catering or flexible catered farmhouse and annexe, sleeps eight
Glendyke Cottage (01260 291970; www.collholidays.co.uk)
Breachacha Bay; self-catering cottage
Lonban Cottage (01879 230461; www.lonban.co.uk)
Lonban; self-catering house, sleeps six

Monadh Ban (01879 230362; www.coll-lochoir.co.uk)
Arinagour; self-catering cottage
Rosebloom (01879 230408)
Arinagour Bay; self-catering traditional cottage, sleeps two
Roundhouse (01879 230378)
Self-catering traditional cottage, sleeps four; open May-Aug
Stronvar (01750 22311; www.stronvaroncoll.co.uk)
Breachacha Bay; self-catering chalet
Tigh na Mara (01879 230354; www.sturgeon.dircon.co.uk)
Arinagour; self-catering cottage, sleeps four

CAMPING AND CARAVANS

Garden House (01879 230374)
Camping/caravan site four and a half miles from Arinagour; open May-Sep; toilets and cold water available
Coll Hotel also has camping (contacts as above)
Greenbank Caravan (01879 230395)
East end of island; luxury caravan, sleeps four
Lochoir (01879 230362; www.coll-lochoir.co.uk)
By Arinagour; mobile home
Totronald Beag Caravan (01879 230382)
West end of island
Uig Residential Caravan (01879 230491)
Four miles south-west of Arinagour; caravan, two bedrooms

PLACES TO EAT

Coll Hotel (01879 230334; www.collhotel.com)
Arinagour; hotel, meals in Gannet Restaurant and bar; open all year
Island Cafe (01879 230262; www.firstportofcoll.com)
Arinagour; cafe/restaurant; self-catering flats also available
Caolas (01879 230438; www.caolas.net)
South-west of island; cream teas and organic food; fishing trips available; also B&B
A burger van, near the pier, is open on boat days, times to coincide with the ferry

Further Information

TRANSPORT

CYCLE HIRE
post office (01879 230400/329)
TAXI
Coll Taxis (01879 230402)
Private tours available including off-road routes

ACTIVITIES AND SPORTS

FISHING
Sea and loch fishing available: check locally
YACHTING AND SAILING
Many yachts anchor at Arinagour
GOLF
Coll Golf Club, Cliad
Nine-hole links course; pay at hotel
Gallanach
Nine-hole course
WALKING/BIRD WATCHING
There are many walks around the island, including
guided walks around RSPB reserve at Cliad
(14.00 Wed): RSPB Warden 01879 230301
TOURS
Coll Taxis (01879 230402)
Private tours available including off-road routes

ARTS AND CRAFTS

An Acarsaid Shop (01879 230400/329)
Acarsaid, by post office; small gift and craft
shop; open boat days
The Art Den
Adjacent to Island Stores
Brigstock & Bodgers (01879 230359)
Kilbride; woodwork workshops available on
Thu; also make and sell hand-made furniture
Coll Ceramics (01879 230382)
Pier, Arinagour; pottery classes available on
Tue; shop open boat days
Isle of Coll Glassworks (01879 230491)
Uig; open daily
The Lighthouse Gallery
Above Arinagour village (signs from the post
office); watercolours of Coll

ADDITIONAL INFORMATION

There is a public toilet and a public telephone at
Arinagour
Grocery store, Arinagour (Island Stores 01879
230484)
post office, Arinagour (01879 230329)
No bank or cash machine on the island
The village hall sometimes has dances, ceilidhs
and other events
Petrol is available at Arinagour, but hours of
service are limited
Winter opening hours are very limited for all
facilities
Summer Saturday mornings there is a car boot
sale opposite the manse in Arinagour. Sales of
local honey, produce and crafts available
Development Coll Office, the island's community
company, is situated on Middle Pier, Arinagour
Wedding ceremonies can be arranged and
conducted by the Island Registrar

EVENTS

Coll Show   1st Friday in August

FURTHER READING

Coll and Tiree (Beveridge, Erskine)
Birlinn, 2001

ACKNOWLEDGMENTS

Thanks to Paula Darnton-Smith and Peter
Mackay for checking the text and supplying
the photos

TIREE

('land of Ith' from Gaelic, or Tir-Iodh, 'land of corn'; also known as Tir fo Thuinn, 'land beneath the waves', as it is so low lying)

www.isleoftiree.com
www.hebrideantrust.org
www.aniodhlann.org.uk (Tiree's historical centre)
www.tiree.zetnet.co.uk/tiree.htm
www.tireewaveclassic.com (surfing)
www.visitscottishheartlands.com (AILLST)

Tourist Information Centre
Oban (mainland) (08707 200630)
Open Jan-Dec

Map Landranger sheet(s): 46 (HIH map page 60)

TRAVEL

The vehicle ferry (CalMac 01631 566688; www.calmac.co.uk) leaves from Oban on the mainland or Arinagour on Coll, and arrives at Scarinish on Tiree. There are services every day from Oban in the summer (less in winter), and the crossing varies between three hours twenty minutes and four hours five minutes from Oban, and fifty-five minutes from Arinagour. There are also services from Castlebay on Barra. There are regular flights (British Airways 0345 222111; www.britishairways.com) from Glasgow to the Reef (www.hial.co.uk/tiree-airport.html), as well as from Barra.

Tiree

DESCRIPTION

Tiree is a very flat and fertile island, hence the name 'land of corn'. Lying twenty miles west of Mull at Treshnish and nineteen miles north-west of Iona, Coll is only two miles to the north-east. Tiree is some twelve miles long, and between one and six miles wide, covering around twenty-nine square miles. Some of Tiree is rougher, and the hill of Ben Hynish (Carnan Mor), to the southwest, rises to 141 metres, while Ben Hough is 119 metres high and stands to the northwest. The island has wonderful beaches around all the coasts, including Traigh Mhor (Gott Bay), Traigh Bhagh and Balephetrish Bay: many surfers come to Tiree. The island is the sunniest place in the UK and has low rainfall, although in the winter it can be battered by gales; but, of course, wind is needed for the surfing. The island had 329 hours of sunshine in May 1975, more than ten hours a day for that month.

The main village is at Scarinish ('sea gull headland' from Norse) to the south-east of Tiree, where the ferry lands. Here there is a hotel at the old harbour, as well as a post office, a supermarket, An Iodhlann (Tiree's historical centre), An Turas ('the Journey': an interesting structure near the ferry landing place and the 2003 Scottish Building of the Year) and a bank.

There are also settlements at Crossapol further west (which has more shops) and is near the island's airstrip. Other settlements are scattered around the coast: Balemartine, Hynish and Balephuil to the southwest; Barrapol, Kilkenneth, Sandaig, and Balevullin to the west; Cornaig and Balephetrish to the north; and Kirkapol, Ruaig and Caolas to the east.

The island has a population of some 750 people or so. There is an extensive road network, although the routes are narrow in places and single track in entirety. Some of the locals have been known to drive in a manner which may seem somewhat hasty to those who do not know the roads so well.

The island still has many distinctive older houses, with the mortar between masonry being whitewashed and with tall roofs like upturned boats.

WILDLIFE

The machair land is very fertile and rich in flowering plants, and is particularly lovely in the late spring and early summer. Many birds can be seen here during the year, some 150 species, including corncrakes, razorbills, arctic skuas and terns; while Loch Bhasapoll has many wild geese and ducks. Like Coll, minke whales, porpoises and dolphins can be seen off the coast, and seals and otters around the shore. Unlike Coll, there are no rabbits on Tiree, none yet having made the two-mile swim from the neighbouring island, although there are hares.

HISTORY

Many prehistoric sites are scattered across Tiree – there are at least fifty identified forts, duns and brochs. The best is Dun Mor at Vaul (see below), to the north-east of the island, although finds from here are kept in the Hunterian Museum in Glasgow. A fine carved cross used to stand at Kirkapol, dating from the fifteenth century, but this was taken by the Campbells and is now in the garden of Inveraray Castle (not on view).

In 565 monks from Iona had found a monastery at Sorobaidh near Balemartine, but this was destroyed by Norse raiders (the site is probably occupied by a later chapel). The island was settled by the Vikings, and hence many of the place names, such as Hynish, Kirkapol and Scarinish. The island was plundered by Magnus Barelegs at the end of the eleventh century.

It was one of the many islands held by the MacDonald Lord of the Isles, but on their forfeiture passed to the MacLeans. Their seat, Castle Loch Heylipol, was on an island in Loch an Eilean [NL 986435], but the castle was later replaced by Island House, built in the eighteenth century as the factor's house for the Dukes of Argyll, into whose possession the island had fallen. A causeway was built out to the island. The house is said to have two ghosts: one the factor, a man called MacLaren, for whom the house was built, although he died before he could enter it; the second a Green Lady or gruagach.

The island is a very fertile place, and at one time supported a population of more than 4,400 people. Due to evictions and hard times around the potato famine in the 1840s, the number of inhabitants had dropped to 2,700 in 1881; five years later the Duke of Argyll sent in police and marines from the mainland in a dispute over land, known locally as the Crofters War. Despite this, the island maintains a relatively large population compared to many of the Western Isles.

The famous Skerryvore Lighthouse, the tallest in Scotland, lies twelve miles southwest of Tiree, and the base station was at Hynish, where there is now a museum. The lighthouse was completed in 1842, and stands some thirty metres high, although it is now automated.

The mainstays of the island are now sheep and cattle farming, lobster fishing, and tourism, and, unlikely as it might seem to some, Tiree is now a centre for windsurfing, having both exceptional beaches and a reliable source of wind and surf (the Atlantic).

Tours

SCARINISH TO BARRAPOL (B8065)

As mentioned above, Scarinish has most of the island's facilities, including the hotel by the old harbour off the 'main' road through the village, a Co-op (01879 220326; open Mon-Sat) which can get surprisingly busy, a butcher, a small post office, An Iodhlann, the island's historical centre (01879 220793; www.aniodhlann.org.uk; open Jul-Sep, Tue-Fri 12.00-17.00; Oct-Jun, Mon-Fri 10.30-15.30) and the award-winning structure (near the landing place and waiting room) An Turas (meaning 'The Journey' and 2003 Scottish Building of the Year: it is looking a little worse for wear but does provide shelter for nesting birds). Art House Gallery and Craft Shop is also located at Scarinish Old Pier (www.dorinda johnson.co.uk; open Mon-Sat 13.00-17.30).

The road leaves to the south, passing through Heanish and Baugh, where there is Rustics, selling home-made chut-

House, Tiree

ney, jam and scarves (01879 220961). This road passes the fine beach at Traigh Bhagh, and the southern edge of the airstrip and passes through Crossapol, where there are also shops (I & F MacLeod: 01879 220347; open Mon-Sat and Skinners: 01879 220066; open daily, Sun 14.00-16.00). Also at Crossapol is the Rural Centre (01879 220677; open Mon-Fri, 10.30-17.00, Sat 12.00-17.00), which houses an exhibition on crofting and the environment as well as a cafe.

The road goes near to Loch an Eilean and Island House (see above), and then on to Heylipol and Barrapol. At the crossroads between the two settlements is Heylipol Church [NL 964432] (or Eaglais na Mointich, 'church of the moss'), which is open daily. It dates from 1902 and is cruciform with a tower.

Near Balinoe is an impressive standing stone [NL 973426], which is pointed and stands more than three metres high. There is another standing stone near the end of the B8065 at Barrapol [NL 947430].

BARRAPOL TO CORNAIGMORE (UNLISTED ROAD)
The road runs near the coast to the Sandaig Museum, a thatched crofter's cottage with a byre and barn, which is staffed entirely by volunteers (01879 220677; open Easter-Sep, Mon-Fri 14.00-16.00). There are also thatched cottages at Middleton, Scarinish, Kilmoluaig and Kenovay. Opposite the museum at Sandaig are the remains of a kelp factory, a once thriving industry. The Glassary restaurant is located at Sandaig.

At Kilkenneth, by the edge of the dunes, is a prehistoric burial cairn [NL 939445], and the remains of an old chapel [NL 943448], dedicated to St Coinneach (Kenneth). South-east of Hough are two stone circles and a cairn [NL 958451], although most of the stones have fallen.

Near Hough is Ben Hough, from which there are fine views, and there are wonderful swathes of sand along this stretch of coast. There are two islands in Loch Bhasapoll, near Cornaigmore, which are the remains of crannogs; there are also the remains of a mill [NL 978472]. The loch has many geese and ducks which winter here.

HEYLIPOL TO HYNISH (B8066)
From Heylipol this road leads to Sorobaidh, near Balemartine. The old parish church [NL 984416] dated from the thirteenth century, but only footings survive of the building. In the burial ground are medieval carved stones, an early cross-slab and a broken cross-shaft. The cross was erected by Anna MacLean, prioress of the nunnery on Iona in the sixteenth century. Sorobaidh was probably the site of a monastery founded by monks from Iona in the sixth century.

At Balemartine is Blue Beyond (01879 220510; www.bluebeyond.uk.com; open Mon-Fri 13.00-17.00), a gallery featuring paintings, textiles, raku pottery and cards. Further on is the Hynish Centre, the Signal Tower and Historic Lighthouse Shorestation, with an exhibition, including on the building of the Skerryvore Lighthouse, and trail (01879 220726; open summer, daylight hours). The lighthouse is twelve miles away but can be viewed from the museum.

Along the coast towards West Hynish is Dun Shiadair [NL 964388] and Dun na Cleite [NL 974385], the ruins of a fort on a strong site.

BALEMARTINE TO BALEPHUIL (B8067)
The B8067 runs down to Balephuil, near to Ben Hynish, the highest hill on Tiree. To the east are the wonderful sands and dunes of Traigh Bhi; and Ceann a' Mhara, the headland beyond the beach, has the remains of prehistoric forts or duns: Dun

nan Gall [NL 935409], An Dun, and Eilean Dubh [NL 936412] which are accessible only at low tide, and Eilean Na Ba [NL 934401]). Also here are the ruins of an old chapel in an oval enclosure [NL 937403], dedicated to St Patrick and with cross-incised stones, as well as fine views to South Uist and Barra (on a good day).

SCARINISH TO BALEPHETRISH, CORNAIGMORE AND HEYLIPOL (B8068)

There is a fort on Balephetrish Hill [NM 013472], and another excellent beach at the nearby bay. Between Balephetrish and Vaul is Clach a' Choire [NM 0267487], the Ringing Stone. This granite boulder is indented with many prehistoric cupmarks. When it is struck with a hard object it makes a strange ringing sound. One story is that there is gold in the middle of the rock, but if the stone is split Tiree will sink beneath the sea.

Down an unlisted road to Kenovay is Fiona's Craft Centre and Art Gallery (01879 220801; open summer, Mon-Sat 10.00-17.00; winter, Mon-Sat 13.00-15.00). Another old chapel [NL 994467] stands nearby. The road goes on through Cornaigmore, past an old chapel [NL 994467] and turns to the south of the island near an old mill.

GOTT TO CAOLAS (B8069)

At Gott there is a Surf Shop in the Tiree Lodge Hotel (Open Jun-Sep, Mon-Fri 18.00-19.00; contact 07712 159205 for other times), which also has public and lounge bars.

From Gott it is a short distance to Kirkapol, where there is Cladh Orain [NM 042472], a small burial ground with the remains of a fourteenth-century chapel, which was dedicated to St Columba. Five carved burial slabs, decorated with crosses, date from between the fourteenth and sixteenth centuries. The modern Kirkapol Church [NM 041468] is open to the public. There is also a hotel with cycle hire, the golf course, and a huge stretch of beach called Traigh Mor.

Near Vaul, off an unlisted road to the north of the B8069, is Dun Mor [NM 083476]. This is a ruinous broch with defensive outworks, the walls of which survive to a height of more than two metres. The entrance with a guard chamber and a gallery and start of a stair can be traced.

On the south side of the road to Caolas is an impressive standing stone [NM 077483], which leans but is around three metres high. Off an unlisted road at Caolas is Dun Mor a' Chaolais [NM 083476], another ruined broch with outworks.

HOTELS AND GUEST HOUSES

Crossapol Guest House (01879 220549)
  Crossapol; guest house
The Glassary (01879 220684;
  www.theglassary.co.uk)
  Sandaig; B&B and converted byre restaurant
Glebe House (01879 220758;
  www.glebehousetiree.co.uk)
  Gott Bay; guest house; open all year
Kirkapol House (01879 220729;
  www.kirkapoltiree.co.uk)
  Gott Bay; guest house; open all year
The Lodge Hotel (01879 220368)
  Gott Bay; hotel and restaurant
Tiree Scarinish Hotel (01879 220308;
  www.tireescarinishhotel.com)
  Scarinish; hotel and restaurant; open all year

BED AND BREAKFAST

Balephetrish House (01879 220541)
  Balephetrish; B&B
The Coolins (01879 220314)
  Scarinish; B&B
The Glassary (01879 220684;
  www.theglassary.co.uk)
  Sandaig; B&B
Windway (01879 220423)
  Crossapol; B&B

SELF-CATERING PROPERTIES

House (01631 563711)
  Balephetrish; sleeps six
Cottage (01301 702425; www.tireecottage.co.uk)
  Balephuil; sleeps five-six

Studio (01879 220747)
  Balevullin, sleeps two
Drovers Cottage (01327 860102;
  www.scotland2000.com/drovers)
  Barrapol; sleeps two
House (0141 632 6994)
  Barrapol; sleeps five
House (01977 684115/07754 089841;
  www.tireecottage.com)
  Baugh; sleeps four-five
House (01879 220538)
  Baugh; sleeps two
House (01879 220402/07769 816411)
  Caolas; sleeps four/five
House (01879 220402/07769 816411)
  Caolas; sleeps two/three
House (01879 220412)
  Caolas; sleeps nine/eleven
House (01560 600252)
  Cornaig; sleeps six/eight
House (01866 822365)
  Cornaig; sleeps five
House & cottage (0141 775 1612; www.tiree-
  cottage.co.uk)
  Cornaig; sleeps six/eight
House (0141 574 7949/07733 323587)
  Cornaig; sleeps twelve
House (01879 220627)
  Cornaig; sleeps seven
House (0141 942 2075/07802 213450)
  Crossapol; sleeps eight
Cottage (01879 220427)
  Crossapol; sleeps five/six
House (01631 565242; www.tireecottages.com)
  Heanish; sleeps four
House (01655 750350)
  Hynish; sleeps nine
Morton Boyd House (01879 220726;
  www.hynishcentre.co.uk)
  Hynish; sleeps eight
House (0141 942 0818)
  Kenovay; sleeps five
House (01879 220307)
  Kenovay; sleeps eight
House (01879 220598)
  Kilkenneth; sleeps seven
House & Flat, Tiree Lodge Hotel (01879 220368)
  Kirkapol; sleeps eight & six
Cottage (01301 702425; www.tireecottage.co.uk)
  Mannal; sleeps four/five
House (01835 822104)
  Mannal; sleeps five
House (01592 775419)
  Milton; sleeps two
House (01879 220301)
  Miodar; sleeps four/six
House (01828 670670/01879 220554)
  Scarinish; sleeps six
Flat (01879 220301)
  Scarinish; sleeps four
House (01499 302212)
  Scarinish; sleeps five
House (07742 070422; www.caledonia-
  cottages.co.uk)
  Scarinish; sleeps four/five

House (01968 672903/07721 860095;
  www.tireehouselet.co.uk)
  Scarinish; sleeps four
House (01879 220479)
  Vaul; sleeps six

HOSTELS AND RETREATS

Tiree Mill House (01879 220435;
  www.tireemillhouse.co.uk)
  Cornaig; hostel, sleeps sixteen/eighteen;
  bookings for pony trekking, sand yachting and
  windsurfing can be arranged
Alan Stevenson House (01879 220726;
  www.hynishcentre.co.uk)
  Hynish; group accommodation, sleeps
  twenty-four

CAMPING AND CARAVANS

Camping is possible but get permission from the
crofter or Township Grazing Clerk before
setting up camp or lighting fires (this also
includes over-night parking of camper-vans or
caravans)
Caravan (01879 220412)
  Caolas ; sleeps three
Caravan (01879 220801)
  Kenovay; sleeps four/six

PLACES TO EAT

Tiree Scarinish Hotel (01879 220308;
  www.tireescarinishhotel.com)
  Scarinish Harbour; meals all day
Tiree Lodge Hotel (01879 220368)
  Kirkapol; public bar/lounge bar; lunches,
  evening meals (booking preferred)
The Glassary Restaurant (01879 220684;
  www.theglassary.co.uk)
  Sandaig; lunches/dinners
Rural Centre Tearoom
  Crossapol; Mon-Sat; refreshments and light
  meals

Further Information

TRANSPORT

PETROL, GARAGES AND CAR HIRE
Tiree Motor Company (01879 220469)
  Crossapol; Mon-Sat, 9.00-18.00
MacLennan Motors (01879 220555)
  Pierhead, Scarinish; Mon-Fri, 9.00-17.30; Sat,
  9.00-17.00
TAXIS
John Kennedy Taxis (01879 220419)
  Crossapol
CYCLE HIRE
Mr N MacLean (01879 220428)
  Kenovay
Mrs Judith Boyd (01879 220435)
  Millhouse, Cornaigmore
Tiree Lodge Hotel (01879 220368)
  Kirkapol

ACTIVITIES AND SPORTS

BOAT TRIPS
Skipinnish Sea Tours (01879 220009/07843
250445; www.skipinnish-sea-tours.co.uk)
Skipinnish, Ruaig; boat trips, including to Coll
and the Skerryvore Lighthouse and
circumnavigation of the island, of one to four
hours and fishing trips; private charters,
including for diving

SURFING AND SAND YACHTING
Sand Yachting (01879 220317)
Gott Bay; times vary with wind and tide;
bookings preferred
Wild Diamond Windsurfing and Kite Surfing
(01879 220399/07712 159205/07711 807976;
www.surfschoolscotland.co.uk)
Loch Bhasapoll and Gott Bay

GOLF
Vaul Golf Club (01879 220729)
Kirkapol; nine-hole golf course
Clubs can be hired from the Tiree Lodge Hotel at
Kirkapol (01879 220368)

FISHING AND ANGLING
Tiree Anglers Club (01879 220334)
Loch Bhasapoll; permits from MacLeods Shop
at Crossapol (01879 220347) or Mrs J. Boyd
(01879 220435)

HORSE RIDING
Tiree on Horseback (01879 220881;
www.tireeonhorseback.co.uk)
Caolas; two- and four-day tours on horseback

TOURS
Guided Island Tours (01879 22054)
Balephetrish
Thursday Island Tours (01879 220684)
Bus tour of the island at 12.15, including lunch
at the Glassary Restaurant

LOCAL PRODUCE

SHELLFISH
Kevin and Myra Brown (01879 220654)
Balephuil
Iain Hamilton (01879 220929)
Cornaigbeag
Sandy MacIntosh (01879 220829)
Urvaig, Caolas

ARTS AND CRAFTS

Blue Beyond (01879 220510 ;
www.bluebeyond.uk.com)
Balemartine; paintings, textiles, raku pottery,
cards and fine art prints; Apr-Oct, Mon-Fri or
by appt
Dorinda Johnson Studio (01879 220747;
www.dorindajohnson.co.uk)
Balevullin; paintings, sculptures, ceramics,
cards etc inspired by Tiree; open Mon-Fri
Tiree Images (www.tireeimages.com)

VISITOR ATTRACTIONS AND MUSEUMS

An Iodhlann (01879 220793;
www.aniodhlann.org.uk)
Scarinish; historical centre and seasonal
exhibition; open Jul-Sep, Tue-Fri 12.00 -17.00;
winter, Mon-Fri 10.30-15.30
Hynish Centre (01879 220726
Hynish; Signal Tower and Lighthouse Shore
station with exhibition and heritage trail; open
summer, dawn to dusk
Rural Centre (01879 220677)
Crossapol; exhibition of crofting and the
environment; cafe; open Mon-Sat
Sandaig Museum (01879 220677;
www.aniodhlann.org.uk)
Sandaig; thatched croft cottage, byre and barn;
open Easter-late Sep, Mon-Fri, 14.00-16.00

ADDITIONAL INFORMATION

BANK
Royal Bank of Scotland, Scarinish (no Cashline
machine)

POST OFFICES
Scarinish Main Office (01879 220301)
Balinoe (01879 220450)
Kilmoluaig (Cornaig, 01879 220550)

Public toilets are located at Scarinish and
Crossapol (Rural Centre)
There are public telephones at Balephuil,
Balevullin, Baugh, Caolas, Cornaigmore,
Crossapol, Heylipol, Kenovay, Mannal,
Middleton, Pierhead, Scarinish, and the end of
Vaul Road

EVENTS

Tiree Agricultural Show   late July
Tiree Wave Classic (windsurfing championships;
www.tireewaveclassic.com)   October

FURTHER READING

Coll and Tiree (Beveridge, Erskine)
Birlinn, 2001

ACKNOWLEDGMENTS

Thanks to Catriona McLeod, Archivist for An
Iodhlann, for reading over the text

Mull, Iona, Erraid, Ulva, Staffa, Treshnish Isles and Neighbouring Islands

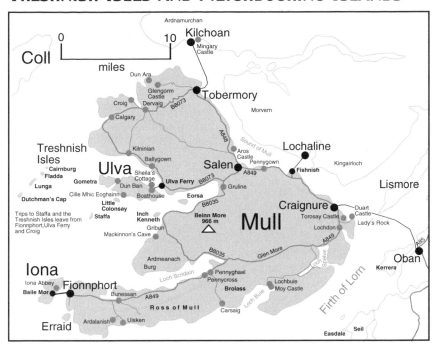

Mull from the ferry

MULL

(probably 'bare hill' from Gaelic maol, or possibly from meall, Gaelic for a rounded hill, which might refer to Ben More.)

www.holidaymull.org
www.isle-of-mull-accommodation.co.uk
www.accommodation.mull.com
www.mull.zynet.co.uk
www.tobermory.co.uk
www.tobermory.mull.com
www.bunessan.bordernet.co.uk
www.pennyghael.net
www.roundandabout-mull.co.uk
www.mict.co.uk
www.mullbirds.com
www.mullgenealogy.co.uk
www.brown-whittaker.co.uk
www.mullchamber.org
www.visitscottishheartlands.com (AILLST)

Tourist Information Centres
Tobermory (08707 200625)
    Open Apr-Oct
Craignure (08707 200610)
    Open Jan-Dec

Map Landranger sheets: 46, 47, 48 (HIH map page 73)

TRAVEL

Vehicle ferries (CalMac 01631 566688 (Oban)/01688 812343 (Craignure); www.calmac.co.uk) leave Oban on the mainland for Craignure on the east coast of Mull. There are up to five crossings daily all year, with up to seven (or more some dates) in the summer. The crossing takes forty-five minutes, and there are fewer trips on Sundays. Oban has a railway station (www.firstgroup.com/scotrail; 08457 484 950), and a full range of amenities and facilities, including a tourist information centre, distillery, banks, supermarkets, leisure centre and much else.

A vehicle ferry (CalMac 01631 566688; www.calmac.co.uk) makes the journey between Lochaline on the south coast of Morvern (A884) on the mainland and Fishnish on the north-east coast of Mull. There are up to fourteen crossings per day, which take fifteen minutes, with fewer on a Sunday.

A vehicle ferry also goes between Kilchoan (B8007) on the south coast of Ardnamurchan on the mainland and Tobermory, the capital and main settlement on the north-west end of Mull. Up to seven trips are made Monday to Saturday, with five crossings on a Sunday, but the latter only sail from May-August. The crossing takes thirty-five minutes. The Ardnamurchan peninsula is a lovely part of Scotland, and there is the ruined Mingary Castle near Kilchoan.

Mull also has ferries for Iona (Fionnphort on the A849), Ulva (Ulva ferry on the B8073), Staffa and the Treshnish Isles. See the respective islands for details.

DESCRIPTION

Mull is the third largest in the Western Isles, covering some 353 square miles, and being about thirty miles long at most, and twenty miles wide. It lies off the mainland across the Firth of Lorn from Oban, and the narrow Sound of Mull from Morvern and Ardnamurchan. The island is deeply indented by the sea lochs of Loch na Keal and Loch Scridain (the latter runs along the thin southern peninsula of the Ross of Mull, at the end of which is Iona); and by Loch Buie and Loch Spelve to the south.

The island is dominated by the frowning mass of Ben More, a Munro at 966 metres, although often the higher parts are shrouded in cloud. There are several other hills over 700 metres, and the centre is very impressive, especially on the road through Glen More. There are cliffs along the southern coast and Brolass but there also lovely beaches, including at Ardalanish, Uisken and Scoor on the coast of the Ross of Mull, and a beautiful stretch of sand at Calgary Bay to the west. Several large caves are dotted along the coasts, including MacKinnon's Cave near Gribun, and the Nuns' Cave at Carsaig, where there is also a natural arch and a good beach. There is also a fossilised tree near Burg, an area also known as the Wilderness, which has stepped cliffs.

Mull also has tracts of good land, particularly in the north and parts of the coasts; and there are many forestry plantations but also woods of native species. Mull is mostly a very green and lush place, explained by fertile volcanic soil and the large amount of rain that falls here (May is the driest month), especially over the hills and higher parts. This can also give rise to that least welcome of summer visitors: the midge and (even more evil) the cleg or horsefly.

The main village and administrative centre is Tobermory ('well of St Mary') to the north and east, one of the most attractive of villages in all the islands with its brightly painted houses. Tobermory has a wide range of amenities, including places to stay and eat, shops, banks, as well as a distillery and a golf course above the town.

Craignure is at the eastern side and where the ferry from Oban lands, and is near to two of Mull's major tourist attractions, Duart Castle and Torosay Castle. About

Ben More

half way between Craignure and Tobermory is Salen and Aros. Dervaig is to the north and west; Ulva Ferry is further south; and to the south of Mull, on the Ross of Mull, are Bunessan and Fionnphort and the ferry to Iona.

Most of the roads are single track, except for the A849 north of Craignure, but there are also some lovely winding routes between Tobermory and Gruline (B8073); along the shore of Loch na Keal between Gruline and Loch Scridain (B8035); and down to Lochbuie and the castle. The journey through Glen More is also lovely, but it can be busy with traffic and coaches bound for Fionnphort and Iona.

The population is now around 2,500 people, although boosted in the summer by holiday home owners and many visitors and tourists.

As mentioned above, Tobermory is famous for its vibrantly painted houses. In recent times it has come to national importance, at least among the very young, as the location of *Balamory*, the CBeebies favourite. Spencer the Painter's house can be seen; the vivid orange was only originally chosen for the show, but the owner grew so fond of it that he did not paint over it after filming. Josie Jump's house is the Harbour Heights Hotel (yellow was its colour before *Balamory*); while 'Pocket and Sweet' is red in the programme, but is returned to its normal blue when it resumes its function as the box office for the Mull Theatre. Edie McCreadie's House is actually the Tobermory Chocolate shop: a good place to frequent, old or young. Unfortunately the pink castle is not on Mull at all and is actually Fenton Tower, near North Berwick; nor is Fenton Tower strident pink, of course: it is a rather duller beige. Souvenirs and *Balamory* clothing can be bought from most shops in Tobermory (further information can be found at www.tobermory-balamory-gifts.co.uk; on-line shopping is available).

WILDLIFE

Many different kinds of birds can be seen, some depending on season, including golden eagles and white-tailed sea eagles (there is a hide at Loch Frisa, to the north-west of Salen), peregrine falcons, buzzards and owls; colonies of puffins and fulmars; and divers, razorbills, guillemots, shags, skuas and merlins. On the hills are red and fallow dear and mountain hares, and there are feral goats, polecats, otters, slowworms and adders. Colonies of seals live around the coasts, and further out are porpoises, dolphins, minke whales, and even killer whales and basking sharks (there is a visitor centre in Tobermory; www.whaledolphintrust.co.uk). There are also boat trips to view puffins.

HISTORY

Mull has a good selection of prehistoric monuments (although not on the scale of some of the other islands), including the stone circle at Lochbuie and many stone settings, such as at Dervaig; burial cairns; and many duns and brochs, such as Dun Aisgain, near Burg, and Dun nan Gall and Dun na Fheurain.

The island was held by the Vikings, and was plundered by Magnus Barelegs in 1100. It later became part of the wide territories of the Lords of the Isles. Iona was a great centre of Christianity from the sixth century, and in medieval times there were a huge number of pilgrims who crossed Mull to get to St Columba's shrine at the abbey on Iona. Iona has its own entry, but the pilgrims are believed to have made their way from Grass Point [NM 748310] to Fionnphort. A series of standing stones marked the way, and many of these monoliths survive, including at Uluvalt [NM 547300], Rossal [NM 543282], Taoslin [NM 397224], Suidhe [NM 371218], Tiraghoil [NM 353224], and Achaban [NM 313223]. The final stone at Catchean, by Fionnphort, was destroyed in an accident of 1863. There are no great ecclesiastical buildings on Mull, but the ruined chapels at Pennygown, Kilvickeon and Inchkenneth are interesting and picturesque.

If Mull is lacking in prehistoric or ecclesiastical remains, it has two of the best castles in Scotland, both held by branches of the MacLeans, who were pre-eminent on Mull.

Duart Castle stands in a fantastic (and strategic) position on a rocky crag overlooking the Firth of Lorn and the Sound of Mull. The present building dates from the twelfth century and, although restored in the first part of the twentieth century, it is everyone's idea of a grim but photogenic Highland stronghold.

On a much smaller scale is Moy Castle at Lochbuie, the plain derelict tower of the MacLaines of Lochbuie, which stands in one of the most beautiful settings in Scotland.

The shattered ruins of Aros Castle stand near Salen, and this was once one of the most important places on the island; there were also small strongholds at Dun Ara and on Eilean Amalaig in Loch Spelve, where the MacLeans marshalled their galleys.

The MacLeans fought a fierce engagement, known as the Battle of Bloody Bay, in 1480 during a dispute between the Lord of the Isles and his illegitimate son, which also involved the Lowland forces of the earls of Huntly and of Crawford. The MacLeans were on the losing side.

Moy Castle

After the defeat of the Spanish Armada in 1588, many ships ended up being blown out of their way up the west coast of Britain. One, *Florenica* or *San Juan de Sicilia*, ended up moored in Tobermory Bay, reputedly with £300,000 of gold bullion on board. The Spaniards got involved in the machinations of the MacLeans of Duart, and the ship ended up at the bottom of the sea, where it is reputed the gold still lies. There are several other wrecks around the coast of Mull, and these are visited by many divers.

Mull was another island to suffer grievously during the Clearances, despite periods of relative prosperity with fishing and kelp gathering. The population was recorded as being more than 10,000 in 1821 but by 1969 it had dwindled to 2,100: it is now around 2,700. There are several cleared townships, including those at Cille Mhuire, Kildavie, Shiaba and Tir Fhearagain.

Tours

CRAIGNURE TO BUNESSAN, FIONNPHORT AND IONA (A849)

The main ferry from Oban on the mainland lands at Craignure, where there are a

Duart Castle

post office and shop, a pub, a hotel, a bistro and the narrow-gauge steam railway to Torosay Castle. There is also a tourist information office, ferry office and a regular bus service to Tobermory and to Fionnphort for the ferry across to Iona.

Two miles south of Craignure an unlisted road runs to the east, passing the cemetery at Kilpatrick [NM 738741] before arriving at Duart Castle (01577 812309; www.duartcastle.com; open Apr-Oct, Sun-Thu 11.00-16.00). This, the ancient seat of the MacLeans, is beautifully sited on Duart Point (Duart is from Dubhard, meaning 'black height'). The castle dates from the twelfth century, has a massive keep, and was restored in the twentieth century, after being bought back by Fitzroy MacLean, twenty-sixth chief, in 1911.

The sixth chief, Red Hector, was slain at the bloody Battle of Harlaw in 1411 in the act of killing Sir Alexander Irvine of Drum. Lachlan Cattanach, eleventh chief, had his wife (the lady was the daughter of the Earl of Argyll) marooned on the Lady's Rock, between Lismore and Duart, in an attempt to rid himself of her. Unfortunately for him, she was rescued and was avenged when Sir John Campbell of Cawdor killed MacLean in his bed some years later. In 1674 the MacLeans' lands were secured by the Campbells, and Duart was only sporadically garrisoned until by the end of the nineteenth century it was a ruinous shell. Now back to its former glory, among its many other attractions are the dungeon where officers from the Spanish galleon (see Tobermory) were imprisoned, displays on MacLean clan history, and a shop and tearoom in the old byre near the castle.

From Craignure the narrow-gauge Isle of Mull Railway (01680 812494; www.mullrail.co.uk; open Easter-mid Oct) runs to Torosay Castle. Both steam and diesel engine run on the line, which is just over one mile long – a trip takes twenty minutes. The journey goes through woodland, and there are panoramic views of the Firth of Lorn, even over to Ben Nevis.

Torosay Castle (01680 812421; www.torosay.com; house open mid Apr-Oct, daily 10.30-17.00; gardens open all year) can be reached either by the railway or by road. It is an imposing castellated mansion of 1858, designed by David Bryce for the Campbells of Possel. It was soon sold to the Guthries, with whose descendants it remains. The twelve acres of fine gardens were laid out by Sir Robert Lorimer in 1899, and there are formal terraces, an Italian statue walk, Japanese garden, a walled garden and woodland walks. The principal rooms of the house are also open to the public, and there is a tearoom and shop.

Also at Torosay Steadings is Isle of Mull Weavers (01680 812381), weavers of high-quality Tweeds. At Achnacroish House, near Torosay, is Wings Over Mull (01680 812594; www.wingsovermull.com; open Easter-Oct, daily 10.30-17.30 or by appt; flying displays, daily 12.00, 14.00 and 16.00) which is a conservation centre and has birds of prey: hawks, falcons, eagles, kites and owls.

At Barr Leathan near Lochdon, south of Craignure and located on moorland to the west of the road, is a standing stone [NM 726342] more than two metres high. Several miles south of Lochdon at Port Donain [NM 737292] are two burial cairns. The larger is thirty metres long and ten wide. It has been robbed of stones, and the chamber, kerb and facade can be seen; there is also the remains of cist. To the north-west is a small round cairn.

Lochdon has possibly the smallest post office in Britain, as well as a restaurant; and beyond Lochdon, the road runs for a while along the banks of Loch Spelve, where the MacLeans harboured their birlinns or galleys. On an islet, Eilean Amalaig [NM 708298], are the remains of a small stronghold; this is recorded as the sacred isle of the MacLeans. Sir Lachlan MacLean was warned not to sail his galleys anticlockwise around the island. He ignored this, of course, and invaded Islay and was slaughtered along with his men at the Battle of Traigh Gruinart in 1598. A little further on is the turn-off for Lochbuie and Moy Castle.

The main road then travels into the interior of Mull towards Glen More, passing Loch Squabain. On an island at the northern end is a crannog [NM 632307], which is believed to have been the residence of Ewen MacLaine. In 1538 he fought with his father, Ian the Toothless, chief of the MacLaines of Lochbuie, over his inheritance, a battle in which the MacLeans of Duart got involved. At the fight, Ewen's head was hewn off with an axe and his headless corpse, still upright in the saddle of his horse, rode on for several miles down Glen More. The legend then goes that, when one of the MacLaines of Lochbuie was near to death, Ewen's ghost, a decapitated apparition on a black horse, was seen to ride down the glen, sometimes accompanied by a large black dog ...

The road is an impressive route and runs between the two hills of Ben More and Ben Buie before emerging out of the glen at the eastern end of Loch Scridain. The B8035 runs north, a beautiful route up to Salen and the north; while the main road runs along the north coast of Brolass and the Ross of Mull.

At Pennyghael there is a shop, hotel and a small pottery run by Norman Salkeld (01681 704229). An unlisted road leads south to Carsaig, where there is a nice beach. A rough footpath leads west, below the high cliffs, to the Nuns' Cave or, in Gaelic, Uamh nan Cailleach. The story goes that nuns driven out from Iona sought shelter here, and hence the name. The walls are inscribed with crosses, perhaps dating from the sixth century, tridents, a ship, and masons' marks. The difficult path goes on to the Carsaig Arches, natural arches at Malcolm's Point, one of which is full of rocks that boom with the swell.

Just north of Pennycross is a sixteenth-century cross, Crois an Ollaimh [NM 506263], which commemorates the Beatons of Mull, celebrated physicians in medieval times. They lived at Pennycross.

At Bunessan is a Spar shop and post office and a grocer, as well as a hotel and a restaurant; and in a portacabin is the Ross of Mull Historical Centre (open Apr-Oct, Mon-Fri 10.30-16.30; Nov-Mar by appt; 01681 700659; www.romhc.org.uk) with a mine of information on local history and people as well as walks around the Ross of Mull.

An unlisted road goes west to Kilvickeon Church [NM 413196], which dates

Beach, Uisken

from the thirteenth century and has a very weathered Sheila na Gig. The site was probably dedicated to St Ernan, nephew of Columba, and there are some old memorials in the cemetery. There is a beach at Scoor, and further west is a cave which has crosses and tridents carved in the walls.

Another route from Bunessan runs south to two lovely beaches at Uisken (where there is a hotel) and Ardalanish. Above Ardalanish Bay is Dun an Fheurain [NM 370187] perched on a rocky promontory above the sands. This was a strong fort, protected by the steepness of the approaches and by a series of ramparts.

At Fionnphort is the Ferry Shop and post office with souvenirs, crafts and a bookshop; and hardware and internet access. There are also restaurants, and the St Columba Centre (01681 700640; open Apr-Sep, daily 11.00-17.00) which focuses on the life and work of St Columba and Iona with displays including a model of a curragh, a small boat in which he and his followers rowed to Scotland. Also here is Eleanor MacDougall (01681 700780), who features traditional silversmithing techniques. To the east of the village is a tall standing stone at Pottie [NM 325222].

This is also, of course, the ferry point to Iona (which has its own entry), and there is a huge car park: visitors' cars cannot be taken onto the island.

Off the south-west side of the Ross of Mull is the small tidal island of Erraid.

CRAIGNURE TO SALEN AND TOBERMORY (A849 AND A848)

The road from Craignure runs north, past the Craignure Golf Club and then a spur (A864) at Fishnish from where the ferry crosses to Lochaline. This road runs through a forestry plantation and there is a car park, forest walk and a picnic area in a pretty spot. The campsite at Balmeanach has a cafe.

Further east on the A849 is the ruinous chapel at Pennygown [NM 604432], which dates from the thirteenth century. In the chapel is the finely carved shaft of a sixteenth-century cross; and in the interesting graveyard are two slabs with the stone effigies of a man and a woman, as well as eighteenth-century markers.

At Salen is a supermarket, a licensed grocers, a post office, a petrol station, a hotel and tea rooms; the B8035 goes west while the A848 heads north to Tobermory.

Near the A848, a mile or so north of Salen, is the crumbling and overgrown ruin of Aros Castle on a picturesque site above the sea. It is hard to believe now that at one time this was the most important place on Mull. This is a large site, although the ruin of the thirteenth-century hall-house is the most prominent of the remains, and was probably built by the MacDougalls of Lorn. It passed to the MacDonald Lord of the Isles, then the MacLeans of Duart, and later again to the Campbells. Aros lost out in importance to Tobermory, partly because its harbour was not nearly as good. The castle may be visited, but seek permission first. It was off Aros that island chiefs were entertained aboard ship in 1608. Under the orders of James VI, they were then seized, carted off to Edinburgh and imprisoned until they saw the error of their ways – or said they had at least.

An unlisted but scenic route runs up through Glen Aros and eventually arrives down at Dervaig to the north of the island. There is a waterfall near the road; and at Carrachan [NM 504463] is a setting of four standing stones, up to two metres high.

Back on the main road, and in a clearing in the forest on the north side of the Aros River, is Cill an Ailein [NM 546456], the shell of a thirteenth-century chapel and burial ground. There are several old burial markers, including a medieval grave slab. To the west of the road at Ardnacross are two cairns [NM 542492] and settings of standing stones, although only one monolith remains standing. The more impressive of the cairns is four metres in diameter and has a kerb of large boulders.

On the coast near Ardnacross is An Sean Caisteal [NM 551499], the remains of a broch (the name means 'the ancient castle') consisting of a mound rising to a couple of metres. The entrance can be seen and traces of a defensive outwork. There are good views from here down the Sound of Mull.

The large forestry plantation south of Tobermory has a series of forest walks, picnic spots, and there are picturesque waterfalls. Near Baliscate [NM 500541] are three standing stones, although one is now prostrate. The biggest stone is two and

Tobermory

a half metres high. The main road run down into Tobermory, while the B8073 heads west to Dervaig and Calgary.

Tobermory has an excellent sheltered harbour, and is also one of the most attractive villages on the island (or, indeed, in the Western Isles). The village has many good shops, hotels, places to eat, lots of places to stay, a Co-op supermarket and a branch of the Clydesdale Bank, as well as a tourist information centre. A ferry from here travels across the narrow sound to Kilchoan Pier on Ardnamurchan. This trip is worthwhile, even if only to visit the ruins of Mingary Castle. Tobermory is used as the backdrop for the BBC show *Balamory*, as mentioned earlier.

On the Main Street is the Mull Museum (01688 302208; open Apr-Oct, daily 10.00-17.00, Sat 10.00-13.00), a small establishment which is packed with artefacts, photographs and documents about the island's history, archaeology, geology and wildlife, plus a reference library. By the shore is the Tobermory Distillery (01688 302645; www.burnstewartdistillers.com; open all year, Mon-Fri 10.00-17.00; other times by appt), which was first established in 1798. It produces the Tobermory Single Malt Scotch Whisky, which is fresh, smooth and medium dry. There are distillery tours and a well-stocked distillery shop.

Many boat trips are available on Mull, and on the Main Street there is also the Hebridean Whale and Dolphin Trust (01688 302620; www.whaledolphintrust.co.uk; open summer, Mon-Fri 10.00-17.00, Sat-Sun 11.00-17.00), which has a visitor centre with an exhibition and gift shop. Also not to be missed is Tobermory Chocolate (01688 302526; www.tobchoc.co.uk), which has a shop with chocolate and gifts for sale as well as a cafe; chocolate can also be purchased on-line.

Above the Main Street is An Tobar (01688 302211; www.antobar.co.uk; 'the well'), an arts centre with live music events, gallery exhibitions, ceilidh evenings, music and dance classes, plus a cafe and shop featuring local arts and crafts. There is a range of art galleries selling work as well as craft shops in and around Tobermory, including Angus Stewart Paintings and Prints (01688 302024; www.mullart.com); Lee's Studio (01688 302602); The Picture Gallery (01688 302426); Mull Pottery (01688 302347; www.mullpottery.com), which has a cafe and bistro; Starfish Ceramics; Whigmaleerie Wood and Horn Craft (01688 302173); and Isle of Mull Silver and Goldsmiths (01688 302345; www.mullsilver.co.uk). The box office of the Mull Theatre is located in Tobermory (01688 302828; www.mulltheatre.com). Several boat trips run from the harbour, and to the north of the village is the Tobermory Golf Club.

TOBERMORY TO DERVAIG, ULVA FERRY AND SALEN (B8073)

An unlisted road runs north out of Tobermory to Glengorm Castle, passing through forestry plantations: there is a forest walk. Bloody Bay is the site of a murderous sea battle between the Lord of the Isles and his illegitimate son. Accommodation is available at Glengorm Castle (01688 302321; www.glengormcastle.co.uk), and there is also a large market garden with a shop, tearoom and art gallery. The name means 'blue glen', and the story goes that the builder first chose the spot for the building because of the blue haze he found here, not realising that this was from the smoke of burning crofts as local people were cleared from the land.

Near the castle are three standing stones [NM 435571], each about two metres high. On a track to the north is the ruin of Dun Ara [NM 377452], originally an Iron Age fortress but occupied as late as the seventeenth century. This was the seat of the MacKinnons, who held lands here from 1354. The remnant of a wall surrounds the highest part of the rock, and there are foundations of what was probably a hall, as well as a boat landing.

Near Glengorm is Isle of Mull Cheese (01688 302235; www.btinternet.com/

-mull.cheese/index.html) at Sgriob-Ruadh Farm Dairy. They produce a traditional farmhouse cheese, and the farm can be visited, and there is a cafe; cheese can also be purchased using on-line ordering.

The B8073 wanders its way west, and on the way into the attractive settlement of Dervaig (from the east) are three groups of standing stones. The first is near the burial ground at Kilmore [NM 438517], where there are four one-metre monoliths. Another setting can be found within the forestry plantation at Cnoc Fada [NM 439521]: there were at least five stones but only two, more than two metres high, are erect. At Maol Mor [NM 436351], far into the trees, are two more upright monoliths, with a third fallen.

Dervaig is a pretty village, which has a distinctive white-washed church with a round tower (www.kilmore.org.uk); and also hotels, a pub, restaurants, a post office and shop. It is also home to the Mull Theatre (01688 302828; www.mulltheatre.com), which was founded in 1966 and, at time of writing, is the smallest professional theatre in Great Britain, seating forty-three people. The theatre features a programme of repertory theatre, new work and touring shows, although it may be looking for a new home from 2006. The box office is in Tobermory.

Near here is the Old Byre Heritage Centre (01688 400229; www.old-byre.co.uk; open Apr-Oct, Wed-Sun, 10.30-18.30), which is housed in a converted byre, and features two videos (shown on alternate days) and 'Mull in miniature', twenty-five exquisite models of the island through the ages. There is also a tearoom and gift shop. There are boat trips from Croig harbour with Inter Island Cruises (01688 302916; www.jenny.mull.com).

Near Dervaig are further standing stones; a three-metre monolith is near Mingary [NM 414552], north of the village; while to the west, near the unlisted road to Sunipol, is another tall standing stone [NM 377535].

At Calgary is a fantastic clean sandy beach (and public toilets); and nearby is the Calgary Art in Nature woodland sculpture walk. Also here is the Carthouse Gallery (01688 400256; www.calgary.co.uk), a handy source of local art from Mull, including

Beach, Calgary

watercolours, etchings, pottery, wood and ironwork, and there is also a cafe and summer art workshops are available for children; as well as a hotel and restaurant. While Colonel J. F. MacLeod stayed at Calgary Castle (a petite mansion) in 1879, he met and fell in love with the fetching young daughter of the house. In memory of where he met her, MacLeod named the settlement on the western seaboard of Canada and so Calgary (in Canada) got its name. Self-catering accommodation is available in the castle (01449 741066; www.calgary-castle.com)

South of Burg is Dun Aisgain [NM 427577], on a rocky outcrop above the sea. This is the well-preserved ruin of a round dun, the walls surviving to a height of about three metres. Some of the lintels are still in place above the entrance passageway. At Kilninian is a standing stone [NM 392456] by the road; a large burial cairn [NM 394454], twenty metres in diameter and two metres high; and the parish church [NM 397456] dating from 1755 in an old graveyard. The site was dedicated to St Ninian, and there are graveslabs, which date from the fourteenth century or earlier, housed in the vestry and lying in the burial ground.

At Ballygown are two ruinous Iron Age strongholds. On a small headland is Dun nan Gall [NM 433432], a reduced but well-preserved broch. The entrance, a mural cell and a stair lobby can be seen. Above the road further east is Dun Choinichean [NM 441431], overgrown and ruinous, but the entrance and a gallery are still evident. There are impressive waterfalls known as Eas Fors (meaning 'waterfall' in both Gaelic and Norse) further along the road.

The island of Ulva (which has its own entry) lies close to the shore and the ferry goes from Ulva Ferry, from where there are also boat trips to Staffa and the Treshnish Isles (Turus Mara Seabird and Wildlife Cruise Tours; 08000 858786; www.turusmara.com).

The road goes on to Gruline, where there is the turn-off for the B8035, and then heads to Salen.

GRULINE TO BROLASS (B8035)

Gruline is the location of the Macquarie Mausoleum. Lachlan Macquarie, who owned the Gruline estate, was Governor of New South Wales, and is important enough in its history to be known as 'the father of Australia', although presumably not to the aboriginal population. Macquarie was born at Ulva Ferry in 1761 and died in 1824. The mausoleum is owned by the National Trust of Australia.

Two monoliths stand on opposite sides of the road. One standing stone [NM 543398] is about two-and-a-half metres in height; the other is 200 metres away [NM 546396].

This route is one of the most beautiful to be found in the Western Isles, and runs along the north shore of Loch na Keal with Ben More looming to the east; a good place to climb the mountain from is Dhiseig. Eorsa, a small island in the loch rising to 98 metres, is more like something from the Mediterranean than the Hebrides.

There is a good beach at Gribun, with Inch Kenneth (see below) just off shore, and it is near here that a boulder is said to have tumbled from the hillside and crushed a newly wed couple in their cottage. Along the coast south of Gribun is Mackinnon's Cave [NM 440323], the deepest cave in the islands (even more so than Fingal's Cave on Staffa) at some 183 metres (a torch is recommended). This was reputedly occupied by Christian hermits, who used the huge slab, known as Fingal's Table, as an altar. One story (similar tales are told of many other caves) has a piper and his dog entering the cave in an attempt to beat the fairies in a piping competition. Only the terrified dog returned, the piper having been seized and taken to the 'other world' of the fairies; one version has him emerging out of the other side of the hill, others that only the dog survived but all its hair had been burned off. Dr Johnson visited the cave.

Burg is one of the least tamed parts of Mull, and is also known as the Wilderness. The grand stepped cliffs were formed by cooling lava, which also overwhelmed MacCulloch's fossil tree [NM 403278], the impression of the trunk being preserved in the rock. The 1,405 acres of Burg (01631 570000) are owned by the National Trust for Scotland, and there is a car park at Tiroran (no cars beyond this). The fossil tree is a seven-mile walk, in some parts difficult, followed by a descent down an iron ladder: the site can only be reached at low tide, and dogs cannot get down the ladder. Two large burial cairns [NM 428265] by the shore near the settlement of Burg lie about one hundred metres apart.

The main road runs along the north shore of Loch Scridain, before joining the A849 near Kinloch.

STRATHCOIL TO LOCHBUIE (UNLISTED ROAD)

Lochbuie is reached down an unlisted road from the A849 at Strathcoil. It climbs up and over a wooded height before running along the north bank of Loch Spelve and then Loch Uisg, before coming to Lochbuie.

Lochbuie is a beautiful place, between the mountains and the sea, with a sweep of sand around the bay. There is an impressive stone circle [NM 618251], the only extant one on Mull, which consisted originally of nine stones, eight of which are still in place. The tallest monolith is two metres. There are outlying standing stones: one three metres away; the second 100 metres to the southwest [NM 617251] and three metres high; a third four hundred metres to the north [NM 616254]; and the last 350 metres to the southwest [NM 619251], although the upper part has been broken off.

Along the shore is the gaunt ruin of Moy Castle [NM 616247], a plain tower house which is derelict but intact to the wallhead. This was the ancestral seat of the MacLaines of Lochbuie (also see Glen More above). MacLean of Duart wanted

Moy Castle, Lochbuie

85

the lands for his own and imprisoned the chief of the MacLaines, Ian the Toothless, (whose heir Ewen was slain in a battle and his headless ghost is said to ride along Glen More) on the island fortress in the Treshnish Isles. MacLaine was eventually killed, but in the meantime got a serving woman pregnant, and her son eventually became chief. The MacLaines fought along with Bonnie Dundee in 1689, but the castle had been abandoned by 1752, and was later replaced by a Georgian mansion. The MacLaines sold the property in the twentieth century. A chapel [NM 626236] has their burial vault and there are several old memorials.

A rough track goes west along the coast of Loch Buie, passing several caves, to Rubha Dubh and eventually reaching Carsaig Bay, which is another very pleasant spot.

INCH KENNETH

Inch Kenneth ('island of Kenneth' – believed to be named after a monk from Iona, who died in 600) is a small island, lying off the west coast at Balnahard, at the mouth of Loch na Keal, two miles south of Ulva. The island is about one mile long, and there are many sandy beaches, as well as rocks and reefs, around the coast. The island is visited by seabirds, including barnacle geese, eider ducks, shags, oystercatchers, curlews, razorbills, redshanks and guillemots

The island was held by the nunnery on Iona, and is said to have produced corn for the monks of Iona, but passed to the MacLeans in 1547. It was visited by Dr Johnson and Boswell in 1773 and, although they enjoyed their visit, Boswell is said to have been scared by a ghost. Their host was Sir Allan MacLean, who was drowned soon after their visit in a boating accident. The island was later held by Lord Redesdale, father of the controversial Mitford girls.

The ruins of a small rectangular chapel [NM 4373540] stand in an old burial ground. The building dates from the thirteenth century, and was dedicated to St Kenneth (Cainneach of Aghaboe). Several fine carved burial slabs are protected in the chapel, dating from the fourteenth and fifteenth centuries, as well as a sixteenth-century ring-headed cross, carved from slate. The finely carved stone of Sir Allan MacLean shows him in his armour with a dog at his feet. The chapel is in the care of Historic Scotland, but there does not appear to be any regular service to get to the island.

There is also a grass-covered prehistoric burial cairn [NM 443359] to the east of the island.

Places to Stay

HOTELS AND GUEST HOUSES

Achaban House (01681 700205; www.achabanhouse.com)
Fionnphort; guest house; self-catering cottage also available; open all year

Ardachy House Hotel (01681 700505; www.ardachy.co.uk)
Uisken; hotel, meals; self-catering accommodation also available; open Mar-Oct

Ardbeg Guest House (01688 400254; www.ardbeghouse-mull.com)
Dervaig ; guest house

Argyll Arms Hotel (01681 700 240; www.isleofmull.co.uk)
Bunessan; hotel and restaurant (booking advisable); open all year

Baliscate Guest House (01688 302048; www.baliscate.com)
Tobermory; guest house; open all year

Bellachroy Hotel (01688 400314; www.bellachroyhotel.co.uk)
Dervaig; hotel in historic drovers' inn, dating from sixteenth century; open all year

Calgary Hotel (01688 400256; www.calgary.co.uk)
Calgary, near Dervaig; hotel, restaurant and tearoom; ; self-catering accommodation also available; open Apr-Oct, wknds Nov and Mar

Caol-Ithe Guest House (01681 700375; www.caol-ithe.co.uk)
Fionnphort; guest house and two self-catering cottages, sleep four-six; open all year

Carnaburg Hotel (01688 302479; www.carnaburg-tobermory.co.uk)
Tobermory; hotel

Craignure Inn (01680 812305; www.craignure-inn.co.uk)
Craignure (near ferry); eighteenth-century hotel and bar; open all year
Drimnin View (01688 392545; www.tobermory.co.uk/drimninview/)
Tobermory; guest house
Druimard Country House Hotel (01688 400345; www.druimard.co.uk)
Dervaig; hotel and restaurant in Victorian country house; open Mar-end Oct
Druimnacroish Hotel (01688 400274; www.druimnacroish.co.uk)
Dervaig; hotel and restaurant; open all year
Fairways Lodge (01688 302238)
Tobermory; guest house; open all year
Glenforsa Hotel (01680 300377; www.glenforsa.com)
Salen, by Aros; hotel, restaurant and bar; open Easter-Oct
Gruline Home Farm (01680 300581; www.gruline.com)
Gruline, near Salen; guest house; open all year
Harbour Heights (01688 302430; www.harbourheights.mull.com)
Tobermory Bay; guest house
Highland Cottage Hotel (01688 302030; www.highlandcottage.co.uk)
Tobermory; hotel and restaurant; confirm opening off season
Killiechronan House (01680 300403; www.highlandholidays.net)
Killiechronan; hotel and restaurant (jacket and tie preferred); open Mar-Oct
The Kinloch Hotel (www.kinloch.ukgateway.net; 01681 704204)
Pennyghael; hotel
Mishnish Hotel (www.mishnish.co.uk; 01688 302009)
Tobermory; hotel and bar; open all year
Old Mill Cottage (01680 812442; www.oldmill.mull.com)
Lochdonhead; guest house and restaurant; self-catering (Mill Cottage), sleeps six-eight; open all year
Pennyghael Hotel (01681 704288; www.pennyghaelhotel.com)
Pennyghael; hotel and self-catering cottages; open all year
Pennyghael Lodge Guest House (01680 812333)
Pennyghael; guest house; open all year
Salen Hotel (01680 300324)
Salen; hotel; open all year
Staffa House (01681 700677; www.staffahouse.co.uk)
Fionnphort; guest house
Sunart View Guest House (01688 302439; www.sunartview.co.uk)
Tobermory; guest house; open all year
Tigh-na-Lochan (01681 700247; www.tighnalochan.com)
Bunessan; guest House; open all year
Tiroran House (01681 705232; www.tiroran.com)
On Craignure-Iona road; hotel; open Apr-Oct

Tobermory Hotel (01688 302091; www.thetobermoryhotel.co.uk)
Tobermory; hotel and restaurant; open all year
Ulva Hotel (01688 302044)
Strongarbh, Tobermory; hotel; open Mar-Nov
Western Isles Hotel (01688 302012; www.mullhotel.com)
Tobermory; hotel, restaurant and bar; open all year except Christmas

BED AND BREAKFAST

Abbey View (01681 700723; www.abbeyviewmull.f9.co.uk)
Fionnphort; B&B
Achaban House (01681 700205; www.achabanhouse.com)
Fionnphort; B&B
Ach-na-Brae Cottages (01681 700260; www.islofmullholidays.com)
Near Fionnphort; two self-catering cottages, sleeps six; open all year
Ardfenaig Farmhouses (01681 700260; www.isleofmullholidays.com)
Ross of Mull; two self-catering houses, open all year
Ardness House (01681 700260; www.isleofmullholidays.com)
Ardness, between Bunessan and Fionnphort; B&B; open Easter-Oct
Baliscate Guest House (01688 302048; www.baliscate.co.uk)
Tobermory; guest house in 1.5 acres of gardens; closed Christmas
Birchgrove (01 680 812364; www.isle-of-mull.demon.co.uk)
Birchgrove, Lochdon; B&B; open Mar-Oct
Brockville (01688 302741; www.tobermory.co.uk/brockville/)
Tobermory; B&B; open all year
Bruach Mhor Bed and Breakfast (01681 700276; www.mullchamber.org)
Near Fionnphort; B&B
The Cedars (01688 302096; www.tobermory.co.uk/Thecedars)
Tobermory; B&B
Clachan House (01680 812439; www.clachanhouse.freeserve.co.uk)
Lochdon; B&B; open all year
Copeland Guest House (01688 302049; www.copelandhouse.com)
Tobermory; B&B
Creagan Cottage (01688 302251; www.islandholidaycottages.com)
Tobermory; B&B and self-catering cottage
Cuidhe-Leathain (01688 302504/07770 628582; www.cuidhe-leathain.co.uk)
Tobermory; B&B
Fairways Lodge (01688 302792; www.fairwaysmull.com)
Tobermory; B&B
Fascadail (01688 300444; www.fascadail.co.uk)
Salen; B&B
Glenaros Lodge (01680 300301/07786 091089; www.glenaroslodge.net)
Salen; B&B

Glengorm Castle (01688 302321;
www.glengormcastle.co.uk)
Glengorm, near Tobermory; B&B and self-
catering; market garden and coffee shop;
accommodation available all year
Glengrant (01688 302205; http://
www.tobermory.co.uk/glengrant/index.htm)
Tobermory; B&B – also available as self-
catering
Gorsten Farm (01680 812332;
www.gorstenfarm.co.uk)
Loch Don; B&B and self-catering
Gruline Home Farm (01680 300581;
www.gruline.com)
Gruline B&B and self-catering cottages
Inverlussa (01680 812436)
Near Craignure; B&B; open Apr-Oct
Island House (01681 700256)
Bunessan; B&B
Killiemor (01680 300302;
www.killiemormull.fsworld.co.uk)
Killiemor, between Salen and Ulva Ferry; B&B
Maolbhuidhe (01681 700718;
www.maolbhuidhe.co.uk)
Near Fionnphort; B&B
Newcrofts (01681 700471/07733 483142)
Bunessan; B&B; open all year
Rockcliffe (01672 851104; http://
www.tob302075.freeserve.co.uk/rockcliffe.htm)
Tobermory; B&B and evening meals
Seaview (01681 700235/07708 556311; www.seaview-
mull.co.uk)
Fionnphort B&B; closed 24-26 Dec
Shore House (01681 700631; www.isleofmull-
uk.co.uk)
Fionnphort; B&B
Staffa House (01681 700677)
Fionnphort; B&B; open Mar-Oct
Torr Buan House (01688 500121;
www.torrbuan.com)
Ulva Ferry; dinner B&B
Uisken Croft (01681 700307)
Uisken, near Bunessan; B&B; open Feb-Nov

SELF-CATERING PROPERTIES

Achaban House (01681 700205;
www.achabanhouse.ndo.co.uk)
Loch Pottie; Fionnphort; B&B and self-
catering
Ach-na-Brae Cottages (01681 700260;
www.isleofmullholidays.com)
Fionnphort; two self-catering cottages, each
sleep six
Achnadrish House (01688 400 388;
www.aboutscotland.com/mull/achnadrish.html)
Dervaig Road; B&B and two self-catering
properties in eight acres, sleep four and two;
open all year
Anchor Cottage (01887 829839/07950 255877;
www.tob302075.freeserve.co.uk/anchor.htm)
Tobermory; self-catering property, sleeps
two-four
Ardfenaig Farmhouses (01681 700260)
Tiraghoil, Bunessan; two farmhouses; open
all year

Ardnacross Farm (www.ardnacross.com)
Ardnacross, Aros; three self-catering houses,
sleep twelve, six and two
Ardtun House (01681 700264)
Bunessan; self-catering house; open all year
Argyll House (01680 300555; www.argyll-
house.co.uk)
Salen; self-catering cottage and studio, sleep
two-four; open all year
Argyll Self Catering (01972 510262;
www.argyllselfcatering.co.uk/
www.steading.co.uk)
Self-catering properties
Arle Lodge (01680 300299; www.arlelodge.co.uk)
Arle, Aros; self-catering accommodation, twenty-
four beds
A ros Mains (01688 500210; www.lambert-
holiday-mull.co.uk)
Aros Mains, Salen; self-catering cottage
Bacca Cottage (02072 678702;
www.mull.zynet.co.uk/bacca)
Gribun, Loch na Keal; self-catering cottage,
sleeps four
Braeside House (01623 477670;
www.tobermory.co.uk/braeside/)
Tobermory; self-catering house, sleeps ten
Braeside Cottage (01623 477670;
www.tobermory.co.uk/braeside/
braesidecottage.html)
Tobermory; self-catering cottage, sleeps six
Burg Beag (01821 640253;
www.tob302075.freeserve.co.uk/burg.htm)
Torloisk, Ulva Ferry; self-catering cottage,
sleeps four-six
Burnside (020 8947 3181)
Near Craignure; self-catering house, sleeps
eight+; open all year
Calgary Castle (01449 741066; www.calgary-
castle.com)
Calgary; self-catering baronial mansion dating
from the seventeenth century, sleeps twelve-
sixteen
Callachally Farmhouse (01680 300424;
www.holidaysonmull.co.uk)
Glen Forsa, Salen; B&B and two self-catering
cottages, sleep nine and six
Caol-Ithe Guest House (01681 700375; www.caol-
ithe.demon.co.uk)
Fionnphort; guest house and self-catering
cottages
Carthouse Lofts (01688 400256;
www.calgary.co.uk)
Calgary Hotel; self-catering loft, sleeps two-
four; open all year; hotel and restaurant nearby
Clachan Cottage and Lodge
(www.mullholidays.co.uk)
Dervaig; self-catering cottage, sleeps six; lodge,
sleeps four
Coach House (01681 700071; 07867 861925;
www.holidaymull.org/members/coachouse)
Argfenaig; self-catering property, sleeps four+
Caol-Ithe (01681 700375; www.caol-ithe.co.uk)
Fionnphort; guest house with two self-catering
cottages, sleep four-six; open all year

Corrachan Cottage (01697 3 22843; www.self-catering-mull.co.uk)
Dervaig; self-catering cottage, sleeps four; open all year

Creagan Cottage (01688 302251; www.islandholidaycottages.com)
Tobermory; B&B and self-catering cottage, sleeps four-six

Druimghigha Bothy Cottage (01688 400228)
Dervaig; self-catering house, sleeps six; open all year

Dungrianach (01681 700417)
Fionnphort; self-catering bungalow; open all year

Glenaros (01631 770369; www.glenaros.co.uk)
Glenaros; five self-catering cottages, sleep four-seven; open all year

Glen Cottage (http://self-catering.mull-scotland.co.uk)
Loch Na Cuilce, Dervaig; self-catering cottage, sleeps up to six

Glengorm Castle (01688 302321; www.glengormcastle.co.uk)
Glengorm; B&B and self-catering accommodation in Victorian Castle

Holiday Lodge (01964 543263/01688 400445/07740 796856; www.isle-mull-self-catering.co.uk)
Dervaig; self-catering timber lodge, sleeps up to six

Maple Cottage (0141 6477288; www.tob302075.freeserve.co.uk/maple.htm)
Kintra, near Fionnphort; self-catering cottage, sleeps six-eight

Mill Cottage (01681 700440; www.accommodationsmull.co.uk/millcott)
Bunessan; self-catering cottage

Mill House (01680 812442; www.oldmill.mull.com)
Lochdonhead; guest house and restaurant; self-catering, sleeps six-eight; open all year

Penmore House (01688 302508; www.visitmull.net)
Dervaig; self-catering house, sleeps ten

Penmore Mill (08000 858786; www.mull-self-catering.co.uk)
Dervaig; self-catering renovated mill, sleeps nine

Pennygown Farm (01680 300486; www.pennygownfarm.co.uk
Aros, self-catering farm house, sleeps four-seven

Puffer Aground (01680 300389/472; www.isleofmullcottageflats.co.uk)
Salen; two self-catering properties; open Feb-Dec

Raraig House (01688 302 390; www.silverswift.co.uk/house.htm)
Tobermory, self-catering accommodation, sleeps two

Rock Cottage (01680 300506; www.rockcottage.mull.com)
Salen; B&B; self-catering caravan, sleeps six

Rowan Cottage (0141 6387856)
Salen; self-catering cottage, sleeps five

The Rowans (001-301-924-0595; www.salmonlady.com/selfcatering.html)
Tobermory; self-catering house, sleeps six

Seilisdeir Cottage (01680 812465; www.seilisdeirlochdon.com)
Lochdon; self-catering or B&B; open all year

Steadings (01681 705217)
Tiroran; self-catering accommodation, sleeps six-seven

Tigh Beag (0118 981 2244; www.tighbeag-tobermory.co.uk)
Tobermory; self-catering house

Tigh Beag and Tigh Mor (01256 381275; www.mull-accommodation.co.uk)
Eorabus and Saorphin, Bunessan; two self-catering cottages, sleep ten and eight

Tobermory (01688 302301; www.tobermoryholidays.co.uk)
Tobermory; B&B and self-catering

Tobermory (01688 302075; http://www.tobermory.mull.com/accommodation.htm)
In and around Tobermory; two self-catering bungalows and a caravan

Treshnish Farm (0845 4581971; www.treshnish.co.uk)
Treshnish Point, near Calgary; eight self-catering properties

West Moirre Cottage (01680 300601; www.holidaymull.org/members/westmoirre.html)
Killiechronan, near Craignure; self-catering cottage, sleeps four

HOSTELS AND RETREATS

Arle Bunkhouse (01680 300343)
Aros; self-catering accommodation for up to twenty-six people

Dervaig Hall (01688 400338)
Dervaig; accommodation for up to ten; camping outside hall is also available

Tobermory Youth Hostel (0870 004 1151; www.syha.org.uk)
Tobermory; youth hostel, sleeps thirty-nine; open Mar-Oct

CAMPING AND CARAVANS

Balmeanach Park (01680 300342; www.holidaymull.org/members/balmeanach.html)
Fishnish, near Craignure; camping, accommodation, garden centre and tearoom

Shieling Holidays (01680 812496; www.shielingholidays.co.uk)
Craignure; campsite, shielings, launderette, showers and self-catering cottage; boats, canoes and other activities

Tobermory Campsite (01688 302525; www.tobermory-campsite.co.uk
Near Tobermory; campsite; open Apr-Oct

PLACES TO EAT

Anchorage Restaurant (01688 302313)
Tobermory; restaurant; open Apr-Oct
An Tobar (01688 302211; www.antobar.co.uk)
Tobermory; arts centre with live music events,
gallery exhibitions, ceilidh evenings, music and
dance classes; cafe and shop
Argyll Arms Hotel (01681 700 240;
www.isleofmull.co.uk)
Bunessan; hotel and restaurant (booking
advisable)
Argyll Restaurant (01681 700291)
Bunessan; cafe/restaurant
Assapol House (01681 700445)
Bunessan; dinner only
Balmeanach Park (01680 300342;
www.holidaymull.org/members/
balmeanach.html)
Fishnish, near Craignure; tearoom in campsite
and garden centre
Calgary Hotel (01688 400256; www.calgary.co.uk)
Calgary; hotel and restaurant
The Carthouse Gallery (01688 400256;
www.calgary.co.uk)
Dervaig; excellent sources of local art from
Mull: watercolours, etchings, pottery, wood and
ironwork; cafe
Coffee Pot (01680 300555)
Salen
Craignure Inn (01680 812305)
Craignure; open all year
Druimard Country House Hotel (01688 400345;
www.druimard.co.uk)
Dervaig; hotel and restaurant
Druimnacroish Hotel (01688 400274;
www.druimnacroish.co.uk)
Dervaig; hotel and restaurant
Duart Castle (01680 812309;
www.duartcastle.com)
Duart; there is a tearoom and shop by the
castle
Gannet's Restaurant (01688 302203)
Tobermory
Glenforsa Hotel (01680 300377;
www.glenforsa.com)
Salen, by Aros; hotel and restaurant
Glengorm Castle (01688 302321;
www.glengormcastle.co.uk)
Glengorm, near Tobermory; B&B and self-
catering; market garden and coffee shop
Highland Cottage Hotel
(www.highlandcottage.co.uk; 01688 302030)
Tobermory; hotel and restaurant; open Dec-
Oct
The Keel Row (01681 700458)
Fionnphort; pub and restaurant; open all year
Killiechronan House (01680 300403;
www.highlandholidays.net)
Killiechronan; hotel and restaurant (jacket and
tie preferred); open Mar-Oct
Lochinver Restaurant (01688 302253)
Tobermory; open late Mar-early Oct
MacGochan's (01688 302821)
Tobermory; cafe and bistro bar

MacGregor's Roadhouse (01680 812471)
Craignure; open all year
Mull Pottery (01688 302347;
www.mullpottery.com)
Tobermory; pottery with cafe and bistro
The Old Byre Heritage Centre (01688 400229;
www.old-byre.co.uk)
Dervaig; museum in a converted byre with two
videos and models; licensed tearoom and gift
shop; open Apr-Oct, Wed-Sun, 10.30-18.30
Old Mill Cottage (01680 812442;
www.oldmill.mull.com)
Lochdonhead; guest house and restaurant
Posh Nosh Cafe and Takeaway
Tobermory
Red Bay Cottage (01681 700396)
Fionnphort; restaurant
Sagar Balti House (01688 302422)
Tobermory
Torosay Castle (01680 812421; www.torosay.com)
Torosay; tearoom and shop
Western Isles Hotel (01688 302012;
www.mullhotel.com)
Tobermory; hotel and restaurant

Further Information

TRANSPORT

BUSES
There are regular trips between Craignure and
Tobermory, and Craignure and Fionnphort, and
also a service between Tobermory and Dervaig
and Calgary. Postbuses (www.royalmail.com/
postbus) make trips on less well-used routes. A
Mull Area Transport Guide, with ferry and bus
times, is available locally.
Bowman's Coaches (01680 812313)
R. N. Carmichael (01688 302220)
Highlands and Islands Coaches (01680 812510)

CAR HIRE
Mackay's Garage (01688 302103;
www.mackaysgarage.fsnet.co.uk)
Ledaig, Tobermory; car hire
Bayview Garage (01680 812444;
www.bayviewgarage.com)
Craignure; car hire; garage services

CYCLE HIRE
On Yer Bike (01680 300501/812487)
Craignure and Salen; cycle hire
Tom a' Mhuillin (01688 302164)
Tobermory; cycle hire
Brown's Hardware Shop (01688 302020)
Tobermory; cycle hire
Blazing Saddles Cycle Hire (01681 700235;
www.iona-bed-breakfast-mull.com/
cycling_mull_iona/cycle_hire.htm)
Fionnphort; mountain, ladies' and children's
cycles available

TAXIS
Richard Atkinson (01680 300441)
Aros, near Salen
Jimmy Polson (01688 302204)
Tobermory; taxi
David Greenhalgh (01681 700507)
Bunessan

ACTIVITIES AND SPORTS

BOAT TRIPS

Alternative Boat Hire (01681 700537;
www.boattripsiona.com)
Boat trips around Iona
Craignure Charters (01680 812332)
Trips to uninhabited islands and fishing; open
May-Oct
M. V. *Amidas* (01688 302048; www.mv-
amidas.co.uk)
Tobermory; sea Fishing and wildlife/scenic boat
trips
Edge of the World (01688 302821; www.edge-
ofthe-world.co.uk)
Tobermory; powerboat excursions and wildlife
trips
Hebridean Adventure (01688 302044;
www.hebrideanadventure.co.uk)
Tobermory; cruises and charters
Inter Island Cruises (01688 302916;
www.jenny.mull.com)
Croig Harbour, Dervaig; whale watching,
wildlife and island sightseeing cruises
Sea Life Surveys (01688 302916;
www.sealifesurveys.com)
Tobermory; boat trips to see whales and
dolphins and boat charter
Silverswift (01688 302 390; www.silverswift.co.uk)
Tobermory; diving and fishing charters; boat
trips
Turus Mara Seabird and Wildlife Cruise Tours
(08000 858786; www.turusmara.com)
Ulva Ferry; boat trips to the Treshnish Isles,
Staffa

SAILING AND YACHTING

Tobermory has an excellent harbour and moorings
are available (www.tobermory.mull.com/
moorings.htm)
Western Isles Yacht Club (01688 302371;
www.tobermory.mull.com/sailing.htm)
Tobermory; yachting club with races and
regattas
Seafare (01688 302277; mysite.wanadoo-
members.co.uk/divemull)
Tobermory; chandlery shop with diving gear
and air

DIVING

There are many wrecks scattered around the
coast.
Seafare (01688 302277; mysite.wanadoo-
members.co.uk/divemull)
Tobermory; chandlery shop with diving gear
and air
Arle Lodge (01680 300299; www.arlelodge.co.uk)
Arle, Aros; self-catering accommodation,
twenty-four beds (see website)
Silverswift (01688 302 390; www.silverswift.co.uk)
Tobermory; diving and fishing charters; boat
trips
Seamore Diving (01681 700462; 07776 080676;
mysite.wanadoo-members.co.uk/divemull)
Scuba-diving courses, guided dives and
information on diving and marine life

TOURS

Discover Mull (01688 400415;
www.discovermull.co.uk)
Dervaig; landrover tours on Mull
Isle of Mull Landrover Wildlife Expeditions
(01688 500121; www.scotlandwildlife.com)
Ulva Ferry; landrover wildlife expeditions;
lunch provided

WALKING

There are many excellent walks on the island,
from the brooding mass of Glen More to
coastal routes and forest paths: guides are
available locally. Glen More is a relatively easy
Munro to scale, although from sea level, and
there are access points at Dhiseig on Loch na
Keal or at the eastern end of Loch Scridain.
Care should still be taken, along with a
compass and map; and appropriate clothing
and footwear worn. The hill can often be misty.
Mull and Iona Ranger Service (01680 300640)
Salen

FISHING AND ANGLING

Mull has excellent fishing: enquire locally
Tobermory Angling Association (01688 302020;
www.tob302075.freeserve.co.uk/
fishing.htm)
Tobermory; permits for Mishnish Lochs, Aros
Loch and Loch Frisa, boat hire
Tackle and Books (01688 302336)
Tobermory; permits available
M. V. *Amidas* (01688 302048; www.mv-
amidas.co.uk)
Tobermory; sea Fishing and wildlife/scenic boat
trips

GOLF

Craignure Golf Club (01680 300402;
www.tobermory.co.uk/Golf/craignure.htm/)
Scallastle, Craignure; nine-hole course with
eighteen tees; clubhouse open dawn to dusk
Tobermory Golf Club (01688 302338;
www.tobermory.co.uk/Golf/tobermory.htm
North of Tobermory; nine-hole course: green
fees may be paid at Brown's Shop, Tobermory,
the Western Isles Hotel, and Fairways Lodge

BIRDING

www.mullbirds.com
Wings Over Mull (01680 812594;
www.wingsovermull.com)
Achnacroish House, Torosay; birds of prey and
conservation centre with hawks, falcons,
eagles, kites, falcons and owls; open Easter-
October, daily 10.30-17.30 or by appt; flying
displays, daily 12.00, 14.00 and 16.00

MOTOR SPORT

The Tour of Mull takes place at the beginning of
October.

LOCAL PRODUCE

Croggan Oyster Farm (01680 814224)
Croggan; retail and wholesale oysters
Isle of Mull Cheese (01688 302235;
www.btinternet.com/-mull.cheese/index.html)

Sgriob-Ruadh Farm Dairy, near Tobermory; traditional farmhouse cheese; the farm can be visited, and there is a cafe; cheese can also be purchased using on-line ordering

Tobermory Chocolate (01688 302526; www.tobchoc.co.uk)
Tobermory; renowned locally produced chocolate; shop with chocolate and gift for sale and cafe; chocolate can be purchased on-line

Tobermory Distillery (01688 302645; www.burnstewartdistillers.com)
Tobermory; distillery tours and well-stocked shop; open Easter-Oct, Mon-Fri 10.00-17.00; other times by appt

Tobermory Fish Company (01688 302120; www.tobermoryfish.co.uk)
Baliscate, Tobermory; fish, trout, haddock, smoked and whisky-cured salmon, chocolate, cheese; hampers and baskets; retail and mail order (on-line)

ARTS AND CRAFTS

Airgiod Gu Leor (01680 300494)
Willow Cottage, Salen; nine carat gold and silver Celtic crosses

Angus Stewart Paintings and Prints (01688 302024; www.mullart.com)
Tobermory; watercolour landscapes, more than thirty-five as prints; open Tue and Thu 10.00-22.00; also available at the

Carthouse Gallery at Calgary, Bellachroy Hotel and Iona Pottery

An Tobar (01688 302211; www.antobar.co.uk)
Tobermory; arts centre with live music events, gallery exhibitions, ceilidh evenings, music and dance classes; cafe and shop with local arts and crafts

Barbara Bisset (01681 700430)
Knockan; pastel landscapes of Mull and Iona

The Carthouse Gallery (01688 400256; www.calgary.co.uk)
Calgary, near Dervaig; excellent source of local art from Mull: watercolours, etchings, pottery, wood and ironwork; cafe; open Apr-Oct

Eleanor MacDougall (01681 700780)
Aridhglas, Fionnphort; traditional silversmithing techniques, the designs incorporate Celtic patterns and shapes and forms inspired by nature.

Isle of Mull Silver and Goldsmiths (01688 302345; www.mullsilver.co.uk)
Tobermory; quaichs, christening spoons, and jewellery; open all year

Isle of Mull Weavers (01680 812381)
Torosay Steadings; weavers of high-quality Tweeds

Lee's Studio (01688 302602)
Unit 3 Baliscate, Tobermory; paintings, prints, cards; batik workshops Fri 10.00-12.00

Mull Pottery (01688 302347; www.mullpottery.com)
Tobermory; hand-thrown ceramics inspired by Mull coastal waters; cafe and bistro; open all year

Mull Theatre (01688 302828; www.mulltheatre.com)
Dervaig (theatre) and Tobermory (box office); shows and theatre

Norman Salkeld (01681 704229)
Tigh na h'Abhainn, Pennyghael; small pottery workshop making gas-fired ash-glazed functional stoneware and other individual pieces; also available from Pennyghael Stores

The Picture Gallery (01688 302426)
Tobermory; original paintings and limited edition prints by Ronnie Leckie.

Starfish Ceramics
Unit 3 Baliscate, Tobermory; wide range of tableware, one-off pieces and hand-made tiles; paint-a-pot workshops held three times weekly

Tackle and Books (01688 302336; booksandtackle.seekbooks.co.uk)
Tobermory; books and fishing tackle

Whigmaleerie Wood and Horn Craft (01688 302173)
Tobermory; walking sticks and crooks in wood and horn; turned and carved wooden items.

VISITOR ATTRACTIONS AND MUSEUMS

Duart Castle (01577 812309; www.duartcastle.com; also see www.maclean.org)
Duart; magnificent old castle, ancient seat of the MacLeans, shop and tearoom; open Apr-Oct, Sun-Thu 11.00-16.00

Hebridean Whale and Dolphin Trust (01688 302620; www.whaledolphintrust.co.uk
Tobermory; visitor centre with an exhibition and gift shop; open summer, Mon-Fri 10.00-17.00, Sat-Sun 11.00-17.00

Isle of Mull Railway (01680 812494; www.mullrail.co.uk)
Craignure; narrow-gauge railway: runs from Craignure to Torosay

Mull Museum (01688 302208)
Tobermory; a good little museum packed into a small space; open Easter-mid Oct, daily 10.00-17.00, Sat 10.00-13.00

The Old Byre Heritage Centre (01688 400229; www.old-byre.co.uk)
Dervaig; museum in a converted byre with two videos and Mull in miniature; licensed tearoom and gift shop; open Apr-Oct, Wed-Sun, 10.30-18.30

Ross of Mull Historical Centre (01681 700659; www.romhc.org.uk)
Bunessan; information on local history and people; open Apr-Oct, Mon-Fri 10.30-16.30; Nov-Mar by appt

St Columba Centre (01681 700640)
Fionnphort; modern interpretation centre focusing on the life and work of St Columba; open Apr-Sep, daily 11.00-17.00

Tobermory Distillery (01688 302645; www.burnstewartdistillers.com)
Tobermory; distillery tours and well-stocked shop; open Easter-Oct, Mon-Fri 10.00-17.00; other times by appt

Torosay Castle and Estate (01680 812421;
www.torosay.com)
   Craignure; Victorian castle and gardens,
   tearoom, shop; house open mid Apr-Oct, daily
   10.30-17.00; gardens and cafe open all year
Wings Over Mull (01680 812594;
www.wingsovermull.com)
   Achnacroish House, Torosay; birds of prey and
   conservation centre with hawks, falcons,
   eagles, kites, falcons and owls; open Easter-
   October, daily 10.30-17.30 or by appt; flying
   displays, daily 12.00, 14.00 and 16.00

ADDITIONAL INFORMATION

Petrol is available at Craignure, Tobermory, Salen,
   and between Bunessan and Fionnphort
There are public toilets at Tobermory, Dervaig,
   Salen, Craignure, Bunessan, Fionnphort; in the
   summer only and Calgary and Ulva Ferry
There is a branch of the Clydesdale bank in
   Tobermory with a cashline machine; mobile
   banks tour the rest of the island
There are post offices at Tobermory, Craignure,
   Fionnphort, Salen, Bunessan, Dervaig, Loch
   Don, Lochbuie and Kinloch

Publications about Mull are available from Brown
   and Whittaker (01688 302381/302336;
   www.brown-whittaker.co.uk

EVENTS

Mull Music Festival	April
Mull and Iona Wildlife Week	May
Mull and Iona Provincial Mod	June
MacLean clan gathering	June
Tobermory Yacht Race	June
Mendelssohn on Mull Festival	June/July
Tobermory Highland Games	July
Bunessan Show and Salen Show	August
Mull Half Marathon	August
The Sound of Mull	September
Taste of Mull and Iona Food Festival	September
Tour of Mull Rally (www.2300club.org)	October

FURTHER READING

The Heart of Mull (Crumley, Jim)
   Colin Baxter Photography, 1996
Island Voices: Traditions of North Mull
   (Mackenzie, Anne (ed.))
   Birlinn, 2002
Island of Mull (MacCormack, John)
   1923
The Isle of Mull: Placenames, Meanings and Stories
   (Maclean, Charles)
   1997
Mull (Macpherson, John)
   Birlinn, 2006
Mull Monuments and History (Whittaker, Jean)
   Brown and Whittaker, 1999
Mull and Iona (MacNab, Peter Angus)
   Pevensey Press, 1995
Mull and Iona: Highways & Byways
   (MacNab, Peter Angus)
   Luath, 2005
Mull: a Traveller's Guide (Weiner, Christine)
   S. Forsyth, 1991
Mull: the Island and its People (Currie, Jo)
   Birlinn, 2001
The Story of Mull and Iona (Hesketh, Nick)
   Mercat Press, 1988
Tall Tales from an Island: Mull (Macnab, Peter)
   Luath Press, 1994
The Terror of Tobermory (Baker, Richard)
   Birlinn, 2005
Traditional Tales of Mull (Macnab, Peter)
   Brown and Whittaker, 1998
A Treasure Lost (Brown, Olive and Jean Whittaker)
   Brown and Whittaker, 2000
Walking on North Mull (eighth edition) (Brown,
   Olive and Jean Whittaker)
   Brown and Whittaker, 2002
Walking on South Mull and Iona (Brown, Olive and
   Jean Whittaker)
   Brown and Whittaker, 2005

ACKNOWLEDGMENTS

Thanks to Anne Cleave for reading over the first
   part of the text

IONA

(from 'Icolmkill': the island of St Columba)

www.isle-of-iona.com
www.iona.org.uk
www.visitscottishheartlands.com (AILLST)

Tourist Information Centres
Tobermory (08707 200625)
  Open Apr-Oct
Craignure (08707 200610)
  Open Jan-Dec

Map Landranger sheet: 48 (HIH map page 73)

TRAVEL

A passenger ferry (CalMac 01688 700559 (Fionnphort); www.calmac.co.uk) makes the crossing between Fionnphort (A849 from Craignure) on Mull and Iona. Frequent trips are made daily from morning until around 18.00, and the crossing takes ten minutes. There are fewer crossings on a Sunday, and these are hourly from early morning to about 18.00. Visitors' cars are not permitted on the island but there is plenty of parking at Fionnphort (where the Columba Centre (01681 700640; open Apr-Sep, daily 11.00-17.00) features an exhibition about the early church, Iona and St Columba, as well as information on the local area.

There is an 'out of hours' ferry service (after the CalMac ferry has finished for the day) during the summer months on the MV *Volante* (01681 700362; www.volanteiona.com).

Day tours to Iona are available in the summer from Oban.

Boat trips can be taken from Iona to Staffa and the Treshnish Isles (see the entries for those islands).

DESCRIPTION

Iona is a beautiful and peaceful little island, located off the west coast of the Ross of Mull, across the narrow Sound of Iona. The island is three and a half miles long by about half as wide, covering some 2,000 acres, and is green and fertile

Beach, Iona

in places, and rough and rocky in others. The highest point is 100 metres at Dun I, at the north end, and there are excellent views from the top. There are several fine sandy beaches, including at Traigh Mor, about one mile south of the pier. The light and scenery here are exceptional, and favoured by many artists, including the Scottish Colourists.

Baile Mor is the only village, and has most of the island's facilities, with hotels, eateries, a post office, well-stocked shops, crafts, and public toilets (details can be found in the More Information section). Iona formerly had a population of more than 500, but it is now around 120.

WILDLIFE

Birds which visit or breed on Iona include corncrakes, cormorants, shags, eider ducks, buzzards, oystercatchers, geese, ring plovers, lapwings, gulls, yellowhammers, terns, grey plovers, sanderlings and godwits. Otters and seals can be seen around the coasts, and further out dolphins, whales and basking sharks visit the waters.

HISTORY

Iona was to become one of the foremost centres of Christianity in early Christian times, not only in what would become Scotland, but in the whole of Great Britain. It is possible that the island was already important to the druids (one of the island's hills is called Cnoc Druidean) or an earlier religion, but it was the arrival of St Columba in 563 which began its prominence in recorded history. Columba, from Ireland, was a missionary and holy man, and is credited with converting the northern Picts. He, and then his followers, spread and consolidated Christianity in the north of Britain. One of his monks was Aidan, who founded Lindisfarne off the coast of Northumberland, and was instrumental in bringing the faith to the north of England.

Iona became a centre of learning, stone carving and manuscript illustration: it is believed that the fantastic *Book of Kells* (on display in Trinity College, Dublin), often

Iona Abbey

thought to have been produced in Ireland, was actually created at Iona. Columba died in 597, and little or nothing survives from this period, except perhaps the ditch or vallum (most impressive to the north-west) which had surrounded his community. More information can be found at the Columba Centre at Fionnphort on Mull. Exceptional carving can be seen in the crosses outside the church and in the Abbey Museum.

Iona became prey to Viking raids between the eighth and tenth centuries, and was repeatedly plundered. There are also stories that the abbot and monks were slaughtered, hence the name of Martyrs Bay – one tale is that all the brothers were slain here by Norsemen. The continued raiding caused the abbey to be abandoned, and it was not until the twelfth century that the establishment was refounded, possibly on the orders of St Margaret, wife of Malcolm Canmore; it later became a Benedictine abbey under the patronage of Reginald, the son of the famous Somerled. A nunnery was also founded nearby in the twelfth century.

Iona was not only a religious centre: it became important as the burial place of many kings, as well as the Lords of the Isles (and in recent times John Smith, leader of the opposition when he died in 1990). In Reilig Odhrain, by the Street of the Dead, forty-eight Scottish (including both Macbeth and Duncan), eight Norwegian and four Irish kings were reputedly buried.

The abbey was dissolved at the Reformation, but was reused as the Protestant Cathedral of the Isles for a while. It then became ruinous, and it was not until 1899 the work began to restore the church, and the cloister and surrounding ranges were rebuilt between 1938 and 1967 for the Iona Community. Guests are welcome at the abbey (see below).

Iona, itself, was a property of the MacDonald Lords of the Isles, but passed to the MacLeans in the fifteenth century, then to the Campbells of Argyll, along with much of Mull. Most of the island was given to the National Trust for Scotland in 1979, and the abbey buildings were recently put into the care of Historic Scotland. More than 200,000 people visit the island annually.

Tours
ROUTE TO ABBEY AND NORTH OF THE ISLAND
The ferry lands at the pier between Martyrs Bay and St Ronan's Bay, near Baile Mor, the island's village with most of the facilities. There is a short walk to the abbey.

The route to the abbey leads first to the pleasant nunnery and the adjacent museum, which is housed in the former parish church, built in the thirteenth century and dedicated to St Ronan. The nunnery is a picturesque collection of ruins built from pink granite, within a flower garden, and is the best preserved in Scotland. It was an Augustinian establishment dating from 1208, and there is a very weathered Sheila nan Gig (a very suggestive female fertility symbol) adorning one wall. The fine carved tombstone of one of the prioresses, Anna MacLean, is now in the Abbey Museum. In the old manse, designed by Thomas Telford, is the Iona Heritage Museum (01681 700328; open Mon-Sat 10.30-16.30), which has displays and exhibits on the island and its people down the ages, including crofting, fishing, island life, geology, flora and fauna.

Further along the road is MacLean's Cross, a fine carved cross dating from the fifteenth century and some three metres tall, which was commissioned by one of the MacLean clan. The route then leads by Reilig Odhrain, reputedly the burial place of kings, and the restored eleventh-century St Oran's Chapel, possibly built on the orders of St Margaret and burial place of the Lords of the Isles. The best of the ancient graveslabs are in the Abbey Museum. St Oran was cousin to St Columba, but was traditionally buried alive in the cemetery which now bears his name to consecrate the ground. His grave was opened some time after his internment, and he was found to still be alive but raving in madness: so he was sealed up again. This is a strange story to be associated with a Christian site. The Street of the Dead is a paved roadway along which the monarchs and personages were taken for burial.

Outside the front of the abbey church are three outstanding examples of early Christian sculpture. St Martin's Cross, St John's Cross (a replica: the original is in the Abbey Museum) and the stump of St Matthew's Cross are fabulous pieces, and date from between the eighth and the

St John's Cross, Iona Abbey

tenth centuries. Just to the left of the main door into the church is St Columba's Shrine, which incorporates the oldest part of the building, some of which may date from the ninth century. This is believed to be where St Columba was buried. The church was used as the Cathedral of the Isles by Protestant bishops after the Reformation in the middle of the sixteenth century.

Iona Abbey (01681 700512; open all year: Apr-Sep, daily 9.30-18.30; Oct-Mar, daily 9.30-16.30) is a beautiful collection of buildings in a fabulous setting. The cruciform church has a central tower, and manages to retain a feeling of serenity and peace despite the many visitors. In the Abbey Museum, housed in the former infirmary, is one of the largest and best collections of early Christian carved stones and burial slabs anywhere in the country. There is a gift shop in the restored cloister with locally produced arts and crafts, and a coffee shop on the way to the abbey. The Iona Community (01681 700404; www.iona.org.uk) was founded in 1938 by the Reverend George MacLeod. It is an ecumenical Christian community of men and women from different traditions in the Christian church that is committed to seeking new ways of living the gospel of Jesus Christ.

The Iona Community have three residential centres on Iona and Mull: the abbey itself, the MacLeod Centre on Iona, and the Camas Centre on Mull.

Southeast of the abbey church are the ruinous remains of St Mary's Chapel, while to the north is Tigh an Easbuig ('bishop's house'), and further northeast is Cladh an Diseart [NM 288248], the 'cemetery of the hermitage'.

Following the road beyond the abbey, passing a cross (memorial to the wife of the eighth duke of Argyll), there is a rough track near Auchabhaich farm to the summit of Dun I, from where there are wonderful views. Excellent beaches can be found on both the north-east and north-west coasts.

SOUTH AND WEST OF THE ISLAND

The fine sandy beach of Traigh Mor is along the road south of Baile Mor, past Sligneach. At the Spouting Cave, on the west coast and south of the golf course, spray can be sent far up the cliff, when the conditions are right: a westerly wind. At Port na Curaich, on the south coast, is the bay where St Columba is said to have first landed on Iona. The shingle mounds are believed to have been made as a devotional act by pilgrims. Further along the east shore at Rubha na Carraig-geire are the ruins and remains of a marble quarry [NM 273223], including the gunpowder store, machinery, quay and reservoir. The communion table in the abbey church is constructed from this marble.

There are the slight remains of Dun Cul Bhuirg [NM 265245], an Iron Age fort with a defensive wall, on a rocky outcrop north-west of the golf course.

HOTELS AND GUEST HOUSES

Iona Community (01681 700404; www.iona.org.uk) was founded in 1938 by the Rev George MacLeod. It is an ecumenical Christian community of men and women from different traditions in the Christian church that is committed to seeking new ways of living the gospel of Jesus Christ

The Iona Community have three residential centres on Iona and Mull: at the abbey itself, sleeping up to forty-five; and the MacLeod Centre on Iona, with fifty more; and at the Camas Centre on Mull. The Camas Centre has basic accommodation for up to sixteen.

Argyll Hotel (01681 700334; www.argyllhoteliona.co.uk)
Hotel and restaurant; near the pier; open Feb-Nov
St Columba Hotel (01681 700304; www.stcolumba-hotel.co.uk)
Hotel; on the road to the abbey; open Apr-Oct

BED AND BREAKFAST

Clachan Corrach (01681 700323)
Centre of island; B&B in Croft House on working croft
Duncraig (01681 700202; www.duncraigiona.org)
B&B; three-day minimum stay policy
Beannachd (01681 700525)
Ten minutes from ferry; B&B; open Mar-Oct; Christian home
Cruachan (01681 700523)
Half a mile from ferry; B&B
Dalantober (01681 700776)
Five minutes from ferry; B&B; open all year
Finlay Ross Ltd (01681 700357; www.finlayrossiona.co.uk)
Martyrs' Bay, close to ferry; B&B; open all year
Iona Cottage (ck@ionacottage.freeserve.co.uk)
Close to ferry; B&B
Shore Cottage (01681 700744; www.shorecottage.co.uk)
Close to ferry; B&B; open all year; dinner available in winter

SELF-CATERING PROPERTIES

Bishops Walk (01681 700329)
Two self-catering flats
Greenbank (01681 700330)
Self-catering house; B&B available on request; suitable for retreats for individuals and small groups; healing massage available
Iona Holiday Cottages (01681 700338)
Self-catering houses, sleep five-six; one week minimum let in July and August; otherwise three-night minimum
Iona Hostel (01681 700781; www.ionahostel.co.uk)
Hostel sleeping twenty-one people in rooms of two-six with self-catering kitchen/living room
Lagandorain (01681 700642; www.lagandorain.com)
North side of island; self-catering cottage, sleeps four
Tighshee (01681 700309 Mar-Oct/0131 343 2070 Nov-Feb)
Self-catering house, sleeps six
Traighmhor (01681 700596)
Self-catering, sleeps six
Traighmhor Bungalow (01681 700596)
Self-catering, sleeps four

HOSTELS AND RETREATS

RETREATS

Cnoc a' Chalmain (01681 700369; www.catholic-iona.com)
Roman Catholic House of Prayer; three single rooms available for pilgrims of all faiths, on private retreat
Iona Community Accommodation (01681 700404; www.iona.org.uk)
Accommodation at the MacLeod Centre and Abbey: the community caters for guests (one week minimum) to share life in the community: discussion, relaxation, crafts, work and worship. Simple accommodation is located in the cloister of the abbey and in the modern MacLeod Centre; food is available, mostly vegetarian
Bishops House (01681 700800; www.scotland.anglican.org/retreats)
Retreat for parish groups and individuals; up to twenty-three people in thirteen rooms;

St Columba's Chapel, the Episcopal Church on Iona, is open to all for private prayer and daily services

CAMPING AND CARAVANS

It is possible to camp on Iona, but permission should first be sought from the landowner or crofter or telephone 01681 700341). There are services for campers, including a laundry and washing facility (Finlay Ross, 01681 700357)

PLACES TO EAT

Argyll Hotel (01681 700334; www.argyllhoteliona.co.uk)
Booking advised; open Apr-Oct
Heritage Tearoom, Iona Heritage Centre
Open Mon-Fri, 11.00-16.00
Martyrs Bay Restaurant and Bar (01681 700382)
Open Feb-Nov, daily
St Columba Hotel (01681 700304; www.stcolumba-hotel.co.uk)
Restaurant; open Feb-Nov
Spar Shop (Gordon Grant Ltd) (01681 700321)
Snacks available

Further Information

TRANSPORT

CYCLE HIRE
Finlay Ross (01681 700357; www.finlayrossiona.co.uk)
TAXI
Iona Taxi (01681 700776/07810 325990)
Four passengers; tours of Iona available

ACTIVITIES AND SPORTS

BOAT HIRE AND FISHING TRIPS
Inshore trips (01681 700537; www.boattripsiona.com)
Maximum eleven passengers
M. V. *Volante* (01681 700362; www.volanteiona.com)
Booking for angling necessary; advised for sightseeing and wildlife trips
Boat trips to Staffa and the Treshnish isles are available (see respective islands for details)
GOLF
There is an 'informal' course on the island
LOCAL TOURIST GUIDE
Jean Black (01681 700605; www.aitga.co.uk)
ACTIVITIES
Iona Arts (01681 700567)
Music, theatre, children's shows, poetry and dance from May-Oct in the village hall and local library

ARTS AND CRAFTS

Finlay Ross (01681 700357; www.finlayrossiona.co.uk)
Celtic jewellery, gifts, books, maps, knitware

iloveiona (01681 700643; www.iloveiona.com)
Range of greetings cards
Iona Community Shop (01681 700404)
Jewellery, gifts, souvenirs, Wild Goose publications
Iona Gallery and Pottery (01681 700439; www.ionagallery.com)
Gallery and pottery workshop in converted croft house; open approx Mon-Sat 11.00-16.00
Iona Scottish Crafts (01681 700001)
Celtic silver jewellery, knitwear, pottery, scarves, books and cards etc.
Iona Tapestries (01681 700335; www.isle-of-iona.com/celtic_tapestries)
Designs taken from the *Book of Kells* and carved stones
Mhiann Arts (01681 700652; www.aosdanaiona.com)
Celtic-style jewellery, woven artwork and handmade cards; open from Easter-Oct, Mon-Fri 10.00-17.00, Sat-Sun 12.00-16.00
Oran Creative Crafts (01681 700700; www.orancrafts.co.uk)
Greetings cards, framed photographs, jewellery, knitwear, candles, soaps etc
Spar Shop (Gordon Grant Ltd) (01681 700321)
Open all year

VISITOR ATTRACTIONS AND MUSEUMS

Iona Abbey (01681 700512; www.historic-scotland.gov.uk)
Open all year (depending on ferries): Apr-Sep, daily 9.30-18.30; Oct-Mar, daily 9.30-16.30; tearoom and gift shop
Iona Heritage Centre (01681 700328)
Displays illustrating the islanders' lives over the past 200 years, plus exhibits on geology, flora, art and Celtic art etc: open Mon-Sat 10.30-16.30

FURTHER READING

Columba's Island: Iona from Past to Present (MacArthur, E. Mairi)
Edinburgh University Press, 1995
Iona (MacArthur, E. Mairi)
Colin Baxter Photography, 1997
Iona (McNeill, Marion F.)
Blackie, 1959
Iona: The Living Memory of a Crofting Community (MacArthur, E. Mairi)
Polygon, 2002
Mull and Iona (MacNab, Peter Angus)
Pevensey Press, 1995
The Story of Mull and Iona (Hesketh, Nick)
Mercat Press, 1988

ACKNOWLEDGMENTS

Thanks to Kirstine Shanks of the Argyll Hotel for reading over the entry

ERRAID

www.erraid.com
www.visitscottishheartlands.com (AILLST)

Tourist Information Centres
Tobermory (08707 200625)
    Open Apr-Oct
Craignure (08707 200610)
    Open Jan-Dec

Map Landranger sheet: 48 (HIH map page 73)

TRAVEL
The island is accessible at low tide off a minor road from the A849 at Fionnphort on Mull. Care should be taken if visiting as it is possible to become stranded.

DESCRIPTION, WILDLIFE AND HISTORY
Erraid lies off the western tip of the Ross of Mull, and is about one mile long and wide. A long strip of sandy shore, which floods at high tide, separates it from the main island of Mull.

Erraid, the inspiration for five of Robert Louis Stevenson's books, was where David Balfour, the hero of *Kidnapped*, was shipwrecked. Balfour then crossed Mull back to the mainland. Stevenson had spent some of his boyhood here while his father (his family were famous civil engineers and architects) was involved in building a lighthouse: Erraid was the shore station.

The island is now managed by the Findhorn Foundation.

PLACES TO STAY
Guests are always welcome to stay with the community, minimum duration one week. Please contact 01681 700384 or bookings@erraid.fslife.co.uk or see www.erraid.com for details

ACKNOWLEDGMENTS
Thanks to Paul for reading over the text

ULVA

('wolf island' or 'Olaf's island' from Norse)

www.ulva.mull.com
www.visitscottishheartlands.com (AILLST)

Tourist Information Centres
Tobermory (08707 200625)
   Open Apr-Oct
Craignure (08707 200610)
   Open Jan-Dec

Map Landranger sheets: 47, 48 (HIH map page 73)

TRAVEL

The passenger ferry (01688 500226) leaves from Ulva Ferry on Mull, which is on the B8073, between Gruline and Calgary. There are crossings on demand Mon-Fri, 9.00-17.00 all year and Sun from June to August. There is no service on a Saturday. The trip takes a few minutes. There is parking at the ferry, but no direct bus service, although the Postbus (01680 300321; www.royalmail.com/postbus) or taxis can be used. The tracks on Ulva are rough and not really suitable for anything other than walking or mountain bikes.

DESCRIPTION

Ulva lies off the west coast of Mull, across the narrow Sound of Ulva, eleven miles west of Salen and ten miles south and west of Tobermory. The island is some five miles long and up to three wide, covering 4,500 acres, and is joined by a bridge to the neighbouring island of Gometra.

Like Staffa, the island has hexagonal basaltic columns. Ulva is very hilly, particularly to the west, and Beinn Chreagach rises to 313 metres in height. The east side has better land and areas are wooded. A sandy beach, Traigh Bhan, lies to the south of Ulva. Parts of the island can become overgrown with bracken, making it difficult to find routes or sites.

On the island and near where the ferry lands is the reconstructed Sheila's Cottage and the Boathouse (01688 500241), a tearoom and restaurant which also has an interpretative display about Ulva. There are waymarked walks.

WILDLIFE

Many birds can be seen here during the year (some 123 species have been recorded), including puffins, terns, corncrakes, herons, oystercatchers, eider ducks, buzzards and even golden eagles and sea eagles. Seals and otters sometimes frequent the coasts, and there are hares and red deer. There are also many interesting plants, such as rare orchids.

HISTORY

Excavations in Livingston's Cave [NM 431384] found items from the Mesolithic and early Neolithic period, including midden material, flint, pottery and bone implements. There are two prehistoric standing stones [NM 403390], one more than one and a half metres high, near Craigaig. The island was held by the Vikings, hence the name, then by the MacQuarrie clan from 1473, or perhaps from as early as the ninth century, until 1777, when the island was sold. General Lachlan Macquarie emigrated to the New World and is credited with being the founder of modern Australia (also see the Macquarie Mausoleum, which is near Gruline on Mull).

The clan's war cry was 'the Red Tartan Army', and they fought at Bannockburn in 1314, Inverkeithing in 1651 and Culloden in 1746, where many of them were killed, a stone at the battlefield marking their burial place. The chiefs of the MacQuarries had a house near the present Ulva House, and there was also a castle or fort, Dun Ban or Glackindaline Castle [NM 384417], on a rocky islet between Ulva and Gometra, which is connected by a causeway. Ulva was also home to the MacArthur's piping college: the MacArthurs were pipers to the MacDonalds at Duntulm on Trotternish in Skye. The remains of a chapel and burial ground can be seen at Cille Mhic Eoghainn [NM 395389]. The site was dedicated to St Ernan, a nephew of Columba, and there are some old burial markers.

The island had a thriving kelp industry, but was brutally cleared of many of its people in the nineteenth century when many inhabitants were burnt out of their crofts and were not even allowed to take their beasts or possessions. The population was 604 in 1837, 204 in 1851, 46 in 1891; and the island is now home to sixteen inhabitants. Cattle, sheep, oyster and fish farming, as well as tourism, are the mainstays. The only settlement on Ulva is at the east of the island, but there are many abandoned townships. The island passed through several hands, and is now owned by the Howard family. Famous visitors include Dr Johnson and Boswell in 1773, Sir Walter Scott and Beatrix Potter.

The heritage centre features Sheila's Cottage (01688 500241), a faithful reconstruction of a traditional thatched croft house, which was last lived in the early twentieth century by Sheila MacFadyen. There are displays on the island from the Mesolithic period to the present day.

Gometra

The nearby island of Gometra ('Godman's isle'), reached via a bridge from Ulva, is two miles long by one wide. Gometra also has basaltic columns, and a series of terraces, and rises to 155 metres. On a rocky hillock is Dun Eiphinn [NM 358402], an Iron Age fort, defended by the steepness of the cliffs and the remains of a wall.

The island was once productive and is said to have provided Iona with corn. It was held by the abbey before passing to the MacDonalds of Staffa and then the Campbells. It was put up for sale at the same time as Ulva and the two islands have since been under the same ownership.

Little Colonsay ('little St Columba's isle') lies to the south of Ulva, and rises to 61 metres at Torr Mor. The island was cleared in the 1840s and now has no permanent residents.

Places to Stay

For accommodation queries contact 01688 500224/241/226 or www.ulva.mull.com
Camping on the island can be arranged (01688 500264)

Places to Eat

The Boathouse (01688 500241)
Tea room and restaurant: open 9.00-16.30; menu includes salmon, oysters and other shellfish

Further Information

There are way-marked trails around the island
Turus Mara (01688 400242/08000 858786; www.turusmara.com) offers boat trips from Ulva ferry to Staffa and the Treshnish Isles (see these islands for more details)
There is a public toilet (Portaloo) at Ulva ferry

Acknowledgments

Thanks to Jamie Howard for checking the entry

STAFFA

('isle of staves or pillars' from Norse, describing the rock formations)

www.nts.org.uk
www.visitscottishheartlands.com (AILLST)

Tourist Information Centres
Tobermory (08707 200625)
   Open Apr-Oct
Craignure (08707 200610)
   Open Jan-Dec

Map Landranger sheets: 47, 48 (HIH map page 73)

TRAVEL

Several operators run boat trips to the island (landing on the island is dependent on weather and tide):

Turus Mara (08000 858786; www.turusmara.com) offers boat trips from Ulva Ferry on Mull (B8073 between Gruline and Calgary)

C. Kirkpatrick (01681 700358; www.staffatrips.f9.co.uk) leaves from Fionnphort on Mull and Iona

Gordon Grant Tours (01681 700338/01631 571112/01631 562842; www.fingals-cave-staffa.co.uk) leaves from Fionnphort on Mull (A849: the ferry to Iona also sails from here)

Inter-Island Cruises (01688 302916; www.jenny.mull.com) leave from Croig harbour, near Dervaig (off B8073 seven miles west of Tobermory)

Ardnamurchan Charters also run trips (01972 500208; 07799 608199; www.west-scotland-tourism.com/ardnamurchan-charters)

Sensible footwear and waterproof clothing are recommended: getting soaked is a possibility. There are no facilities on the island.

DESCRIPTION

Staffa is some seven miles to the west of Mull, and about six miles from Iona. It is a small, now uninhabited island, covering eighty-two acres and rising to forty-two metres.

Despite its size, Staffa is one of the most famous places in the Highlands due to the hugely impressive rock formations: (mostly) hexagonal basalt columns formed by the cooling of lava. The Giants Causeway leads to the magnificent Fingal's Cave (named after the legendary Irish hero), a huge structure, also known in Gaelic as An Uamh Ehinn ('the musical cave'). It was formed from the erosion of the columns, is some eighty metres deep and twenty metres high, and is accessible at low tide. There are also other impressive caves: Boat, Cormorant, Clamshell, and Mackinnon's (called after one of the abbots of Iona).

WILDLIFE

Seals can be seen around the coasts, while there are porpoises, dolphins and whales in the waters. Staffa has a large breeding colony of puffins, guillemots and razorbills, and a diverse fauna of some 300 different species. The island is a National Nature Reserves (www.nnr-scotland.org.uk/reserve).

Staffa

HISTORY

The island was a property of the MacQuarries of Ulva, but was sold in 1777. It had a population of sixteen in 1784, and oats, potatoes and barley were grown here. The island was abandoned about 1800.

Staffa has had many famous visitors, not least Felix Mendelssohn, who composed the 'Hebrides Overture' after being inspired by the sound of the sea in Fingal's Cave. J. M. W. Turner, Wordsworth, Tennyson and Keats, Wagner, Queen Victoria and Prince Albert, Jules Verne, Sir Walter Scott, David Livingstone and Robert Louis Stevenson are some of the others who have visited the island.

Staffa is now owned by the National Trust for Scotland, and was made a National Nature Reserve in 2001.

TRESHNISH ISLES

('headland peninsula' from Norse)

www.hebrideantrust.org/treshnish.htm
www.visitscottishheartlands.com (AILLST)

Tourist Information Centres
Tobermory (08707 200625)
   Open Apr-Oct
Craignure (08707 200610)
   Open Jan-Dec a

Map Landranger sheets: 47, 48 (HIH map page 73)

TRAVEL

Several operators run boat trips to the islands, including some landing on Lunga
(landing on the island is dependent on weather and tide):

Turus Mara (08000 858786; www.turusmara.com) offers boat trips from Ulva Ferry
   on Mull (B8073 between Gruline and Calgary)

Gordon Grant Tours (01681 700338/01631 571112/01631 562842; www.fingals-cave-
   staffa.co.uk) leaves from Fionnphort on Mull (A849: the ferry to Iona also sails
   from here)

Inter-Island Cruises (01688 302916; www.jenny.mull.com) leave from Croig harbour,
   near Dervaig (off B8073 seven miles west of Tobermory)

Ardnamurchan Charters also run trips (01972 500208; 07799 608199; www.west-
   scotland-tourism.com/ardnamurchan-charters)

Sensible footwear and water-proof clothing are recommended: getting soaked is a
possibility. There are no facilities on the islands.

DESCRIPTION

The chain of islands lies five miles north and west of Staffa and two miles west of
Mull, and is spread out over six miles.

   The most easterly are the small isles of Cairn na Burg Mor and Cairn na Burg
Beg, which once had an important castle [NM 305447], little of which remains.
When the monastery on Iona was dissolved, the library and other papers were kept
here. It seems, however, they did not escape the siege by Cromwell's forces in the
1650s. The castle was still garrisoned during the 1745-6 Jacobite Rising, having been
held by the MacDougalls, the MacDonalds and the MacLeans. It was here that the
chief of the MacLaines of Lochbuie was imprisoned and eventually killed, although
he managed to make a serving woman pregnant in the meantime. She escaped the
island, and her son became the next chief of the MacLaines. The Hebridean Trust
bought the isles in 2000.

   Fladda is a small island, and is the flattest, as the name suggests.

   Lunga, the largest of the Treshnish groups at one mile long and the main bird
sanctuary, rises to 103 metres. Rabbits live on the island, many of which are black in
colour. There is also a population of house mice. The remains of an abandoned
township, occupied until 1834, survives.

   Dutchman's Cap or Bac Mor is the most distinctive and recognisable island, the
rock formation, created by an ancient volcanic eruption, is said to look like a
Dutchman's Cap.

WILDLIFE

The islands are a Site of Special Scientific Interest and are a Special Protection Area under the European Union Directive on the conservation of wild birds. There are breeding colonies of razorbills, guillemots, shags, fulmars, cormorants, kittiwakes, storm petrels, skuas, puffins and barnacle geese. Seals can be seen around the coasts, while there are porpoises, dolphins and whales in the waters between the islands.

FURTHER INFORMATION

The Hebridean Trust's management plan for the islands can be seen at www.hebrideantrust.org

ACKNOWLEDGMENTS

Thanks to Frances Buckel for checking the entry

Seil, one of the Slate Isles (see next section)

Lismore, Kerrera, and Seil, Easdale and Luing (Slate Isles), and Neighbouring Islands

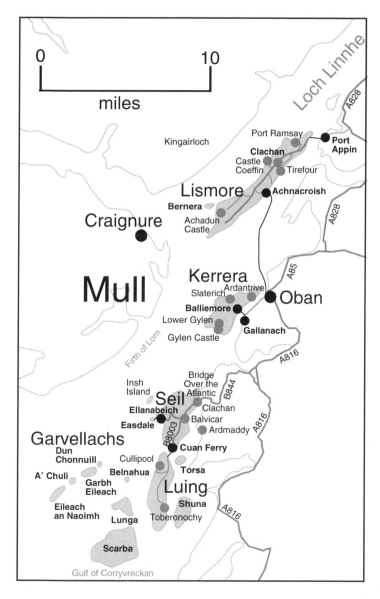

0 — 10

miles

Loch Linnhe

A828

Kingairloch

Port Ramsay

Port Appin

Clachan

Castle Coeffin

Tirefour

Lismore

Achnacroish

Bernera

A828

Achadun Castle

Craignure

Mull

Kerrera

Ardantrive

A85

Slaterich

Oban

Balliemore

Lower Gylen

Gallanach

Gylen Castle

Firth of Lorn

A816

Bridge Over the Atlantic

Insh Island

B844

Seil

Clachan

Ellanabeich

Balvicar

A816

Easdale

Ardmaddy

Garvellachs

B8003

Cuan Ferry

Dun Chonnuill

Cullipool

A' Chuli

Belnahua

Torsa

Garbh Eileach

Luing

Eileach an Naoimh

Shuna

A816

Lunga

Toberonochy

Scarba

Gulf of Corryvreckan

LISMORE
('big garden'; Lios Mor is Gaelic; pronounced 'Lissmore')

www.isleoflismore.com
www.visitscottishheartlands.com (AILLST)

Tourist Information Centre
Oban (mainland) (08707 200630)
  Open Jan-Dec

Map Landranger sheet: 49 (HIH map page 107)

TRAVEL
A vehicle ferry (CalMac 01631 566688; www.calmac.co.uk) sails from a slipway just along from the main pier at Oban on the mainland. It runs twice daily six days a week, with an extra sailing Tuesday, Thursday, and Saturday. Monday has a very early extra sailing, known as the scholars' boat, which operates during school term, and on Friday there is a later extra ferry. There is no ferry on Sundays. The trip takes fifty minutes, and sails to Achnacroish, on the middle of the island, which is a good place from which to explore the island. Taking the car across is, however, expensive and for the moderately fit walking or taking a bike may be a better option.

A frequent passenger ferry (Argyll and Bute Council; 01631 562125) also sails from Port Appin to Point, the northern-most tip of Lismore; more people visit the island using this route. It takes only ten minutes and bikes can be ferried across. The ferry runs approximately hourly, with a reduced service on Sundays and outwith peak periods. Port Appin can be reached down a single-track road from the main A828 road between Oban and Ballachulish (and Fort William). There is parking at Port Appin, a shop and two hotels.

DESCRIPTION
The island lies to the west of Benderloch in Argyll, some miles north-west of Oban at the mouth of Loch Linnhe, across the body of water known as the Lynn of Lorn. Lismore is about ten and a half miles long, and around one mile wide. The island is very lush and green, and is fertile, hence its name in Gaelic, the 'great garden'. The highest point of the island is Barr Mor at 127 metres, which has excellent views.

Port Ramsay, at the north end of the island, has a row of lime kiln workers' cottages, built in the eighteenth century, and is now a conservation village. There are also settlements at Achnacroish, Clachan and Kilcheran, but these are no more than a scattering of houses. The population is a little more than 170 (at one time it was more than 3,000). A listed narrow single-track road (B8045) runs from the northern tip to near the southern end of the island.

WILDLIFE
There are a great variety of wild flowers and plants growing on the island. There are also many different breeds of bird, such as buzzards, hawks, harriers and owls; terns, razorbills, plovers, gulls and oystercatchers; and geese, guillemots, lapwings, swans, corncrakes and even curlews as well as sea eagles. There are also hares, and otters and seals around the coasts. Unfortunately there are also mink on the island, decimating ground-nesting birds, although also exterminating the brown rat population. Lismore is one of the last places to see the Marsh Fritillary butterfly. See the wildlife section of www.isleoflismore.com for more information.

HISTORY

There are many excellent prehistoric sites on the island, including fourteen Bronze Age burial cairns, the most impressive of which is Cnoc Aingil, near Bachuil; and good duns, forts and brochs, the best of which is Tirefour Castle, actually an Iron Age broch, although it is likely it was still in use in medieval times. In addition there are two medieval castles: the thirteenth-century Castle Coeffin, near Port Castle on the northern side of the east shore; and Achadun, at the south end, the thirteenth-century palace of the Bishops of Argyll and the Isles.

It has always been desirable to live on Lismore, and there is a story that in the sixth century St Columba squabbled with St Moluag over its possession. St Columba was paddling towards the island, but St Moluag pipped him by cutting off his small finger and throwing it onto the island, thereby claiming he had arrived first. Like Columba, St Moluag was from Ireland and was an early missionary to the west coast of Scotland. He is believed to have died at Rosemarkie, near Inverness, but his body was reputedly returned to Lismore, and his staff (known as the Bachuil Mor) is still kept on the island at Bachuil House (the staff can be viewed but only by appointment: 01631 760256; bachuil@talk21.com). The island became the centre

Parish church, Clachan, Lismore

for the Bishopric of the Isles in 1236 and part of the thirteenth-century Cathedral of the Isles is used as the parish church at Kilmoluag.

The island was a property of the MacDougalls, then the Stewarts of Appin but, like many other parts of Argyll, passed to the Campbells. There was once a thriving lime industry, which employed many people, although a large number of trees were felled to fuel the kilns: there are the remains of lime kilns at Port Ramsay, Sailen and at Kilcheran. There was also a flax industry, and the population was more than 1700 in the 1800s.

The south of the island was cleared by its then owner, and the population dwindled through emigration to the Carolinas, Nova Scotia, Cape Breton and other parts of Scotland. John Stuart McCaig, who was a banker, essayist and philanthropist, was born (one of a family of eleven children) on the island and his relatives are still resident here today. He was responsible for building McCaig's folly above Oban. Most of the land is now used for farming sheep and cattle, though some of the inhabitants work at the quarry at Glensanda.

Tours
ACHNACROISH TO CLACHAN AND PORT APPIN FERRY (NORTH)
The ferry from Oban lands at Achnacroish, where there are toilets. There is currently a small museum about the island at Achnacroish, although it is to move to near Tigh Iseabel Dhaidh (see below, possibly as early as autumn 2006). An unlisted road leads up to the main road, which runs up the spine of the island.

The northward branch leads towards Clachan, passing both the Lismore Community Hall and the island shop and post office (01631 760272; open Mon-Tue and Thu-Fri 9.00-17.30, Wed and Sat 9.30-13.00, closed Sun). The well-stocked shop also sells souvenirs. Beyond this is Tigh Iseabel Dhaidh (01631 760257/285), a rebuilt eighteenth to nineteenth century traditional thatched cottage, which is usually open to the public in the summer or by appointment. This is closed, however, until September 2006 when the Lismore Museum and Heritage Centre, including a cafe and shop,

Tigh Iseabal Dhaidh

is due to be completed.

Just before Clachan is a track (signposted) running west from the road. This leads about a mile to Caisteal Coeffin [NM 804392], the shattered ruins of a thirteenth-century castle. It is thought that the site was also a Norse stronghold, dating from Viking times. Tradition has it that one Beothail, sister of one of the owners, Caifen (hence the name) was heartbroken when her lover was slain. She was buried on Lismore, but her unhappy ghost tormented those in the castle until her remains were taken and buried beside her love in Norway. The castle was later held by the MacDougalls, Stewarts and the Campbells, and was probably abandoned in the seventeenth century.

Beyond this, back on the main road, is St Moluag's Parish Church, formerly the Cathedral of the Isles, now much reduced in size but the fourteenth-century choir is still used as the parish church [NM 861434]. It had been 137 feet long, and was dedicated to St Moluag. It stands in a pleasant spot and has an interesting burial ground, and houses the fragments of an eight-century cross-slab, indicating that the cathedral was built on the site of an earlier Christian settlement. James MacGregor, who was the Dean of Lismore in the sixteenth century, compiled an important anthology of Gaelic poetry and history *The Book of the Dean of Lismore*. Behind the church is Carn Mor [NM 859436], a prehistoric burial cairn, from which both Tirefour Castle and Cnoc Aingil can be seen.

Over the road is a sanctuary stone within which criminals and debtors were safe from prosecution. Another site associated with the saint is St Moluag's Chair [NM 870441], half a mile north of the church (signposted). There are excellent views from here, and it is said that the saint used to sit on the stone chair to appreciate them. Sitting here is also said to help alleviate the symptoms of rheumatism. His pastoral staff is kept at Bachuil.

Cnoc Aingil [NM 864440], just beyond Bachuil, is the largest cairn in Lorn, measuring forty-two metres in diameter and seven metres in height. This is a prehistoric burial cairn, but is now covered in grass.

One mile north of the church a (signposted) track leads south from the road one mile to the impressive Tirefour Castle [NM 867429], the remains of an Iron Age

Tirefour Castle (or Broch)

broch, which was probably used well into medieval times. The overgrown walls survive to a height of more than three metres, and some detail of the entrance and the mural gallery can be seen. There are also excellent views from here, but it is a bit of a scramble up to the ruins.

A couple of miles further on from Clachan, back on the main road, is the turn-off to the north on an unlisted road which leads to Port Ramsay. There are the remains of a lime kiln, and lime was quarried here for shipment to the mainland.

The road winds north until it reaches the jetty for the ferry from Port Appin and is a pleasant walk or bike ride. There is a waiting room and public toilet at the terminal.

SOUTH OF ACHNACROISH

Returning to the main road where it joins the unlisted road from Achnacroish, the southern branch leads, via an unlisted road (signposted to Achinaduin) and rough track down to Achadun Castle [NM 804392], a ruined stronghold of the Bishops of the Isles, dating from the thirteenth century. They moved to Saddell in Kintyre in 1510. Bernera Island, which is beyond the castle, is accessible at low tide (care should be taken not to get stranded).

There are several more prehistoric burial cairns, including three cairns at Aon Garbh [NM 802375], two more at Barr Mor [NM 802375], and others at Baligrundle [NM 840396]. Beyond the end of the main road, near Dalnarrow, is Dun Chruban [NM 793360], an Iron Age fort, the walls of which survive to a height of more than three metres in places.

PLACES TO STAY

(also see www.isleoflismore.com)
Achnaduin (01631 760336)
Achnaduin; guest house and dinner
The Schoolhouse (01631 760262)
Baligarve (two miles from Port Appin ferry);
B&B and dinner

SELF–CATERING

No 3 Achnacroish (01381 621076)
Achnacroish; self-catering, sleeps six
Achuran House (www.scottish-country-cottages.co.uk; www.isleoflismore.com)
Near Point, north of island; self-catering, sleeps eight
An Aird (01631 760213)
Tirefour, to north of island; self-catering, sleeps eight-ten
Baligrundle Cottages (www.isleoflismore.com)
Near Achnacroish; check availability
Balnagowan (01631 760247)
Middle of island; self-catering, sleeps six
Calgary (www.isleoflismore.com)
North of island; self-catering, sleeps five
Daisy Bank (0141 339 5433/01631 760251)
Middle of island; self-catering, sleeps ten
Lark Rise (01661 886277)
Port Ramsay; north of island; self-catering, sleeps four
Marsh Cottage (01631 760392)
One mile from Achnacroish; self-catering house, sleeps six; open May-Sep
Pier Cottage (01631 760221)
Achnacroish; sleeps six
Point Steadings (01631 760236/330)
North of island; self-catering; two cottages, sleeps six; bicycles available with House Two
No 1 Port Ramsay (01381 621076)
North of island; self-catering, sleeps five + three children
Stokers Cottage (0207 609 2718)
Balnagowan, middle of island; sleeps four
Tigh-an-Uillt (www.isleoflismore.com)
Port Ramsay; self catering

PLACES TO EAT

Lismore Museum and Heritage Centre Cafe - expected to open in late September 2006 (01631 760346; lismore-museum@btconnect.com for enquiries)

Post Office and Shop (01631 760272)
Refreshments and snacks can be purchased; open Mon-Tue and Thu-Fri 9.00-17.30, Wed and Sat 9.30-13.00, closed Sun
The Schoolhouse (01631 760262)
Baligarve; evening meals for both residents and non-residents
At Port Appin on the mainland there is also the Pierhouse Hotel and Seafood Restaurant (01631 730302; www.pierhousehotel.co.uk), which is (as the name suggests) by the pier and, further into Port Appin, the swanky Airds Hotel (01631 730236; www.airds-hotel.com)

FURTHER INFORMATION

CYCLE HIRE

(book in advance)
Cycle Hire (01631 760213)
Port Appin Bike Hire (01631 730391)

TAXI

Taxi service available (01631 760220)

BUS

Postbus operates on Lismore (08457 740740; www.royalmail.com/postbus)
The community bus can be hired by groups or individuals (01631 760205)

INTERNET ACCESS

Post Office and Shop (01631 760272)

There are public telephones at Achnacroish, Clachan, Port Ramsay and near the jetty for the ferry to Port Appin
No petrol on Lismore

FURTHER READING

Isle of Lismore (Ritchie, Walter M.)
  Lismore Kirk Session, 1995
Lachann Dubh a' Chrogain (Lachlan Livingstone and his Grandsons) Bards of Mull and Lismore (MacDonald Lobban, Margaret)
  New Iona Press, 2004
Lismore in Alba (Carmichael, Ian)
  D. Leslie, 1947
Sgeul neo dha as an Lios – Tales from the Garden: A Look from the Inside (Black, Donald)
  2006

ACKNOWLEDGMENTS

Thanks to Pauline Dowling and Cait McCullagh for checking the text

KERRERA

('copse-water island'; pronounced Kerr-e-ra: the emphasis is on the first syllable)

www.kerrerabunkhouse.co.uk
www.undiscoveredscotland.co.uk/kerrera/kerrera/
www.visitscottishheartlands.com (AILLST)

Tourist Information Centre
Oban (mainland) (08707 200630)
    Open Jan-Dec

Map Landranger sheet: 49 (HIH map page 107)

TRAVEL

From Oban, take the turn-off signposted for Gallanach (past the main ferry terminal for Oban); two miles on, just before Gallanach, is the ferry. The passenger ferry runs every half hour or so, and only takes a few minutes. There are no toilets or facilities at the pier or on Kerrera itself except for a public telephone. Stout footwear and protective clothing is advised. Number 431 bus service from Oban connects with the 10.30 and 16.00 ferries in the summer.

Trips around Kerrera can be made in a rigid inflatable boat from Oban (07786963279; 01631 563664; www.kerrerasea.co.uk; Apr-Oct).

DESCRIPTION

The island is just over four miles long and just under two wide, and it rises to 189 metres at Carn Breugach. The land is mostly used for farming, both sheep and cattle, which wander freely in places; the island shelters Oban Bay, and there are many boats moored in its lea at Ardantrive Bay. The only settlement is Balliemore, and there is a sandy beach at Slatrach.

Kerrera

WILDLIFE

There are wild goats, as well as many birds, such as gulls, mute swans, gannets, eider ducks, guillemots, buzzards, peregrine falcons and even red kites. In places otters can be seen, and there is a seal colony off the west coast. Porpoises, dolphins and whales are sometimes sighted in the waters around Kerrera.

HISTORY

The island has long been a property of the MacDougalls, the clan being descended from Dougal, son of the great Somerled. The clan were subject to the Norse king despite an expedition by Alexander II, King of Scots, in 1249. His force is said to have sheltered in Horseshoe Bay, and Alexander fell ill and died on the island. King Hakon marshalled his forces here before sailing south to defeat at the Battle of Largs in 1263, and three years later Kerrera and the Western Isles passed into the kingdom of Scots. The MacDougalls built Gylen Castle to the south of the island, which was later burnt and looted.

Although sleepy now, there was once a substantial community of more than 200 people on Kerrera (the population is now about forty and the school closed in 1997), and cattle were driven across the island from Barr nam Boc on their way to markets in the south. Most of the island is still owned by the MacDougalls of Dunollie on the mainland (near Oban).

Tour

A map of the island is available on the ferry: a track, rough, sometimes steep and possibly muddy in places, circles most of the island. Sensible footwear is appropriate. There are wonderful views from various points around the island, including over to Mull and the mainland. The complete route is easier attempted anticlockwise (the slope is less steep), although this is a longer and more difficult way to the Tea Garden. There is a good sandy beach at Slatrach [NM 815295].

There are the remains of a prehistoric burial cairn at Slaterich [NM 820296], and a beaker, food vessel and quartz pebbles were found in one of the cists. In 1249, Alexander II, King of Scots, died on Kerrera at Dalrigh [NM 825285] near Horseshoe Bay (or perhaps at Gylen), while on an expedition to recover the area from the Vikings. King Hakon of Norway held court here on his way south to defeat at the Battle of Largs in 1263.

At Lower Gylen, near the track for the castle, is the excellent tea garden and bunkhouse (01631 570223; www.kerrerabunkhouse.co.uk;

Gylen Castle

open Apr-Sep, Wed-Sun), which offers hot and cold , mostly organic, refreshments, and accommodation. There are also toilets for Tea Garden customers.

The island was long a property of the MacDougalls, and there is an impressive stronghold called Gylen Castle ('fortress of springs') to the south of the island [NM 805265], standing on cliffs above the sea. This is an elegant ruin of 1587 on an older site, although it was captured and torched by a Covenanter army in 1647 when the garrison was slaughtered. It has being undergoing restorations in the past few years, which are due to be completed in the summer of 2006; there are tours from the Tea Garden. It was from here that the 'Brooch of Lorn', once owned by Robert the Bruce, was stolen by the Campbells of Inverawe. They held it for nearly 200 years before finally returning it to the MacDougalls in 1825.

The monument to the north of the island [NM 845310], and seen from the ferry to Mull, commemorates David Hutcheson, one of the founders of the ferry company Caledonian MacBrayne (CalMac). Just north of this are the earthworks of a cashel [NM 842313], an early Christian monastery known as Cladh a' Bhearnaig.

PLACES TO STAY

There is a bunk house in eighteenth-century converted stables, organic restaurant and customer toilets at Lower Gylen [NM 285270] (01631 570223; www.kerrerabunkhouse.co.uk)
Accommodation also is available at Ardentrive Farm (01631 567180)

PLACES TO EAT

Tea Garden, Lower Gylen (01631 570223; www.kerrerabunkhouse.co.uk)
Tea garden with mostly hot and cold organic refreshments; open Apr-Sep, Wed-Sun

FURTHER INFORMATION

SAILING AND YACHTING
The anchorage at Ardantrive Bay has moorings, boat yard and slipway

OTHER INFORMATION
There is a public telephone at Balliemore
Shiatsu is available from a practitioner on the island

ACKNOWLEDGMENTS

Thanks to Andy Crabb for checking the text

SEIL

(perhaps from 'Seil', a personal name, or from Gaelic for 'willow' or 'yellow iris'; pronounced 'Seal')

www.seil.oban.ws
www.slate.org.uk
www.visitscottishheartlands.com (AILLST)

Tourist Information Centre
Oban (mainland) (08707 200630)
Open Jan-Dec

Map Landranger sheet: 55 (HIH map page 107)

TRAVEL

From Oban, take the A816 south (Lochgilphead Road), then, after six miles, the B844 (signposted Easdale). This is a single-track road (although wide enough to be used by coaches). On the way to Seil, a narrow turn-off from the B844, three miles beyond Kilninver, leads down to Ardmaddy Castle [NM 780165], which has a fine walled garden and woodland walks. The main road crosses the sound to Seil via Clachan Bridge.

DESCRIPTION

This is one of a beautiful and accessible group of islands in the Firth of Lorn, known as the Slate Islands, and a short journey south of Oban. The island of Seil is about four miles long and two miles across at its widest. The west of the island is hilly and picturesque, and bluebells and yellow irises are widespread in the spring. There are four settlements: Clachan with its bridge in the north; Balvicar in the centre; Ellanabeich and Easdale to the west; and North Cuan with the ferry to Luing in the south. Argyll Transport runs a bus to Cuan and Ellanabeich. Four trips daily; varies with season.

Ellanabeich, Seil

WILDLIFE

The fairy foxglove *Erinus alpinus* grows in the masonry of the bridge at Clachan. Ballachuan hazel wood at Kilbrandon (www.swt.org.uk; park in the road opposite the church; no parking in the private road to Kilbrandon House) is one of the few remaining natural hazel and oak woods in Scotland. The island also has a variety of bird life, including herons, buzzards and even sea eagles, and seals, otters, dolphins and basking sharks visit the waters around the island.

HISTORY

The island was long held by the MacDougalls, who had a castle at Ardfad [NM 7691945] (not open to the public), but it passed to the Campbells of Breadalbane. Seil, the offshore island of Easdale and Luing and Belnahua became renowned for their slate quarries (and hence are known as the Slate Isles): slates from the area are identifiable by the large amount of iron pyrites found in them (which sparkles in the sun). Eleven million slates were produced annually at peak periods in the nineteenth century. There are several flooded quarries, remains of tramways and buildings, and slate spoil: a fascinating industrial landscape in a place of much natural beauty. There are attractive villages at Balvicar, Ellanabeich, Toberonochy and Cullipool on Luing, and Easdale island, where there are rows of whitewashed miners' houses. One of the quarries on Easdale was devastated in a great storm of November 1881 when the sea-wall was breached, and the industry declined until the last quarries closed at Balvicar on Seil and on Luing in the 1950s and 1960s.

The population was more than 650 at one time. Unlike many islands, the number of people living here has actually grown in recent times, from around 300 people in 1961 to some 550 in 2001.

Tours
CLACHAN SOUTH TO BALVICAR, ELLANABEICH AND EASDALE (B844)

Clachan Bridge (known widely in tourist guides as 'the bridge over the Atlantic') is a very impressive high-arched bridge, built in 1782 by the Stephenson brothers of Oban to a design of Robert Mylne, the duke of Argyll's architect (not the designs of Thomas Telford). Near the bridge is Tigh na Truish, the 'house of the trousers', a hotel and public house. Soldiers returning from Highland regiments were obliged to remove their kilts and put on trousers as part of measures following the Jacobite Rising of 1745-6. There is parking at Clachan. There are two places to eat at Clachan: Tigh na Truish and the Willowburn Hotel (both of which offer accommodation). It was in the narrow and shallow sound that a twenty-five metre whale was stranded in 1835, and a colony of pilot whales also came to grief here. There is a good anchorage

Clachan Bridge, the 'Bridge Over the Atlantic'

at Puilladobhrain (pronounced 'Pol-dor-an') at the north end of the island, with a footpath to Clachan.

The road (B844) continues south and branches at Balvicar, where there is an excellent shop and post office (open daily, until 19.30 in summer, except Sun; 01852 300373; www.balvicarstores.co.uk), a phone box, and a nine-hole golf course. Just south [NM 764167] is an old burial ground with interesting markers. Sealife Adventures (01631 571010/01852 300203; www.sealife-adventures.com) run boat trips from Balvicar to the Corryvreckan whirlpool, the Garvellachs and the Firth of Lorn.

One branch of the road goes south to Cuan and the ferry for Luing (B8003), while the 'main' road turns west to Ellanabeich and the small offshore island of Easdale. The road climbs to a stunning viewpoint with vistas over the Firth of Lorn to Scarba, Luing, Lunga, the Garvellachs and Mull (with seating and parking), then continues down past Dunmor (where Highland games are held in July) to Ellanabeich. On entering the village there is the beautiful garden of An Cala with its huge sheltering wall. The garden was begun in 1930, covers some five acres, and is open to the public in the spring and summer.

The village itself (variously spelled Ellanabeich, Ellenabeich and Ellanbeich) has rows of single-storey miners' cottages: there is a small but interesting museum housed in one of them, by the shop, run by the Scottish Slate Island Heritage Trust (01852 300370; www.slate.org.uk; open Apr-Sep, daily), with models, photographs and artefacts charting the heritage of the islands. There is the Oyster Bar and Brewery with restaurant in the square, as well as the shop and post office, telephone and public toilets. There is plenty of free parking, and also Highland Arts, which offers the visitor a unique experience, with a putting green. There are several cottages available for rent at Ellanabeich, as well as other accommodation on the island.

Sea.fari (www.seafari.co.uk) run expeditions in inflatable boats from the pier to some of the nearby islands, such as Belnahua, Scarba, Lunga and the Garvellachs, plus the famous whirlpool of Corryvreckan. The passenger ferry across to Easdale also runs from the pier here.

BALVICAR TO CUAN FERRY (NORTH CUAN) (B8003)

The B8003 branches to the south from the road to Ellanabeich and Easdale and runs down to North Cuan and the vehicle ferry to Luing, passing the church at Kilbrandon [NM 757155] with its fine stained-glass windows; it was built in 1866 and is open to the public.

Ballachuan hazel wood at Kilbrandon (park in the road opposite the church; no parking in the private road to Kilbrandon House) is one of the few remaining natural hazel and oak woods in Scotland and has been established since the last Ice Age.

The vehicle ferry for Luing, parking and public toilets are at North Cuan, but not much else, although the currents between Seil and Luing can be impressive.

In a remote and difficult spot on the west coast, Dun Mucaig [NM 751554], stands on a rock, the remains of an Iron Age stronghold.

HOTELS AND GUEST HOUSES

Tigh An Truish (01852 300242; www.tigh-an-truish.co.uk)
Clachan Seil; pub and B&B; lunches and evening meals
Willowburn Hotel (01852 300276; www.willowburn.co.uk)
Clachan Seil; accommodation and licensed restaurant: booking advised; open Mar-Dec

BED AND BREAKFAST

Clachandubh Farmhouse (01852 300317)
Balvicar; B&B
Dunfillan (01852 300258)
Cuan Ferry; B&B
10 Ellanabeich (01852 300202)
Ellanabeich; B&B

Innish (01852 300423; www.innish.com)
Clachan Seil; B&B
Mutiara (01852 300241)
Clachan Seil; B&B; open May-Nov

SELF-CATERING PROPERTIES

Achnacroish Cottage (020 8661 1834;
www.achnacroish.fsnet.co.uk)
Achnacroish, near Balvicar; self-catering
cottage, sleeps two-four
Annexe (0870 1976420;
www.welcomecottages.com)
Ellanabeich; self-catering ground-floor
apartment, sleeps two-four
Ardara (01852 300379/07919 808098;
www.seil.org.uk)
Clachan Seil; self-catering
Am Baile (01852 200274)
Clachan Seil; self-catering, sleeps seven
Balvicar Chalets (01852 300221;
www.balvicarchalets.uk.com)
Balvicar; seven chalets, each sleeps four; open
all year
Caolas (01852 300329)
Ellanabeich; self-catering, sleeps two-three
27 Ellanabeich (01852 300522)
Ellanabeich; self-catering cottage, sleeps two
Insh Cottage (01852 300573;
www.ellenabeich.com)
Ellanabeich; self-catering, sleeps two-four
Innish (01852 300423; www.innish.com)
Clachan Seil; self-catering, sleeps four
Innishmore (01852 300222)
Ellanabeich; self-catering
Kilbride Croft (01852 300475;
www.kilbridecroft.co.uk)
Near Balvicar; two cottages, sleep four and six;
open all year
Misty Isles (01852 300121/269)
Ellanabeich; self-catering, sleeps two
Monaveen (01852 300273/320)
Ellanabeich; two properties, sleep two-three
and four
Oban Seil Croft Cottage (01852 300457)
Clachan Seil; self-catering traditional cottage,
sleeps four; open all year
Oban Seil Steadings (01852 300245/058;
www.obanseilfarm.com)
Clachan-Seil; four properties, one sleeps two,
others four; open all year
Old Clachan Farmhouse (01852 300493)
Clachan (before bridge); self-catering house
One Seaview (01852 300 358; www.seaviewone-
easdale.co.uk)
Easdale; self-catering, sleeps four-five
Otter Cottage (www.unique-cottages.co.uk)
Balvicar; self-catering, sleeps four
Sea Breezes (01631 565213)
Ellanabeich; self-catering, sleeps three
Seil Island Cottages (01852 300440)
Seil; self-catering
Tramway Cottages (01852 300112;
www.tramwaycottages.com)
Ellanabeich; two cottages, both sleep four;
open all year

Tigh An Truish (01852 300242)
Clachan Seil; three properties, each sleeping
two

PLACES TO EAT

Tigh An Truish (01852 300242; www.tigh-an-
truish.co.uk)
Clachan Seil; lunches and evening meals; also
sells petrol and diesel; B&B; self catering
Willowburn Hotel (01852 300276;
www.willowburn.co.uk)
Clachan Seil; lunches and evening meals
Oyster Bar and Brewery (01852 300121;
www.oysterbrewery.com)
Ellanabeich; bar and restaurant with brewery
(products can be bought on-line)

FURTHER INFORMATION

BUSES
Buses run between Oban and Seil (Cuan and
Ellanabeich) (01631 582856;
www.westcoastmotors.co.uk)

YACHTING AND SAILING
There are anchorages at Puilladobhrain (with a
footpath to Clachan), Balvicar and in Easdale
Sound

BOAT TRIPS
Sealife Adventures (01631 571010/01852 300203)
Balvicar; trips to Corryvreckan whirlpool, the
Garvellachs and Firth of Lorn
Sea.fari (01852 300003; www.seafari.co.uk)
Trips in an RIC from Ellanabeich to
uninhabited islands and the Corryvreckan
whirlpool
Westward Quest (01852 300 379;
www.westwardquest.co.uk)
Charter sailing trips and cruises around the
west coast of Scotland

GOLF
Isle of Seil Golf Club (01852 300373)
Balvicar; nine-hole course

There is a post office and shop at Balvicar and at
Ellanabeich
Petrol is available at Clachan by the parking
opposite Tigh an Truish

FURTHER READING

*The Islands that Roofed the World: Easdale, Belnahua,
Luing and Seil* (Withall, Mary)
Luath Press, 2001
Seil: a Portrait (third edition) (Shaw, Michael)
2001

EVENTS

Highland Games (Dun Mor)   July

ACKNOWLEDGMENTS

Thanks to Mary Withall for checking the text

EASDALE

('horse dale'; pronounced 'Easedale')

www.easdale.org
www.stoneskimming.com
www.slate.org.uk
www.visitscottishheartlands.com (AILLST)

Tourist Information Centre
Oban (mainland) (08707 200630)
   Open Jan-Dec

Map Landranger sheet: 55 (HIH map page 107)

TRAVEL
This small but lovely island, located over a narrow sound from Ellanabeich on Seil, is reached by a passenger ferry (Argyll and Bute Council; 01631 562125) from the pier. The ferry runs regularly during the day, but has breaks, including at lunchtime: check before crossing. The trip takes just a few minutes.

DESCRIPTION, WILDLIFE AND HISTORY
Another of the Slate Islands, Easdale is compact but has many points of interest: not least the attractive village with its whitewashed single-storey houses and interesting harbour, flooded slate quarries up to sixty metres deep, tracks of railways, ruinous mining buildings, and the overgrown remains of gardens, plus being in a fantastic location. The island was a centre of slate mining for hundreds of years until a great storm of 1881 flooded one of the quarries, after which the industry declined. Easdale gave its name to the belt of slate which stretches from Jura north towards Inverness and includes Ballachulish, whose quarries were initiated by men from Easdale. Some 450 people lived on Easdale island in the 1860s.

Easdale Island

There is a fine walk around the island, including up to a viewpoint from which there are brilliant panoramic views. Care should be taken as paths can be rough or slippy in wet weather and there are deep drops into the quarries (one of which is often used as a swimming pool in the summer).

In the village is the award-winning Easdale Island Folk Museum (www.slate.org.uk; open Apr-Oct, daily 10.30-17.30), which has displays on life on the islands, and The Puffer (www.pufferbar.com), a bar and restaurant, which serves meals in a friendly and cosy atmosphere. Meals are not served from October to March, while the bar is only open some evenings over the same period and not during the day.

Insh or Innisch Island lies to the north of Easdale and west of Seil and is uninhabited.

PLACES TO STAY

An Rubha (07831 838717)
    Sleeps four-five
Ardpoll House (01985 846 536)
    Sleeps four
4 Easdale Island (01852 300508)
    Sleeps six
13 Easdale Island (01253 723004)
    Sleeps four
Stonesthrow Cottage (01852 300019)
    Sleeps two-four

PLACES TO EAT

Puffer Bar and Restaurant (www.pufferbar.com)
    Bar and restaurant open Apr-Sep, daily 10.30-17.30; bar only open some evenings during the winter (Oct-Mar)

FURTHER INFORMATION

The world stone skimming championships (www.stoneskimming.com) are held here in September, the flooded quarries and abundance of slate making it an ideal site. The winning stone in 2003 reached 54 metres! There is a public phone in the village, and the Village Hall hosts a variety of events, both cultural and musical, please visit www.easdale.org for details
The island sells its own labelled whisky; Eilean Eisdeal Whisky (www.easdale.org/whisky_description.htm)

FURTHER READING

Island: Diary of a Year on Easdale (Waite, Garth and Vicky Garth)
    Mainstream, 1995
The Islands that Roofed the World: Easdale, Belnahua, Luing and Seil (Withall, Mary)
    Luath Press, 2001

ACKNOWLEDGMENTS

Thanks to Jess and Donald Melville for checking the text

Viewpoint, Easdale Island

LUING

('long island' or 'boat island'; pronounced 'Ling')

www.isleofluing.co.uk
www.isleofluing.org
www.visitscottishheartlands.com (AILLST)

Tourist Information Centre
Oban (mainland) (08707 200630)
Open Jan-Dec

Map Landranger sheet: 55 (HIH map page 107)

TRAVEL

The island lies to the south of Seil, and is reached by a vehicle ferry (Argyll and Bute Council; tel.: 01631 562125) from Cuan. This runs every thirty minutes between 07.30 to 18.00, and there is a limited evening passenger service, with later crossings in the summer: check before crossing. Although it is possible to take cars across to Luing (the roads are single-track but passable), the moderately fit may prefer to walk or to take a bike. Bike hire is available from the Sunnybrae Caravan Park (contact in advance: tel. 01852 314274; www.luingbikehire.co.uk)

DESCRIPTION

Luing is some six miles long, and stretches to about 1.5 miles at the widest. The island rises to around 90 metres at Binnein Furachail, from where there are fine views. It is fertile and hilly, and was also a centre of slate mining, with attractive villages at Cullipool to the north-west and Toberonochy to the south-east.

There is a tidal race between Seil and Luing in Cuan Sound, which can reach a speed of six to eight knots.

Cottages, Toberonochy

WILDLIFE

Birds which can be seen here include buzzards, peregrine falcons, hen harriers and possibly golden eagles. Otters live on the island as do hares. There are no rabbits on Luing. Seals, dolphins and porpoises can be found in the waters around the coast.

HISTORY

The island was part of the extensive possessions of the Lords of the Isles, and passed through the hands of the MacDougalls, MacDonalds, MacLeans and the Campbells. Like the other Slate Isles, slate was quarried here. The last mines closed in the 1960s, but there are many reminders of the industry. The island is now mostly used for farming, while fishing for scallops, prawns and lobsters is a mainstay. A breed of cattle, a cross between Highlands and Shorthorns, was developed on Luing and bears the island's name.

The population was once more than 600 people, but is now around 200. There are the remains of an abandoned township at Port Mary, to the north of the island.

Tours

LUING

The unlisted single-track road runs south from the ferry, and then branches, one going to Cullipool in the west, the other running down to Toberonochy.

The Cullipool branch passes by an old well [NM 742123] and the well-stocked island shop (01852 314243) near Bardrishaig, which also sells crafts. By the shop is what is claimed to be the smallest coffee shop in the world, and it also makes a handy shelter from adverse weather. The road goes on to the village of Cullipool – which is larger than might be expected. There are public toilets in the village. There is a walk north from here back to Cuan, and to the north of Cnoc Dhomhnuill, the highest point of the Luing.

The south branch of the road runs down to Toberonochy, passing the ruinous

Kilchattan

church at Kilchattan [NM 744090], which stands in a pleasant spot with good views. There are several points of interest in the graveyard, including old markers, a memorial to those lost when the *SS Helena Faulbaums* sank off Belnahua in 1936, and seamen's graffiti on one of the church walls. There is also a stone in the graveyard wall which commemorates the 'piety' of the 'Covenanter' Alexander Campbell . He founded a very strict branch of the Presbyterian church in 1787, only to eventually throw out and excommunicate all the other followers for not strictly adhering to his beliefs. Among the many things of which he disapproved were 'play actors and pictures', 'dancing schools' and 'men [who] have whiskers like ruffian soldiers'.

The attractive village has many white-washed cottages, and Kilchattan Kirk [NM 734104], the parish church of Toberonochy and built in 1936, is open to the public. There are fine views across to Shuna and the mainland from the harbour.

At Leccamore [NM 750107], about one and a half miles north of the village, are the impressive remains of an Iron Age dun, the walls of which stand to a height of three metres. Entrances, cells and the beginning of a stair can be seen. There is another fort at Ardinamir, known as Ballycastle Dun [NM 753121], and an old healing well, Tobar na Suil, the waters of which were used for curing diseases of the eye [NM 753114] (permission should be sought from the farmer before visiting).

GARVELLACHS, LUNGA, TORSA AND SCARBA

Boat trips can be arranged from Balvicar on Seil (Sealife Adventures 01631 571010/ 01852 300203 or Sea.fari Adventures 01852 300003) to visit the Garvellach Isles and the other islands which lie some miles west of Luing.

The Garvellachs have several points of interest including a thirteenth-century castle on Dun Chonnuill [NM 680125], a property of the MacLeans of Duart; and the remains of an early monastic settlement founded by St Brendan in 545 – St Columba's mother is said to be buried here – on Eileach an Naoimh [NM 640097]. St Columba is said to have loved the island and he often visited. Garbh Eileach has the remains of an old fort and a herd of red deer.

Other neighbouring islands to Luing include Torsa, east of Cuan, which had a castle, Casiteal nan Con [NM 765136], at its northern end – a property also of the MacDougalls and probably used as a hunting lodge. It is possible to rent a holiday home on the island, sleeping four to five (01852 314274; www.torsa-island.co.uk), which also includes the use of a boat.

There is also the wooded island of Shuna, lying offshore at Toberonochy (see separate entry); there are holiday cottages on the island (www.islandofshuna.co.uk).

Scarba (see next page) and the Firth of Lorn

The impressive and high Scarba ('isle of cormorants' or 'hilly island'), to the south-west of Luing, rises to 449 metres and is often shrouded in cloud. It lies between Jura and Luing. The island formerly had a population of fifty but there are no permanent residents now except Luing cattle, sheep and wildlife. There are the remains of an old chapel at Kilmory [NM 718057], and Kilmory Lodge is occasionally used.

Lunga and Belnahua are another two small islands in the Firth of Lorn: slate was also mined here but the islands are now abandoned. Fladda is a small island with a lighthouse.

The Corryvreckan whirlpool lies between Scarba and Jura (George Orwell was nearly sucked into Corryvreckan when his boat capsized), although the waters and the Grey Dogs between Luing and Scarba can also be treacherous. Boat trips go to the whirlpool, including Sealife Adventures from Balvicar (see Seil), Sea.fari from Ellanabeich (see Seil), from Crinan (www.gemini-crinan.co.uk), and from Craobh Haven with Farsain Cruises (01852 500664) who run trips to the Gulf of Corryvreckan, Scarba and some of the other islands.

PLACES TO STAY

Ben More (book through Hamster Cottages: www.hamstercottages.co.uk/properties/AL51/AL51.asp)
  Cullipool; cottage, sleeps two
Creagard House (0141 639 4592; www.scottishcountrycottage.co.uk)
  Cullipool; traditional quarriers cottage; sleeps six-seven
Cullipool (01852 314300)
  Two cottages, sleep five/six; leaflet with further information available
Sunnybrae Caravan Park (01852 314274; www.oban-holiday.co.uk)
  South Cuan; seven mobile homes, sleep four-six; bike hire available

FURTHER INFORMATION

BUSES
The Postbus can be used to get around the island: check timetable (www.royalmail.com/postbus)
SAILING AND YACHTING
There is a good anchorage at Ardinamir

FURTHER READING

The Islands that Roofed the World: Easdale, Belnahua, Luing and Seil (Withall, Mary)
Luath Press, 2001

ACKNOWLEDGMENTS

Thanks to Mike Barlow for checking the text

SHUNA

(perhaps 'fairy island' but not certain)

www.islandofshuna.co.uk
www.visitscottishheartlands.com (AILLST)

Tourist Information Centre
Oban (mainland) (08707 200630)
  Open Jan-Dec

Map Landranger sheet: 55 (HIH map page 107)

TRAVEL

Arrangements will be made for those taking holiday accommodation, the boat trip taking twenty minutes from the mainland. Boat crossings to the island can be arranged through the owners (01852 314244).

DESCRIPTION

Shuna lies just east of its bigger neighbour Luing and the mainland of Argyll. It is three miles long and just over one wide at most, and covers about 1,000 acres. Unlike most of the isles, it is heavily wooded with many native species of trees; and the land rises to about ninety metres. Also, unlike the neighbouring islands, it did not have any useable slate.

WILDLIFE

On the island are many deer (red, roe and fallow); otters and seals can be seen around the coasts, and dolphins and porpoises in the waters around Shuna. There are also many seabirds, plus golden eagles, buzzards, woodcock and snipe.

HISTORY

The island has evidence of occupation from prehistoric times, including a burial cairn [NM 763064] to the south on Shuna Point, and three more cairns near Shuna Cottage to the southwest. The island was held by the MacLeans from the seventeenth century, but it passed from them around 1800.

At one time, stone was used for lime production, and there are remnants of the industry, including lime kilns. Shuna House [NM 770095] is a ruinous Gothic mansion, which was unroofed in the 1980s. The island had a population of more than sixty at one time, but now has only one resident family. It is a working estate, used to farm sheep and cattle; and there are also fish farms.

PLACES TO STAY

Four holiday cottages (01852 314244;
  www.islandofshuna.co.uk)
There is no electricity; appliances and lighting
  work by gas
Use of a boat is included with holiday lets

FURTHER INFORMATION

There are no facilities on Shuna

ACKNOWLEDGMENTS

Thanks to Phil Lloyd for checking the text

ISLAY

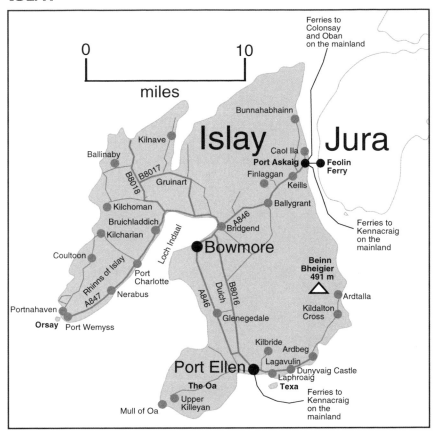

- Ferries to Colonsay and Oban on the mainland
- 0
- 10
- miles
- Bunnahabhainn
- **Islay**
- Kilnave
- Caol Ila
- **Jura**
- Ballinaby
- **Port Askaig**
- **Feolin Ferry**
- B8017
- B8018
- Finlaggan
- Gruinart
- Keills
- Kilchoman
- Ballygrant
- Bruichladdich
- A846
- Kilcharian
- Bridgend
- Ferries to Kennacraig on the mainland
- Coultoon
- Loch Indaal
- **Bowmore**
- **Beinn Bheigier 491 m**
- Port Charlotte
- Rhinns of Islay
- Duich
- B8016
- Ardtalla
- A847
- Nerabus
- A846
- Kildalton Cross
- Portnahaven
- Glenegedale
- **Orsay** Port Wemyss
- Kilbride
- Ardbeg
- Lagavulin
- **Port Ellen**
- Dunyvaig Castle
- **The Oa**
- Laphroaig
- **Texa**
- Upper Killeyan
- Ferries to Kennacraig on the mainland
- Mull of Oa

Dunyvaig Castle and Texa, Islay

ISLAY

('Ile's island' from Norse, Ile may have been a Viking princess; pronounced 'Eye-la', not 'Eye-lay')

www.isle-of-islay.com
www.islay.co.uk
www.isleofislay.info
www.visit-islay.com
www.ileach.co.uk
www.islaywildlife.freeserve.co.uk
www.islaybirding.co.uk
www.visitscottishheartlands.com (AILLST)

Tourist Information Centre
Bowmore (08707 200610/01496 810254)
   Open Jan-Dec

Map Landranger sheet: 60 (HIH map page 127)

TRAVEL

A vehicle ferry (CalMac 01880 730253 Kennacraig;01496 840620 Port Askaig;01496 302209 Port Ellen; www.calmac.co.uk) leaves from Kennacraig (on the A83 Lochgilphead to Campbeltown road, five miles south-west of Tarbert) and sails to Port Askaig on the east coast or Port Ellen on the south coast of Islay. The crossing takes two hours five minutes or two hours twenty minutes respectively, and the service runs every day. Please note that all there is at Kennacraig is the ferry terminal: there are no amenities except public toilets.

There is also a service from Colonsay and Oban to Port Askaig on Islay.

Flights (Loganair 01667 462445; booking 0870 850 9850; www.ba.com) can be made to the island's airstrip at Glenegedale (Islay Airport 01496 302022; www.hial.co.uk/islay-airport.html; on A846 half way between Port Ellen and Bowmore) from Glasgow Airport (0141 887 1111). The service is twice daily from Mon-Sat, taking thirty-five minutes. Extra flights are operational in the summer.

From Port Askaig on Islay a vehicle ferry (Argyll and Bute Council 01496 840681) crosses to Jura. There are many crossings a day, taking around five minutes.

DESCRIPTION

Islay is one of the most beautiful of Scottish islands, and lies some twenty miles from the west coast of Kintyre and twenty three miles north of Northern Ireland. Jura is just to the west across the narrow Sound of Islay, and Colonsay and Oronsay are to the north.

Port Ellen

128

Islay is some twenty-five miles from south to north and nineteen miles from east to west, covering 246 square miles. A wide variety of landscapes is found here, from hills and rough moorland, sheltered woodland and good pasture, and sandy beaches to high cliffs and treacherous skerries. The climate is warm with frosts being rare and, along with the island having much good land, and its strategic importance being within easy reach of Scotland, England and Ireland, this was why Islay became very important in medieval times as the base of the Lords of the Isles.

The north-east and south-east are hilly, and the highest point is at Beinn Bheigier, 491 metres high, to the east and south of the island. There are beautiful beaches, such as Traigh Mhachir and Saligo Bay to the west of the island (currents can make bathing on these beaches dangerous), along with Laggan Bay and Traigh Cill an Rubha to the south and west. There are large tracts of peat, useful for fuel and for whisky distilling.

There are several very attractive villages and settlements, most of them planned, including Bowmore (at the head of Loch Indaal towards the middle of Islay) with its round church, leaving no corners for Satan to lurk in; Port Charlotte, a pretty village of 1828; Portnahaven; Port Wemyss (all three of which are on the east coast of the Rhinns of Islay) and Port Ellen (on the south coast). Other villages include Ballygrant (in the middle); Bridgend (east of Bowmore); Port Askaig (on the east coast); and Bunnahabhain (further north). The population of the island is around 3,400 people.

Islay is famous for the eight whisky distilleries on the island, producing millions of gallons of whisky in a year and generating huge amounts of duty and tax, leading some to claim that the island is the most heavily taxed part of Britain.

WILDLIFE

As many as 250 different species of birds have been reported, either living, breeding or visiting the island. These include barnacle, scaup and whitefronted geese, as well as golden eagles, guillemots, cormorants and shags, arctic terns, black throated and great northern divers, eider ducks and gannets, as well as choughs. There is a RSPB bird sanctuary at Loch Gruinart (to the north), where there is a visitor centre, a hide and a closed-circuit camera system to watch the birds. Walks and events are held throughout the year (01496 850505). There is another RSPB reserve at Upper Killeyan Farm on The Oa.

Other wildlife includes wild goats, red and roe deer; otters and seals around the coasts; and dolphins and porpoises offshore. Islay also has a wide range of plant species, including 900 species of flowering plants.

HISTORY

Islay has a wealth of prehistoric monuments, including many tall and impressive standing stones, not least the stone at Ballinaby, which is just less than five metres high (one of the tallest in Scotland); the broch at Dun Bhoraraic; and the extensive ramparts of the fort of Dun Nosebridge. The island was held by the Norsemen from the ninth century until 1156, and many place names date from this occupation. As mentioned above, the name Islay is reputed to be from the 'island of Ile', Ile being a Viking princess who died here and a standing stone to the east of Port Ellen, near Ardilistry Bay, is said to mark her grave.

Scattered across the island are the remains of ancient chapels and burial grounds, along with four upright carved crosses. The finest and oldest of these is the magnificent cross at Kildalton with a plainer example, the Thief's Cross, nearby; while the cross at Kilchoman is also impressive and beautifully carved. The fourth is at Kilnave (Cill Naoimh) on the western shore of Loch Gruinart, although it is broken and very weathered.

There was a kingdom of the isles, subject to Norway from about 900. Somerled was of mixed Norse and Celtic blood, and in the twelfth century he set about establishing himself along the western seaboard of Scotland. He wrested Islay, Jura and many other territories from the Vikings, and was powerful enough to assert himself against the kings of Scots. Raising a large army, he marched to Renfrew meaning to engage the forces of Malcolm IV. In what was apparently an act of treachery, he was assassinated in his tent before any battle could be fought.

His wide possessions passed to his sons: Kintyre and Islay to Reginald; Lorn, Mull and Jura to Dugald (from whom the MacDou-

Burial slab, Kildalton

galls were descended); and Bute, Arran and north Argyll to Angus.

There then followed a campaign by successive kings of Scots to make the western seaboard part of Scotland, and in 1263 the Norwegians were defeated at the Battle of Largs. Angus Og ('young Angus') MacDonald was grandson of Donald, a son of Reginald. Angus was a friend and supporter of Robert the Bruce, and fought with him at the Battle of Bannockburn in 1314. The MacDougalls had been enemies of Bruce, and the MacDonalds were to benefit at their expense, gaining much of their lands. Angus died at Finlaggan in 1328. His son, John of Islay, was the first of the family to use the title 'Lord of the Isles'.

The Lords of the Isles became extremely powerful, certainly enough to be a threat to the kings of Scots. The second Lord led a campaign which led to the bloody Battle of Harlaw in 1411, in a dispute over the Earldom of Ross; and the third Lord was twice imprisoned by James I. In 1461 John, fourth Lord and also the Earl of Ross, signed a pact with the English king, Edward IV, and the Earl of Douglas whereby they agreed to divide Scotland between them (Treaty of Westminster-Ardtornish, 1461). James IV was strong enough to confront the Lords, and brought forces to bear in 1493. The last of the MacDonalds to hold the title was forced to surrender himself, and was imprisoned in Paisley Abbey until his death in 1503.

The MacDonalds retained much of Islay and Jura, but the Rhinns of Islay were given to the MacLeans of Duart. The MacDonalds were angry and after much skirmishing this came to battle. The MacLeans landed on the island but were routed at the Battle of Traigh Gruinart in 1598. Lachlan MacLean of Duart, chief of his clan, was among the slain. The MacDonalds were not to profit from the fighting, however, and Islay was given to the Campbells of Cawdor in the reign of James VI.

The MacDonalds did all they could to re-establish their power, including seizing the island in 1615, but it all came to nothing. The Campbells could not be ousted. In May 1847, during the times of the Clearances, the *Exmouth*, a ship carrying emigrants to north America was shipwrecked on the north-west coast with the loss of hundreds of lives. During the First World War in 1918 two American troop carriers were torpedoed by a German submarine with the loss of 266 lives. A monument on the Mull of Oa (pronounced 'Oh') commemorates the tragedy.

As there are many treacherous rocks around the coast, several lighthouses were built around the island in the nineteenth century. Notable among these are the lighthouse on Orsay, a small island off the southern coast of the Rhinns of Islay, and those at Rhuvaal, MacArthur's Head and Loch Indaal.

The population of Islay was once 16,000, but this had reduced from 12,300 in 1851 to 7,375 in 1891 to around 3,400 today. Parts of Islay became depopulated in the nineteenth century, and there are the remains of the abandoned townships of Tokamal and Grasdal and Lurabus on The Oa.

Tours

PORT ELLEN TO KILDALTON (A846 AND UNLISTED ROAD)

Ferries from Kennacraig land at Port Ellen, the largest settlement on Islay; and in the village are hotels, shops, a cyber cafe (01496 302693) on Mansfield Place, and the dive centre. Port Ellen is a pleasant place, and was established in 1831 by Walter Frederick Campbell of Islay and named after his wife.

Several exceptionally tall standing stones lie to the north of the A846. Just to the east of Port Ellen, near the unlisted road to Kilbride, is a very tall standing stone [NR 372456], some three and a half metres high, said to commemorate the site of an ancient battle. At the end of this unlisted road, at Kilbride, is another three-metre stone [NR 384466], near the ruins of Kilbride Chapel [NR 384465], a rectangular building that was dedicated to St Bride. At Achnacarran are two impressive standing stones [NR 389461], one two and a half metres tall, the other, which is less lofty, is about six metres away. A third stone has fallen.

At Laphroaig is the first of the three distilleries along this stretch of road. Laphroaig Distillery was first founded in 1815, and the whisky produced here is probably the most distinctive of malts, with peaty, iodine and even medicinal flavours. The distillery is open to visitors by appointment only, and there is a shop (01496 302418; www.laphroaig.com).

A mile further east is Lagavulin with the second distillery and the remains of Dunyvaig Castle. Lagavulin Distillery is housed in a picturesque collection of white-washed buildings, and whisky production began here in 1816. It is open to the public also by appointment only, and there is a gift shop (01496 302400).

Nearby Dunyvaig Castle [NR 406455] is a crumbling and shattered ruin but remains a very lovely place. This was for centuries a stronghold of the MacDonalds, but passed to the MacIans, then to the Campbells with the MacDonalds as tenants. The MacDonalds were eventually forfeited following the Battle of Traigh Gruinart in 1598, and the island and castle were then held by the Campbells. The castle was besieged several times in the middle of the seventeenth century, and was occupied until about 1677 when the Campbells moved to Islay House near Bridgend.

The island of Texa lies just off the coast, and has the remains of an old chapel [NR 391438] as well as a holy well. A sculpted stone found here dates from the fourteenth century and has the inscription 'This is the cross of Reginald, son of John of Islay' from whom the MacDonalds of Clanranald were descended. The stone is now in the Museum of Scotland. Bluebells flourish on Texa in the spring, and there is a colony of feral goats.

The distillery at Ardbeg is just a mile beyond Lagavulin, and was also founded in 1815. Ardbeg is a peaty whisky, with sweetness from the malt. In the original kiln and malt barn are displays from the distillery's past, and along with a distillery tour there is a coffee shop and gift shop (open all year, Mon-Fri 10.00-16.00; Jun-Aug, daily 10.00-17.00; 01496 302244). A standing stone, at Clachan Ceann Ile [NR 437483], is said to mark the burial place of the Norse princess Ile but lies in woodland.

An unlisted road continues towards Ardtalla from the end of the A846. In a pleasant spot at Kildalton is probably the finest piece of early Christian sculpture in Scotland. The Kildalton Cross [NR 214631] dates from the eighth century, and the magnificent ringed cross is carved from a single slab of stone. Beneath the cross was reputedly found the remains of a Norse ritual killing when *Kildalton Cross*
the site was excavated in 1890. The adjacent ruinous chapel was dedicated to St John, and within the walls are carved medieval graveslabs, some with stone effigies of knights. Also nearby, enclosed by railings, is the fine fifteenth-century Thief's Cross, presumably marking an area of sanctuary for criminals and debtors.

Off the unlisted road at Trudernish is Dun Trudernish [NR 468526], a prehistoric fort on a promontory, defended by three walls, one of which is vitrified in places.

PORT ELLEN TO THE OA (UNLISTED ROAD)

The Oa (pronounced 'Oh') is the peninsula to the west of Port Ellen.

One mile from Port Ellen is Kilnaughton [NR 344452], the remains of a fifteenth-century chapel in a lovely spot. The site was dedicated to St Nechtan, and there are several medieval sculpted graveslabs. The road runs past an excavated chambered cairn [NR 329451] at Lower Cragabus, and a two-metre-high standing stone at Glac a' Charraigh [NR 297432] beyond Lenavore.

There is a monument [NR 270416] to the 266 American service personnel who were killed near here when the ship *Tuscania* was torpedoed by the Germans during the First World War in 1918. Many more lives were lost when the *Otranto* sank in a storm the same year after colliding with another ship when in a convoy. There is car parking near the monument, and the RSPB have a reserve at Upper Killeyan Farm, a good place to see choughs. There are some remains of Dun Athad [NR 284406], on a stack connected to the mainland by a narrow ridge above the sea, a mile or so south-east of Upper Killeyan. This was first built during the Iron Age, but was used by Sir James MacDonald when he tried to reclaim the island for his clan in 1615.

By the unlisted road to Kintra at Carraigh Bhan is a large standing stone [NR 328478], more than two metres in height. This is said to mark the burial place of the Viking King of Man, Godred Crovan.

The Oa once had some 4,000 inhabitants, now the population of the whole of Islay; and there are abandoned townships near the north coast at Grasdal and

Tokamal [NR 300476 & NR 300472] with an old chapel [NR 299474], reached along a track from Kintra; and the south coast at Lurabus [NR 337435], accessed by a footpath from the track beside the chapel at Kilnaughton.

PORT ELLEN TO BOWMORE AND BRIDGEND (A846 OR B8016)

The A846 (Low Road) runs inland from the sandy beach along the coast of Laggan Bay, and past the island's golf course at Machrie (Islay Golf Club 0141 580 6091/ 01496 300094 www.btinternet.com/-islay.golf/), where there is also a hotel. At Glenegedale is the airport (01496 302361), where there is a cafe.

Bowmore is a pretty village, dominated by the round parish (the parish is Killarrow) church and bell-tower at the top of Main Street, which was built in 1767 and has no corners in which the devil can lurk. The building can hold 500 people (open all year, 9.00-18.00). The village was laid out a year after the building of church, as the Campbells wanted to move the villagers away from their mansion, Islay House, which is near Bridgend.

Another attraction is Bowmore Distillery, one of the oldest in Scotland and first licensed in 1779. Along with guided tours, there is a video explaining the production of whisky and a gift shop (open May-Sep, Mon-Fri guided tours 11.30-15.00, Sat 10.30; closed Sun; Oct-Apr, Mon-Fri 10.30 and 14.00; groups by appointment; 01496 810441; www.morrisonbowmore.co.uk). The waste water from the distillery is used to warm the water for the village's Mactaggart Leisure Centre, with a twenty-five metre swimming pool with a sauna and launderette (01496 810767).

Bowmore has a range of shops (including C & E Roy's Celtic House www.roysceltichouse.com; 01496 810304; and Islay Celtic Crafts), a post office, hotels and bars, and eating places, including an Indian restaurant.

Dun Nosebridge [NR 372603], to the south-west of Bowmore, is a very impressive fort defended by a series of earthen ramparts and a wall.

At Bridgend is a hotel and shop, and the burial ground of Killarrow [NR 335625], near the policies of the impressive Islay House, the seat of the Campbells and dating from 1677. In the cemetery are several fine carved burial slabs, one with the stone effigy of a clergyman. Near Bridgend is Elizabeth Sykes Batiks (01496 810147 for opening times), the Candle and Card Shop, and Islay Quilters in Islay House Square. Islay House is not open to the public.

The B8016 (High Road) runs across the island from the turn-off from the A846 near Port Ellen, rejoining the A846 between Bridgend and Bowmore. The road crosses Duich Moss, a wide expanse of peat moorland, which is a National Nature Reserve.

BRIDGEND TO PORT ASKAIG AND BUNNAHABHAIN (A846 AND UNLISTED ROAD)

At Bridgend is a hotel and shop. Just beyond the village is a turn-off for the Islay Woollen Mill [NR 352632], an early Victorian mill, which produces a range of woollen products (including the tartan for the film *Braveheart*) for sale, and has an original spinning jenny and weaving demonstrations (01496 810563; www.islay woollenmill.co.uk; open all year, closed Sun).

Before Ballygrant is Kilmeny Parish Church [NR 353636], which stands in wooded grounds and lies a quarter of a mile from its medieval predecessor [NR 388653]. The church dates from 1828 (open Jul-Aug, Thu 10.30-12.30 and 1400-16.00).

Three miles south of Port Askaig, off tracks in the Dunlossit Estate (from whom permission to visit can be sought), are the remains of Dun Bhoraraic [NR 417658], an impressive broch on a small hill, which was later reused by the MacDonalds as a stronghold in the seventeenth century.

133

Finlaggan

Finlaggan [NR 388681], reached by unlisted roads from the A846, is now a quiet and pleasant place, but was once the seat of the powerful MacDonald Lord of the Isles. They had a large and sophisticated court, but all that remains are ruins and foundations on Eilean Mor, the bigger of the islands in Loch Finlaggan, and on Eilean na Comhairle ('island of council'). Several carved slabs marked the burials of relatives of the Lords of the Isles, who were themselves buried in St Oran's Chapel on Iona. Excavations and consolidations are ongoing, and on the shore is a visitor centre with finds from the islands (01496 810629; www.islay.com; open Apr-Oct; confirm opening). The islands are connected to the mainland by a wooden board walk.

At Keills, a mile west of Port Askaig is the shaft of a carved cross [NR 417687] and nearby is a ruined chapel [NR 415686], which was dedicated to St Columba.

Just after Keills is the turn-off onto an unlisted road for the quiet village of Bunnahabhain, where another distillery is located. Near the turn-off is the Persabus Pottery (01496 840753; www.persabuspottery.co.uk). Bunnahabhain Distillery is the most northerly of the Islay distilleries, and there are wonderful views across the Sound of Islay to the Paps of Jura. The distillery is open to visitors by appointment all year, and also has a gift shop (01496 840646). By the shore, to the south of the village, is the wreck of the *Wyre Majestic*, its rusting hull particularly evocative against the backdrop of the Paps of Jura.

Caol Isla, another distillery, is reached from another unlisted road from the A846, and it also stands in a pleasant location by the sea. It was founded in 1846, and the whisky, along with its own malt, is used in the Bells brand. There is a visitor centre and gift shop, and tours of the distillery are available by appointment (01496 840207).

Port Askaig has a sixteenth-century hotel and a shop, and the ferry from Kennacraig and Colonsay and Oban calls in here. The ferry across to Jura also leaves from here. The Lifeboat Station is regularly open to the public (01496 840245).

BRIDGEND TO PORTNAHAVEN AND KILCHIARAN (A847 AND UNLISTED ROAD)

Beyond the turn-off for the B8017, just to the north of the A847, is a three-metre-high standing stone [NR 294634].

Bruichladdich lies on the coast and is the site of another distillery, which was founded in 1881. Tours of the distillery are available by appointment (01496 850821).

At the pretty village of Port Charlotte is the excellent Museum of Islay Life (open Apr-Oct, Mon-Sat 10.00-17.00, Sun 14.00-17.00; 01496 850358/310), housed in an old church and with displays covering all aspects of island life, including an important collection of carved stones. There is also a library as well as extensive archives. Also in the village is the Islay Natural History Trust (01496 850288; www.islaywildlife.freeserve.co.uk; open Apr-Oct daily 10.00-15.00, except closed Sat and Wed, open Jul-Aug until 17.00) with displays, a good library and a lecture room. The Croft Kitchen, a cafe, is open in the summer; and there is a large hotel.

Just south of the village, to the east of the A847 near the shore, is a disturbed chambered burial cairn [NR 248576]. The remains of the chambers can be traced, and finds from excavations here are in the Museum of Islay Life.

At Nerabus [NR 225549] is an ancient burial ground with a collection of fine medieval graveslabs, dating from the fourteenth and fifteenth centuries. The graveslabs have been raised up for protection. Nearby are the ruins of a small chapel.

Portnahaven and Port Wemyss are two more attractive villages lying further to the south.

To the west of the unlisted road between Portnahaven and Kilchiaran are the remains of Cultoon (or Coultoon) Stone Circle [NR 224604]. This small circle stands in a fine location, but perhaps the most interesting thing about it is that it was abandoned in the middle of being built. Sockets for stones have been located, but the stones were never erected.

Kilchiaran is in a beautiful location, and there are the ruins of Kilchiaran Chapel [NR 204602] along with several carved graveslabs and the base of a cross-shaft. The dedication was to St Kieran or Ciaran, but one tale has St Columba landing here (as on Colonsay) after leaving Ireland in exile, but then continuing his journey north as Ireland could still be seen from the hills of Islay.

Off the unlisted road between Kilchiaran and Port Charlotte is a prominent standing stone [NR 224604], around three metres tall; while another tall stone [NR 211594] lies to the south of Kilchiaran in Gleann Droighneach.

BRIDGEND TO KILCHOMAN AND KILNAVE (B8017, B8018 AND UNLISTED ROADS)

The RSPB Nature Reserve is at Loch Gruinart, where there is a hide, a visitor centre and toilets, as well as weekly guided walks on a Thursday from May-October (visitor centre open all year, 10.00-17.00; 01496 850505).

Near Loch Gruinart are several sites associated with the Battle of Traigh Gruinart. This took place in 1598, when a force of MacLeans was defeated by the MacDonalds. Lachlan MacLean of Duart, chief of the MacLeans, was killed and a small stone, Clach Mhic-'Illean [NR 274674], north of B8017 between Gruinart and Loch Gorm, marks where he was buried. Following the battle, a remnant of the MacLeans sheltered in Kilnave Chapel [NR 285715], on the western shore of Loch Gruinart, which was then burned down and all of them perished except one man. By the chapel is a broken and very weathered cross, which dates from about 750.

In Loch Gorm, which has good fishing, are the slight remains of Gorm Castle [NR 235655], built in the fifteenth century. This was held by the MacDonalds, but passed with the Rhinns to the MacLeans. It was besieged by the MacDonalds in 1598, used by them in 1615, then garrisoned by the Campbells at least until the 1640s.

A large prehistoric burial cairn [NR 240672] lies just east of the road at Carnduncan, some sixteen metres in diameter and two metres high.

Taking the unlisted road to Kilchoman, at Ballinaby, and in a prominent position, is one of the most striking standing stones [NR 219672] in Scotland (approach by foot from Ballinaby farm). It is very thin but around five metres tall; another three metre stone is positioned nearby. The stone is said to have been used to track phases of the moon.

Kilchoman stands in a lovely location above the sands of Traigh Mhachir. In the burial ground of the now derelict church is the elegantly carved Kilchoman Cross [NR 214631]. One side has a depiction of the Crucifixion, with horseman and knotwork. At the foot of the cross are four indentations and a stone. The stone should be placed in the indentations sunwise for good luck or for the granting of wishes. The cross is said to have been raised to commemorate Margaret, second wife of John of Islay, although it appears to date from the fifteenth century. There are also several carved

Kilchoman Cross

memorials, and the Sanctuary Cross. At Rock-side farm is the Kilchoman Distillery (01496 850011; www.kilchomandistillery.com; open Mar-Oct, Mon-Sat 10.00-17.00; Jul-Aug, daily 10.00-17.00; tour times 11.00 and 15.00; winter, bookings by appt only), a small independent farm-sized distillery with a visitor centre, cafe and shop.

Beyond the end of the B8018 is a fine beach at Sanaigmore, while to the west at Alt nan Ba [NR 218712] is a promontory defended by a series of walls on the landward side. The wall survives to a height of just less than two metres, and the entrance can be seen. On the promontory is a roofed beehive cell, and this is presumably the remains of an early Christian monastery within an older fort.

HOTELS AND GUEST HOUSES

Abbotsford Guest House (01496 850587)
 Bruichladdich; guest house; open all year
Ballygrant Inn and Restaurant (01496 840277;
 www.ballygrant-inn.co.uk)
 Ballygrant; hotel and restaurant; open all year
Bowmore Hotel (01496 810416;
 www.bowmorehotel.co.uk)
 Bowmore; hotel and restaurant
The Bothy (01496 302391)
 Port Ellen; guest house; open all year
Bridgend Hotel (01496 810212; www.bridgend-
 hotel.com)
 Bridgend; hotel, restaurant and bar; open
 all year
Glenegedale House (01496 302147;
 www.glenegedalehouse.co.uk)
 Glenegedale, near Port Ellen; hotel in
 seventeenth-century farmhouse; open all year

Glenmachrie Country Guest House (01496
 302560; www.glenmachrie.com)
 Port Ellen; guest house in family-run
 farmhouse; open all year
Greenside Guest House (01496 810615)
 Cruach, fourteen miles from Bowmore; B&B
Harbour Inn and Restaurant (01496 810330;
 www.harbour-inn.com)
 Bowmore; hotel and restaurant; open all year
Kilmeny Country Guest House (01496 840668;
 www.kilmeny.co.uk)
 Ballygrant; dinner, B&B ; open all year
Lambeth House Guest House (01496 810597)
 Centre of island; guest house
Lochindaal Hotel (01496 850202)
 Port Charlotte; hotel
Lochside Hotel (01496 810245/4?;
 www.lochsidehotel.co.uk)
 Bowmore; hotel; open all year

Machrie Hotel (01496 302310; www.machrie.com)
Machrie, between Port Ellen and Bowmore; hotel dating from 250 years ago; golf course; self-catering cottages also available; open all year

Marine Hotel (01496 810324)
Bowmore; hotel

Meadowside (01496 810479)
Bowmore; guest house

Port Askaig Hotel (01496 840245; www.portaskaig.co.uk)
Port Askaig; 400-year-old inn and bars; open all year

Port Charlotte Hotel (01496 850360; www.portcharlottehotel.co.uk)
Port Charlotte; hotel and restaurant; open all year except 25/26 Dec

Trout Fly Guest House (01496 302204)
Port Ellen; guest house; open all year

White Hart Hotel (01496 300120; www.whiteharthotelislay.com)
Port Ellen; hotel

BED AND BREAKFAST

Anchorage (01496 850540)
Bruichladdich; B&B

Askernish (01496 302536; www.islay.co.uk/askernish/)
Port Ellen; B&B

Carraig Fhada Farm (01496 302114)
The Oa; B&B

Caladh Sona (01496 302694; www.islay-maltwhisky.co.uk)
Port Ellen; B&B; open Mar-Oct

Ceol na Mara (01496 850371)
Bruichladdich; open Mar-Nov

66 Frederick Crescent (01496 302420)
Port Ellen; B&B

Kintra Farmhouse (01496 302051; www.kintrafarm.co.uk)
Port Ellen; B&B, bunkhouse and camping and caravan site

Loch Gruinart House (01496 850212)
Gruinart; B&B; open all year

Lyrabus Croft (01496 850374)
Gruinart; B&B

The Monachs (01496 850049; www.islayguesthouse.co.uk)
Nerabus, near Port Charlotte; B&B; open all year except Xmas and New Year

Mulindry Cottages (01496 810397)
Bridgend; B&B

Octofad (01496 850225)
Nerabus by Port Charlotte; B&B

Old School House (01496 860242)
Portnahaven; B&B

Shieling (01496 810634)
Bowmore; B&B; open all year

Sornbank (01496 810544; www.sornbank.co.uk)
Bridgend; B&B; also self-catering; open all year

Tigh na Suil (01496 302483)
Lagavulin; B&B

SELF-CATERING PROPERTIES

Ardtalla Estate Holiday Cottages (01496 302441; www.ardtallacottages.co.uk)
Ardtalla estate; four individual self-catering properties

Ballimony Cottage (01496 860354; www.ballimonycottage.co.uk)
Portnahaven; self-catering cottage, sleeps five Ballimony

Ballivicar Farm (01496 302251; www.ballivicar.co.uk)
Port Ellen; two self-catering apartments, sleeping four and two; open all year

Black Park (01496 810376; www.assc.co.uk/blackparkcroft/index.shtml)
Bridgend; self-catering house, sleeps eight & two self-catering flats, sleeps four

Bowmore (01496 810235; www.lagganestate.co.uk)
Bowmore; self-catering lodge and two bungalows, sleep four-ten

Bowmore Distillery Cottages (01496 810671; www.bowmore.com)
Bowmore; five cottages; open all year

Bridgend Hotel (01496 810212; www.bridgend-hotel.com)
Bridgend; self-catering cottage, sleeps ten

Cardhu Cottage (01496 810729; www.cardhucottage.co.uk)
Bowmore; self-catering cottage, sleeps six

Carnain Cottage (0131 347 8853; www.islay-holidays.co.uk)
Bridgend; self-catering cottage, sleeps six

Clachan (01496 810440; www.clachancottages.co.uk)
Two self-catering cottages, sleep four-six

Coillabus Cottage (0131 553 1911; www.islay-cottage.co.uk)
Port Ellen; self-catering cottage, sleeps six-eight

The Corran (01496 850434; www.ileach.co.uk/calasith)
Port Charlotte; self-catering house, sleeps six

Corray Cottage Self Catering (01496 810229; www.corrary.co.uk)
Bowmore; self-catering cottage, sleeps five

Coullabus Keepers Cottage (01496 810293; www.keeperscottageislay.co.uk)
Bridgend; self-catering cottage, sleeps six

Coull Farm (01496 850317)
Self-catering cottage and flat

Craigard Apartments (01496 810728; www.craigard-islay.co.uk)
Ballygrant; self catering cottage and three flats
Prices :

Cross House West Holiday Cottage (07798 695764; www.crosshousewest.freeserve.co.uk)
Bridgend; self-catering, sleeps six-eight

Cuil Sith (01496 302560)
Ballygrant; self-catering, sleeps four; open all year

Easter Ellister Farmhouse (01506 881046; www.easterelister.co.uk)
Portnahaven; self-catering accommodation

Glenmachrie Country Guest House (01496 302560; www.glenmachrie.com)
Self-catering caravan, sleeps six
Helenvale Cottage (0141 8814439)
Port Charlotte; self catering, sleeps six-eight
The Inns (01496 810532; www.theinnsoverby.co.uk)
Bowmore; four self-catering flats
Islay Rhind (01496 810532)
Bowmore; four self-catering flats, sleep four-six
Kilchoman House Cottages (01496 850382; www.kilchomancottages.co.uk)
Near Bruichladdich; six self-catering cottages; open all year
Kintra Farmhouse (01496 302051; www.kintrafarm.co.uk)
Port Ellen; three self-catering cottages; sleep four-six, four and six; open all year
Knocklearach Farm (01496 840209)
Ballygrant; self-contained apartments, sleep three-eight; open all year
The Little House, Glenegedale (01496 302030; www.islayselfcatering.com)
Port Ellen: self-catering; open all year.
Lochindaal Hotel (01496 850202)
Port Charlotte; self-catering cottage
Lochindaal House (01835 870779)
Port Charlotte; self-catering house (lighthouse keeper's house), sleeps six
Lochview Cottage (01496 810147)
Port Charlotte; self-catering, sleeps four
Lorgba Holiday Cottages (01496 850208)
Port Charlotte; five self-catering cottages, sleep two-six; open all year
Neriby Farm (01496 810274)
Bridgend; self-catering cottage, sleeps six; open all year
Newton Cottage (01496 810414)
Bowmore; two self-catering flats, sleep four
Octomore Farm Self Catering (01496 850235)
Port Charlotte; self-catering farm cottage, sleeps six
Persabus Farm Cottage and Pottery (01496 840243; www.persabus.co.uk)
Port Askaig; self-catering farmhouse, sleeps six
Port Askaig Apartment (01496 840245; www.portaskaig.co.uk)
Port Askaig, sleeps four-five
School House (01496 302030; www.islayselfcatering.com)
Self-catering accommodation; two properties: The Annexe and the Little House, both sleep four; open all year
Sgioba House (01496 850334)
Self-catering studio cottage, sleeps two-four
9 Shore Street (0141 956 5743; www.zyworld.com)
Port Charlotte; self-catering flat, sleeps four
Sornbank (01496 810544; www.sornbank.co.uk)
Bridgend; self-catering, also B&B; two flats; open all year
Tigh Cargaman (01496 302345; www.tighcargaman.com)
Port Ellen; three self-catering cottages, sleep two-four
Tigh-Na-Speur (01496 810592)
Loch Gruinart; self-catering, sleeps six

HOSTELS AND RETREATS

Islay Youth Hostel (01496 850385; www.syha.org.uk)
Port Charlotte; housed in former distillery, sleeps forty-two; open May-Sep
Kintra Bunk Barns Hotel (01496 302051; www.kintrafarm.co.uk)
Near Port Ellen; B&B, bunk house (open Apr-Sep), and camping and caravan site

CAMPING AND CARAVANS

Kintra Farmhouse (01496 302051; www.kintrafarm.co.uk)
Port Ellen; campsite and caravan site, facilities; open Apr-Sep

PLACES TO EAT

Also see list of hotels and guest houses

An Sabhal (01496 860308)
Portnahaven; bar meals; open Mar-Oct
Cottage Restaurant (01496 810422)
Bowmore; licensed restaurant, coffee shop and takeaway; open all year, Mon-Sat
The Croft Kitchen (01496 810422)
Port Charlotte; licensed restaurant; open Apr-Oct

Further Information

TRANSPORT

BUSES
Service 450
Portnahaven to Ardbeg to Portnahaven
Service 451
Port Askaig to Ardbeg to Port Askaig
Service 456
Port Askaig to Bowmore to Port Askaig
CYCLE HIRE
(see www.thewashingmachinepost.net for information about cycling on Islay)
Bowmore post office (01496 810366)
Bowmore; cycle hire
Macaulay and Torrie (01496 302053)
Port Ellen; cycle hire
Mick Stuart (01496 302391)
Port Ellen; cycle hire
Mountain Bike Hire (01496 850488)
Port Charlotte; cycle hire
Port Ellen Playing Fields Association (07831 246911)
Open May-Sep, daily 12.00-21.00; also putting, tennis, pitch and putt, bowls, refreshments
TAXIS
Carol Macdonald (01496 302155/0777 5782155; www.carols-cabs.co.uk)
Fiona's Taxis (01496 302622/07808 303200)
Lamont Campbell Taxis (01496 810449/07899 756159)
Jim Davis (01496 810398/07762 590055)

CAR HIRE
McKenzie (01496 810206)
Bowmore
D. & N. Mackenzie (01496 302300)
Glenegedale (airport)

ACTIVITIES AND SPORTS

GOLF
Islay Golf Club (01415 806091/01496 300094;
www.btinternet.com/-islay.golf/)
Machrie; eighteen-hole course (also see
Machrie Hotel)
SPORT
Port Ellen Playing Fields
Open May-Sep, daily 12.00-21.00; putting,
tennis, pitch and putt, bowls, refreshments,
cycle hire
MacTaggart Leisure Centre (01496 810767)
Bowmore; twenty-five metre swimming pool
with a sauna and launderette
DIVING
There are many wrecks around the coasts
BOAT TRIPS
Islay Sea Safari (07768 450000;
www.islayseasafari.co.uk)
Charter trips around the islands and distilleries
BIRD WATCHING
RSPB Nature Reserve: Loch Gruinart (01496
850505)
Visitor centre and toilets open all year, daily
10:00 17:00; guided walks, May -Oct, Thu
10:00; Nov-Apr, please book in advance
Islay Birding (01496 850010;
www.islaybirding.co.uk)
Port Charlotte; daily birding safaris and bush-
craft courses
WALKING
Walkers Information Line (01496 810810)
Year-round outdoor information: a message
gives details of stalking, outdoor activities and
sensitive areas; calls charged at normal rates
NATURAL HERITAGE
Scottish Natural Heritage (01496 810711)
Main Street, Bowmore; a guide to wildlife and
landscapes available
Islay Wildlife Information Centre (01496 850288)
Port Charlotte; open Apr-Oct daily 10.00-
15.00, except closed Sat and Wed, open Jul-Aug
until 17.00
PONY TREKKING
Ballivicar Farm Pony Trekking (01496 302251;
www.ballivicar.co.uk)
Ballvicar Farm, Port Ellen; all ages and abilities
Rockside Trekking Centre (01496 850231)
Rockside Farm; all ages and abilities
SHOOTING
Islay Estates (01496 810221)
Stalking
Cultoon Shooting Ground (01496 860323;
www.cultoonshootingground.co.uk)
Cultoon Farm, Portnahaven; open all year, PM
Also enquire locally
FISHING AND ANGLING
Dunlossit Estate (01496 840232)

Foreland Estates (01496 850211)
Islay Estates (01496 810221)
Islay Marine Charters (01496 850 436;
www.islaymarinecharters.co.uk)
Sea fishing
Port Ellen Angling Association (01496 302264)

LOCAL PRODUCE

Bunnahabhain (pronounced Bu-na-ha-ven) (01496
840646)
Bunnahabhain; guided tours by arrangement
Caol Ila (pronounced Coll-eela) (01496 840207)
Port Askaig; guided tours by arrangement
Bowmore (01496 810441;
www.morrisonbowmore.co.uk)
Bowmore; open for guided tours May-Sep
except Sun, 11.30-15.00; Oct-Apr, Mon-Fri
10.30 and 14.00 only
Bruichladdich (pronounced Broo-ich-laddie)
(01496 850821)
Bruichladdich; guided tours by arrangement
Kilchoman (pronounced Kilhoman) (01496
850011; www.kilchomandistillery.com)
Rockside farm, near Bruichladdich; farm
distillery with visitor centre, cafe and shop;
open Mar-Oct, Mon-Sat, 10.00-17.00; Jul-Aug,
daily 10.00-17.00; tour times 11.00 and 15.00;
winter, bookings by appt only
Ardbeg (01496 302244)
Ardbeg; open all year, Mon-Fri 10.00-16.00;
Jun-Aug 10.00-17.00; last full tour 15.30; also by
appointment
Lagavulin (pronounced Lag-a-voo-lin) (01496
302400)
Near Port Ellen; open all year but tours by
appointment only
Laphroaig (pronounced La-froyg) (01496 302418;
www.laphroaig.com)
Near Port Ellen; open all year but tours by
appointment only
Islay Whisky Shop (01496 810684;
www.islaywhiskyshop.com)
Bowmore; specialises in Islay whisky
Islay Whisky Society
(www.islaywhiskysociety.com)
Ballygrant

Islay Fine Food Company
Rockside Farm; smoked food and fresh local
meat

ARTS AND CRAFTS

C & E Roy's Celtic House (01496 810304;
www.roysceltichouse.com)
Bowmore; arts events
Elizabeth Sykes Batiks (01496 810147)
Purchase from the Machrie shop or from the
Batik studio at Islay House Square near
Bridgend
Islay Craft Shop and Gallery
Bowmore; range of locally produced paintings
and crafts, souvenirs and gifts

Islay Heathers Gift Shop (01496 302147)
Port Charlotte; workshop and shop selling
crafts and gifts; open all year
Islay Woollen Mill (01496 810563;
www.islaywoollenmill.co.uk)
Bridgend; rare Slubbing Billy in seventeenth-
century mill; weaving demonstrations; scarves,
caps, skirts, jackets, rugs and much more
Persabus Pottery (01496 840753;
www.persabuspottery.co.uk)
Port Askaig; hand-crafted jugs, vases and
bowls; can be purchased on-line

Islay Arts and Crafts Guild (01496 30254)
Organises arts and crafts fairs

VISITOR ATTRACTIONS AND MUSEUMS

Also see the whisky section in Local produce

Finlaggan (01496 810629; www.islay.com)
Finlaggan; remains of building associated with
the Lords of the Isles on two islands; visitor
centre; open Apr-Sep: tel. to confirm opening
Museum of Islay Life (01496 850358/310)
Port Charlotte; museum with displays on all
aspects of island life; library and extensive
archives; open Apr-Oct, Mon-Sat 10.00-17.00,
Sun 14.00-17.00

EVENTS

Islay Festival of Malt and Music
(www.islayfestival.org)   May/June
Islay Half-Marathon (www.islayhalfmarathon.co.uk)
                                           August
Jazz Festival (www.islayjazzfestival.co.uk)
                                           September

FURTHER READING

Birds of Islay: A Celebration in Photographs
(Langsbury, Gordon and Malcolm Ogilvie)
Lochindaal Press, 2006
*The Book of Islay: Documents Illustrating the History of
the Land* (Smith, G. Gregory (ed.))
1895
Dive Islay Wrecks (Blackburn, Steve)
Bucknall Publications, 1986
The Early History of Islay (Lamont, W. D.)
Burns and Harris, 1966
A Guide to Islay and Jura (Booth, C. Gordon)
1984
Islay (Newton, Norman S.)
David and Charles (Pevensey), 1995
Islay and Jura (Robertson, George)
Birlinn, 2006
Islay, Jura and Colonsay: A Historical Guide
(Caldwell, David)
Birlinn, 2001
Islay: Biography of an Island (Storrie, Margaret C.)
House of Lochar, 1997
*Peat Smoke and Spirit: A Portrait of Islay and Its
Whiskies* (Jefford, Andrew)
Headline, 2005

ACKNOWLEDGMENTS

Thanks to Brian Palmer at Ileach.co.uk, Colin
Roy at the Celtic House and Katherine
Urquhart for checking over the text

Paps of Jura and the Sound of Islay from Islay

Jura, and Colonsay and Oronsay

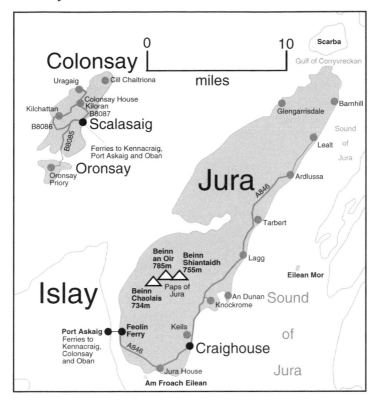

Colonsay

0 ——————— 10

miles

Scarba

Gulf of Corryvreckan

Uragaig · Cill Chaitriona

Colonsay House
Kiloran
Kilchattan · B8087

B8086 · Scalasaig

B8085

Ferries to Kennacraig,
Port Askaig and Oban

Oronsay

Oronsay
Priory

Islay

Jura

Glengarrisdale

Barnhill

Sound

Lealt of

Jura

Ardlussa

A846

Tarbert

Beinn
an Oir
785m
Beinn
Shiantaidh
755m

Lagg

Eilean Mor

Beinn
Chaolais
734m
Paps of
Jura

An Dunan Sound
Knockrome

Port Askaig · Feolin
Ferry
Ferries to
Kennacraig,
Colonsay
and Oban

A846

Keils

of

Craighouse

Jura House

Am Froach Eilean

Jura

Feolin Ferry, Jura

141

JURA

(from Norse 'dyr-ey', 'deer island' or 'Doirad's island'; perhaps 'udder island', also from Norse (the Paps of Jura); or from the giants Diu and Ra; pronounced 'Joora')

www.theisleofjura.co.uk
www.juradevelopment.co.uk
www.jura.visit-islay.com
www.visitscottishheartlands.com (AILLST)

Tourist Information Centre
Bowmore (08707 200610/01496 810254)
    Open Jan-Dec

Map Landranger sheet: 61 (HIH map page 141)

TRAVEL

The vehicle ferry (Argyll and Bute Council 10496 840681) leaves from Port Askaig (A846) on Islay (also see section on Islay) to Feolin Ferry on Jura. The crossing takes only a few minutes, with up to eighteen crossings on weekdays and six on Sundays. There are no facilities at Feolin Ferry except a telephone and public toilets and a new research centre, although there is a hotel and shop at Port Askaig.

Boat trips also go to Jura from Crinan (www.gemini-crinan.co.uk) and from Colonsay (*Lady Jayne of Colonsay*, contact: 01951 200320; www.colonsay.org.uk). Sea.fari at Easdale also run trips to the Corryvreckan Whirlpool, which lies off the north coast of Jura.

DESCRIPTION

Jura is the fourth biggest of the islands, and is one of the last great wildernesses in Great Britain. The island covers more than 150 square miles, but has a population of less than 180 people, although more than 4,500-5,500 deer. The climate is very mild and frosts are rare (palm trees are grown at Craighouse), although it can be windy and wet.

Jura lies just four miles from the west coast of Argyll at its northern end, and just east of Islay. It is some twenty-eight miles from north to south and eight miles wide at most. Jura is almost cut in two at Tarbert, about midway up the island, where the land is only one mile between the sea at Tarbert Bay and Loch Tarbert.

Most of the island is very rugged and rough and dramatic. The south is dominated by the three Paps

Paps of Jura

('breasts', from their apparent resemblance to such things) of Jura, the highest hills on the island. Beinn an Oir ('mountain of gold') rises to 785 metres, while Beinn Shiantaidh ('holy or storm mountain') is 755 metres and Beinn Chaolais ('mountain of the kyle') is 734 metres; from their summits it is possible to see Ireland and even the Isle of Man on a clear day. The north end is not as high but is more remote, and the main road runs out just north of Lealt. The south and east of the island has better land, and there are several large forestry plantations and areas of woodland.

Excellent sandy beaches are dotted along the coasts, although some in very out-of-the-way places, as well as caves, arches, raised beaches and cliffs. The unspoilt west coast is especially beautiful. To the north of Jura, between it and the island of Scarba, is the famous Corryvreckan (from Corrie Bhreacan, the 'cauldron of Breckan') Whirlpool. It is most impressive when there is a westerly or southerly wind. Boat trips are available to the whirlpool from Seil and Crinan: care should be taken – George Orwell was nearly drowned here.

The only settlement is at Craighouse, which has a shop, a post office, a hotel, and a distillery. The main road (A846) runs around the south side and then up the east coast. It is single track but easily passable by cars, although caravans are not recommended; the west and north only has a few rough tracks (where there are any paths at all). Jura is divided into eight sporting estates, and much of the land is used for hunting and shooting.

WILDLIFE

As mentioned above, there are many red deer on the island, but otters and seals can also be seen around the coasts; and there are also wild goats, hares, stoats and many rabbits. Many birds visit or live on the island, including snipe, golden eagles, sea eagles, falcons, owls, buzzards and choughs, and many seabirds such as puffins.

HISTORY

Jura was occupied at least from Mesolithic times, and there are many prehistoric sites to the south and east of the island, including standing stones, burial cairns and forts and duns. Tradition has it that there was a battle in 768 (or perhaps 678) between the Britons and the Scots from Ireland. Jura was long held by the Vikings, although the only evidence of their presence is in some place names and burials.

Like Islay and much of the western seaboard, Jura was one of the possessions of the MacDonald Lord of the Isles after Somerled had driven out the Norsemen. Jura passed to Reginald his son, then to his grandson Donald, from whom the MacDonalds were descended. The clan had a stronghold, Claig Castle, on the small island Am Fraoch Eilean, which sits in the mouth of the Sound of Islay, and it was from here they are said to have extorted payment out of people needing to use the sound. Even after the fall of the Lord of the Isles, the MacDonalds of Dunyvaig retained Jura but, like so much else of Argyll, it eventually came into the possession of the Campbells.

The north of Jura was a property of the MacLeans, whose seat was at Aros Castle in Glen Garrisdale. The Campbells accused the MacLeans of raiding their lands, and in 1647 a battle ended in the rout and defeat of the MacLeans. Apart from Ardlussa, the whole island was held by the Campbells. It has since been divided and sold off. The population was never large as there is a shortage of good land, but it has dwindled from around 1,300 in the middle of the nineteenth century to less than 200 today.

Jura is also associated with George Orwell, who stayed at Barnhill on the north of the island between 1946 and 1949. Here he wrote his famous novel *1984* (the

143

house is not open to the public). The famous Corryvreckan whirlpool can be seen from the northern tip of Jura: Orwell was nearly drowned when travelling around Jura in 1949.

Tours
FEOLIN FERRY TO CRAIGHOUSE (A846)

The ferry crosses from Islay to Feolin Ferry, where there are public toilets but little else except for the Feolin Centre, across the narrow Sound of Islay. The Feolin Centre (director@theisleofjura.co.uk) is a new research facility, which survives on donations by supportive islanders and has no public funding; it has the largest database on Jura anywhere in the world.

The only road is single track but quite passable. To the south of the road, near Camus an Staca, is a prominent three-metre-high standing stone [NR 464048]. Further along the coast, off the road, is the island of Am Fraoch Eilean, which has the remains of Claig Castle [NR 472627]. The stronghold of the MacDonalds dates from the thirteenth century and was still in use in the sixteenth century, reputedly as a prison. The castle was also used to extort tolls from shipping using the sound. The MacDonald clan slogan is 'Fraoch Eilean'.

At Ardfin is Jura House Walled Garden [NR 486636], which has a wide variety of unusual plants and shrubs, including a large Australasian collection. There are also woodland and cliff walks and, although Jura House (which was built by the Campbells and dates from the 1800s) is not open to the public, it can be rented as holiday accommodation. From June to August there is also a tea tent (garden open all year, daily 9.00-17.00; 01496 820 315; www.jurahouseandgardens.co.uk).

Craighouse, more than eight miles from Feolin Ferry, has most of the island's facilities. There is the

Palm trees, Craighouse

Jura Hotel, a post office, a general store (01496 820231; www.stores.demon.co.uk), and petrol (01496 820243). Also at Craighouse is the Isle of Jura Distillery, which was first founded in 1810 on a site where distilling has taken place for 300 years. Tours can be made of the distillery, but by appointment only, and there is a shop (01496 820240; www.isle ofjura.com). The parish church, which dates from 1776 but was altered in later years, is also open to the public, and there is a photographic exhibition of Old Jura in a gallery behind the church.

Above Craighouse is Kilearnadil Burial Ground [NR 524687], which has some interesting memorials as well as the Campbell mausoleum. St Earnan, Columba's uncle, is believed to be buried here, although the village here was reputedly devastated by the plague. A crofting township survives at nearby Keils [NR 525683].

CRAIGHOUSE TO LEALT (A846 AND UNLISTED ROAD)

Several miles north of Craighouse at Knockrome [NR 547715] are four standing stones, two of which stand close together just south of the unlisted road. These are said to be the markers of the graves of two giants, traditionally Diu and Ra, giving the island its name. It is believed to be lucky to pass between the two stones. Further down the unlisted road and then a track is An Dunan [NR 578730] on the north side of Lowlandman's Bay. This is an Iron Age fort on a rocky point.

At Tarbert is a standing stone [NR 605823] by the side of the road, and nearby are the remains of Kilmhoire Chapel and Burial Ground [NR 609822]. There are some interesting markers as well as a standing stone which has been decorated with crosses.

Far to the north and west is the site of Aros Castle [NR 645968?] in Glen Garrisdale, although the exact location is not known. This was a stronghold of the MacLeans from 1330, but the clan were defeated by the Campbells in 1647. The castle was still in use in 1690, when the Campbell constable took action against MacLeans who had not taken the Oath of Allegiance to William and Mary, but its exact site is not known. Nearby was MacLean's Skull Cave [NR 647970], called after the tradition that the severed head of one of the MacLeans was mounted, along with

Standing stone, Tarbert

two limb bones, on top of a cairn for many years following the slaughter.

There are many walks and climbs, some easy, some challenging, around the island. Details can be obtained from the Jura Hotel (01496 820243; www.jurahotel.co.uk).

EILEAN MORE

Eilean More ('big island') is a small island lying in the Sound of Jura, three miles offshore at Kilmory Knapp. Several sites on the isle are associated with St Cormac, a contemporary of St Brendan and St Columba. The ruins of a thirteenth-century chapel [NR 666752] consist of a barrel-vaulted chancel, which was later used as an inn. The chapel was dedicated to the saint, and there is a stone effigy of a priest beneath a canopy in the building.

A broken and weathered cross [NM 667753], decorated with animals, people and interlace, is believed to mark the spot where the saint was buried; while a cave, Uamh nam Fear [NR 666750], is also associated with Cormac: one of the walls has an early Christian cross.

Keills, south of Tayvallich on the mainland and four miles north of Eilean Mor, is also associated with the saint.

PLACES TO STAY

Jura Hotel (01496 820243; www.jurahotel.co.uk)
 Craighouse; hotel, restaurant and bar; lunches
 and evening meals
The Manse (George Campbell 01496 820384)
 B&B
Roberto Waldteufeul (www.wylliedraughts.com/jura)
 B&B

SELF CATERING

Angus Cottage (01496 820393;
 www.juraholidays.co.uk)
 Inverlussa; self-catering cottage, sleeps four;
 open all year
Boiden Cottage (01496 820393;
 www.juraholidays.co.uk)
 Ardfarnal; self-catering cottage, sleeps six;
 open all year
Braeside Cottage (www.juraholiday.org.uk)
 Craighouse
Corran House (01496 820243)
Crackaig Cottages (01496 820396; www.crackaig.co.uk)
 Craighouse; two self-catering cottages, each
 sleeps four; open all year
Charles Fletcher (01496 820323)
 Also trout and salmon fishing
Barnhill House (LENNIESTON@AOL.COM;
 Barnhill link from www.theisleofjura.co.uk)
Burnbank Cottages (www.juraselfcatering.com)
 Balard
Kate Johnson (01496 820327)
Jura House (Miriam Cool 01496 820315;
 www.jurahouseandgardens.co.uk)
 Ardfin; historic house with walled garden;
 sleeps up to fifteen
Jack Paton (01496 820242)
 Bungalow; sleeps two
Seaview Cottage (01688 302251; www.ileach.co.uk/
 seaview.html)
 Craighouse; self-catering cottage, sleeps six
Small Isles House (01695 557122;
 www.juracottage.co.uk)
 Craighouse; self-catering house, sleeps six;
 open all year
Stalkers Cottage (01496 810023;
 www.ileach.co.uk/stalkers_cottage/index.html)
 Tarbert; self-catering cottage, sleeps six-eight;
 open all year
Bunkhouse (07899 912116)
 Also Exploration Jura (Guided tours, walks)

It is possible to camp on the island, including in a
field by the Jura Hotel (01496 820243;
www.jurahotel.co.uk)

PLACES TO EAT

Jura Hotel (01496 820243; www.jurahotel.co.uk)
 Craighouse; restaurant and bar; lunches and
 evening meals
There is also a tea tent at Jura House during the
 season

Further Information

TRANSPORT

BUS SERVICE
A minibus (01496 820314/221) operates from
 Feolin Ferry to Craighouse and as far as
 Inverlussa

CYCLE HIRE
Bikes are for hire available from the hotel at
 Craighouse (01496 820243;
 www.jurahotel.co.uk) and Jura Bike hire (01496
 820192)

ACTIVITIES AND SPORTS

WALKING AND CLIMBING
Guides from the hotel: access to some parts of
 Jura may not be possible depending on the
 season: check with the Jura Hotel (01496
 820243). Many of the walks and climbs may be
 difficult, or at least tough going, as there are
 few tracks in the wilder parts of the island

FISHING, ANGLING AND SHOOTING
These are available, but check locally, including at
 the hotel (01496 820243; www.jurahotel.co.uk)

YACHTING AND SAILING
There is an excellent sheltered anchorage at
 Craighouse; shower and laundry facilities are
 available at the hotel

LOCAL PRODUCE

Isle of Jura Distillery ((01496 820240; www.isle
 ofjura.com)
 Craighouse; whisky distiller: tours by appt
Jura Fine Foods (01496 820223)
Products from Jura or about the island can be
 purchased on-line from
 www.isleofjuragifts.com, including books and
 guides, souvenirs, jewellery and gifts

ARTS AND CRAFTS

Pier Chandlery (01496 820273)
Traditional Spinning and Weaving (01496 820313)

ADDITIONAL INFORMATION

Petrol is available at Craighouse (01496 820243)
There are public telephones at Feolin Ferry,
 Ardfin, Craighouse, Knockrome, Lagg and
 Inverlussa
A mobile bank (Royal Bank of Scotland) visits the
 island on Thursday
Ceilidhs and other events are held at the village
 hall in Craighouse

EVENTS

Isle of Jura Fell Race (www.hillrunning.com)   May
 Gruelling fell race, covering sixteen miles and
 seven peaks
Jura Music Festival   September

FURTHER READING

A Guide to Islay and Jura (Booth, C. Gordon)
1984

Hebridean Islands: Colonsay, Gigha and Jura
(Mercer, John)
Blackie, 1982

Islay and Jura (Robertson, George)
Birlinn, 2006

Islay, Jura and Colonsay: A Historical Guide
(Caldwell, David)
Birlinn, 2001

Jura: A Guide for Walkers (Wright, Gordon)

Jura: Island of Deer (Youngson, Peter)
Birlinn, 2002

Jura: Language and Landscape (McKay, Gary)
House of Lochar, 2004

Jura: an Island in Argyll (Budge, Donald)
Smith and Son, 1960

Jura's Heritage (Wright, Gordon)

The Long Road: a Driver's Guide to Jura
(Youngson, Peter)
1987

ACKNOWLEDGMENTS

Thanks to Donald Ewen Darroch for checking
the text

Wreck of the Wyre Majestic *and the Paps of Jura*

COLONSAY AND ORONSAY

('St Columba's Isle' and 'St Oran's Isle' or 'tidal island')

www.colonsay.org.uk
www.visitscottishheartlands.com (AILLST)

Tourist Information Centres
Oban (mainland) (08707 200630)
  Open Jan-Dec
Tarbert (mainland) (08707 200624)
  Open Apr-Oct

Map Landranger sheet: 61 (HIH map page 141)

TRAVEL

A vehicle ferry (CalMac 01631 566688; www.calmac.co.uk) leaves from Oban on the mainland and sails to Scalasaig on Colonsay. The ferry makes crossings on Mondays, Wednesdays, Thursdays, Fridays and Sundays, and takes two hours and fifteen minutes. There is also a service from Kennacraig (CalMac 01880 730253; www.calmac.co.uk) A83 between Tarbert and Campbeltown), which also calls at Port Askaig on Islay. It is possible to make a day trip, and spend some six hours on the island – the service leaves from Kennacraig on a Wednesday, but only runs during the summer peak. The services are seasonal so checking information is essential.

Vehicles can be taken onto Colonsay, but caravans, trailers and motor-homes are not permitted.

Oronsay can be reached from Colonsay via a tidal causeway, depending on tide and weather.

Trips can be made from Colonsay to Mull, Jura and Islay on *Lady Jayne of Colonsay* (01951 200320; www.colonsay.org.uk). Gemini Cruises, based at Crinan on the mainland, run charter trips to Colonsay (01546 83028; www.gemini-crinan.co.uk).

Beach, Colonsay

DESCRIPTION

Colonsay lies twelve miles south of the Ross of Mull, nine miles west
miles north of Islay. It is a small island, some eight miles from nort
about three miles wide. One of the finest beaches on the isles ca
Kiloran Bay in the northwest of the island, and there are other god
sand on both Colonsay and neighbouring Oronsay. The highest poi... ... ...
Eoin, also to the north, which rises to 143 metres; and there are excellent views to
be had from Beinn nan Gudairean (136 metres) in the centre. Although parts are
rough and there are dramatic cliffs down the west coast, there are also extensive
areas of fertile land and woods. The climate is relatively warm and sunny, although
it can be wet and windy.

The only settlements of any size are at Scalasaig, where the ferry lands and which
has a well-stocked shop and post office (01951 200323), and a hotel, restaurant and
bar; and Kiloran, which is near Colonsay House with its gardens. There are also
townships at Uragaig and Kilchattan. The population is around 100 people (although
there are more than 4,000 sheep and a herd of Highland cattle), and the roads are
good but single track.

Oronsay lies just offshore to the south of Colonsay. It is a tidal island and can be
reached across the sands known as The Strand by a causeway at low tide (check
tides locally before venturing across). Oronsay is about three miles long and a couple
wide, and mostly flat. Good stretches of sand can be found around the coasts, while
the south is very rocky.

WILDLIFE

Many species of birds have been seen (some 214, it has been claimed), including
golden eagles, sea eagles, falcons, shearwaters, fulmars, guillemots, razorbills,
kittiwakes, shags, gulls, great northern and red-throated divers, terns, oystercatchers,
merlin, swans, geese, choughs and corncrakes. Wild goats also live here, survivors
(it is said) of animals carried on a Spanish Armada ship which was wrecked here;
and otters and seals live around the coasts. The islands are also rich in flowers and
plants, including old woodland, as there are many different types of habitat.

HISTORY

Both islands have many archaeological and historical remains. Mesolithic shell
mounds, some 7,000 years old, survive near the east coast of Oronsay, and there are
standing stones, burial cairns and forts and duns. Viking burials have also been
found with coins, weaponry, horse and boat.

This is one of the places where St Columba and his followers, including St Oran,
are said to have stopped after leaving Ireland. Columba had decided that he would
not rest until he was out of sight of his home, but as it was still possible to see the
coast of Donegal in Ireland from Colonsay, he set off again and eventually settled
on Iona. Oronsay may be named after St Oran (who was buried alive on Iona), and
there is a well that is known as Tobar Oran near Colonsay House. Oronsay has one
of the best-preserved medieval monastic complexes in Scotland. The buildings date
from the fourteenth century, and this became a centre of learning and stone carving.
One of the attractions is the Oronsay Cross, along with thirty impressive decorated
burial slabs.

The islands were long a property of the MacDuffie or MacPhee clan, who had
strongholds at Dun Eibhinn and Loch an Sgoltaire, but passed to the MacDonalds
in the first quarter of the seventeenth century, then the Campbells of Argyll, then
in 1701 to the MacNeills. They moved to Colonsay House, which dates from 1722,

...e house was extended in the nineteenth century and has excellent gardens. ...e island has been owned by the lords Strathcona since 1905, and the mainstays of ...e economy are farming, crofting, tourism and some fishing.

Tours

SCALASAIG TO KILORAN AND COLONSAY HOUSE (B8086)

The ferry lands at Scalasaig to the east of the island. Single-track roads lead from near the pier: both go to Kiloran and Colonsay House, the B8087 taking the more direct route.

At Scalasaig are many of the island's facilities, including the general store and post office (01951 200323), and the hotel (01951 200316; www.thecolonsay.com) and the Pantry (01951 200325), which both offer meals. The Gallery features exhibitions during the season as well as a heritage centre (opening times on the notice board outside the gallery). Colonsay Parish Church (01951 200320) was built in 1802 and stands on the site of an ancient chapel. It is usually open to the public. There is also an old well [NR 391939], which was used by the fisherman and sailors to secure a favourable wind, known as Tobar nan Gaeth Deas ('well of the south wind').

Above Scalasaig is Dun Eibhinn [NR 382944], the well-preserved remains of an ancient fort, named after Eyvind, a Norseman. The wall and entrance can be seen, along with the remains of buildings within the fort. This was apparently used as a strong point by the MacDuffies in medieval times.

Taking the B8086 south through Scalasaig, and by the hotel, the road comes to the turn-off for Oronsay (B8085), then goes by the landing strip and the golf course to Kilchattan. There are several sandy beaches down the west coast. Some remains survive of an old chapel [NR 363950] dedicated to St Catan, but more impressive are two standing stones [NR 367949], known as Fingal's Limpet Hammers, after the ancient hero. One of the stones is more than three metres high, while the other is just less than that; and these are the only survivors of a stone circle. Another old chapel [NR 377958], dedicated to St Mary, is located just to the north of the road.

At Kiloran is Colonsay House [NR 395968] and the rhododendron and woodland garden (01951 200221/369; garden open Apr-Sep, Wed 12.00-17.00, Fri 15.00-17.30; lunches and afternoon teas are available on these days, and there is also a shop

Colonsay House and gardens

selling local crafts and produce; accommodation is also available), which covers some twenty acres. Many tender and rare shrubs grow here, and there are also more formal walled gardens. The house was the home of Lord Strathcona. The big house on Colonsay is said to have had a gruagach, a fairy woman or brownie.

The house was built in 1722 on the site of an old chapel, dedicated to St Oran, and hence the name Kiloran. St Oran's Cross and Well are located near the house. The cross dates from the early Christian period and is decorated with the face of a man; the well is covered and is reached via a flight of steps.

To the north-west of Kiloran is Loch an Sgoltaire, and on an island in the loch are some remains of a castle [NR 386972] of the MacDuffie family, which was reused by the MacDonalds in 1615. The site may have been later utilised as a summer house.

The road runs on to an unlisted road which goes to the beautiful sandy Kiloran Bay. Some other points of interest to the north are Carnan Eoin, the highest hill; Dunan nan Nighean [NR 415976], a ruinous dun on a small crag; Clach na Gruagach [NR 415997], an unshaped boulder with a small indent in the top where milk was left here for the gruagach or fairy woman; and Cill Chaitriona [NR 421998], the remains of a small chapel in an enclosure with four cairns. A cross is built into the wall of the enclosure, and may date from as early as the seventh century.

The B8087 takes a more direct route back to Scalasaig.

Scalasaig to Oronsay (B8086, B8085 and Unlisted Road)
Off the road at Milbuie are the remains of a round prehistoric burial cairn [NR 387929]. Some of the kerb stones can be seen. Further south is Dun Cholla [NR 377913], a prehistoric fort, protected on three sides by the steepness of the crag. On the other side is a ruinous wall and entrance.

At the end of the road is a causeway which crosses the sandy expanse of The Strand for Oronsay. This is a tidal causeway, and should only be used when the tide and weather are favourable – check locally.

On Oronsay are several Mesolithic shell mounds [NR 373891, 360886 & 358880] and Clach Thuill [NR 365896], the 'hole stone'. Legend has it that it was used to cure consumption. There are several stretches of sand along the rocky coastline. The island is very flat, and part is used as a landing strip.

Oronsay Priory

The most important place on the island is, however, the remains of Oronsay Priory [NR 349889]. This was an Augustinian establishment, founded by John, Lord of the Isles, in the fourteenth century and dedicated to St Columba. There may have been an early monastery here, which may have been associated with St Oran. Large parts of the priory church, cloister and other buildings survive, although they are roofless. Items of note include the Oronsay Cross, carved in 1510 and decorated with a crucified Christ figure and patterns of foliage. The inscription translates as 'the cross of Colinus, son of Cristnus MacDuffie'. More than thirty grave slabs, some finely carved, are kept protected in the Prior's House, and there are also several stone effigies. The priory was used as a burial place by both the MacDuffies and the MacNeills.

Places to Stay
HOTELS AND GUEST HOUSES

The Colonsay (01951 200316;
www.thecolonsay.com)
Scalasaig; 1750 listed building; bar and restaurant; nine bedrooms; open all year
Seaview Guesthouse (01951 200315)
Kilchattan; working croft

BED AND BREAKFAST

Donmar (01951 200223)
Uragaig; B&B
Glaic na Craoibhe (01951 200253)
Scalasaig; B&B
Glassard (01951 200354)
Scalasaig; B&B
Hannah (01951 200150)
Uragaig; B&B

SELF-CATERING PROPERTIES

Balnahard Farmhouse (07860 763192)
Balnahard; traditional farmhouse, sleeps up to ten
Calcraig Cottage (01855 811087/07747 805683)
Kilchattan; self-catering cottage, sleeps six-seven
Cill a' Rubha (01951 200320)
Uragaig; modern cottage, sleeps four-five
Colonsay Estate Cottages and Flats (01951 200312)
More than twenty traditional houses and cottages, as well as flats in Colonsay House; sleep two-twelve; open all year
Colnatarun Crofthouse (01951 200355)
Kilchattan; self-catering house, sleeps up to eight
Corncrake Cottage (01951 200303)
Kilchattan; self-catering cottage, sleeps seven
Druim Buidhe (01951 200229)
Kiloran; self-catering modern cottage, sleeps up to six
Drumclach Crofthouse (01951 200238)
Drumclach; self-catering house, sleeps six
Isle of Colonsay Lodges (01951 200320)
Scalasaig; four chalets, sleeping two-three and five-six; open all year

Pairc Molach (01350 727778)
Kilchattan; new house, sleeps six to eight
Scruiten Croft House (01951 200304/200300)
Kilchattan; sleeps seven
Seaview Croft (01951 200315)
Kilchattan; three cottages, sleep two-six; open all year
Sgreadan Crofthouse (01951 200304/300)
Sgreadan; self-catering house, sleeps seven
Uragaig Crofthouse (01505 350139)
Uragaig; self-catering house, sleeps six

HOSTELS AND RETREATS

Keepers Backpackers' Lodge (01951 200312)
Kiloran, three and a half miles from pier; hostel; transport to the hostel from the pier can be arranged; bikes can be hired

CAMPING AND CARAVANS

Camping and caravanning are not usually allowed

PLACES TO EAT

The Colonsay (01951 200316)
Scalasaig; 1750 listed building; bar and restaurant (open to non-residents), lunch and evening meals
The Pantry (01951 200325)
Scalasaig (near pier); tearoom; open all year: confirm winter opening days and times
Colonsay House Gardens (01951 200221/369)
Wed and Fri only

Further Information
TRANSPORT

CYCLE HIRE
Cycles can be hired (01951 200355 or 01951 200312)
GUIDED TOURS
(01951 200320)
BUSES
Postbus (01951 200323; www.royalmail.com/postbus)

Service Bus (01951 200341)
Circular route: Kilchattan-Machrins-Scalasaig-Kiloran
Private hire (01951 200320)

TOURS
Tours of the island are available (01951 200320)

ACTIVITIES AND SPORTS

BOAT TRIPS/ FISHING TRIPS
Lady Jayne of Colonsay (01951 200320; www.colonsay.org.uk)
Boat and fishing trips, private hire and Lorn ferry service
Gemini Cruises
Based in Crinan; charter trips to Colonsay (01546 83028; www.gemini-crinan.co.uk)

YACHTING AND SAILING
There is a good anchorage at Scalasaig

FISHING
Colonsay Fly-Fishing Association
Loch fishing available mid Mar-Sep; membership available at Colonsay Hotel (01951 200316) or at the Office of Colonsay Estate (01951 200312)

GOLF
Colonsay Golf Club (eighteen-hole course)
Membership is essential: available at Colonsay Hotel (01951 200316) or at the Office of Colonsay Estate (01951 200312); the course is on machair land to the west of the island

CLAY PIGEON SHOOTING
Available: enquire locally

LOCAL PRODUCE

Locally produced oysters and honey can be purchased, either locally or on-line (01951 200365; www.colonsay.org.uk), as can beef and lamb (01951 200303; dialspace.dial.pipex.com/prod/dialspace/town/estate/ahd18/colonsaylambandbeef)

ARTS AND CRAFTS

BOOKSHOP AND PUBLISHER
House of Lochar (01951 200232; www.houseoflochar.com), publisher of Scottish books, is located on the island, and produces books about Colonsay and Oronsay, and much else; there is a small bookshop selling a range of titles, including of local interest

VISITOR ATTRACTIONS AND MUSEUMS

Colonsay House Gardens (01951 200221/369)
Open Apr-Sep, Wed 12.00-17.00, Fri 15.00-17.30; lunches and afternoon teas are available on these days, and there is also a shop selling local crafts and produce; accommodation is also available

ADDITIONAL INFORMATION

General store and post office (01951 200323)
Scalasaig; information about the island

FURTHER READING

The Book of Colonsay and Oronsay (Grieve, Symington)
Oliver and Boyd, 1923
Colonsay and Oronsay (Newton, Norman S.)
David and Charles (Pevensey), 1990
Colonsay and Oronsay in the Isles of Argyll (Loder, J. de V.)
Oliver and Boyd, 1935 (repr 1995?)
Colonsay: Elements of an Island (Hindmarch, Brian)
House of Lochar, 2003
Colonsay: One of the Hebrides (McNeill, Murdoch)
House of Lochar, 1910 (facs 2001)
Hebridean Islands: Colonsay, Gigha and Jura (Mercer, John)
Blackie, 1982
Islay, Jura and Colonsay: A Historical Guide (Caldwell, David)
Birlinn, 2001

ACKNOWLEDGMENTS

Thanks to Rhona at the Colonsay Hotel and Restaurant for checking the entry. Images Courtesy Colin Palmer (www.buyimage.co.uk)

Gigha

('good island' or 'God island';
pronounced 'Gee-ah')

www.gigha.org.uk
www.visitscottishheartlands.com
(AILLST)

Tourist Information Centre
Tarbert (mainland) (08707 200624)
   Open Apr-Oct

Map Landranger sheet: 62

Travel

The vehicle ferry (CalMac tel.: 01880 720253; www.calmac.co.uk) sails from Taylinloan, which is on the main Lochgilphead to Campbeltown (A83) road, sixteen miles south of Tarbert. The crossing takes twenty minutes, and arrives at Ardminish on Gigha. Cars (but not caravans) can be taken across, but this is expensive, and for the moderately fit walking or taking a bike may be a better option (bicycle hire is available on the island from the post office at Ardminish). In the summer there is one sailing an hour (except 13.00) from 8.00 on school days and 9.00 at other times, and the last crossing back from Gigha is at 17.30, or 16.30 on Sundays. There are fewer crossings in the winter. There is an inn and post office at Tayinloan village, and regular mainland bus services connect with the ferry arrival and departure times. British Airways has two flights a day from Glasgow to the nearby airport of Campbeltown further south on Kintyre.

Boat trips to Cara can be arranged: ask for details locally.

Beach, Gigha

DESCRIPTION
This lovely island, one of the most southerly of the Western Isles, lies three miles off shore from the west of the Kintyre peninsula, and is six miles long and about two wide at its broadest. It is mostly a fertile place, although the west coast is rougher; the climate is warm and frosts are rare. The highest point of the island (Creag Bhan) is 100 metres high, and there are excellent views from here to Kintyre, Islay and Jura, and even as far as Ireland (on a clear day). Good clean beaches with white sand can be found at Druimyeon Bay and Ardminish Bay.

The only settlement is Ardminish, where there is a well-stocked shop (selling, among many other things, the excellent Taste of Gigha cheeses) and the Gigha Hotel (01583 505254). An unlisted road runs virtually the length of the island. The population is about 140 people, although in 1801 it was more than four times this. There has, however, been a fifty percent increase in population since 2002, at the time of the community buy out, when there was a population of 89.

WILDLIFE
Many birds (some 120 species) can be seen on Gigha, including mute and hooper swans, guillemots, different kinds of gulls, eider ducks, shelducks, fulmars, divers and snipes. There is good land and the island has many cows, sheep, and rabbits, as well as seals and otters around the coast. There are many wild flowers and plants in the spring, including carpets of bluebells in woods and yellow irises in marshy areas.

HISTORY
King Hakon of Norway is said to have held court on the island in 1263 before going on to defeat at the Battle of Largs, his longships being marshalled in the Sound of Gigalum. The defeated king also returned this way after the battle.

Gigha was a property of the MacDonald Lords of the Isles from the fourteenth century but in the middle of the next century it passed to the MacNeills of Taynish, although there was trouble between the MacNeils, the MacDonalds and the MacLeans over possession. The island was ravaged in 1530, when the laird was slain by pirates, and then again in 1551. Branches of the MacNeills held the island until the middle of the nineteenth century. It then changed hands several times, including being owned by Sir James Horlick, who developed the fine gardens at Achamore. Gigha was bought by its inhabitants in 2002.

Tours
ARDMINISH AND THE SOUTH (UNLISTED ROADS)
The ferry lands near Ardminish, on the east side of the island, below the village. This is the only settlement, and at the village can be found the post office and well-stocked shop (01583 505251/07876 468498; www.gighastores.co.uk), petrol pumps, the excellent Gigha Hotel, and the Boathouse Restaurant (open Easter-Sep). Gigha and Cara Parish Church was built in 1923 and has fine stained-glass windows (01583 505245).

Turning south, the road runs past the hotel and comes to a track to the west. This leads to Kilchattan [NR 644482], the ruins of a chapel dating from the thirteenth century and dedicated to Catan, a contemporary of St Columba. There are several carved grave slabs, one identified as being for Malcolm MacNeill of Gigha, who died in 1493; and an octagonal font from here is now in the parish church at Ardminish.

Nearby on a ridge is a standing stone [NR 642481] which has an Ogham inscription, probably dating from the seventh century. It is believed to read 'Fiacal son of Coicelle' and may be a grave marker. Beyond the end of the track is the peaceful bay at Cuddyport, where there is a prehistoric burial cairn [NR 631482] on a small headland. Seals can be seen in the bay.

Not much further south on the 'main' road, or by a track from near the old church, are Achamore Gardens (open all year, dawn-dusk) laid out over fifty acres, a fine woodland garden featuring rhododendrons and azaleas. The garden was created by Sir James Horlick, who purchased the island in 1944. Many of the plants were brought from his home in Berkshire in laundry baskets. Sub-tropical plants flourish, and there is a walled garden for less hardy specimens. Achamore House, a baronial mansion of 1884 built by a Captain Scarlett, is probably on the site of a much older residence of the MacNeills, and offers B&B accommodation.

The small island of Cara (see below) is to the south of Gigha.

NORTH OF ARDMINISH (UNLISTED ROAD)

The road runs north from the turn-off for the ferry past the island's nine-hole golf course. There are fine beaches at Ardminish and Druimyeon Bay to the east, while beyond Druimyeonbeg is Dun Chibhich [NR 645500], the remains of an Iron Age fort. One legend has this as the stronghold of Keefie, who absconded with the wife of Dairmid, the Fingallian hero. Dairmid pursued them to Dun Chibhich and slew them here.

Also to the west of the road is the highest point of the island, Creag Bhan (accessible from the track opposite Druimyeon More Farm), from where there are fine views; and near the track is a ruinous dun [NR 649507]. The track leads to Ardailly (a self-catering property), then on to an old water mill [NR 642508].

To the east of the road and not easy to find, before Tarbert, is a broken and weathered cross [NR 655516], that dates from the tenth century; nearby is an early Christian stone, the Holy Stone [NR 654515], decorated with crosses; and further to the northeast is Tobar a' Bheathaig [NR 656519], a spring, the water of which was said to have great benefit, including securing a fair wind for mariners.

Giant's Tooth, Tarbert

At Tarbert the land narrows to an isthmus and there is a leaning standing stone, over two metres high, locally known as the Giant's Tooth [NR 655523] (alternative names are the Druid's Stone and the Hanging Stone, the latter from a tradition that people were executed here). There are also two prehistoric burial cairns [NR 656524], although these are covered in bracken. The road continues to the northern tip of Gigha. East of here are two fine beaches at Port Mor, while Eilean Garbh, to the west, is also picturesque and has many nesting seabirds.

CARA

Cara ('Kari's island' or possibly 'island of the rock', both from Norse: Kari is a Viking name) is a small island, half a mile south of the southern end of Gigha, and about one mile long. The island has been long held by the MacDonalds of Largie (descendants of the Lords of the Isles), but Cara House, their seat, dating from the eighteenth century, is now ruinous. The house and island is said to have had a brownie, a bearded fellow clad in brown. There is a ruinous chapel [NR 642444], dedicated to St Fionnlugh and believed to be the site of an early Christian monastery. The island was infamous for smuggling in the eighteenth century, but has had no permanent residents since the 1940s.

There is a colony of wild goats on the island, and rabbits, otters and many birds.

PLACES TO STAY

Gigha Hotel (01583 505254; www.gigha.org.uk) Ardminish; accommodation, bar and restaurant; self-catering accommodation also available

Achamore House (01583 505385; 01583 505385; www.AchamoreHouse.com) Achamore; B&B in the fine mansion; by the famous gardens; open all year

The post office House (01583 505251/07876 468498; www.gighastores.co.uk) Ardminish; B&B and self-catering accommodation available

Tighnavinish (01583 505378/07810 302127; www.gigha.net) 0.5 miles north of Ardminish; B&B

There are several self-catering properties around the island: check websites for details or contact the Gigha Hotel

Camping is available at the boathouse with toilets, showers and a laundry

PLACES TO EAT

Gigha Hotel (01583 505254; www.gigha.org.uk) Ardminish; accommodation, bar and restaurant; open all year

The Boathouse Restaurant Ardminish; open Easter-Sep

FURTHER INFORMATION

CYCLE HIRE
Available from the post office (01583 505251/07876 468498; www.gighastores.co.uk)

GOLF
Druimyeonbeg (01583 505242) 0.5 miles north of Ardminish; nine-hole golf course

SAILING AND YACHTING
There are maintained moorings in Ardminish Bay with showers and drying facilities in the boathouse by the catwalk

FISHING AND ANGLING
Contact Gigha Hotel (01583 505254; www.gigha.org.uk)

Petrol is available on the island: check at the post office

There is a publisher on the island (01583 505233; www.ardpress.co.uk)

Other businesses include International Flower Essence Repertoire based at Achamore House, Sea Safari Tours also run from Achamore House, and Laura MacKenzie a Massage and Alternative Therapist

FURTHER READING

Antiquities of Gigha (Anderson, R. S. G) Galloway Gazette, 1978 (reprint)

Hebridean Islands: Colonsay, Gigha and Jura (Mercer, John) Blackie, 1982

The Isle of Gigha (Tulloch, Vie) 1988

The Story of Gigha: the Flourishing Island (Philip, Kathleen) K. Philip, 1979

ACKNOWLEDGMENTS
Thanks to Lorna Andrew at the Isle of Gigha Heritage Trust for checking the entry

Bute and Cumbrae

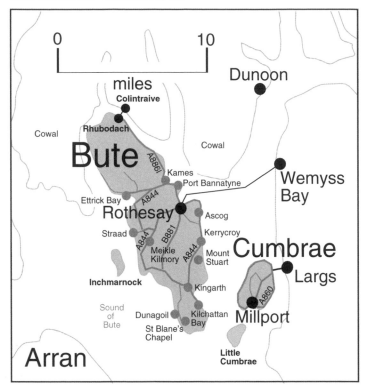

St Blane's Chapel, Bute

BUTE

('fire' or 'beacon fire' or 'victory isle')

www.visitbute.com
www.isle-of-bute.com
www.butesonsanddaughters.com
www.kilchattan-bay.co.uk
www.bute-gateway.org
www.cowal-dunoon.com
www.wemyssbay.net
www.visitscottishheartlands.com (AILLST)

Tourist Information Centre
Rothesay (08707 200619)
   Open Jan-Dec

Map Landranger sheet: 63 (HIH map page 158)

TRAVEL

Vehicle ferries depart from Wemyss Bay (on the A78) to Rothesay on Bute (CalMac 01700 502707 (Rothesay); 01475 520521 (Wemyss Bay); www.calmac.co.uk). Crossings take thirty-five minutes and run every forty-five minutes from early morning until the evening. There are fewer crossing on Sundays. Wemyss Bay has a railway station (www.firstgroup.com/scotrail; 08457 484 950) with trains from Glasgow Central, and a range of facilities and amenities, including places to eat and stay.

There is also a vehicle ferry (CalMac 01700 841235) from Colintraive on Cowal (A886) to Rhubodach in the very scenic north of the island. The trip takes just a couple of minutes and runs frequently from early in the morning until evening.

DESCRIPTION

The island lies five miles west of the Ayrshire mainland at Largs and nestles into the southern part of Cowal, where it is only 300 or so metres from the mainland. The island is some fifteen miles long and between three and five broad, and covers about forty-eight square miles.

The northern part of the island is hilly, rising to 278 metres at Windy Hill and is mostly moor and woodland with raised beaches, while the south of the island is more fertile, except for the southern tip. The Highland fault runs through the island, dividing it through from Rothesay to Scalpsie Bay, hence the difference in the landscape. The island is mostly used for cattle and sheep farming; and Bute has a population of about 7,000 people.

There are good beaches at Ettrick Bay, St Ninian's Bay and Scalpsie Bay, on the west coast, and Kilchattan Bay to the southeast. The scenery and views to Arran and down the Firth of Clyde are particularly fine at the southern end of Bute; while the area around Scalpsie Bay and the Kyles of Bute is also very picturesque.

The island has excellent roads, and the main town on the island is Rothesay, which has most of Bute's amenities and facilities. To the north of this is Port Bannatyne, and at the southern end of the island are the villages of Kingarth and Kilchattan Bay. Many people live in Rothesay and on the east coast, and most of the island's facilities are in the town, including the ferry terminal, winter garden, Victorian gents' toilets, banks, tourist information centre, shops, many places to stay and eat, library, swimming pool, museum and much more.

WILDLIFE

A large variety of birds can be seen, as many as 150 species. In winter there are greylag, barnacle and greenland geese and ducks, while in the summer there are wheateaters, woodwarblers, redstarts and blackcaps. Other birds include hawks, buzzards, oystercatchers, redshanks and eider ducks, as well as teal and goldeneye ducks. There is a hide at Loch Fad, and Scalpsie Bay is a good place to see seals.

HISTORY

The island has many prehistoric monuments, including standing stones or circles, such as those at Ettrick Bay, Largizean and Blackpark Plantation, and the remains of several chambered cairns. There are also forts and duns, and Little Dunagoil was

occupied through the Bronze Age, and then later again by the Vikings when they held Bute in the twelfth and thirteenth centuries.

Before this, St Blane had established a monastery near Kingarth in the sixth or seventh century. It is in a wonderful location with fine views, and there are ruins from the ancient monastery as well as from a later chapel.

As mentioned above, the island was part of the western seaboard that was held by the Vikings and the moated Rothesay Castle was besieged by them in 1263. The Norsemen lost the Battle of Largs the same year, and the territory was incorporated into the kingdom of Scots. The Stewarts were (and are) the major family and landowners on the island, and they developed Rothesay Castle down the cen-

Standing stone, Blackpark

turies, before moving to Mount Stuart. This later house is a grand gothic mansion, is still a property of the Stuart Marquesses of Bute, and is open to the public. There were several other strongholds on the island, including Kames Castle [NS 064676], held by the Bannatynes; Wester Kames [NS 062680], a property of the MacKinlays, Spences and Grahams; Meikle Kilmory [NS 051611], held by the Jamiesons; Kelspoke [NS 106541]; and Ascog House [NS 105633], which was held by the Glass family, Fairlies and Stewarts, can be rented through the Landmark Trust.

The main town on the island is Rothesay, which was made a royal burgh by Robert III in 1400. In the eighteenth century there was a thriving herring fleet (some 500 boats) as well as a textile industry, but it was tourism that was to become the town's mainstay.

Rothesay has a gentle climate, being warm and frosts being rare. It mostly dates from Victorian times and later, and sweeps round Rothesay Bay and Bogany Point to Ascog. It was extremely popular with holidaymakers from Glasgow until the 1950s, and at one time nineteen different steamers called here per day, some more than once.

Tours

ROTHESAY

Rothesay is the main settlement on the island, and is perhaps more like a town in the Lowlands than on one of the islands; there are many Victorian villas. The ferry from Wemyss Bay lands here and the burgh is often a bustling place. Features include the Winter Garden and Isle of Bute Discovery Centre, the Victorian gents' toilets, banks, shops, many places to stay and eat, library, swimming pool, and museum.

The most impressive building in the town, at the south end of the High Street, is the ruinous Rothesay Castle (01700 502691; open Apr-Oct, daily; reduced hours in winter; Historic Scotland), consisting of a unique round wall with four towers, surrounded by a water-filled moat, and with a later gatehouse block. The oldest part dates from the twelfth century and was completed in the sixteenth century by James V. The castle is floodlit at night.

The castle was besieged and seized by Norsemen in the 1230s, but was recovered by the Scots after King Hakon of Norway was defeated at the Battle of Largs in 1263. It also saw action in the Wars of Independence, and was a favourite residence of Robert II and Robert III; the latter may have died here. In 1401 Robert III made his son duke of Rothesay, a title given to the heir of the throne ever since and currently held by Prince Charles (although the first *Rothesay Castle*
holder, David, came to sticky end, being starved to death at Falkland Palace). The castle was long held by the Stewarts, besieged several times, and left a ruin after being torched in 1685. It was consolidated in the nineteenth century by the Marquess of Bute, and finds from the site, including cannon balls and keys, are in the Bute Museum. The castle is now in the care of Historic Scotland, and there is an audio-visual presentation about the Viking influence on Bute.

Nearby is the Bute Museum (01770 502033; www.butemuseum.org.uk; open all year, Apr-Sep, Mon-Sat 10.30-16.30, Sun 14.30-16.30; Oct-Mar, Tue-Sat 14.30-16.30) in Stuart Street, housed in galleries covering the geology, archaeology, history, wildlife and natural history of the island. Displays include models of Clyde steamers, a collection of early Christian crosses (including from Inchmarnock), and finds from prehistoric burial cairns: the jet necklace (also from Inchmarnock) being particularly notable; and there are also children's activities. Trinity Parish Church (01700 502781; www.isle-of-bute.com/trinity/index.htm), on Castle Street, is a fine building and open to the public.

In the High Street is the eighteenth-century Bute Estates Office, which was formerly the town house of the Stuarts of Bute; and the Castle Gallery (0170050015; www.thecastlegallery.com), which sells an interesting range of island, Scottish and international arts and crafts.

The pier dates from the eighteenth century, while the Winter Garden on the Esplanade dates from the 1920s and now houses a cafe and a cinema, as well as the Isle of Bute Discovery Centre (08707 200619; open all year), which highlights the attractions of the island, using multimedia, games and graphics. It is also home to a genealogy centre, TIC and shop. Mention must also be made of the stunning Victorian Toilets (www.isle-of-bute.com/victoriantoilets/) which have mosaics, tiles and urinals lined with black vitreous china. It was built in 1899, and there is a leaflet describing the wonders. The loos are only for men and women must use a less plush toilet.

At the north end of the High Street (B881, about 500 metres from the castle) is the High Kirk, dating from the end of the eighteenth century, which replaced an older building. Adjacent to the building is St Mary's Chapel, dating from the thirteenth century. Inside the building are two fine stone effigies: one of a warrior, probably a Stewart of Menteith; the other of a mother and child. The well-kept burial ground has the Marquesses of Bute Mausoleum, as well as some outstanding Victorian funerary memorials and statues. A spring, housed in a small building, is known as St Mary's Well.

At Townhead is Rothesay Creamery (01700 503186; www.mclelland.co.uk) with cheese-making demonstrations and a shop.

To the east of the town at Craigmore is Ardencraig Garden (01700 504644; open May-Sep), which has an interesting Cactus House, with many varieties, and a colourful Fuchsia House, plus a small aviary, stream and fish pond.

ROTHESAY TO KINGARTH (A844)

Along the A844, about a mile east and then south of Rothesay, is the village of Ascog. Built around 1870, Ascog Hall Fernery (01770 504555; www.ascoghallfernery.co.uk; open Apr-Oct, Wed-Sun) and Garden has a collection of subtropical ferns and there is fine rock work and water pools. The oldest fern is believed to be 1,000 years old. Ascog House incorporates an old tower house, dating from the sixteenth century, and was held by the Glass, Fairlie and Stewart families. It can be rented through the Landmark Trust.

There is a pleasant beach at Kerrycroy. Five miles south of Rothesay is the Victorian Gothic Mount Stuart House (01700 503877; www.mountstuart.com; open Easter, then May-Oct, except Tue and Thu – tel. to confirm), a palatial stately home with fine interior decoration, built in 1877 for the third Marquess of Bute by the Scottish architect Robert Rowand Anderson; the Stuarts had moved here in the eighteenth century from Rothesay. The house was the first to have electricity in Scotland, as well as a heated swimming pool. There are 300 acres of grounds and gardens, and a tea room, gift shop and a meadery. A special day return ticket is available from Glasgow.

A branch of the A845 at Kingarth (B881) leads down to Kilchattan Bay, passing the excellent beach. There are slight remains of a castle at Kelspoke [NS 106541]. A post office and general store and a hotel can be found at Kilchattan Bay; at nearby Kingarth is the Kingarth Trekking Centre (01700 831295; www.kingarth trekkingcentre.co.uk) and another hotel.

Just beyond Kingarth is a turn-off (unlisted) to St Blane's Church (signposted). Half a mile south, by the road in a forestry plantation, are the remains of a prehistoric stone circle [NS 092556], one stone is around three metres high; while half a mile to the west of the road is a setting of three standing stones [NS 092556], the tallest two metres high. There are the remains of two forts at Dunagoil [NS 085531 and NS 087532] (Accessible from a lay-by opposite Dunagoil Farm). The larger has the remains of a vitrified wall; while the other was reused by Norsemen and occupied until the thirteenth century. Remains of longhouses were excavated, and finds from both sites are in the Bute Museum.

There is a car park for St Blane's Church [NS 094353], and a short walk (300 metres) leads to the site. There are the remains of a sixth-century monastery, dedicated to St Blane, who is also associated with Dun-

St Blane's Chapel, near Kingarth

blane, near Stirling. It is located in a wonderful, tranquil and picturesque spot. The most striking building is the ruin of a small twelfth-century chapel within an old burial ground. The cemetery is divided into upper and lower parts, the upper being for men, the lower for women. There are other ruins, including an enigmatic structure known as the 'devil's cauldron', and part of an ancient boundary wall. A spring, reputedly a holy and wishing well, is known as St Blane's Well.

KINGARTH TO ETTRICK BAY (A844)

The A844 takes a circular route from Kingarth around the island, going up the west side. Four miles beyond Kingarth, the road branches and the A845 returns to Rothesay, passing Loch Fad, where there is a hide from which birds can be watched.

The A844 passes the fine beach at Scalpsie Bay and there are good views looking south and then east. The road passes the scant remains of a castle (a turret) at Meikle Kilmory [NS 051611]. This was a property of the Jamiesons, hereditary coroners of Bute, although it later passed to the Stuarts. About one mile from the road is Bicker's Houses [NS 061604], a long cairn, some twenty-five metres in length and more than ten wide. The entrance to the burial chamber can be traced.

The road continues north (another turn-off (B878) returning to Rothesay) eventually arriving at Ettrick Bay after a left turn. St Ninian's Bay also has a fine beach, and there are two standing stones and the remains of a chapel [NS 035613], which was dedicated to the saint (park at settlement at Straad).

There is a stone circle [NS 044668] near the road on the way to Ettrick Bay, consisting of four small upright stones and other broken ones, as well as other standing stones. Nearby is St Colmac Cross [NS 045673], a large stone with an incised cross. The beach at Ettrick Bay is particularly fine, and there is a cafe and parking. An unlisted road continues up the scenic west coast and the West Island

163

Way, which leads north around the top of Bute and then back to Port Bannatyne.

Beyond the end of the unlisted road, at Kilmichael, are the remains of two chambered burial cairns [NR 994704 and NR 997705] and an old chapel [NS 992705], dedicated to St Michael or Macaille. There is a spring here known as the Lovers' Well. The remains of a fort [NR 994713], with a wall up to two metres high, stand above a gorge. It can be difficult to find when it is overgrown.

The A844 returns to Rothesay via Port Bannatyne, which is a characteristically Victorian village.

ROTHESAY TO RHUBODACH (A844 AND A886)

The main road north out of Rothesay arrives at Port Bannatyne, and rounds Kames Bay. Port Bannatyne was a busy port for Clyde steamers, and midget submarines exercised in the bay during the Second World War. A turn-off here (A844) goes to Ettrick Bay and the south of the island.

Near the junction is the impressive fourteenth-century Kames Castle [NS 064676], owned by the Bannatynes of Kames until around 1780. Near Kames is also Wester Kames Castle [NS 062680], a small restored tower house, formerly held by the MacKinlays and the Spences. About one mile south of Kames Bay is Dun Burgidale [NS 063660], the ruins of an Iron Age broch or fort. The walls survive to a height of about three metres, and the entrance can be identified.

The road (A886) continues up the west side of the Kyle of Bute, with Windy Hill and Kames Hill (267 metres) to the west. The views are panoramic from both. After several miles the road runs out at Rhubodach, where there are toilets, and the vehicle ferry for Cowal. This is a very scenic route, and seems rather remote after the bustle of Rothesay.

INCHMARNOCK

The name comes from the 'isle of Marnock', a saint and contemporary of St Columba, who lived on the island.

The small island lies about one mile from the west coast of Bute at St Ninian's Bay, and rises to some sixty metres. It is about two miles long, flat and fertile, and there are fine views from the ridge running down its centre.

Inchmarnock was a property of Saddell Abbey (north of Campbeltown in Kintyre), and there are some ruins of an ancient chapel [NS 025597], which was dedicated to St Marnock. The burial ground is said to have had a similar division for men and woman as that at St Blane's. There is also a large prehistoric burial cairn [NS 020613] at Northpark, to the north of the island. The skeleton of a young woman was found here, and the remains were reinterred but can be seen through a glass panel. The skeleton was found with a fine jet necklace and a flint knife, which (along with fragments of carved crosses and a Viking stone from Inchmarnock) are held in the Bute Museum.

The population of the island was 30 in 1871 but it has since dwindled and is now uninhabited. A postage stamp was issued from Inchmarnock in 1999.

HOTELS AND GUEST HOUSES

Ardbeg Lodge Hotel (0 1700 505448; www.ardbeglodge.co.uk) Rothesay; hotel; open all year

The Ardmory House Hotel (01700 502346 www.ardmoryhousehotel.co.uk) Ardbeg; hotel and restaurant; open all year

The Ardyne-St Ebba Hotel (01700 502052; www.rothesay-scotland.com) Rothesay; hotel and restaurant; open all year

Bayview Hotel (01700 505411; www.bayviewhotel-bute.co.uk) Rothesay; hotel; open Feb-Nov

Cannon House Hotel (01700 505725; www.cannonhousehotel.co.uk) Rothesay; hotel and restaurant; open all year

The Commodore (01700 502178;
www.commodorebute.com)
Rothesay; guest house; open all year
Glendale Guest House (01700 502329)
Rothesay; guest house; open all year
Kingarth Hotel (01700 831662
www.kingarthhotel.com)
Kingarth; hotel and restaurant; open all year
Lyndhurst Guest House (01700 504799)
Guest house; open all year
Palmyra Guest House (01700 502929; www.isle-of-
bute.com/palmyra/)
Rothesay; guest house; open all year
The Port Royal/Russian Tavern (01700 505073;
www.butehotel.com)
Port Bannatyne; hotel and Russian restaurant
The Regent Hotel (01700 502006;
www.theregent.co.uk)
Rothesay; hotel, bar and restaurant
St Blane's Hotel (01700 831224;
www.stblaneshotel.com)
Kilchattan Bay; hotel and bar with meals

BED AND BREAKFAST

Ascog Farm (01700 503372)
Ascog; B&B (200-year-old farm house); open
all year
Balmory Hall (01700 500669;
www.balmoryhall.com)
Ascog; B&B (Victorian villa in ten acres of
grounds); open all year
The Boat House (01700 502696
www.theboathouse-bute.co.uk)
Rothesay; Boutique-style B&B
Glecknabae Farmhouse (01700 505655
www.isleofbuteholidays.co.uk)
North Bute; B&B plus self-catering cottage;
open all year
The Moorings (01700 50 2277; www.isle-of-
bute.com/themoorings/)
Rothesay; B&B (Victorian lodge of 1850); open
Mar-Dec
The Riversdale (01700 503240; www.isle-of-
bute.com/riversdale/)
Rothesay; B&B
Sunnyside House (01700 502351)
Rothesay; B&B; open all year

SELF-CATERING PROPERTIES

Ardencraig Self Catering Holidays (01700 504550;
www.ardencraig.com)
Rothesay; self-catering
Ascog House (01628 825925;
www.landmarktrust.org)
Ascog, Rothesay; self-catering house, dating
from the sixteenth century
Balmory Hall (01700 500669;
www.balmoryhall.com)
Ascog; three self-catering apartments in
country home and one cottage; also B&B; open
all year
Bannatyne (0131 466 3353; www.isle-of-bute.com/
bannatyne/)
Kilchattan Bay; self-catering

Birgidale Crieff (01700 831236; www.isle-of-
bute.com/birgidale/)
Kingarth; self-catering
Daisy Cottage (01700 503177; www.isle-of-
bute.com/daisycottage/)
Ardbeg; self-catering
East Colmac Farm (01700 502144)
North Bute; two self-catering apartments in
working farm, sleeps four; open all year
Glecknabae (0 1700 505655)
North Bute; self-catering; open all year
The Guest Wing (01700 504798; www.isle-of-
bute.com/theguestwing/)
Rothesay; self-catering
Harbourside Apartments (01700 503770
www.harbourside-bute.co.uk)
Rothesay; self-catering apartments; open all year
Morningside (01700 503906;
www.isleofbuteholidayflats.co.uk)
Rothesay; self-catering; open all year
Prospect House (01700 503526;
www.prospecthousebute.co.uk)
Rothesay; luxury self-catering; open all year
Sea View Apartment (0141 574 8174;
www.seaviewapartmentbute.com/)
Rothesay; self-catering
Shalunt Farm (01700 841387)
North Bute; self-catering flat in farmhouse,
sleeps two-five; open all year
Stewart Hall (01700 500006 www.visitbute.co.uk)
Luxury self-catering cottage with views to
Arran
West St Colmac Farm Apartments (01700 502144;
www.isle-of-bute.com/colmac)
Ettrick Bay; self-catering

Several properties available in Rothesay,
Kilchattan and Ardbeg (01700 503906;
www.jpsbute.com)

CAMPING AND CARAVANS

Roseland Caravan Park (01700 504529)
Rothesay; caravans (also to let), tourers and
tents; open Mar-Oct

PLACES TO EAT

The Ardyne-St Ebba Hotel (01700 502052;
www.rothesay-scotland.com/index.htm)
Rothesay
Brechin's Brasserie (01700 502922 www.brechins-
bute.com)
Open all year Tue-Sat
Butes Italy (01700 500099)
Pizza and Pasta on Bute, licensed
The Ardmory House Hotel and Restaurant
(01700 502346)
Ardbeg
The Bistro, The Isle of Bute Discovery Centre
(01700 505500)
The Black Bull (01700 502366)
Rothesay; Rothesay's oldest pub; open all year
The Pier at Craigmore(01700 502867)
Rothesay; open all year

Ettrick Bay Tearoom (01700 500223; www.isle-of-
bute.org.uk/ettrickbay)
 Ettrick Bay; tearoom; open winter, daily except
 closed Mon and Fri
The Waterfront (01700 505166)
 Rothesay; licensed cafe and restaurant.
The Kettledrum (01700 505324)
 Rothesay; bistro/cafe; open all year
The Kingarth Hotel and Restaurant (01700
 831662)
 Kingarth; Smiddy Bar
The Port Royal Hotel (01700 505073;
 www.butehotel.com)
 Port Bannatyne; restaurant and award-winning
 pub
Tea-Pot Tearoom (01700 503603)
 Port Bannatyne

Further Information

TRANSPORT

BUSES

West Coast Motors (01700 502076)
 Local services
Grand Island Tour (01700 502076)
 Open-top bus tours of Bute
Argyll and Bute Council (01546 604695)

TAXIS

AA (01770 502275)
David Gaston (01700 505050)
McKirdy and McMillan (01700 502317)
Sandy Ross Taxis (01770 504224)
Stewart Sweet (01770 504000)

CYCLE HIRE

David Zan-Kreyser (01770 504499)
 Cycle Hire and Tours

ACTIVITIES AND SPORTS

WALKS

Details of walks, including the West Island Way
 (twenty-six miles in total) are available from
 the Isle of Bute Discovery Centre. The Way
 traverses some of the most remote parts of the
 island, leading from the south of the island,
 round to the north to Port Bannatyne (or vice
 versa)

HORSE RIDING AND TREKKING

Kingarth Trekking Centre (01700 831295;
 www.kingarthtrekkingcentre.co.uk)
 Tuition, rides out & accommodation; Kingarth
 Old School, Kilchattan Bay

GOLF

Port Bannatyne Golf Club
 (www.portbannatynegolf.co.uk)
 Port Bannatyne; thirteen holes
Rothesay Golf Club (01700 502244;
 www.rothesaygolfclub.com)
 Rothesay
Bute Golf Club (http://butegolfclub.com/
 index.html)
 Kingarth; nine holes

ANGLING AND FISHING

Angling can be arranged on Loch Fad, Quien
 Loch, Loch Ascog and Greenan Loch

Loch Fad Fishing (01700 504871
 www.lochfad.com)
Bute Art and Tackle, Rothesay (01700 503598)

SAILING AND YACHTING

Isle of Bute Sailing Club (01700 505808)
Bute Sailing School (01700 504881; 07779 800737;
 www.butesail.com)
 Port Bannatyne; instruction, tuition and
 excursions as far as St Kilda

SWIMMING AND SPORTS

There is a sports centre with a twenty-five metre
 pool in Rothesay (01700 504300), which also
 has a fitness suite, sauna etc; and there is
 badminton, table tennis and snooker at the
 Moat Centre, also in the burgh; and two
 bowling clubs

CINEMA

Isle of Bute Discovery Cinema (01700 502151)
 Rothesay

LOCAL PRODUCE

James McIntyre (01700 503762)
 Rothesay; sells island cheeses, Bute honey,
 haggis and game; open Tue-Sat
Rothesay Creamery (01700 503186)
 Townhead, Rothesay; cheese-making
 demonstrations and shop

ARTS AND CRAFTS

Bute Crafts (01700 502555)
 Local arts and crafts, artist supplies
The Castle Gallery (0170050015;
 www.thecastlegallery.com)
 Rothesay; Scottish and international art gallery
 and craft shop
The Grapevine (01700 504414)
 Rothesay; sells health foods, gifts, local pottery
 and hand-made soaps

VISITOR ATTRACTIONS AND MUSEUMS

Ardencraig Garden (01700 504644)
 Craigmore, Rothesay; garden with Cactus
 House, Fuchsia House, aviary, stream and fish
 pond; open May-Sep
Ascog Hall Fernery and Garden (01770 504555;
 www.ascoghallfernery.co.uk)
 Ascog, Rothesay; collection of subtropical
 ferns; open Apr-Oct, Wed-Sun
Bute Discovery Centre (08707 200619)
 Winter Garden, Rothesay; information centre,
 cafe and cinema
Bute Museum (01770 502033;
 www.butemuseum.org.uk)
 Rothesay; open all year, Apr-Sep, Mon-Sat
 10.30-16.30, Sun 14.30-16.30; Oct-Mar, Tue-Sat
 14.30-16.30
Mount Stuart House (01700 503877;
 www.mountstuart.com)
 Five miles south of Rothesay; magnificent
 home of the marquesses of Bute with 300 acres

of grounds, and a tearoom, gift shop and a meadery; open Easter, then May-Oct, confirm opening with house

Rothesay Castle (01700 502691)
Rothesay; open Apr-Oct, daily; reduced hours in winter; Historic Scotland

ADDITIONAL INFORMATION

Petrol available in Rothesay (seven days)

Banks, branches in Rothesay (Royal Bank of Scotland and Bank of Scotland)

Somerfield, Spar and Co-op supermarkets in Rothesay

EVENTS

Isle of Bute Jazz Festival	May
Royal Rothesay Regatta	June
Bute Live Music & Arts Festival	July
Bute Highland Games	August
Horticultural Show	September
Country Music Festival	September
Cycling Weekend	September

FURTHER READING

Arran and Bute (Weiner, Christine)
S Forsyth, 1996

Bute in the Olden Time (Hewison, James King)
Blackwood and Sons, 1893-5

History of Bute (revised edition)
(Marshall, Dorothy N.)
1992

The Isle of Bute (Newton, Norman)
Pevensey Island Guides, 1999

ACKNOWLEDGMENTS

Thanks to Andy Walters for checking over the text

Kames, Bute

CUMBRAE

('isles of the Britons' or 'refuge')

www.millport.org
www.argyll.anglican.org/cumbrae.htm
www.largsonline.co.uk
www.ayrshire-arran.com (Ayrshire and Arran Tourist Board)

Tourist Information Centres
Millport (Cumbrae Card and Gift Shop) (0845 2255121 (central no))
    Open all year
Largs (mainland) (0845 2255121 (central no))
    Apr-Oct

Map Landranger sheet: 63 (HIH map page 158)

TRAVEL

The vehicle ferry sails from Largs (on the A78) to Cumbrae slip (Portrye) at the north of Great Cumbrae (CalMac 01475 674134 (Largs) 01475 650100 (Gourock); www.calmac.co.uk). The crossing takes ten minutes and runs every thirty minutes (fifteen minutes from end May-mid Aug) from 9.00 until about 20.00 in the evening; there are earlier less-frequent crossings. There are slightly fewer crossings on Sundays. Largs has a railway station (08457 484950; www.firstgroup.com/scotrail) with an hourly service from Glasgow Central; and there is a regular bus service to cover the three miles from Cumbrae slip to Millport. There is a WC, telephone and shelter at the slip, but nothing else.

Little Cumbrae is apparently not accessible to the public without prior permission. Cumbrae Voyages (0845 257 0404; www.cumbraevoyages.co.uk) have trips around the Cumbraes and to Little Cumbrae in a rigid inflatable dinghy. Trips leave from Largs.

DESCRIPTION

There are two neighbouring islands: Great Cumbrae to the north; and the smaller Little (or Lesser or Wee) Cumbrae to the south across the narrow kyles known as The Tan.

Great Cumbrae lies two miles south-west of the mainland at Largs, and four miles east of southern Bute. It is about four miles long and more than two across at its widest. The highest point is 127 metres at Glaid Stone, from where there are excellent panoramic views in all directions (perhaps except south towards Hunterston and the nuclear power station). There are a range of habitats from good farmland to health land, woodland and moor. The only settlement is Millport, to the south of the island, which has many places to stay and eat.

The population of Great Cumbrae grew in the nineteenth century as the island became popular with holidaymakers from Glasgow and the Clyde, from about 500 in 1801 to more than 1,700 in 1891. It is now about 1,400.

WILDLIFE

The island has many species of birds, including eider ducks, swans, lapwings, oystercatchers, shelducks, fulmars, buzzards, sparrow hawks, kestrels and tawny owls. Seals can seen in Millport Bay. There are also many species of wild flowers and ferns, and nine different types of orchids can be found on the island. Rabbits are numerous, including some that are black in colour, and there are also ferrets, polecats, hedgehogs, voles, slow worms, lizards and newts.

HISTORY

The island was held by the Vikings, until they were defeated at the Battle of Largs in 1263: King Hakon of Norway is said to have watched the defeat of his troops from Cumbrae at Tormont End.

Much of the island was held by the Montgomerys in the eighteenth century, and they had a castle or seat at Ballikillet [NS 172560], but it was later divided between the Stuarts of Bute and the Boyle earls of Glasgow, with the Stuarts in charge by the beginning of the twentieth century. The island was put up for sale in 1999, when most tenants bought their land.

Tours
MILLPORT

Millport dates from Victorian times, and is elegantly ranged around Millport Bay. It has a very fine sandy beach, which has a painted stone, this one known as the Crocodile Rock, at Newton Beach. The Garrison House (which formerly housed the Museum of the Cumbraes) was originally built to house the crew of a ship used to prevent smuggling, which was rife in the area, but has been burned out and is being restored. The museum is said to be rehoused in some huts.

Millport is home to the Cathedral of the Isles, on College Street, believed to be Britain's smallest cathedral, seating less than 100 people, and built in 1851 by the architect William Butterfield. The building has fine stained glass, and there is a collection of early carved stones from Mid Kirkton (01475 530353, www.argyll.anglican.org/cumbrae.htm; open all year, daily). As well as the smallest cathedral, Millport also boasts the narrowest house, known as The Wedge, which has a frontage of only 47 inches (1.1 metres).

Most of the facilities on the island are in Millport, including shopping, chippies, cafes, places to stay, cycle hire, post office, bank, bowling green, cinema, bingo and a funfair.

CLOCKWISE AROUND THE ISLAND (A860)

On the way out of Millport on the A860 to the west is Golf Road, which leads to the island's golf course. On this road is an old cemetery [NS 157551], where there were a succession of churches from the seventh century. Some carved stones from here are kept at the Cathedral of the Isles. The road also leads to a track and an excellent walk to Fintray Bay.

The main road runs up to Fintray Bay, which has a good beach, a cafe, and loos, past Indian's Face, painted on a cliff, and then on to the north of the island and White Bay, which also has fine sands. At Tormont End is a monument to two drowned mariners from *HMS Shearwater,* which foundered in 1844; and two prehistoric burial cairns [NS 183592], which are 300 metres apart. One is known as Lady's Grave, reputedly the burial place of a lady who lost her husband at the Battle of Largs. This is also said to be from where, in 1263, King Hakon watched the Battle of Largs and the defeat of his army.

The road turns south down the east side of the island, past the slip for CalMac ferries and Scotland's National Water Sports Centre. About two miles south, near Butter Lump, is a spring, which is reputed to be a wishing well. The well is reached down steps on the sea side of the road (parking). Further on is Lion Rock, a sandstone formation which has been eroded into the shape of the beast; then the Marine

Biological Museum (01475 530581; www.gla.ac.uk/acad/marine/; open all year, Mon-Fri, also Sat, Jun-Sep). This is a research centre for the universities of Glasgow and London, first founded in 1887. The museum and aquarium house a number of unique displays from the world of marine science. The road then returns to Millport.

MILLPORT TO GLAID STONE (UNLISTED ROAD & B899)

An unlisted road climbs out of Millport to Glaid Stone, from where there are fantastic views and a plaque indicating landmarks. Nearby is a spring [NS 168573], formerly a mineral drinking well. The unlisted road turns to the south, joins the B899, then passes (on the west in woodland) the Druids Stone at Craigengour [NS 176564], a two-metre standing stone said to commemorate Vikings killed at Largs; and (on the east, by the farm) the site of a castle or seat of the Montgomery family at Ballikillet [NS 172560]. This road returns to Millport via Ninian Brae.

LITTLE (OR LESSER OR WEE) CUMBRAE

The island (which is privately owned and not accessible without permission: contact Cumbrae Estate, PO Box 1, Millport KA28 0AA) is located about two miles south of Millport, and is about two miles wide and up to one wide. The island is hilly, rising to over 100 metres (123 metres at Lighthouse Hill) and covering some 770 acres. There are fine views. Cumbrae Voyages (0845 257 0404; www.cumbrae voyages.co.uk) have trips from Largs to the island in a rigid inflatable dinghy.

There are three burial cairns, two of them large, on the northern tip at Sheanawally Point [NS 155529], one of which apparently held a suit of armour.

The island was a property of the Hunters of Hunterston, then the Montgomery Earls of Eglinton after the Hunters lost a dispute with the Crown over the ownership of falcons. On a small island to the east of Little Cumbrae are the impressive ruins of a castle [NS 148518], which was visited by Robert III and was sacked by Cromwell in the 1650s.

The island is also associated with St Vey or Beye, a 'Scottish virgin and saint' said to have died here in 896, and was a place of pilgrimage. There are scant remains of a chapel [NS 148518] dedicated to her, and a rectangular structure [NS 147518] is reputed to be her burial place.

The island has the second oldest lighthouse in Britain. This lighthouse [NS 143515] was coal fired, and dates from the middle of the eighteenth century. It was replaced by a later building, in the same century, to the west of the island.

Places to Stay
HOTELS AND GUEST HOUSES

Ambler Guest House (01475 530532; www.millport.org/ambler.html)
Millport; guest house
Cir Mhor Guesthouse (01475 530723)
Millport; guest house
Denmark Cottage (01475 530958/530918)
Millport; guest house
Eastneuk Guest House (01475 530799)
Kames Bay, Millport; guest house
Glencoe House (01475 530350)
Millport; guest house
Islands Hotel (01475 530397)
Millport; hotel
Kelburn House (01475 530062)
Millport; guest house

Millerston Hotel (01475 530480; www.millport.org/millerstonhotel.html)
Millport; hotel; also self-catering caravans
The Royal George Hotel (01475 530301)
Quayhead; hotel, restaurant and bar meals

BED AND BREAKFAST

College of the Holy Spirit (01475 530353; www.scotland.anglican.org/retreats)
Millport; B&B and half-board; open all year
Westbourne House (01475 530000; www.westbourne-house.com)
Millport; B&B

SELF-CATERING PROPERTIES

3 Clyde Street (01475 530102/07855 615419)
Millport; self-catering

Cumbrae Holiday Apartments Ltd (01475 530094)
Self-catering; various central locations; open all year
Downcraig Ferry House (01475 530550, www.holidaymillport.co.uk)
Near ferry terminal; self-catering
Garden Flat (01475 672031)
Millport; self-catering
1 Guildford Street (01324 551570; www.1-guildford-street.co.uk)
Millport; self-catering
Orchard Cottage (01475 530000; www.westbourne-house.com)
Millport; self-catering

CAMPING AND CARAVANS

Caravan (0141 883 0032/07747 041143)
To let/self-catering
Millport Holiday Park (01475 530370)
Millport; caravan sales/hire; tourers welcome
Westbourne Caravan Park (01475 530000; www.westbourne-house.com)
West Bay Road; caravan park

PLACES TO EAT

There are cafes and restaurants (Deep Sea Chippie, Millerston Hotel, Royal George Hotel, Dancing Midge Cafe, Ritz Cafe) in Millport, and there is a tearoom (01475 530426) at Fintray Bay

Further Information

TRANSPORT

TAXIS
Caldwell's Newsagent (01475 530344)
Millport
CYCLE HIRE
Bremner's Stores (01475 530707/530309)
Millport
Mapes of Millport (01475 530444; www.mapesmillport.co.uk)
Millport (also fishing tackle)
A. T. Morton (01475 530478; www.sandymillport.fsnet.co.uk)
Millport

ACTIVITIES AND SPORTS

Cumbrae has been particularly recommended for those with families. For the moderately fit, cycling or walking is an ideal way to see the island, which is just over ten miles in circumference. Bikes can be hired in Millport; but cyclists should stay on the roads as off-roading is currently discouraged. The coast road (A860) is very flat, while the interior, up to Glaid Stone, is much hillier and challenging

WALKS
There are several pleasant walks from Millport: details available locally and there is a leaflet or from www.millport.org
GOLF
Millport Golf Club (01475 530305/01475 530306; www.millportgolfclub.co.uk)
Millport; eighteen holes and fine views
ANGLING AND FISHING
Fishing tackle available from Mapes of Millport (see Cycle Hire)
SAILING AND WATER SPORTS
Scotland's National Water Sports Centre (01475 530757; www.sportscotland.org.uk)
Cruising, dinghy, catamaran, canoeing, power boating, windsurfing, VHF courses and diesel maintenance (all instructors RYA qualified)

ADDITIONAL INFORMATION

Tourist Information is located in Cumbrae Cards and Gift Shop in Millport (www.millportscotland.com)
Cumbrae's Card and Gift Shop (www.millportscotland.com)
Millport; internet access, souvenirs
Petrol: available in Millport (seven days except PM Wed & Sun)
Bank: Millport
Garage Services: 01475 530567

EVENTS

Millport Country & Western Festival (September) (01475-531106; www.wildwest.org.uk)
The Festival Office, 19 Cardiff Street, Millport (1–3 Sep 2006)

ACKNOWLEDGMENTS

Thanks to Laura McAlees from Millport.org for checking over the text

Arran, Holy Island, Sanda and Ailsa Craig

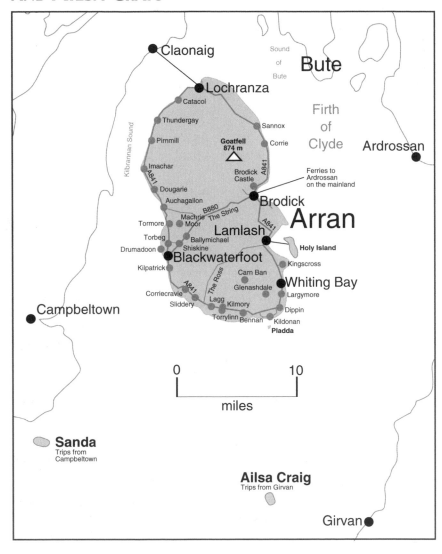

Claonaig

Sound of Bute

Bute

Lochranza

Catacol

Firth of Clyde

Thundergay

Sannox

Ardrossan

Pirnmill

Goatfell 874 m

Corrie

Kilbrannan Sound

Imachar

A841

Brodick Castle

A841

Ferries to Ardrossan on the mainland

Dougarie

Auchagallon

Brodick

Arran

Tormore

B880

The String

Machrie Moor

Lamlash

Torbeg

Ballymichael

A841

Drumadoon

Shiskine

Holy Island

Blackwaterfoot

Kilpatrick

Kingscross

Carn Ban

The Ross

Glenashdale

Whiting Bay

Corriecravie

A841

Largymore

Sliddery

Lagg

Kilmory

Dippin

Campbeltown

Torrylinn

Bennan

Kildonan

Pladda

0   10

miles

Sanda
Trips from
Campbeltown

Ailsa Craig
Trips from Girvan

Girvan

ARRAN

('peaked hill' or 'high')

www.visitarran.net
www.arrantourism.com
www.arran-hideaways.co.uk
www.ayrshire-arran.com/arran.htm
www.tastetrail.com
www.taste-of-arran.co.uk
www.arran.uk.com
www.arransites.co.uk
www.arranart.com
www.sliddery.com
www.ayrshire-arran.com (Ayrshire and Arran Tourist Board)

Tourist Information Centres
Brodick (0845 2255121 (general no))
    Open Jan-Dec
Lochranza (Community Hall) (0845 2255121 (central no))
    Seasonal

Map Landranger sheet: 69 (HIH map page 172)

TRAVEL

The vehicle ferry (CalMac 01294 463470 (Ardrossan), 01770 302166 (Brodick); www.calmac.co.uk) leaves from Ardrossan in Ayrshire and crosses to Brodick on Arran. Ardrossan is on the A78, there is a direct rail service (08457 484 950; www.firstgroup.com/scotrail) from Glasgow Central, and there are a range of shops and services in the town. The crossing to Arran takes fifty-five minutes, and there are up to six services a day from Monday to Saturday and four on Sunday. There are fewer crossings in the winter.

There is also a vehicle ferry (CalMac 01770 302166) which sails from Claonaig on Kintyre to Lochranza to the north of Arran. There are up to nine crossings a day, and the trip takes thirty minutes.

Claonaig is on the B8001, off the A83 Tarbert to Campbeltown road; the turn-off is near Kennacraig, the terminal for ferries to Islay, Jura and Colonsay. Argyll and Bute Council (01546 604695) runs a bus between Claonaig and Kennacraig. There are no facilities at Claonaig except a car park and toilets (although there are excellent views). Just along the coast is Skipness, which has a ruined castle, a chapel with carved graveslabs (both of which are in the care of Historic Scotland and open at all reasonable times), and a shop. Nearby Tarbert has a full range of amenities.

The ferry for the Holy Isle leaves from Lamlash (01770 600349/600998).

DESCRIPTION

Lying fourteen miles off the west coast of the Ayrshire mainland and five miles from Kintyre across the Kilbrannan Sound, Arran nestles in the Firth of Clyde. It is an island of contrasts, and is sometimes called 'Scotland in Miniature' because of the variety of landscapes. It is one of the larger of the Western Isles, and is some twenty miles long by about ten wide, covering 165 square miles. From the ferry from Ardrossan, the island is said to resemble a 'Sleeping Warrior', like an ancient warrior laid out on a bier.

Arran

The north of the island is very hilly and rugged with moorland and glens; and Goatfell ('windy mountain', from Norse) rises to 874 metres, and there are several other summits over 800 metres, including Caisteal Abhail at 859 metres and Ben Tarsuinn at 825 metres. Spectacular views can be had from the top of Goatfell on a clear day. This area is popular with walkers and climbers, and there is also the Isle of Arran Coastal Way (www.coastalway.co.uk).

The south of the island is much flatter and more fertile, although large areas are covered by coniferous forestry plantations. Details of forest walks can be obtained from the TIC in Brodick or from the Forestry Commission (01770 302218). There are fine sandy beaches at several places around the coast.

Arran has a population of around 5,000, but this is greatly increased in the summer by the many visitors who come here. Most islanders live around the coasts. Brodick, lying halfway down the east coast, is the main village on Arran, but there are also villages at Lamlash and Whiting Bay to the south-east; Kildonan, Kilmory, Torrylinn, Lagg and Sliddery to the south; Blackwaterfoot, Shiskine and Dougarie to the west; Pirnmill and Thundergay to the north-west; Catacol and Lochranza to the north; and Sannox and Corrie to the north-east. Unlike some of the islands, there are many amenities as well as places to eat and stay: this can mean, however, that the island and routes can be busy, at least in places.

The island has excellent roads, and the A846 circumnavigates the island, keeping mostly to the coast. The String Road (B880) cuts across the island from Brodick to Blackwaterfoot; while the unlisted Ross Road runs from Lamlash to Sliddery – there are excellent views from here (in the right weather conditions).

WILDLIFE

Because of the variety of habitats, Arran is home to, or is visited by, as many as 200 species of birds, including heron, mallard, shelduck, merganser and eider duck, as well as widgeon, goldeneye and teal. Other birds which can be seen here are ptarmigan, red grouse, curlew, cuckoo and red-throated diver. As there are no foxes on Arran there are many raptors: buzzards, peregrines, kestrels, hen harriers, sparrowhawks, short-eared owls and even golden eagles. Red deer can be found in the hills; and, by Brodick Castle, there is a colony of red squirrels. Around the coasts are otters and seals, and basking sharks can sometimes be seen offshore. Palm trees also thrive at many points around the island, indicating the island's warm and largely frost-free climate.

HISTORY

Arran has a good selection of prehistoric sites, mainly on the southern half of the island. The best of these is the arrangement of stone circles, standing stones and burial cairns on Machrie Moor, which is also a lovely location. On other parts of the island are the remains of chambered cairns, impressive standing stones, and Iron Age fortifications.

Arran was raided by Vikings at the end of the eighth century, and was then settled and held by them. This was one of the many territories claimed by the Norwegian king Magnus Barelegs (his nickname was because he dressed in plaid like the Scots) in 1098: anything around which he could sail he appropriated (cleverly adding Kintyre by dragging his boat across the isthmus at Tarbert). Some place names on the island are Viking in origin, not least Brodick (brethir vik), which means 'broad bay'.

Somerled forced the Vikings out of the western seaboard of Scotland, including Arran, but he was killed at Renfrew in 1164. Arran finally became part of the kingdom of Scots in 1266 after King Hakon of Norway was defeated at the Battle of Largs three years earlier. Hakon had marshalled his longships off Arran, probably in the sheltered anchorage at Lamlash, but a storm and bad luck led to his defeat.

Arran has associations with Robert the Bruce, and the King's Cave, on the west coast of the island near Drumadoon, may be where he was inspired by the persistence of the spider. He certainly did seize Brodick Castle in 1306, and it was from Kingscross Point that he and Sir James Douglas launched their ultimately successful campaign to drive the English from Scotland.

The island was held by the Stewarts of Menteith, then for some years by the Boyds of Kilmarnock, before being given to the Hamiltons in 1503, with whom it was to have a long association. The Hamiltons were one of the most important families in Scotland, and they were made both earls of Arran and eventually dukes of Hamilton. Their seat on Arran was Brodick Castle, which was developed down the years into a splendid castle and mansion, and is now in the care of the National Trust for Scotland. Lochranza Castle lies to the north of the island, and is a fine ruin in a very scenic location. There is also the small ruin of another castle at Kildonan; the two towers which defended Lamlash Bay have completely gone.

Much of the island was cleared for sheep in the nineteenth century, and cattle are also farmed; good cheese is produced. Herring fishing was formerly also important, especially to the economy of the north of the island, but the boats are long gone. Arran became very popular with holidaymakers from Glasgow and the west going 'doon the watter' in the nineteenth century, and tourism remains a mainstay of the island economy. There is also a whisky distillery at Lochranza.

Tours

BRODICK AND BRODICK CASTLE TO LAMLASH AND WHITING BAY (A841)

The ferry from Ardrossan lands at Brodick, on the east coast in the centre of the island. Brodick has a good range of shops, supermarkets, hotels, and other places to eat, as well as banks, a post office, a tourist information centre, a library and petrol.

Brodick Castle

It also has a good beach. The Burnside (01770 303888; www.theburnside.com) is a mixed-media art gallery.

First place to visit on any trip to Arran will probably be Brodick Castle (which is one and a half miles north of the village itself; 01770 302202; www.nts.org.uk; castle open Apr-Oct, daily 11.00-16.30, closes 15.30 in Oct; country park and Goatfell open all year; National Trust for Scotland), the grand mansion and stronghold of the Hamiltons, both earls of Arran and dukes of Hamilton. A stronghold was first built in the thirteenth century, and was seized and held by the English in the Wars of Independence until captured by Robert the Bruce. Arran passed to the Hamiltons at the beginning of the sixteenth century. The old castle was extended and remodelled into a magnificent mansion when the eleventh Duke of Hamilton married Princess Marie of Baden. In 1958 the building and tracts of Arran were given to the National Trust for Scotland. The castle is also said to have a ghost, a Grey Lady, the spirit of a girl who committed suicide when she found herself pregnant (or was imprisoned because she was thought to have plague).

There is access to Goatfell from Brodick Castle, as well as fine gardens with a large collection of rhododendrons, a walled garden, a nature trail, country park, reception centre, gift shop and restaurant.

Straddling the road out of Brodick Castle are three impressive standing stones [NS 006374], one of which is more than three metres high, while the other two are around two and a half metres. Another prominent stone [NS 018355] is south of the Arran Heritage Museum at Stronach, to the north of Brodick and the golf course. This one is three metres high; while another [NS 018355] at Mayish to the south of Brodick is a similar height.

On the road between Brodick and Brodick Castle is the Arran Heritage Museum (01770 302636; www.arranmuseum.co.uk; open Apr-Oct, daily 10.30-16.30) at Rosaburn. This features an original eighteenth-century croft farm along with a smiddy, cottage, dairy, coach house and stables. Displays also cover geology, archaeology, the Vikings and local history; and the museum has a gift shop and tea room.

Also to the north of Brodick, at Home Farm, is Arran Aromatics (01770 302595; www.arran-aromatics.co.uk; open daily 9.30-17.30, confirm winter hours), who make a range of soaps, beauty products and candles. There is a factory tour and shop. The Island Cheese Company (01770 302788; www.islandcheese.co.uk; open all year) is also located here, with demonstrations of cheese making and a factory shop, along with other shops, and Creelers, a seafood restaurant. Nearby at the Cladach Visitor Centre (01770 302977) is the Arran Brewery (01770 302353; www.arranbrewery.com), as well as a leather workshop and a bar and bistro.

Leaving Brodick, the main road goes south through a large forestry plantation, which has a series of walks. By the road at Blairmore Glen [NS 019334] is an arrangement of four massive boulders, some one metre high. A burial cist was found between the stones.

Lamlash is a large village and sweeps around Lamlash Bay, itself dominated by the Holy Island (see separate entry); it is from here that the ferry sails to that island. There is a good anchorage for yachts, and this is home to the Arran Yacht Club; diving is also available. The village has a full range of services, including shops, hotels, other places to eat, a bank and a golf course. There is also Island Porcelain (01770 601230; www.islandporcelain.com) producing a range of ornamental ceramic figures.

To the north-east is Kilbride [NS 033323], the shell of an old church, dedicated to St Bride and dating from the fourteenth century. Sculpted stones and gravestones are built into the walls, and lie in the interesting cemetery.

Kilbride, Lamlash

One is believed to be for James Hamilton, third Earl of Arran, who died in 1609. Lamlash Parish Church [NS 026309] (01770 600787; church open by arrangement) has a twenty-five metre tower and dates from Victorian times, having been built by the twelfth Duke of Hamilton. An old cross and font are in the front of the church, and are believed to have been brought here from the Holy Isle.

In the village is Studio 4 (01770 600919), which sells contemporary jewellery by Barbara Young, as well as other Scottish crafts. Nearby is Paterson Arran (01770 600606; www.paterson-arran.com), housed in the old mill, which produces a range of mustards, jams, preserves and sauces.

Between Lamlash and Whiting Bay is a headland known as Kingscross Point. It is from here that in 1306 Robert the Bruce set out on his quest to gain the throne of Scotland. A stone [NS 056282] is said to commemorate the event. Nearby are the remains of an Iron Age dun [NS 056283], by which is a mound [NS 056282]. When this mound was excavated, it was discovered that this was a Viking grave, and human bones, rivets from a boat, a decorated whalebone and a ring were recovered.

Whiting Bay is a long village along the bay, and has shops, a tea room, restaurant and hotels, as well as a youth hostel. There is also a golf course, and several forest walks start from here (see below); boats and cycles can be hired.

WHITING BAY TO KILDONAN, TORRYLINN AND BLACKWATERFOOT (A841)
Much of the south of Arran is covered in coniferous forestry plantations, and there are several signposted forest walks through the trees. One from the south of Whiting Bay leads to the impressive Glenashdale Waterfalls which fall some thirty metres, while another branch goes to Giants Graves [NS 043247]. These are the remains of two chambered burial cairns. Another cairn can be found nearby at Torr an Loisgte [NS 040248].

At Dippen Head, south of Whiting Bay, are the massive ramparts of an Iron Age fort [NS 051224], cutting of the headland. The entrances can be seen, and there are fine views from here.

Kildonan (called after St Donan) is off the main road, and has a post office and shop. There are the slight remains of an ancient castle [NS 037210], which was built in the thirteenth century. It was held by the MacDonald Lord of the Isles, then the Stewarts and the Hamiltons. Paragliding is available, based at Kildonan (01770 820292; 07984 356149; www.flyingfever.net). Offshore at Kildonan is Pladda Island, which has associations with St Blaise of Pladda, and a colony of seals. The island has had a lighthouse since 1790, which had keepers until the 1980s but is now automated. Two miles beyond Kildonan is South Bank Tearoom (01770 820206).

Far within the trees of a forestry plantation (and in a remote location) is Carn Ban [NR 991262], a large prehistoric burial cairn, about thirty metres long and eighteen wide, with a forecourt. The cairn survives to a height of more than four metres.

At Torrylinn, near Kilmory, are several prehistoric burial cairns. The most impressive of these is Torrylinn Cairn [NR 955211], which is about two metres high and twenty in diameter. The chambers of the cairn can be traced, and the remains of six people were found here, including two children. Further to the west, near Clachaig, is another large cairn [NR 949212], the mound of which is up to three metres high.

Torrylinn is home to the Torrylinn Creamery (01770 870240; www.tastetrail.com/foodproc/torrylinn.htm; open all year, daily), which has been making cheese since 1947. Cheese-making can be viewed and there is a shop. At Kilmory, along with post office and shop, is the Kilmory Workshop (01770 870310), which features woodwork, furniture, toys and stoneware pottery made on the premises. The Lagg Inn is a good hotel, built in the eighteenth century, and has fine gardens.

South of Corriecravie, and reached by a footpath, is Torr a' Chaisteal [NR 921232], the slight remains of an Iron Age dun with an outer rampart.

One mile south of Kilpatrick are the ruins of a drystone settlement [NR 906262] with a later wall. It is not certain from which period the remains come. There is a half-mile walk to the site.

Blackwaterfoot has shops including a post office, and nearby are Shiskine golf course, and Cairnhouse Riding Centre (01770 860466), which offers pony trekking. The leisure centre at the Kinloch Hotel has a swimming pool, snooker and a sauna and is open to non-residents.

BLACKWATERFOOT TO CATACOL AND LOCHRANZA (A841)
The Shiskine golf course (which also has tennis courts and a cafe) is to the north-west of Blackwaterfoot, and there is a fine sandy beach at Drumadoon Bay. To the north is The Doon or Drumadoon [NR 886292] a very large prehistoric fort,

defended by a now ruinous wall. A standing stone [NR 886293] is within the fort.

Further north, in cliffs by the shore, are several caves, one known as the King's Cave [NR 884309]. One story is that Robert the Bruce sheltered here after defeat on the mainland. He was ready to abandon his claims to the Scottish throne when he saw a spider keep trying to weave a web, despite many failures and setbacks. This inspired him to redouble his efforts and he eventually became King of Scots. This cave was, however, apparently called Fingal's Cave as late as the eighteenth century, and may have been a Christian retreat or hermitage (Rathlin Island has been given as an alternative setting for Bruce and the spider). Kirk Sessions were held here, and the cave was also used as a school. There are carvings in the walls, including crosses, figures and animals. Bars are fitted across the cave to prevent entry as the cave has been vandalised.

To the east of Tormore is Machrie Moor and a fine group of prehistoric monuments; burial cairns, hut circles and a series of unusual and atmospheric stone circles. The most impressive [NR 921324] now consists of only three stones, but the tallest is around five metres in height. Another circle is Suidhe Coire Fhionn [NR 909323], 'Fingal's Cauldron Seat' after the old hero. There are two rings of boulders, the inner consisting of eight stones, the outer of another fifteen stones. A third circle [NR 912324] has an alternate arrangement of granite boulders and taller slabs; a fourth [NR 910324] has only one upright stone, although this is four metres high; and the fifth [NR 910323] is a setting of four low boulders. There was at least one other circle [NR 912324], while on the walk to the site is Moss Farm Road Cairn [NR 901326], a Bronze Age burial cairn, some twenty metres in diameter, surrounded by kerb stones. There is a walk of about a mile to the main site.

Four miles north of Blackwaterfoot, near the main road at Machrie, is Auchagallon Cairn [NR 893346]. This dates from the Bronze Age, and the cairn is enclosed by a circle of kerbstones or standing stones, the tallest of which is two metres high. There are fine views across Kilbrannan Sound to Kintyre.

At Auchencar is a tall standing stone [NR 891363] on a small hill, known as the

Machrie Moor

Druid Stone, which is nearly five metres in height. Near here is the Old Byre Showroom (01770 840227; www.oldbyre.co.uk), which features Scottish knitwear, sheepskin and tartan rugs.

Around Catacol Bay is the small but attractive village of Catacol with a row of white-washed cottages known as the Twelve Apostles, and a hotel.

Lochranza ('loch of the rowans') is a picturesque hill-clad place, with a post office and shop, tourist information in the community hall, hotel, camping site and golf course. The ferry for Claonaig on Kintyre leaves from here. The village is dominated by the interesting and imposing ruin of Lochranza Castle [NR 933507] (open all year: key available locally), which stands on a low peninsula surrounded by the sea on three sides. Much of it dates from the thirteenth or fourteenth century, although it was later remodelled. It was used as a hunting lodge by the kings of Scots, may have been visited by Robert the Bruce, and was held by the Montgomerys for many years. The castle was used by James IV in 1493 during his campaign against the MacDonald Lord of the Isles.

Also here is the Isle of Arran Distillery (01770 830634; www.arranwhisky.com; open mid Mar-Oct, daily 10.00-17.00; winter times vary), which went into production in 1995. The visitor centre has interactive displays and a video, which is followed by a tour of the distillery. There is also a gift shop and restaurant, as well as a picnic area and garden. Also in the village is the Lochranza Studio Gallery (01770 830651), which features fine-art paintings by Ian B. Buchanan, as well as selected craft work.

There are fine walks to the very northern part of the island from the village.

LOCHRANZA TO SANNOX, CORRIE AND BRODICK (A841)

Sannox is another small village by the coast and is home to the Corrie Golf Club and a standing stone [NS 016456], and nearby at Laimhrig is the North Sannox Trekking Centre (01770 810222), which offers pony trekking. A fine walk through

Lochranza

Glen Sannox and then Glen Rosa starts from Sannox.

Corrie is a pleasant village with a row of white-washed cottages on the coast, and a hotel and village shop. Based at the shop is Marvin Elliot woodcarving (01770 810209); and also in the village is a basket weaver (01770 810296; www.willowweaver.com) and Three Dimensions (01770 810204), which sells hand-crafted jewellery, clocks and candlesticks.

STRING ROAD (B880) AND ROSS ROAD (UNLISTED)

The String Road (B880) was built by Thomas Telford in 1817, and is so called because it looks like a piece of string draped across the moor when seen from the sea. It goes from just north of the village of Brodick west, through the middle of the island, to Blackwaterfoot.

North of the String Road, south-east of Monyquil, is a large standing stone [NR 941353], more than two metres high, by the remains of a chambered cairn.

Three miles or so from Blackwaterfoot is the Balmichael Visitor Centre (01770 860430; www.thebalmichaelcentre.co.uk; open summer, daily; winter, closed Mon-Tue), housed in converted farm buildings, which has a coffee shop, craft shops (including Arran Ceramics (01770 860430) with a range of stoneware pottery), an adventure playground, indoor play barn and quad bikes for children and adults. Arran Heli-Tours (01770 860526/07909 886385; www.arranhelitours.co.uk) are based here, and offer services such as tours, transfers and emergency collections.

At Shiskine is The Studio (01770 860471; www.alisonbell.co.uk) with painting and printed silks. Shiskine is also reputed to be the burial place of St Molaise (see Holy Island), and there is a roughly carved marker in the graveyard [NR 910294].

The Ross is an unlisted road which runs from Lamlash across to the island in a sweep to emerge at the south of the island between Sliddery and Kilmory. It is a picturesque route, which rises to 300 metres or so, and is well worth a traverse in good weather.

HOTELS AND GUEST HOUSES

Aldersyde Hotel (01770 600219)
Lamlash; hotel and bar
Allandale Guest House (01770 302278; www.allandalehouse.co.uk)
Brodick; guest house; open Feb-Nov
Apple Lodge (01770 830229)
Lochranza; guest house in Edwardian country house; open all year except Xmas and New Year
Arran Hotel (01770 302265)
Brodick; hotel, bar and restaurant
Auchrannie Country House Hotel (01770 302234; www.auchrannie.co.uk)
North of Brodick; hotel, restaurant and leisure centre with swimming pool; open all year
Belvedere Guest House (01770 302397/302088; www.vision-unlimited.co.uk)
Brodick; guest house; open all year
Blackrock House (01770 81028)
Corrie; guest house; open Apr-Nov
Blackwaterfoot Lodge (01770 860202; www.blackwaterfoot-lodge.co.uk)
Blackwaterfoot; hotel and restaurant; open Easter-Oct

Breadalbane Hotel (01770 820284; www.breadalbanehotel.co.uk)
Kildonan; hotel and restaurant; self-catering apartments; open all year
Burlington Hotel (01770 700255; www.burlingtonarran.co.uk)
Whiting Bay; hotel, bar and restaurant; open Easter-mid Oct
Butt Lodge Hotel (01770 830240; www.buttlodge.co.uk)
Lochranza; hotel, bar and restaurant; open all year
Carrick Lodge (01770 302550)
Brodick; guest house; open Mar-Dec
Catacol Bay Hotel (01770 830231; www.catacol.co.uk)
Catacol; hotel
Corrie Hotel(01770 810273)
Corrie; hotel
Douglas Hotel (01770 302155)
Brodick; hotel, bar and restaurant
Dunvegan House (01770 302811)
Brodick; guest house; open all year
Eden Lodge Hotel(01770 700357; www.edenlodgehotel.co.uk)
Whiting Bay; hotel
Fairhaven Guest House (01770 830237)
Catacol, near Lochranza; guest house

Glen Artney Hotel(01770 302220;
www.glenartney-arran.co.uk)
Brodick; hotel; open Mar-Oct
Glenisle Hotel (01770 600559;
www.glenislehotel.com)
Lamlash; hotel, bar and restaurant; open
Mar-Oct
Ingledene Hotel (01770 810225)
Sannox; hotel
Invermay Guest House (01770 700431)
Whiting Bay; guest house
Kildonan Hotel (01770 820207;
www.kildonanhotel.co.uk)
Kildonan; hotel, bar and restaurant
Kilmichael Country House Hotel (01770 302068;
www.kilmichael.com)
Glencloy, by Brodick; hotel and restaurant;
open Mar-Oct
Kinloch Hotel (01770 860444; www.bw-
kinlochhotel.com)
Blackwaterfoot; hotel, indoor swimming pool
and leisure facilities; open all year
The Lagg Inn (01770 870255/870250;
www.arran.uk.com/lagg/inn)
Lagg, Kilmory; eighteenth-century coaching
inn with bar and restaurant; open Mar-Nov
Lillybank Guest House (01770 600230;
www.lilybank-arran.co.uk)
Lamlash; guest house; open Apr-Oct
Lochranza Hotel(01770 830223;
www.lochranza.co.uk)
Lochranza; hotel; open all year
Lochside Guest House (01770 860276)
Blackwaterfoot; guest house
Marine House (01770 600298)
Lamlash; guest house; open Easter-Sep
Ormidale Hotel (01770 302293; www.ormidale-
hotel.co.uk)
Brodick; hotel, bar and restaurant; open
Mar-Oct
Otterburn (01770 870227;
www.smoothhound.co.uk/hotels/
otterburn.html)
Corriecravie; hotel
The Royal (01770 700286; www.royalarran.co.uk)
Whiting Bay; hotel; open Mar-Oct
Sannox Bay Hotel (01770 810225;
www.sannoxbayhotel.co.uk)
Sannox; hotel, bar and restaurant
Stanford Guest House (01770 700313)
Whiting Bay; guest house
Tigh-Na-Mara (01770 302538)
Brodick; hotel

BED AND BREAKFAST

Alltan (1770 302937; www.alltanarran.co.uk)
Brodick; B&B
Argentine Guest House (01770 700662;
www.argentinearran.co.uk)
Whiting Bay; guest house; open all year except
22-27 Dec
Auchrannie Spa (01770 302234)
Brodick; lodges

Bay View (01770 302178)
Brodick; B&B; open all year
Bell View (01770 870364; www.sliddery.com)
Sliddery; B&B
Caberfeidh (01770 830255)
Lochranza B&B; open May-Oct
Castlekirk (01770 830202;
www.castlekirkarran.co.uk)
Lochranza; B&B; gallery; open Mar-Nov
Connemara (01770 302488)
Brodick; B&B; open all year
Craigard (01770 700378)
Whiting Bay; B&B
Croftbank (01770 830201)
Lochranza; B&B; open Mar-Dec
Crovie (01770 302 275)
Brodick; B&B; open Mar-Oct
Ellangowan (01770 700784;
www.ellangowan.me.uk)
Whiting Bay; B&B
Fyne View (01770 830386)
Lochranza; B&B
Glencloy Farm House (01770 302351)
Brodick; B&B; www.smoothhound.co.uk/
hotels/glencloy
Glenn House (01770 302092)
Brodick; B&B; open all year
Gowanlea (01770 810253)
Sannox; B&B
The Greannan (01770 860200)
Blackwaterfoot; B&B; open all year
Hawthorn Cottage (01770 302534)
Glen Sherraig, Brodick; B&B
The Invercloy (01770 302225/495)
Brodick; B&B; open Mar-Oct
Laighbent (01770 860405)
Blackwaterfoot; B&B
Mingulay (01770 700346)
Whiting Bay; B&B; open Feb-Nov
Morvern House (01770 860254)
Blackwaterfoot; B&B; open all year except
Christmas
Ocean Breeze (01770 820275)
Kildonan; B&B
Rosaburn Lodge (01770 302383)
Brodick; B&B
The Shore (01770 600764; www.arran-shore.co.uk)
Lamlash; B&B; open all year
Sunnyside (01770 700 422)
Kings Cross; B&B
View Bank House (01770 700326)
Whiting Bay; B&B
Torlin Villa (www.sliddery.com)
Kilmory; B&B
Westfield (01770 600428)
Lamlash; B&B; open all year

SELF-CATERING PROPERTIES

Alba (01770 600795)
Lamlash; self catering, sleeps four; open all year
An Caladh (01369 870388)
Shiskine; self-catering, sleeps six; open all year
Arnhall Cottage (01770 700654)
Whiting Bay; self-catering house, sleeps six

Arran Coastal Holidays (01770 600590)
Lamlash; accommodation
Auchrannie Country Club (01770 30202;
www.auchrannie.co.uk)
Brodick; lodges, sleeping up to eight
Balnagore Farmhouse (01403 822364/823743)
Machrie; self-catering house, sleeps twelve
Barra (01770 830224)
Lamlash; self-catering bungalow; sleeps six
Beech Cottage (01770 830224)
Lamlash; self-catering cottage, sleeps six
Bellevue Cottages (01770 870238;
www.sliddery.com)
Sliddery; self-catering cottage, sleeps four
Bracklinn House (01770 302303;
www.bracklinn.com)
Blackwaterfoot; self-catering house, sleeps six
Braeside (01770 860219)
Torbeg, Blackwaterfoot; self-catering, sleeps
four; open all year
Blackrock Houses (01770 810282; www.arran.net/
corrie/blackrock)
Corrie; four self-catering houses, sleep two-
fourteen
Breadalbane Hotel (01770 820284;
www.breadalbanehotel.co.uk)
Kildonan; hotel and restaurant; self-catering
apartments
Briar Cottage (01770 860334)
Kilmory; self-catering cottage, sleeps four;
open Jan-Sep
Brodick Castle Shore Lodge (NTS) (01770 302202/
312)
Brodick; self-catering lodge, sleeps fourteen
Burnside Cottage (01728 723629;
www.sliddery.com)
Sliddery; self-catering cottage, sleeps six; open
Mar-Oct
Cairnfield Farmhouse (01403 822364/823743)
Machrie; self catering, sleeps ten
Carraigh Dhubh (01770 700563)
Whiting Bay; self-catering, sleeps four-seven;
open all year
Cir Mhor Cottage (01770 302274)
Glen Rosa; self-catering cottage, sleeps two;
open all year
The Cottage (01770 830224)
Lochranza; self-catering cottage, sleeps six
Craigdhu (01770 820225)
East Bennan, Kildonan; self-catering cottage
Craiglea Court (01770 302377)
Brodick; nine self-catering apartments, sleep
two-five
Dougarie Holiday Cottages (01770 840259/
840266; www.dougarie.com)
Dougarie; self-catering traditional cottages,
sleep five-eight; open Easter-Oct
Drumla Farm (01770 820256)
Kildonan; self-catering, sleeps two-six
Fir Cottage (01770 302378)
Brodick; self-catering cottage, sleeps four;
open May-Sep
Garret Cottage (01770 700396)
Whiting Bay; self-catering, sleeps four

Goatfell View (01770 830224)
Brodick; self-catering flat, sleeps six
Gran's Cottage (01770 302380)
Glen Rosa Farm; seventeenth-century self-
catering cottage, sleeps four; open all year
Kilmichael Deluxe Cottages (01770 302219;
www.kilmichael.com)
Glencloy, by Brodick; self-catering cottage,
sleeps four; open Mar-Oct
Kinneil (01770 600307; www.kinneil.co.uk)
Lamlash; self-catering apartments, sleep seven
Knowe View (01770 830224)
Brodick; self-catering bungalow, sleeps five
Kwathu (01770 830224)
Blackwaterfoot; self-catering house, sleeps
seven
Letter (01770 830224)
Lamlash; self-catering house, sleeps five
Middle Cottage (01770 302564)
Chelan; self-catering cottage, sleeps four-six;
open all year
Monachylebeg (01770 830224)
Brodick; self-catering house, sleeps four
Mulloch Mor (01770 830224)
Lamlash; self-catering house, sleeps six
Norwood Cottage (ekmccormack@hotmail.com)
Whiting Bay; self-catering cottage, sleeps four
Ornsay Cottage (01770 830304)
Lochranza; self-catering cottage, sleeps two;
open Mar-Jan
Rindill (01770 830224)
Blackwaterfoot; self-catering chalet, sleeps four
Rowanbank (01403 822364/823743)
Machrie; self-catering cottage, sleeps four
Sandbraes (01770 700707)
Whiting Bay; self-catering cottage and chalet,
sleep four and six
Seabank (01770 830224)
Lamlash; self-catering house, sleeps seven
Seal Shore Cottage (01770 820320;
www.isleofarran.freeserve.co.uk)
Kildonan; self-catering house, sleeps eight
The Smiddy (01770 700536;
ekmccormack@hotmail.com)
Whiting Bay; self-catering cottage, sleeps four-
six; open all year
Strathwhillan House (01770 302331;
www.strathwhillan.co.uk)
Brodick; self-catering bungalow, sleeps six
Tigh an Droma Lodge (01294 552700)
Kings Cross, Whiting Bay; self-catering house,
sleeps eight/nine
Trafalgar Cottage (01770 700396)
Whiting Bay; self-catering cottage, sleeps four
View Bank House (01770 700326)
Whiting Bay; self-catering bungalow
Willow Cottage (01770 302303;
www.holidaysarranproperties.co.uk)
Whitefarland, Pirnmill; self-catering cottage,
sleeps two
Woodside Cottage (01294 224835)
Lamlash; self-catering house, sleeps ten

HOSTELS AND RETREATS

Lochranza (01770 830631; www.syha.org.uk)
Lochranza; sleeps up to sixty-eight; open Feb-Dec
Lighthouse Bunkhouse (01770 850225)
Pirnmill; bunkhouse
North High Corrie Croft and Annexe (Arran Estate Trust: 01770 302203; www.arranland.net)
Corrie
Whiting Bay (01770 700339; www.syha.org.uk)
Whiting Bay; sleeps up to forty-eight; open Mar-Oct

CAMPING AND CARAVANS

Breadalbane Lodge Park (01770 820210)
Kildonan; caravan and camping site
Ceol-na-mara (01770 600217)
Lamlash; caravan, sleeps four; open May-Oct
Glen Rosa Farm Site (01770 302380)
Near Brodick; campsite; open all year
Lochranza Caravan and Camping Site (01770 830273)
Lochranza; camping and caravan site; open Apr-Oct
Middleton Caravan and Camping Park (01770 600251/600255)
Near Lamlash; camping and caravan site; open Apr-Oct; booking essential
Sandbraes Holiday Park (01770 700707)
Whiting Bay; caravan park; open Mar-Oct
Seal Shore Camping and Touring Site (01770 820320; www.isleofarran.freeserve.co.uk)
Kildonan; site with facilities; open all year

PLACES TO EAT

Most of the hotels listed above have restaurants which are also open to non-residents of the establishments. There are also excellent cafes or restaurants at visitor attractions such as Brodick Castle (01770 302202), Arran Heritage Museum (Cafe Rosaburn 01770 302636), the Balmichael Visitor Centre (01770 860430) and the Isle of Arran Distillery (01770 830264).

Arran Taste Trail (www.tastetrail.com)

Brodick Bar and Brasserie (01770 302169)
Brodick
Butt Lodge (01770 830240; www.butlodge.co.uk)
Lochranza
Caddies (01770 600743)
Lamlash
Carraig Mhor Restaurant (01770 600453)
Lamlash
Coffee Pot (01770 700382)
Whiting Bay
Creelers (01770 302810; www.creelers.co.uk)
Home Farm, Brodick; sea-food restaurant
Drift Inn (01770 600656)
Lamlash
The Lighthouse (01770 850240)
Pirnmill

Machrie Bay Tearoom (01770 840213)
Machrie; also evening meals Mon-Thu; open Apr-mid Sep
Machrie Hall Golf Course Tearoom (01770 840213)
Machrie; open Apr-mid October
The Pantry (01770 700489)
Whiting Bay; open all year
Pier Tearoom and Restaurant (01770 830217)
Lochranza
Southbank Tea Room (01770 820206)
Southbank, near Kildonan
Stalkers Eating House (01770 302579)
Brodick
Taj Mahal (01770 600600)
Lamlash
Trafalgar Restaurant (01770 700396)
Whiting Bay
Wineport (01770 302977)
Cladach Visitor Centre, Brodick

Further Information

TRANSPORT

BUSES

The island has a good bus service, visiting most of the villages, and tickets are available for daily unlimited travel by bus
Strathclyde Transport (0141 332 7133)
Argyll and Bute Council (01546 604695)
Stagecoach West Scotland (01770 302000)
Postbus (08457 740740; www.royalmail.com/postbus)

CYCLE HIRE

Arran Adventure Co (01770 302244)
Brodick
Balmichael Visitor Centre (01770 860430; www.thebalmichaelcentre.co.uk)
String Road, near Shiskine; guided cycle tours
Brodick Cycles (01770 302460)
Brodick
Brodick Boat and Cycle Hire (01770 302 388)
Brodick
Mini Golf Cycles (01770 302272/07968 024040)
Brodick
Spinning Wheels (01770 810 660)
Corrie
Whiting Bay Cycle Hire (01770 700382)
Coffee Pot, Whiting Bay

CAR HIRE

Arran Transport (01770 302121)
Brodick
Blackwaterfoot Garage (01770 860277)
Blackwaterfoot
Glencloy Garage (01770 302224)
Glencloy, near Brodick
Whiting Bay Garage (01770 700345)
Whiting Bay

ACTIVITIES AND SPORTS

GOLF

Seven golf courses (a pass for playing all of them is available 01770 860226)

Brodick Golf Club (01770 302394)
Eighteen holes
Lochranza Golf Club (01770 830273;
www.lochgolf.co.uk)
Nine greens/eighteen tees
Lamlash Golf Club (01770 600296;
www.arran.uk.com/lamlash/golfcourse/
index.html)
Eighteen holes
Whiting Bay Golf Club (01770 700775)
Eighteen holes
Shiskine Golf and Tennis Club (01770 860226;
www.sliddery.com)
Twelve holes; tennis courts; shop and cafe
Machrie Bay Golf Club (01770 840213)
Nine holes
Corrie Golf Club (01770 810223)
Nine holes

WALKING AND CLIMBING

There are many fine hill- and ridge-walks and
climbs, ranging from easy to severe, (including
Goatfell: most visitor begin the climb from
Cladach) as well as the Isle of Arran Coastal
Way (www.coastalway.co.uk)
Continuous route around the island; can be
divided into seven walks; guide book available.
There is also a leaflet on forest walks.
Forestry Commission (01770 302218)
Ranger, Brodick Country Park (01770 302462)
Mountain Rescue (01770 302625 or 999 in an
emergency)

PONY TREKKING

Cairnhouse Riding Centre (01770 860466)
Blackwaterfoot; pony trekking available, range
of experience catered for
North Sannox Farm Park (01770 810222)
Sannox; pony trekking available

YACHTING AND SAILING

Excellent sheltered moorings can be found in
Lamlash Bay and Lochranza, although there are
many anchorages around the coast.
Arran Yacht Club (01770 600470;
www.lamlash.demon.co.uk)
Lamlash pier

BOAT TRIPS AND SEA FISHING

Brodick Boat and Cycle Hire (01770 302868)
Brodick; fishing dinghies for hire with tackle
and equipment
Blackrock Boat Hire and Guest House (enquiries
to) (01770 810282; www.arran.net/corrie/
blackrock)
Corrie 'wee Port'; sightseeing or fishing
Johnston's Marine Stores (01770 600333)
Lamlash
Lamlash Boat Hire and Holy Island Ferry (01770
600349)
Lamlash; fishing trips and sea angling: book in
advance

FISHING AND ANGLING

Fishing is available
Arran Angling Association (01770 302327)
Permits are available from: Tourist Information
Centre, Brodick; Kilmory post office and
General Stores; Bay News, Whiting Bay; Jimmy
the Barber's, Lamlash; Corrie Golf Club,
Sannox.

Port-na-Lochan Trout Fishery (01770 860276)
Blackwaterfoot; permits available from
Lochside Guesthouse, Kinloch Hotel or Bay
News, Whiting Bay

DIVING

Isle of Arran Sub-Aqua Club (01770 600523;
www.lamlash.demon.co.uk)
Lamlash Pier; dives most weekends, weather
permitting
Johnston's Marine Stores (01770 600333)
Brodick; diving equipment; information on
diving around Arran

ACTIVITIES

Arran Adventure Company (01770 302244;
www.arranadventure.com)
Ormidale Park, Brodick; climbing, abseiling,
gorge walking, sailing, survival skills, power
boating
Flying Fever (01770 820292/07984 356192;
www.flyingfever.net)
Kildonan; paragliding

LOCAL PRODUCE

Arran Brewery (01770 302353;
www.arranbrewery.com)
See Cladach Visitor Centre
Arran Chocolate Factory (01770 302873)
Invercloy, Brodick; chocolate and truffles; open
all year
Island Cheese Company (01770 302788;
www.islandcheese.co.uk)
Outskirts of Brodick (Home Farm Shopping
Centre); large variety of locally produced and
flavoured cheeses
Isle of Arran Distillery (01770 830264;
www.arranwhisky.com)
Guided tours, gift shop and restaurant open
daily 10.00-17.00; winter times vary
Paterson Arran (Arran Fine Foods) (01770
600606; www.paterson-arran.com)
Lamlash; mustards, Jams, preserves and sauces;
open all year
Torrylinn Creamery (01770 870240;
www.tastetrail.com/foodproc/torrylinn.htm)
Kilmory; demonstrations of cheese-making and
shop; open all year, daily

Arran Taste Trail (www.tastetrail.com)

ARTS AND CRAFTS

Arran Aromatics (www.arran-aromatics.co.uk)
Home Farm, Brodick; toiletries and candles;
factory tour and gift shop; open daily 9.30-
17.30, confirm winter hours; products from the
Island Cheese Co can be found at Home Farm
Arran Ceramics (01770 860430)
Balmichael Visitor Centre; stoneware pottery
Arran Pottery (01770 850238)
Thundergay, Pirnmill; hand-thrown and
decorated stoneware
Balmichael Visitor Centre (01770 860430;
www.thebalmichaelcentre.co.uk)
String Road; coffee shop, quad bikes, motor

museum, craft workshops, water mill, picnic areas; open summer, daily; winter, closed Mon-Tue

The Burnside (01770 303888; www.theburnside.com)
Brodick; mixed-media gallery

Crafts of Arran (01770 700251)
Whiting Bay; Arran crafts and Scottish gifts

Island Porcelain (01770 601230; www.islandporcelain.com)
Lamlash; ornamental ceramic figures; open Mon-Fri

Julie Gurr Basket Weaver (01770 810296; www.willowweaver.com)
Corrie; basket weaver using willow

Kilmory Workshop (01770 870310)
Kilmory; hand-made pottery and woodwork; open all year, Tue-Fri

Lochranza Studio Gallery (01770 830651)
Lochranza; paintings by Ian B. Buchanan; craft work

Marvin Elliot Woodcarving (01770 810209)
Corrie; wood carving

Old Byre Showroom (01770 840227; www.oldbyre.co.uk)
Auchencar Farm, Machrie; hand-knitted Arran sweaters and gifts; open all year

Roslyn Gibson (01770 870224)
Glenside, Kilmory; painting, drawings and knitware; open by appt

The Studio (01770 860471; www.alisonbell.co.uk)
Shiskine; works in painting and printed silks

Studio 4 (01770 600919)
Lamlash; contemporary jewellery by Barbara Young; Scottish crafts

The Whins Craftshop (01770 830650)
Lochranza; hand-painted stone characters and animals and gifts; open all year

VISITOR ATTRACTIONS AND MUSEUMS

Arran Heritage Museum (01770 302636; www.arranmuseum.co.uk)
Rosaburn, near Brodick; gift shop and tearoom; open Apr-Oct, daily 10.30-16.30

Balmichael Visitor Centre (01770 860430; www.thebalmichaelcentre.co.uk)
String Road; coffee shop, quad bikes, motor museum, craft workshops, water mill, picnic areas; open summer, daily; winter, closed Mon-Tue

Brodick Castle (01770 302202; www.nts.org.uk)
North of Brodick; castle open Apr-Oct, daily 11.00-16.30, closes 15.30 in Oct; country park and Goatfell open all year)

Cladach Visitor Centre (01770 302977)
Near Brodick; bar and restaurant, MacKenzie Leather workshop, Isle of Arran Brewery (01770 302353; www.arranbrewery.com with tours and shop)

South Bank Park Farm
Open Apr-Oct, Sun, Tue and Thu 10.00-17.00

Old Byre Showroom (01770 840227; www.oldbyre.co.uk)
Auchencar, Machrie; Scottish knitwear, sheepskin rugs, tartan rugs

ADDITIONAL INFORMATION

There are petrol stations at Brodick, Lamlash, Whiting Bay, Blackwaterfoot and Corriecravie

There is a Royal Bank of Scotland and a Bank of Scotland in Brodick with Cashline machine

EVENTS

Arran Folk Festival	June
Brodick Castle Victorian Day	August
Brodick Highland Games	August

Hill races: Goatfell (May); Glen Rosa (June); Urie Loch (July)

FURTHER READING

All About Arran (Downe, R Angus)
Blackie & Sons (reprinted by Banton Press), 1933

An Arran Anthology (Whyte, Hamish (ed.))
Mercat Press, 1997

Arran Shipwrecks 1890-99 (Johnston, Donald)
Johnston's Marine Stores, 1997

Arran and Bute (Weiner, Christine)
S Forsyth, 1996

Exploring Arran's Past (third edition) (Fairhurst, Horace)
Central Press, 1988

Isle of Arran (McLellan, Robert)
Pevensey Press, 1995

ACKNOWLEDGMENTS

Thanks to Euan Watterson at VisitArran for checking over the text

Holy Island

(also known as the Holy Isle; previously Eilean Molaise, the 'island of St Molaise' – and from which Lamlash is derived. Holy Island was used to distinguish the village from the island)

www.holyisland.org
www.ayrshire-arran.com (Ayrshire and Arran Tourist Board)

Tourist Information Centre
Brodick (0845 2255121 (general no))
    Open Jan-Dec

Map Landranger sheet: 69 (HIH map page 172)

Travel
The passenger ferry (01770 600349/600998) leaves from Lamlash (which has a full range of services) and runs hourly during the day, provided the weather and tide are suitable. The crossing takes ten minutes. Bus service 323 runs from Brodick on Arran to Lamlash.

Description
The island lies off the east coast of Arran, one mile from Lamlash. It is two miles long and half a mile wide, covering 625 acres, and is very hilly, rising to 314 metres at Mullach Mor ('big top'), from where there are great views. The island protects Lamlash Bay, making it an excellent anchorage.

Wildlife
The island was recently been replanted with thousands of native trees, and wildlife includes wild goats, Soay sheep, Eriskay ponies, rabbits and many birds, including eider ducks and gulls, and raptors such as peregrine falcons and buzzards.

Holy Island

HISTORY

Holy Island was formerly known as Eilean Molaise. Molaise (or Mo Las) was the nephew of St Blane (see St Blane's Chapel near Kingarth on Bute) and may have been educated on Bute around the turn of the seventh century. Molaise is believed to have lived in a cave on the Holy Island, which can still be visited today. The cave [NS 053303] has walls inscribed with several crosses, as well as Norse graffiti. Near the cave is a well which is reputed to have healing properties. Molaise was buried as the first Bishop of Leighlin in Ireland in 640, but tradition also has his grave at Shiskine on Arran.

Lamlash Bay is where King Hakon is believed to have marshalled his longships before going on to defeat at the Battle of Largs in 1263, and there is thought to have been a small tower or castle on the island.

The island had a small population in the nineteenth and twentieth centuries. In the 1970s it was owned by the Universities Federation for Animal Welfare. The private owners who followed sold the island in 1992 to Rokpa Trust, a Tibetan Buddhist charity. At the north of the island there is the Centre for World Peace and Health, which has guest house facilities, as well as an ongoing retreat and course programme. A closed Buddhist retreat is located to the south of the island.

PLACES TO STAY

Centre for World Peace and Health (01770 601100; www.holyisland.org)
Non-denominational accommodation for as many as sixty-four people (twenty-six single rooms, seven twin rooms and three dormitories sleeping eight people); members of the public are welcome to stay in the centre for retreats and holiday breaks; kitchen and dining room

PLACES TO EAT

Free tea and coffee for day visitors is served in the information centre

FURTHER INFORMATION

There is a walk over the mountain and along the west side of the coast

ISLAND RULES

All who visit the island are asked to abide by the **Five Golden Rules**
- To respect life and refrain from killing
- To respect other people's property and refrain from stealing
- To speak the truth and refrain from lying
- To encourage health and refrain from intoxicants (including alcohol, cigarettes and other drugs)
- To respect others and refrain from sexual misconduct

ACKNOWLEDGMENTS

Thanks to Kristine Janson, Holy Island Reception, for checking the text

SANDA

('sandy island' from Norse)

www.sanda-island.co.uk
www.visitscottishheartlands.com (AILLST)

Tourist Information Centre
Campbeltown (08707 200609)
   Open Jan-Dec

Map Landranger sheet: 68 (HIH map page 172)

TRAVEL

The island is reached by boat from the old quay at Campbeltown (Kintyre Marine Charters 01586 554667/551987/553511 (evening)), taking one hour: time ashore three hours. Trips are daily in the summer (fewer in winter), with about four hours ashore. This is also the service for rented accommodation on the island.

DESCRIPTION

Sanda is a small island, about one mile long and covering 400 acres, south-east of the tip of the Mull of Kintyre, two miles from the coast. It is about half way between Campbeltown and Northern Ireland, and has a good anchorage for yachts. To the west of the isle are steep cliffs, and the highest point is 123 metres. There is a double-turret lighthouse with an elephant-shaped rock formation at the side, completed in 1850, on the southern-most tip (the keepers' cottage of which can be rented as holiday accommodation). The island once had a population of around 100 people. *Byron Darnton*, an American liberty ship, struck rocks to the south of the island in 1947, and the fifty-four crew were rescued only after the heroics of the Campbeltown lifeboat.

Lighthouse, Sanda

189

WILDLIFE

Sanda, and the nearby Glunimore Island and Sheep Island, have many seabirds, including colonies of guillemots, razorbills and puffins, manx shearwaters and storm petrels, and seals can be seen around the shore. In July 2003 Sanda Bird Observatory became Scotland's fourth official bird observatory, with facilities and accommodation. There are also many butterflies and moths.

HISTORY

There are the remains of an old chapel [NR 728047], which was dedicated to St Ninian (or St Adamnan) and may be the oldest Christian site in Scotland. The MacDonalds of Sanda were buried here. The island was raided by the Viking king of Norway Magnus Barelegs (or Barefoot) in 1093, was held by the priory of Whithorn, and then passed to the MacDonalds of Sanda, who held it until 1929. The chief of the family was massacred at the siege of Dunaverty Castle in 1647.

Robert the Bruce is said to have stopped here on his way to Rathlin Island, and his brother, Edward, to have kept watch here, hence the name of the southern tip: Prince Edward's Rock.

PLACES TO STAY

Sanda Farmhouse (B&B)
Self-catering accommodation is available in the former cottages and buildings of the lighthouse and other cottages
Bunkhouse (own sleeping bag required)
(07810 356278 (Sanda mobile); 01586 554667/ 551987/553511 (evening); www.sanda-island.co.uk)

PLACES TO EAT

The award-winning Byron Darnton (the island tavern, named after the ship wrecked on the island; 07810 356278 (Sanda mobile))

FURTHER INFORMATION

Fishing trips can be arranged
Helicopter service can be arranged (Arran Helitours: 01586 552571)
Sanda stamps and First Day Covers are available

ACKNOWLEDGMENTS

Thanks to Meg on Sanda for checking the text, and to Andy Gray at Andy Gray Digital (www.andygraydigital.com) for the photos

Byron Darnton Tavern, Sanda

AILSA CRAIG

('fairy rock'; also known as 'Paddy's Milestone')

www.ailsacraig.org.uk
www.ayrshire-arran.com (Ayrshire and Arran Tourist Board)
Tourist Information Centre
Ayr (0845 2255121 (central no))
   Open Jan-Dec

Map Landranger sheet: 76 (HIH map page 172)

TRAVEL

Boat trips to the island can be made in good weather, although it may not be possible to land on the island, especially with easterly winds. The crossing takes about one hour. There are trips from Mark McCrindle (*MFV Glorious*; 01465 713219; www.ailsacraig.org.uk; the only one with permission to land); and ASW Fishing and Diving Charters (*Racheal Claire*; 01294833724).

DESCRIPTION

Ailsa Craig is tall and impressive, although small in area (some 99 hectares), and rises to more than 330 metres. It stands in the Firth of Clyde some eight or so miles off Ardwell Point to the south of Girvan in Ayrshire on the Scottish mainland. The island has spectacular cliffs teeming with seabirds, and there are basaltic columns rising more than 100 metres.

There is a lighthouse on the eastern side. Granite was mined from here for many centuries, and was used for building purposes as well as for curling stones. There are remains of the quarries, railways and cottages, and some 29 people lived on the island in 1881.

The number of rats became such a problem that they had exterminated a colony of puffins and were decimating other birds. Steps were taken to exterminate the rats: this succeeded in 1994 and the bird populations have made a recovery.

WILDLIFE

The island is home to a huge colony of gannets (20,000 breeding pairs), and there are also large numbers of guillemots, kittiwakes, fulmars, razorbills, shags, eider ducks, gulls and puffins. Other visitors include arctic skuas, manx shearwaters and storm petrels.

HISTORY

The island was a property of Crossraguel Abbey from the fourteenth century, and is said to have been a place of imprisonment for wrong-doing monks. It was held by the Kennedys from the Reformation, and they built a castle on the south-east of the island [NX 023995], which is now a ruin. Hugh Barclay of Ladyland seized the island for the Spanish in 1597. Some 5,000 tons of granite was quarried from the island in 2000 and was made into curling stones by Kays of Scotland, the only company in the world who still does this. The island is now managed by the RSPB.

ACKNOWLEDGMENTS

Thanks to Mark McCrindle for checking the text

Lewis

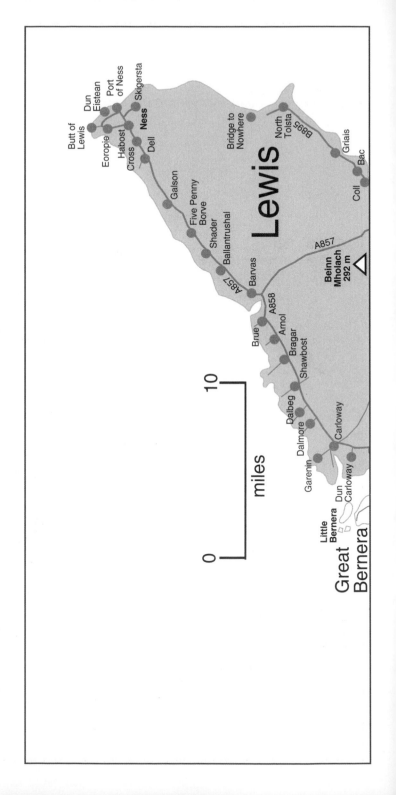

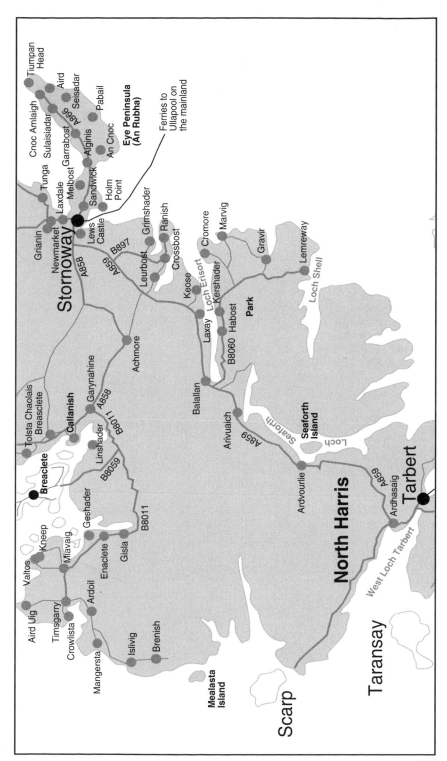

LEWIS

('marshy place' or 'place/house of song' or perhaps from 'Leod's island'; Leodhais in Gaelic; the Lews)

www.isle-of-lewis.com
www.hiddenlewis.org.uk
www.cne-siar.gov.uk
www.stornowayhistoricalsociety.org.uk
www.tolsta.info
www.breasclete.com
www.iomairtnis.com (Ness)
www.lochslewis.org
www.c-e-n.org (Ness Historical Society)
www.ceats.org.uk (West Side Historical Society)
www.barvasandbrue.com (Barvas and Brue Historical Society)
www.hebcon.com (under construction)
www.harristweed.com
www.stornowaygazette.co.uk
www.valewis.org.uk
www.visithebrides.com (Western Isles)

Tourist Information Centre
Stornoway (01851 703088)
    Open Jan-Dec

Map Landranger sheets: 8, 13, 14 (HIH map page 192-3)

TRAVEL
A vehicle ferry (CalMac 01854 612358 or 01851 702361; www.calmac.co.uk) leaves from Ullapool on the mainland and crosses to Stornoway on Lewis. There are two crossings a day from Monday to Saturday (with no service on Sunday, although this is likely to change in the near future); and the trip takes two hours and forty minutes. Ullapool (www.ullapool.co.uk) is on the A835 from Inverness, and has a range of places to eat and stay, shops, amenities and a museum (01854 612987; www.ullapoolmuseum.co.uk; open Apr-Oct, Mon-Sat; restricted opening in winter).
    Lewis and Harris occupy the same island, and there is a road (A859) between the two, although this is narrow in places. The ferry to Tarbert on Harris leaves from Uig on Skye (see Harris) – this may be an easier way to get to Lewis.
    Stornoway has an airport (01851 707400; www.hial.co.uk/stornoway-airport.html), with regular flights from Glasgow and Inverness on the mainland, and Barra and Benbecula in the Outer Hebrides.
    A bridge (B8059) connects Lewis to Great Bernera.

DESCRIPTION
Lewis (and Harris) is the third largest island in the British Isles after the mainland of Britain and of Ireland. Although often thought of as two separate islands, it is one, although nearly divided by the sea lochs Loch Seaforth and Loch Resort and the Harris hills. This is the 'border' between Lewis and Harris, although the division is as much to do with land ownership as any physical barrier.
    The island lies off the western coast of Scotland, west of Sutherland and north of the island of Skye. It is forty-five miles long and some thirty miles across at its

Uig, Lewis

widest, covering 600 square miles. Unlike Harris to the south, much of Lewis is relatively flat, although Beinn Mholach is 292 metres and Muirneag 248 metres, both of which are in the middle of Lewis and offer panoramic views. The south of Lewis is much hillier, and Park to the south-east has several imposing peaks of over 400 metres, with Benmore at 572 metres; Mealisval, near the west coast, is 574 metres. The south has many lochans and inlets of sea eating into the rugged coast. The cliffs at Swordale (Suardail), on the south-west coast of Point (Eye Peninsula or An Rubha) east of Stornoway, rise straight out of the sea and are home to hundreds of seabirds, and the lighthouse at Tiumpan Head (Rubha an Tiumpain) is in an impressive spot. The crashing waves at the Butt of Lewis (Rubha Robhanais) with its lighthouse can be monumental, even on a quiet day.

There are many wonderful stretches of excellent sandy beaches, such as Traigh Mhor at North Tolsta, along the coast of Broad Bay (Loch a' Tuath) at Back (Bac) and round to the Eye Peninsula, Port of Ness and along the north coast of Ness (Nis), Bosta (Bostadh) on Great Bernera, Traigh na Berie near Valtos (Bhaltos) and the fantastic Uig sands, where the famous Lewis chessmen were found. These are just a few of the beaches; there are many more.

Along with being the largest island, Lewis also has by far the largest population at more than 21,000 people. It, and the islands north from Vatersay, have a thriving Gaelic culture, with a local radio station, television programmes and the publisher Acair. Most road signs are also in Gaelic. Many of islanders on Lewis, Harris and North Uist are devoutly Presbyterian, and have deeply held beliefs that Sundays should be days of rest. Consequently shops and petrol stations are closed on the Sabbath, and there are (or were, until recently) no ferries or buses; the airport and ferries starting Sunday services has caused controversy. Restaurants and bars are also closed on Sundays, and meals are only available to residents of hotels.

The main town is Stornoway (Steornabhagh; 'anchor or steering bay' from Norse), on the east coast in the middle of the island. This is where the ferry from Ullapool docks, and there is an airport and a busy harbour. The town has a population of around 8,000 inhabitants, making it the biggest settlement in all the islands of

Western Scotland. There is a full range of places to eat and stay, a leisure centre, museum, public library, banks, hotels, pubs, shops, craft outlets and much else, including a golf course and a hospital, and this is also the home of the Islands' Council, Comhairle nan Eilean. The town is overlooked by Lews Castle, which stands in a wooded park with a cafe and visitor centre. There is a fine beach between Melbost (Mealabost) and the Eye Peninsula where rollers come in off the Minch.

Many islanders live in the Eye (An Rubha) Peninsula, also known as Point, amd there are townships at Aiginis (Aignis), Bayble (Pabail), Garrabost, Sulaisiadar, Seisiadar and Port Mholair. There are many settlements, mostly along the coasts, usually consisting of a smattering of houses and crofts. North of Stornoway, on the east coast and along the A895, are Tunga, Back (Bac), Grais (Griais) and North Tolsta (Tolstadh bho Thuath). There is the 'bridge to nowhere', part of a metalled road which was planned to go up to Ness (Nis) but was never completed.

There is a substantial community at Ness at the northern tip, and coming down the west coast there are townships at Galson (Gabhsann), Borve, Shader (Siadar), Barvas (Barbhas), Arnol, Bragar, Shawbost (Siabost), Carloway (Carlabhagh), Tolsta Chaolais (Tolastadh a' Chaolais), Breasclete (Breascleit) and Callanish (Calanais). Further west are Great Bernera (Bearnaraigh), Enaclete (Einacleit), Carishader (Cairisiadar), Miavaig (Miabhaig), Valtos (Bhaltos) and Kneep (Cnip), Timsgarry (Timsgearraidh), Crowlista (Cradhlastadh), Islivig (Islibhig) and Brenish (Breanais).

To the south and east are Arivruaich (Airidh a Bhruaich), Balallan (Baile Ailein), Laxay (Lacasaigh), Kershader (Cearsiadair), Marvig (Marbhig), Gravir (Grabhair) and Lemreway (Leumrabhagh) in Park (Pairc). Further north are Crossbost (Crosbost), Grimshader (Griomsidar), Leurbost (Luirbost) and Achmore (Acha Mor), which has the distinction of being the furthest inland.

The island has good roads, although there are some stretches which are single-track and they can be narrow in places. One major obstacle to quick passage can be of the woolly variety: sheep on Lewis seem to believe that right of access applies predominantly to the four legged rather than the four wheeled.

Harris Tweed is made on Lewis, despite the name, and weaving, fishing, crofting and tourism are the mainstays of the island.

WILDLIFE

Many different species of birds frequent Lewis, including gannets, terns, cormorants, skuas, fulmars, kittiwakes, oystercatchers, ringed plovers, corncrakes, waders and greylag geese; wintering birds include greenland and white-fronted geese, whooper swans and redwings. Raptors such as eagles and buzzards can also be seen. Otters can be seen around lochs and the coasts, and seals by the shore. Further out, but even sometimes close to the shore, there are dolphins, porpoises, basking sharks and different species of whale, including orcas. Red deer can be found in Park, to the south-east, introduced when it became a sporting estate.

HISTORY

Lewis has three of the foremost prehistoric sites in Scotland, with the standing stones at Callanish (Calanais), the broch at Dun Carloway and the exceptionally tall standing stone at Ballantrushal, and there are many other impressive or fascinating monuments.

The island has a long association with the Vikings, being held by them until 1266, and many of the place names are Norse in origin. Lewis was held by the MacNicols or Nicholsons, but then passed by forcible marriage to the MacLeods of Lewis. The lands were granted to the MacDonald Lords of the Isles, with the MacLeods as vassals, until the fall of the lordship in 1493.

The Fife Adventurers tried to settle on Lewis, but were beaten off by the islanders under the MacLeods: there were expeditions in 1599, 1605 and 1609, all unsuccessful and bloody. James VI then gave the island to the Mackenzies of Kintail, later earls of Seaforth, in 1610. This was resisted by the MacLeods, but after Neil MacLeod was captured and then executed in 1613 resistance withered. The Morrisons of Ness and MacAulays of Uig were other major clans.

Stornoway was a place of some importance from early times as it has an excellent anchorage. It had two old strongholds to guard the harbour. There was a castle

Callanish

at Holm, two miles south-east of Stornoway, known as MacLeod's Castle [NB 442305], which was an old fortress of that clan. This may have been used by the Fife Adventurers in 1599, supported by 600 mercenaries. Their camp was stormed by Lewis men led by Neil and Tormod MacLeod, and many of the adventurers were slain, while their leaders were seized and imprisoned for months. The castle was razed by Cromwell's forces in 1653.

The site of Stornoway Castle [NB 423327] was incorporated into the harbour in 1882. It may have dated from the eleventh century, and was held by the MacNicol family before being seized by a Viking called Leod, from whom the MacLeods were then descended. The MacNicols or Nicolsons then went to Skye. This castle was also destroyed by Cromwell's men, and a small nearby fort was then garrisoned by them. The garrison was to fare as badly as the Fife Adventurers, and they were reputedly slaughtered.

The Mackenzies were forfeited for their part in the Jacobite Rising of 1715 and the lesser-known rebellion of 1719. The sixth earl managed to regain his estates in 1741, and was then prudent enough not to become involved in the last rising, of 1745-6, which ended with disaster at the Battle of Culloden.

The Mackenzies retained Lewis, although they did not live here, and it was managed by a series of tacksmen who exploited the islanders and repeatedly raised rents. The Mackenzies sold the island (along with Great Bernera) to Sir James Matheson in 1844, and he built Lews Castle on the site of Seaforth Lodge, a house of the Mackenzies dating from the seventeenth century. Matheson's factor was responsible for evicting many islanders from their homes and land, leading to growing anger and desperation in both Lewis and Great Bernera. Park (Pairc), also known as South Lochs, was the scene for the Park Deer Raid of 1887: Lewis men drew attention to their problems by killing some of Matheson's deer and occupying land they needed to survive. A cairn commemorates the event, and there are other memorials to the land raids at Aiginis, Back and on Great Bernera near Tobson.

Matheson died in 1878, and in 1918 Lewis was sold to Lord Leverhulme, who was fantastically wealthy and whom some have called a visionary. He spent a small fortune (getting on for £1,000,000) trying to change the prospects of the islands by modernising and developing herring fishing, improving transport links and other schemes. Although few of his plans were to have a lasting impact, he gifted Lews Castle, Stornoway and the adjoining land to the people of Stornoway in 1923. He had found little success for his schemes, sold the rest of the island, and bought the South Harris estate. He was to be no more successful there, and he died in 1925.

Perhaps one of the most bitter-sweet memorials of his failed ambitions is the 'bridge to nowhere', beyond the end of the B895. This was a project to build a road up the east coast to Ness; but, when Leverhulme left, the building of the road was quickly abandoned. A waymarked footpath does lead up to Ness so that neither the bridge nor the route actually do go nowhere ...

One of the saddest events in the island's history must be the sinking of the *Iolaire* off Stornoway harbour. The *Iolaire* was returning with 260 Lewis men after the end of World War One. It foundered near the harbour on New Year's Day 1919, and more than 200 lives were lost. This was a heavy blow as the island had already lost more than 1,000 men during the war: a high proportion of the male population. There is a memorial near Holm Point.

Tours
STORNOWAY TO CALLANISH AND BARVAS (A858)

Stornoway is a relatively large and bustling town (rather less so on a Sunday and perhaps rather too much so on Friday and Saturday nights). There are plenty of places to eat and stay, as well as a full complement of shops and amenities, but it is not perhaps what everyone wants from a visit to the Western Isles. The burgh was built around the excellent anchorage, and Stornoway became a major fishing port from the seventeenth century, although this has since declined.

An Lanntair ('the Lantern') Arts Centre (01851 703307; www.lanntair.co.uk; open all year, Mon-Sat) on South Beach Street, hosts a varied programme of exhibitions and events. It also has a good coffee shop, as well as a gift and bookshop. On Francis Street in the town is the museum for Lewis and Harris, Museum nan Eilean (01851 709266; www. cnesiar.gov.uk/museum/; open sum-mer, Mon-Sat; winter Tue-Fri and Sat morning). This museum holds collections of many objects, photographs and archival material

Stornoway

on Lewis from the earliest times. There are permanent displays on archaeology, fishing and maritime history, domestic life and agriculture, and changing temporary exhibitions. The Lewis Loom Centre (01851 704500; www.lewisloom centre.co.uk; open Mon-Sat) at 3 Bayhead features displays and a guided tour on the history and production of Harris Tweed, including traditional looms, warping, waulking with Gaelic waulking songs, hand spinning and hand carding. On Cromwell Street is Hebridean Jewellery (01871 702372; www.hebridean-jewellery.co.uk) with a range of locally produced jewellery with Celtic and Pictish influences; and Mosaic (01851 700155) featuring Scottish and ethnic crafts and jewellery.

Overlooking the town on the west side of Stornoway harbour is the grand Lews Castle [NB 420332] (www.lews-castle.com), set in the fine wooded grounds and gardens of Lady Lever Park. The castle was built in the mid-nineteenth century by Sir James Matheson, but then was sold to Lord Leverhulme in 1918, who gifted it to the islanders in 1923. It has been vacant since 1997, although there are plans to turn it into a museum and hotel. In the park is Cnoc na Croich [NB 417323], ('gallows hill'), named so because criminals are thought to have been executed here. Nearby are the remains of a chambered cairn. There are shore, woodland, moorland and river walks around the grounds (a leaflet detailing them is available); and the Woodlands Centre (01851 706916; open Mon-Sat) has displays, a tearoom and toilets.

The A858 goes west of Stornoway and across the interior of the island through Achmore. P.Q.A. (01851 860551; open Mon-Thu 10.00-17.00) is at 27 Achmore, and features Harris Tweed crafts, hats, bags, toys and cushion covers.

At Garynahine is the turn-off (B8011) for Great Bernera and the Uig sands. Tigh Mealros (01851 621333), a family-run restaurant is located at Mealros, Garynahine.

At the small township of Callanish on the west coast is one of the most interesting and enigmatic of prehistoric sites; indeed, not just one site but a grouping of stone circles and settings comprising perhaps as many as twenty different monuments.

The most impressive is definitely at Callanish [NB 213330] itself. Here there is

Callanish

an avenue of nineteen upright stones, leading north from a circle of thirteen monoliths, with rows of stones leading to the south, west and east (forming a Celtic cross arrangement). The tallest of the stones, in a central position, is around five metres in height; and there was a small burial cairn in the middle of the monoliths, but this was inserted many years after the stones had first been erected. The stones are accessible to the public all year, and are in the care of Historic Scotland.

It is thought that the stones, along with the outlying settings, are aligned to the phases of the moon, and the winter and summer solstices. The stones had been overwhelmed by a layers of peat over the centuries, and when this was removed in 1857 their true magnitude was revealed. It is thought that the quarry for the stones was at Druim nan Eum [NB 230336], where there are several prostrate slabs.

The Calanais Visitor Centre (01851 621422; www.calanaisvisitorcentre.co.uk; open Apr-Sep Mon-Sat 10.00-18.00; Oct-Mar, Wed-Sat 10.00-16.00) has an exhibition, tearoom, gift shop and toilets; but there is also the excellent Calanais Tearoom (01851 621373) in a black house in the township, which has crafts and knitwear for sale. At Olcote is an archaeological exhibition and publications for sale (Margaret Curtis 01851 621277; www.geo.org/callan.htm).

There are three more accessible stone circles, which would merit more attention were it not for the magnificence of the main setting. Cnoc Ceann a' Gharaidh [NB 222326], sometimes known as Callanish II, is at the end of a track south of the main road. The stones are actually set in an ellipse; five monoliths remain erect, the tallest of which is three metres in height. East of here is Cnoc Fillibhir Bheag [NB 225327], Callanish III, on a footpath south of the main road. This consists of two circles of concentric stones: the outer ring has eight uprights, the tallest less than two metres; the inner has four stones. Ceann Hulavaig [NB 230304], Callanish IV, is to the west of the B8011 one mile south-west of Garynahine. Five monoliths remain in situ, varying in height between two and three metres. Other sites have also been identified and publications are available locally.

Boreas Knitwear (01851 621241; www.thewesternisles.co.uk/woolsweaters.htm; open Mon-Sat) with hand-framed and hand-made knitwear is based at Breasclete.

At Doune Carloway is another of Lewis's outstanding prehistoric monuments, Dun Carloway [NB 190412], the striking ruin of a broch (access at all reasonable

Dun Carloway

times). The wall stands to a height of ten metres, although one half has fallen away to the lintel of the entrance. A covered gallery runs through the wall, and there is a guard cell. In the seventeenth century the broch was being used as a stronghold by the Morrisons of Ness. Their enemies, the MacAulays of Uig, scaled the wall, dropped smouldering heather on the sleeping Morrisons, and suffocated them. Nearby is the unique, almost organic Doune Broch Centre (01851 643338; www.calanaisvisitorcentre.co.uk; open Apr-Sep, Mon-Sat 10.00-17.00).

At the township of Carloway is Clach an Tursa [NB 204430] ('stone of sorrow'), a monolith more than two metres in height. Two fallen stones lie nearby. Towards the sea is the restored blackhouse township of Garenin (Gearrannan), which was only abandoned in 1973. It has a museum, cafe and gift shop (01851 643416; www.gearrannan.com; open all year) in the thatched buildings. Some of the houses can be rented as holiday accommodation, and there is also a hostel and public toilets. Also at Carloway is Taigh nan Creaganan (01851 643356; www.creaganan.com), making hand-made silver jewellery, and there is also a hotel.

Dalbeg is further up the road, and there is a fine sandy beach by the shore of Loch Dalbeg in a lovely spot.

The Shawbost Museum (01851 710212; open Apr-Sep) has displays illustrating the island way of life, with exhibitions on crofting, fishing and domestic life up to 1950. The Mill of the Blacksmiths [NB 244464] is a restored Norse horizontal mill, and straddles the channel for the water wheel. Along with the grain kiln, the mill is thatched. At North Shawbost is Kenneth Macleod Harris Tweed Mill (01851 710251) with guided tours and Harris Tweed for sale. There is also the Shawbost Inn (01851 710632) at Raebhat House.

On an island in Loch an Duna is Dun Bragar [NB 285474], an ancient broch rising more than four metres from the water. It was still in use in the sixteenth or seventeenth century when the fugitive John Roy MacPhail was surprised here. North of Bragar is Teampull Eoin [NB 288488], the remains of a chapel, and a cemetery. There is a shop at Bragar.

Arnol is the next township, and among the houses is the Blackhouse Museum [NB 312495] (01851 710395; open Apr-Sep, 9.30-18.30; Oct-Mar, 9.30-16.30, closed

Arnol Blackhouse Museum

Sun all year), a superbly evocative Lewis dwelling house, constructed without mortar and thatched on a wooden framework: the people lived in one end, their beasts in the other. It was last used as a home in 1964. The central peat fire is kept burning at all times (although there is no chimney) and the building has many of its original furnishings. Hebridean Replicas (01851 710562) features hand-made Lewis chess sets and island miniatures; also here is the Celtic Art Gallery (01851 710531).

At Brue is the Oiseval Gallery, home to James Smith Photography (01851 840240; www.oiseval.co.uk), a gallery with work for sale.

Just beyond here the road joins the A857 from Stornoway and turns north to Ness. There is a petrol station at the junction.

STORNOWAY TO PORT OF NESS (A857)

The road runs north out of the outskirts of Stornoway through the lonely and peaty middle of the island until it reaches Barvas. There are plans afoot to build a large wind-farm with many turbines. The road joins the A858, which goes to Arnol, Carloway and Callanish and to the south, and there is a petrol station. The A857, however, continues north up the west coast.

The Morven Gallery (01851 840216; www.morvengallery.com) is at Upper Barvas. Along with a gallery of paintings, ceramics, sculptures, photographs and textiles by local artists and crafts people, there is also a shop with jewellery, books and gifts and a cafe.

Three miles on from Barvas is Ballantrushal and Clach an Trushal [NB 375538], a hugely impressive standing stone, probably the tallest in Scotland at more than six metres high. Tradition has it that this marks the site of a battle between the MacAulays of Uig and the Morrisons of Ness.

Steinacleit prehistoric site [NB 393541] is at Shader, and is a rather puzzling place, perhaps a stone circle, a robbed cairn or a homestead. There is a dun in the loch, and Clach Stei Lin [NB 396546] is a standing stone less than two metres in height. Just up the road is Borgh Pottery (01851 850345; www.borgh-pottery.com; open Mon-Sat, 9.30-18.00) with hand-made ceramics and a selection of crafts and gifts. Beyond this, at Galson, is Galson Farm Guest House (01851 850492; www.galsonfarm.co.uk), which offers accommodation and evening meals.

The Ness Heritage Centre (01851 810377; www.c-e-n.org; open Mon-Fri, also Sat Jun-Sep) at Habost has collections and archives on the area of Ness, and hosts differing exhibitions. A tenth-century cross is thought to have marked the grave of St Ronan. The Dell Mill [NB 491614] has been restored and retains its equipment and machinery; there are displays on the mill and local grain production and the mill is open by appointment. Taigh Dhonnchaidh Art and Music Centre (01851 810166; www.taighdhonnchaidh.com) is located in a restored cottage and is a venue for workshops, lectures, classes, performance and events, along with a cafe and gift shop (seasonal). There is also the Cross Inn (01851 810152; www.crossinn.com) which is open all year; and there are shops and a fine beach.

At Port of Ness is Harbour View Gallery (01851 810735; www.abarber.co.uk; open Mon-Sat), featuring watercolours and prints by Anthony Barber; and Callicvol Quilts (01851 810681; www.callicvolquilts.com) with hand-crafted patchwork quilts and smaller items. North of here is Dun Eistean [NB 536650], a small island separated from the mainland by a deep ravine, on which there are the traces of buildings and a wall, the stronghold of the Morrisons of Ness, dating from the sixteenth century or earlier. There is a bridge to give access to the island.

Further north at Eoropie is St Molu-ag's Church [NB 519652] (open Easter-Sep during daylight hours), a fine peaceful and atmospheric build-ing. The present church dates from the twelfth century but it was restored in 1912, although it has no electricity.

St Moluag's Church

A small abutting building is believed to have been added so that lepers could witness the service in the church: all that connects the two buildings is a squint or tiny viewing hole. The church probably stands on the site of an early Christian monastery; nearby is a mound, the site of Teampull Ronaidh [NB 523654], and there was also a holy well here. These were dedicated to St Ronan, who also has connections with the remote island of Rona far to the north. Many birds can be seen at nearby Loch Stiapaval, including a breeding colony of black-headed gulls, whooper swans, mallards, tufted ducks and widgeons.

An unlisted road leads to the tall brick lighthouse at the Butt of Lewis, which is some thirty-eight metres high. The waves here can be monumental, even on a relatively quiet day.

Butt of Lewis

Also at Ness is a souterrain at Carnan a' Ghrodhair [NB 512640], which has an underground passage three metres long and the ruin of a cell. The cemetery is nearby, and to the west is Teampull Pheadair [NB 508638], the remains of an old chapel. Beyond Eoropie on a steep rock along the north coast is Luchruban [NB 508660], possibly the site of a hermitage or early Christian oratory as there is a corbelled cell and passageway in an enclosure; the name, however, comes from the tradition that this was the haunt of pygmies or 'little men'.

Stornoway to North Tolsta (B895)

The road runs through Tunga to the good sandy beach at Traigh Chuil, where there is parking and public toilets. At Coll is Broadbay Ceramics (01851 820219; www.broadbayceramics.co.uk; open all year) which features a wide range of pottery and ceramics; and Anna Macneil Crafts (01851 820559). There is another beach at Traigh Ghriais and the ruin of St Aula's church [NB 490415]. Two miles north-west of Griais, on the slope above the river, is Carnan a' Mharc [NB 472439], a large chambered burial cairn, more than thirty metres long and three metres in height.

Traigh Mhor at Tolsta is a fantastic two-mile length of sand, and there are public toilets and parking. Not far beyond here is the 'bridge to nowhere'.

There is a waymarked walk up to Ness, which is around eight miles from the 'bridge to nowhere', although the bridge does actually lead to 'somewhere'.

Stornoway to Arivruaich (A859)

The road leaves Stornoway and swings around to the south. The B897 runs down to Crossbost and an unlisted road to Leurbost, where there is a filling station and shop. Fishing permits can also be purchased.

The Kinloch Museum (01851 830778) is at Laxay, and at Balallan is a cairn [NB

261196], a memorial to the Park Deer Raid of 1887. There is a post office and general store in the settlement.

Just beyond here is the turn-off for Kershader and Park (B8060), a lovely route which meanders off to the east. At Kershader is the Ravenspoint Centre (01851 880236; www.ravenspoint.net) which has a shop with crafts for sale and a tearoom, as well as public toilets. Hostel accommodation is also available. At Gravir is an exhibition on Park (01851 880705; open summer, Mon-Sat) in the old school.

On the north shore of Loch Seaforth and down an unlisted road off the A859, is a stone circle [NB 278166], although only three stones remain upright, the tallest about a metre and half in height. The main road goes through Arivruaich, through remote and lovely country, to Harris and the south.

STORNOWAY TO TIUMPAN HEAD (POINT) (A866)

The A869 runs east past the town's airport and Sandwick, and the turn-off to the south for Holm Point. It was off Holm Point that the *Iolaire* sank with the loss of more than 200 men in 1919, and there is a monument [NB 445305] to those who were lost. At Melbost is Breanish Tweed (01851 701524; www.breanishtweed.co.uk), a small family business hand weaving light-weight pure new wool tweed.

The main road travels along a narrow isthmus bordered on both side by sandy beaches. There is car parking and public toilets. On the Eye Peninsula, also known as An Rubha ('point or headland') or just Point, are the ruins of St Columba's Church [NB 484322] at Aiginis, formerly the parish church of Stornoway, in a lovely spot. This is reputedly the site of a church of St Catan, who was active in the sixth and seventh centuries. The present building, however, dates from the fourteenth century. It was used as a burial place by the MacLeods of Lewis, perhaps nineteen chiefs in all, and there are two stone memorials, which are believed to be for Roderick, the seventh chief, and Margaret, daughter of (another) Roderick MacLeod, who died in 1503. There is a large burial ground with some interesting memorials; and there are fine views from here. There is a monument to the Aiginis Farm Raiders [NB 483321].

There are many townships on the peninsula and at Pabail Iarach (Lower Bayble) is the Barn Gallery (01851 870704; open Mon-Sat), which features paintings by local artists.

The main road runs out towards Rubha an Tiumpan, where there is a lighthouse, the buildings of which are used as a cat and dog home. This is another picturesque spot with excellent views across the waters of the Minch to the mainland.

Lighthouse, Tiumpan

GARYNAHINE TO GREAT BERNERA AND TIMSGARRY (B8011 AND B8059)

At Garynahine the B8011 turns west, passing the Ceann Hulavaig stone circle [NB 230304] (see above). After a few miles the B8059 runs north to Great Bernera and the 'bridge across the Atlantic' to that scenic and interesting island.

The B8011 runs round Little Loch Roag, passing through Gisla where there is Gisla Woodcraft (01851 672371; www.gisla-woodcraft.co.uk) with hand-turned wooden gifts and other crafts. The road runs up to Miavaig, from where Sea Trek (01851 672464; www.seatrek.co.uk) make short trips and longer excursions to islands such as Scarp, Taransay and the Flannan Isles, and even Mingulay, in a RIB.

An unlisted road goes up to Kneep and Valtos, where there are long stretches of beautiful sands with views across to Great Bernera. At Kneep [NB 098366] is a well-preserved wheelhouse, which retains two roofed cells, found when storms stripped away sand dunes.

The B8011 runs through the narrow and lovely Glen Valtos before arriving at Timsgarry, where there is a filling station and general store. At nearby Crowlista is the Uig Heritage Centre (01851 672456; open Jun-Sep), which houses a local history museum and photographic exhibits, plus a tea room and crafts. Across the bay are

Uig sands

the sands of Uig, where the famous Lewis chessmen were found in 1831. This was the domain of the MacAulays of Uig, one of the great clans of Lewis.

Further north at Aird Uig near Gallan Head is Bonaventure (01851 672474; www.bonaventurelewis.co.uk; booking essential), a licensed Scottish-French restaurant with fine views over West Loch Roag.

The white sands at Uig are so dazzling on a sunny day that it can hurt to look at them. On the edge of Uig sands (cross using the bridge if approaching from the car park) is Dun Borranish [NB 050332], a ruinous dun with a causeway on a rocky outcrop looking across the beach. The story goes that this was once the abode of the giant Cuithach, who terrorised the area until slain by a party of heroes. His grave is marked by a setting of stones [NB 035364].

An unlisted road leads to the south and more small townships.

RONA (OR NORTH RONA)

Rona (Ronaidh) may be named after the holy man St Ronan; or it may be Norse and mean 'rocky island'; or perhaps 'seal island' from Gaelic.

This is one of the remotest parts of the British Isles, and lies some forty-four miles north-east of the Butt of Lewis. The men of Ness come all the way to Sula Sgeir ('gannet skerry'), a rock ten miles from Rona, for the 'guga hunting': the harvesting and preserving with salt of young gannets for food. There are a series of interesting sea caves.

On Rona is one of the best-preserved groups of buildings from the early Christian period, probably the seventh or eighth century, consisting of an oratory and cashel. Burial markers incised with crosses date from between the seventh and twelfth centuries; and a stone cross from here is now in the Ness Heritage Centre. The island was last permanently inhabited in 1844.

Rona and Sula Sgeir are a National Nature Reserve, with breeding colonies of seabirds, including guillemots, fulmars, great black-backed gulls, razorbills, kittiwakes, storm petrels, leach's petrels, puffins and gannets (more than 130,000 birds). There are also thousands of seals which calve here, forming the third largest colony in Britain.

It is recommended that Scottish National Heritage should be contacted if landing on the island is envisaged. Contact SNH, 32 Francis Street, Stornoway, Isle of Lewis, HS1 2ND or 01851 705258 (www.nnr-scotland.org.uk; www.snh.org.uk).

Northern Light Charters (01631 740595; www.northernlight-uk.com) and Island Cruising (01851 672381; www.island-cruising.com) make cruises to the island.

FLANNAN ISLES

Flannan Isles ('St Flannan's Isles': St Flannan is believed to have been the half-brother of St Ronan) are a group of lovely islands, some twenty-one miles west and north of Gallan Head on Lewis. The islands are known as the Seven Hunters, and are home to many colonies of seabirds, including puffins, fulmars, petrels, auks and gannets. As at Sula Sgeir and Rona, men from Lewis came to the isles to exploit the birds, at considerable risk to their own lives. Whales and dolphins are often seen in the waters here.

On Eilean Mor, the largest of the group, are the remains of a small corbelled chapel or oratory, dating from the seventh or eighth century. It is associated with the seventh-century St Flannan. Islanders from the west of Lewis are said to have made pilgrimages to the islands, even after the Reformation. There are some remains of an old chapel.

There is a lighthouse on Eilean Mor, and this was the scene of a famous mystery in 1900 when the three keepers disappeared without a trace. No explanation is known as to how they could all vanish, but theories include a monstrous wave, a monstrous serpent or a monstrous argument between the men. The lighthouse is now automatic.

The islands are sometimes visited by Sea Trek (01851 672464; www.seatrek.co.uk; departures from Miavaig jetty, on B8011, nine miles west of Callanish). Several hours can be spent on the islands, depending on sea conditions. Northern Light Charters (01631 740595; www.northernlight-uk.com), Westernedge Charters Ltd (01506 824227/07811 387633; www.westernedge.co.uk) and Island Cruising (01851 672381; www.island-cruising.com) also make cruises to the island.

HOTELS AND GUEST HOUSES

Baile-na-Cille (01851 672242;
www.bailenacille.com)
Timsgarry; guest house
Caberfeidh Hotel (01851 702604;
www.calahotels.com)
Stornoway; hotel; open all year
C Afrin (01851 703482)
Stornoway; guest house
Caladh Inn (01851 702740; www.calahotels.com)
Stornoway; hotel; open Mar-Oct
Caledonian Hotel (01851 702411)
Stornoway; hotel; open all year
Cleascro Guest House (01851 860302;
www.cleascro.co.uk)
Achmore, Lochs; guest house; open all year
County Hotel (01851 703250;
www.activehotels.com)
Stornoway; hotel; open all year
Cross Inn (01851 810152; www.crossinn.com)
Cross, Ness; inn; open all year
Crown Hotel (01851 703181/01851 703734)
Stornoway; hotel and restaurant; open all year
Doune Braes Hotel (01851 643252; www.doune-braes.co.uk)
Doune, Carloway; hotel and restaurant; open all year
Eshcol Guest House (01851 621357;
www.eshcol.com)
Breasclete, Callanish; guest house in eighteenth-century farmhouse, dinners and packed lunches; open all year
Galson Farm Guest House (01851 850492;
www.galsonfarm.co.uk)
South Galson; guest house; open all year
Greenacres Guest House (01851 706383)
Stornoway; guest house; open all year
Hal o' the Wynd Guest House (01851 706073;
www.halothewynd.com)
Stornoway; guest house; open all year
Handa Guest House, Lochs (01851 830334)
Lochs; guest house; open May-Oct
Hebridean Guest House (01851 702268;
www.hebrideanguesthouse.co.uk)
Stornoway; guest house; open all year
Loch Roag Guest House (01851 621357;
www.lochroag.com)
Breasclete, Callanish ; guest house; open all year
Leumadair Guest House (01851 612706;
www.leumadair.co.uk)
7 Callanish; guest house; open Apr-Dec
The Old House (01851 702485)
Stornoway; guest house; open all year
Park Guest House and Restaurant (01851 702485;
www.taste-of-scotland.com/
park_guest_house.html)
Stornoway; guest house (and licensed restaurant which is open Tue-Sat); open all year
Royal Hotel (01851 702109; www.calahotels.com)
Stornoway; hotel, restaurant and bistro; open all year
Seaforth Hotel (01851 702740;
www.activehotels.com)
Stornoway; hotel and restaurant; open all year

BED AND BREAKFAST

Airigh (01851 710478)
South Shawbost; B&B; open Mar-Nov
Alexandra's (01851 703247)
Kildun, Stornoway; B&B; open all year
Bonaventure (01851 672474;
www.bonaventurelewis.co.uk)
Aird, Uig, Timsgarry; B&B
Caladh (01851 820743/07909 556584)
44 Grais; B&B; open all year
Carloway Bed And Breakfast (01851 643482;
www.carlowaybedandbreakfast.co.uk)
28 Knock, Carloway; B&B
Ceol na Mara (01851 870339; www.ceol-na-mara.co.uk)
1a Aiginis, Point ; B&B; open all year
Christina's B&B (01851 704122; www.witb.co.uk/
links/slater.htm)
Stornoway; B&B; open all year
Christine Kennedy (01851 705545)
Stornoway; B&B
Clearview (01851 830472; www.clearview-lewis.co.uk)
44 Balallan, Lochs; B&B; open all year
Craigard (01851 70 6174; www.craigard.co.uk)
Stornoway; B&B; open all year
Mrs Davina Macdonald (01851 703254;
www.davinamacdonald.co.uk)
Stornoway; B&B; open all year
Dolly's B&B (01851 870755)
33 Aiginis, Point; B&B; open all year
Doniver (01851 704194; www.doniver.co.uk)
Stornoway; B&B; open all year
Dunroamin (0845 6448635/01851 704578/07711
853946; www.dunroaminbandb.co.uk)
Stornoway; B&B; open all year
Fernlea (01851 702125; www.witb.co.uk/links/
fernlea.htm)
Stornoway; B&B; open all year
13 Garden Road (01851 705315)
Stornoway; B&B; open all year.
Gledfield (01851 830233; www.gledfield-balallan.co.uk)
5 Balallan, Lochs; B&B; open all year
Hebridean Surf Holidays (01851 705862;
www.hebrideansurf.co.uk)
Stornoway; B&B
Heatherview (01851 850781; www.witb.co.uk/links/
heatherview)
55 North Galson; B&B; open all year
Hebron (01851 702890)
Stornoway; B&B; open all year
Kathryn Murray (01851 705893/701083)
Stornoway; B&B
Kennedy Terrace (01851 702780)
Stornoway; B&B; open all year
Kerry-Croy (01851 706553)
Stornoway; B&B; open all year
Laxay B&B (01851 830432; www.10laxay.co.uk)
10 Laxay (Lacasaigh), Lochs; B&B; open all year
Primrose Villa (01851 703387;
www.primrosevilla.com)
Stornoway; B&B; open all year

Rockvilla (01851 840286; www.rockvilla.org)
Barvas; B&B; open all year
The Rowans (01851 704473; www.witb.co.uk/links/
rowans.htm)
Stornoway; B&B; open all year
Seaside Villa (01851 820208;
www.seasidevilla.co.uk)
Back; B&B; open all year
Sula Sgeir (01851 705893)
Stornoway; B&B; open all year
Thorlee Guest House (01851 705466)
Stornoway; B&B
Westwinds (01851 703408; www.westwinds-
newton.co.uk)
Stornoway; B&B; open all year

SELF-CATERING PROPERTIES

Aignish Self Catering (01851 870258; www.theflat-
aignish.co.uk)
Aiginis, Point; self-contained annexe, sleeps
four; open all year
Aird Cottage (01851 810207; www.witb.co.uk/
links/airdcottage.htm)
South Dell, Ness; self-catering cottage, sleeps
four; open all year
24 Aird Tong (01851 700288)
Tong; self-catering house, sleeps four; open all
year
7a Ardroil (07785 753758; www.7a-ardroil.com)
Ardroil, Uig; self-catering
Balallan Self Catering (01851 830253/449)
Balallan, Lochs; self-catering house, sleeps six;
open all year
Bayview Cottage (01851 700000; www.bayview-
cottage.co.uk)
Stornoway; self-catering cottage
Brae House (01851 850350)
High Borve; self-catering house, sleeps six;
open all year
Braighe Self Catering (01851 702304;
www.visithebrides.co.uk)
21 Braighe Road, by Stornoway; self-catering
cottage, sleeps six; open all year
Calan Maran (01851 612706; www.leumadair.co.uk)
Callanish; self-catering cottage, sleeps four-six;
open Apr-Dec
10 Ceann a Tuath (01851 710640)
Ceann a Tuath; self-catering semi-detached
house, sleeps six; open all year
Ceol Na Mara (01851 810429;
www.ceolnamara.org.uk)
Port of Ness; traditional stone-built croft
house, sleeps four; open all year
Chalet Centre (01851 705771)
Newvalley; self-catering chalet, sleeps four;
open all year
Clach na Cuthaig (01859 520217;
www.scotland2000.com/cuthaig)
Gravir, Lochs; self-catering house, sleeps six-
seven; open all year
Cnoc Cottages (01851 870537)
Knock, Point; four chalets, each sleep four;
open all year

Gearrannan Blackhouse Village (01851 643416;
www.gearrannan.com)
Gearrannan, Carloway; four thatched cottages,
one sleeping up to sixteen; cafe, exhibition and
'working blackhouse' museum; open all year
Glen Gravir Cottage (01851 703575;
www.witb.co.uk/links/maryhill.htm)
Gravir, South Lochs; self-catering house, sleeps
six; open all year
Handa Self Catering (01851 830334;
www.westernisleswelcome.co.uk)
Keose, Lochs; self-catering house, sleeps four;
open all year
Hollyburn (01851 870483; www.hollyburn.co.uk)
Crulivig, near Great Bernera; self-catering
bungalow, sleeps six; open all year
Kabuis Self Catering (01851 710461;
www.kabuis.co.uk)
Shawbost; self-contained wing, sleeps four;
open all year
Kebbock View (01491 641051;
www.kebbockview.co.uk)
Gravir, Lochs; self-catering house, sleeps five;
open all year
Kirklea Chalet (01851 820379;
www.kirkleachalet.co.uk)
Vatisker; self-catering chalet, sleeps five; open
all year
Laxdale Holiday Park (01851 706966/703234;
www.laxdaleholidaypark.com)
Laxdale; self-catering bungalow, sleeps six;
open all year
Longorm Self Catering (01851 710240; www.lon-
gorm.co.uk)
Shawbost; self-catering bungalow, sleeps four;
open all year -
Macrae House (01851 706205; www.witb.co.uk/
links/branahuie.htm)
Stornoway; self-catering semi-detached house,
sleeps four; open all year
The Mollans (01851 705338/07778 784533;
www.mollans.co.uk)
Shawbost; self-catering cottage, sleeps six;
open all year
Number 10 (01851 621722; www.witb.co.uk/links/
granville.htm)
Tolsta Chaolais; self-catering house, sleeps six;
open all year
Oceanview (01851 704751; www.oceanview.org.uk)
Breanish, Uig; self-catering cottage, sleeps six;
open all year
Ocean View (001-613-832-2244; home.istar.ca/
-psutherl/oceanview/index.html)
Brue, Barvas; self-catering, traditional croft
house, sleeps four; open all year
Scaliscro Lodge (01851 672325;
www.scaliscro.co.uk)
Scaliscro; self-catering lodge; open all year
Sea Breeze (01851 672394; www.witb.co.uk/links/
seabreeze.htm)
Sheshader, Point; self-catering cottage, sleeps
four; open all year
Shiant View Self Catering (01851 705283;
www.hebrideanselfcateringholidays.com)
Orinsay, South Lochs; self-catering house,
sleeps six; open all year

Tigh Na Mara (01851 830479;
www.eileanoirceos.co.uk)
Keose, Lochs; self-catering house, sleeps five;
open all year
Tolsta Chaolais (01851 621260)
Tolsta Chaolais; self-catering house, sleeps six;
open all year

HOSTELS AND RETREATS

Galson Farm Bunkhouse (01851 850492;
www.galsonfarm.freeserve.co.uk/bunkhse.htm)
South Galson; sleeps eight; open all year
Garenin Youth Hostel (www.gatliff.org.uk)
Garenin, Carloway; hostel in restored black
house, sleeps fourteen; open all year
Laxdale Bunkhouse Hostel (01851 703234;
www.laxdaleholidaypark.com)
6 Laxdale Lane; bunkhouse, sleeps sixteen;
open all year
Ravenspoint Centre (01851 880236;
www.ravenspoint.net)
Kershader, Lochs; hostel, sleeps fourteen;
kitchen, showers and laundry; shop with local
crafts for sale, tearoom and public toilets on
site
Stornoway Backpackers Hostel (01851 703628;
www.stornoway-hostel.co.uk)
Stornoway; sleeps sixteen; kitchen, showers,
breakfast provided; open all year; booking
essential Dec-Feb

CAMPING AND CARAVANS

Eilean Fraoich Camp Site (01851 710504;
www.eileanfraoich.co.uk)
North Shawbost; ten touring pitches; open
May-Oct
Laxdale Holiday Park (01851 703234/706966;
www.laxdaleholidaypark.com)
Laxdale; forty-two touring pitches (open May-
Nov); three caravans, each sleep six (open Jan-
Dec)

PLACES TO EAT

Many of the hotels listed in the accommodation
section also have restaurants or bar meals.

An Lanntair (01851 703307; www.lanntair.com)
Stornoway; the complex has a coffee shop
Baile na Cille (01851 672242)
Timsgarry; dinners and lunches by
arrangement; confirm opening
Balti House (01851 706116)
Stornoway
Bonaventure (01851 672474;
www.bonaventurelewis.co.uk)
Aird Uig (Gallan Head), Timsgarry; licensed,
Scottish-French restaurant with fine views over
West Loch Roag; booking essential
Caberfeidh Hotel (01851 702604;
www.calahotels.com)
Stornoway; hotel and restaurant

Callanish Tearoom (01851 621373)
The Black House, Callanish; tearoom and
crafts and knitwear
Calanais Visitor Centre (01851 621422;
www.calanaisvisitorcentre.co.uk)
Callanish; exhibition, tearoom, gift shop and
toilets; open summer Mon-Sat 10.00-19.00;
winter 10.00-16.00
The Coffee Pot (01851 703270)
Stornoway
Cross Inn (01851 810152; www.crossinn.com)
Cross, Ness; licensed restaurant with seafood
County Hotel (01851 703250; ;
www.activehotels.com)
Stornoway
Crown Hotel (01851 703181/734)
Stornoway
Doune Braes Hotel (01851 643252; www.doune-
braes.co.uk)
Carloway
Freddie's (01851 702289)
Stornoway
Galson Farm Guest House (01851 850492;
www.galsonfarm.co.uk)
38 South Galson, Ness
Gearrannan Blackhouse Village (01851 643416;
www.gearrannan.com)
5A Gearrannan, Carloway; restored blackhouse
village with museum, cafe and gift shop;
accommodation can be rented in the village
and there is a youth hostel
Park Guest House and Restaurant (01851 702485;
www.taste-of-scotland.com/
park_guest_house.html)
Stornoway; licensed restaurant, open Tue-Sat
Ravenspoint Centre (01851 880236;
www.ravenspoint.net)
Kershader, Lochs; hostel, sleeps fourteen;
kitchen, showers and laundry; shop with local
crafts for sale, tearoom and public toilets on
site
Royal Hotel (01851 702109; www.calahotels.com)
Stornoway; hotel, restaurant and bistro; open
all year
Seaforth Hotel (01851 702740)
Stornoway; hotel, restaurant and bar
Shawbost Inn (01851 710632)
Raebhat House, North Shawbost; restaurant
for up to thirty
Thai Cafe (01851 701811)
Stornoway
Taigh Dhonnchaidh Art and Music Centre (01851
810166; www.taighdhonnchaidh.com)
Ness; cafe and gift shop (seasonal); arts and
music centre; workshops, lectures, classes,
performance and events
Tigh Mealros (01851 621333)
Mealros, Garynahine, near Callanish; family-
run unlicensed restaurant (BYOB); confirm
opening in winter
The Whalers Rest (01851 701265;
www.thewhalersrest.co.uk)
Stornoway

Uig Heritage Centre (01851 672456)
Crowlista, Uig; local history museum and
photographic exhibitions with tea room and
crafts; open Jun-Sep
Woodland Centre (Lews Castle) (01851 706916)
Stornoway; displays, tearoom and public
toilets; open Mon-Sat

Further Information
TRANSPORT

BUSES
(see www.cne-siar.gov.uk/travel/)
Hebridean Transport (01859 502011)
Stornoway Bus Station (01851 704327)
CYCLE HIRE
Alex Dan Cycles (01851 704025;
www.hebrideancycles.co.uk)
Stornoway; hire, sales and repairs
TAXIS (SEVERAL FIRMS INCLUDING:)
Central Cabs (01851 706900)
Stornoway
Express Taxis (01851 702233)
Stornoway
Hebridean Taxis (01851 702708/703599)
Stornoway
Island Taxis (01851 705533)
Stornoway
Stornoway Cabs (01851 702092;
www.stornowaycabs.com)
Stornoway
CAR AND VEHICLE HIRE
Arnol Car Rentals (01851 710548;
www.arnolmotors.com)
Arnol, Barvas; cars and vans for hire
Jackie's Hire-Drive (01851 840343)
Barvas
Lewis Car Rentals (01851 703760; www.lewis-car-
rental.co.uk)
Stornoway; cars for hire
Lochs Motor Transport (01851 705857)
Stornoway
Mackinnon Self Drive (01851 702984;
www.mackinnonselfdrive.co.uk
Stornoway; cars to commercial vehicles for hire
Riddell Autos (01851 706622;
www.riddellautos.co.uk)
Stornoway
Stornoway Car Hire (01851 702658)
Stornoway Airport
Hebridean Campervan Holidays (01851 704578;
www.hebrideancampervanholidays.co.uk)
Stornoway; camper vans for hire

ACTIVITIES AND SPORTS

YACHTING AND SAILING
www.sailhebrides.info
SURFING
Hebridean Surf Holidays (01851 705862;
www.hebrideansurf.co.uk)
Accommodation, information and facilities for
surf holidays

FISHING AND ANGLING
Stornoway Sea Angling Club (01851 702021;
www.stornowaysac.co.uk)
South Beach Quay, Stornoway; sea angling
Stornoway Angling Association (01851 705464;
www.stornoway-angling-association.co.uk
Stornoway; loch and river fishing; no fishing on
Sun
Sportsworld (01851 705464)
Stornoway; sports gear and fishing tackle; day
and evening fishing trips
BOAT TRIPS
Sea Trek (01851 672464; www.seatrek.co.uk)
Miavaig, Uig; short trips and day trips;
excursions to deserted islands such as Scarp,
Taransay and the Flannan Isles; most days in
summer except Sun
An Sulaire Trust (01851 870038;
www.ansulaire.com)
30 Upper Aird, Point; sailing in a traditional
boat, the Ness Skiff, which was developed and
used by the men of Ness, Back and Tolsta
GOLF
Stornoway Golf Club (01851 702240;
www.stornowaygolfclub.co.uk
Lady Lever Park, Stornoway; eighteen-hole
course and clubhouse with full range of
facilities
WALKING
There are many excellent walks, including
waymarked routes from Garenin to Dalbeg and
from North Tolsta to Ness
CLIMBING AND ABSEILING
Sgor (01851 820726; www.sgor.co.uk)
Back; climbing, abseiling and first aid classes
KITE SURFING AND LANDBOARDING
Western Isles Kite Company (01851 672771;
www.extremehebrides.co.uk)
Aird, Uig; kite buggying, kite landboarding and
kite surfing; accommodation available
KARTING
Lewis Karting Centre (01851 700222;
www.outdoorhebrides.com/sports/karting/)
Near Stornoway; karting; open Apr-Oct, Mon-
Fri; Nov-Mar, Sat only
SPORTS AND SWIMMING
Nicholson Lewis Sports Centre (01851 702603;
www.w-isles.gov.uk/nlsc/index.htm)
Stornoway; swimming pool, games hall,
running track, gym, sauna, squash; cafe; open
Mon-Sat

LOCAL PRODUCE

Acair Ltd (01851 703020; www.acairbooks.com)
Stornoway; publisher of books in Gaelic and in
English
Hebridean Brewing Company (01851 700123;
www.hebridean-brewery.co.uk)
Stornoway; fine ales
Hebridean Soap Company (01851 621306;
www.HebrideanSoap.co.uk)
25 Breasclete; hand-made soaps; a retail outlet
is being built (May 2006)

Islander Shellfish (01851 706772)
Stornoway; fresh fish and shellfish and smoked products
Charles MacLeod (01851 702445; www.charlesmacleod.co.uk)
Stornoway; makers of gourmet black pudding
Stornoway Salmon (01851 701349; 07836368232; www.stornoway-salmon.co.uk)
Stornoway; smoked salmon, available locally or on-line
Uig Lodge Smoked Salmon (01851 672396; www.greensalmon.co.uk)
Uig; smoked salmon; purchase from website or by mail order; the lodge and fishing can be booked: www.sport.ckdfh.co.uk/uiglodge.htm
Wild West Foods (01851 67234; www.wildwestjerky.co.uk)
Crowlista; beef jerky specialists

ARTS AND CRAFTS

An Lanntair Arts Centre (01851 703307; www.lanntair.co.uk)
South Beach Street, Stornoway; programme of events and exhibitions, coffee shop, gifts and bookshop; open all year
The Barn Gallery (01851 870704)
2 Eagleton, Lower Bayble; paintings by local artists; open Mon-Sat
Boreas Knitwear (01851 621241)
29 Breasclete; hand-framed and hand-made knitwear; open Mon-Sat
Borgh Pottery (01851 850345; www.borgh-pottery.com)
Borve; hand-made ceramics and selection of crafts and gifts; Mon-Sat, 9.30-18.00
Breanish Tweed (01851 701524; www.breanishtweed.co.uk)
1A Melbost, by Stornoway; hand-woven Tweed cashmere and lambswool
Broadbay Ceramics (01851 820219; www.broadbayceramics.co.uk)
Coll, Back; wide range of pottery and ceramics; craft shop; open all year
Callicvol Quilts (01851 810681; www.callicvolquilts.com)
10 Port of Ness; hand-crafted patchwork quilts and smaller items
Eilean Oir (01851 830479; www.eileanoirceos.co.uk/jewellery/index.html)
Keose, Loch; gold and silver jewellery
Gisla Woodcraft (01851 672371; www.gisla-woodcraft.co.uk)
Gisla, Uig; hand-turned wooden gifts and other crafts
Harbour View Gallery (01851 810735; www.abarber.co.uk)
Port of Ness; watercolours and prints by Anthony Barber; open Mon-Sat
Hebridean Jewellery (01871 702372; www.hebridean-jewellery.co.uk)
Stornoway; range of locally produced jewellery with Celtic and Pictish influences

Hebridean Replicas (01851 710562)
15a Arnol; hand-made Lewis chess sets and Celtic tile boards; island miniature gifts
Kenneth Macleod Harris Tweed Mill (01851 710251)
9 North Shawbost; guided tours and Harris Tweed for sale
Lewis Loom Centre (01851 704500; www.lewisloomcentre.co.uk)
3 Bayhead, Stornoway; features displays and a guided tour on the history and production of Harris Tweed; shop; open Mon-Sat
Morven Gallery (01851 840216; www.morvengallery.com)
Upper Barvas; gallery of paintings, ceramics, sculptures, photographs and textiles by local artists and crafts people; shop with jewellery, books and gifts; cafe
Mosaic (01851 700155)
Stornoway; Scottish and ethnic crafts and jewellery
P.Q.A. (01851 860551)
27 Achmore, Lochs; Harris Tweed crafts, hats, bags, toys and cushion covers; open Mon-Thu 10.00-17.00
James Smith Photography (01851 840240; www.oiseval.co.uk)
Oiseval Gallery, Brue; photographic gallery with work for sale
The Studio Gallery (01851 710460; www.simonrivett.co.uk)
North Shawbost; drawings and paintings inspired by Lewis and Harris; open Apr-Oct
Taigh Dhonnchaidh Art and Music Centre (01851 810166; www.taighdhonnchaidh.com)
Ness; arts and music centre; workshops, lectures, classes, performance and events; cafe and gift shop (seasonal)
Taigh nan Creaganan (01851 643356; www.creaganan.com)
Creaganan Gorm, Carloway; hand-made silver jewellery

VISITOR ATTRACTIONS AND MUSEUMS

Calanais Visitor Centre (01851 621422; www.calanaisvisitorcentre.co.uk)
Callanish; exhibition, tearoom, gift shop and toilets; open Apr-Sep Mon-Sat 10.00-18.00; Oct-Mar, Wed-Sat 10.00-16.00
Doune Broch Centre (01851 643338; www.calanaisvisitorcentre.co.uk)
Carloway; exhibition 'Scenes from the Broch', gift shop, toilets; open Apr-Sep, Mon-Sat 10.00-17.00
Gearrannan Blackhouse Village (01851 643416; www.gearrannan.com)
5A Gearrannan, Carloway; restored blackhouse village with museum, cafe and gift shop; accommodation can be rented in the village and there is a youth hostel
Kinloch Museum (01851 702350)
Laxay

Lewis Loom Centre (01851 704500;
www.lewisloomcentre.co.uk)
   3 Bayhead, Stornoway; features displays and a
   guided tour on the history and production of
   Harris Tweed; shop; open Mon-Sat
Museum nan Eilean (01851 709266; www.cne-
siar.gov.uk/museum/)
   Francis Street, Stornoway; museum for Lewis
   and Harris; open summer, Mon-Sat; winter
   Tue-Fri and Sat morning
Ness Heritage Centre (01851 810377)
   Habost, Ness; open Mon-Fri, also Sat Jun-Sep
Pairc Exhibition (01851 880705)
   Gravir, Park; exhibition
Shawbost Museum (01851 710212)
   Shawbost; displays illustrating island way of
   life; open Apr-Sep
Uig Heritage Centre (01851 672456)
   Crowlista, Uig; local history museum and
   photographic exhibitions with tea room and
   crafts; open Jun-Sep
Woodlands Centre (Lews Castle) (01851 706916)
   Stornoway; displays, tearoom and public
   toilets; open Mon-Sat

ADDITIONAL INFORMATION

Petrol at Stornoway, Barvas, Leurbost and
Timsgarry
There are branches of the Royal Bank of
Scotland, Bank of Scotland and Clydesdale
Bank in Stornoway
Public toilets are available at Aiginis, Bayble,
Callanish, Dalmore, Gearrannan, Kershader,
Kneep, Laxay, North Tolsta, Port of Ness, and
Shawbost
As Sunday is seen as a day of rest on Lewis
because of the strongly held beliefs of the
islanders, it should be assumed that tourist
attractions, arts and crafts outlets, pubs and
restaurants etc. are not open on a Sunday

EVENTS

Feis nan Coisir	March
Piping Competition	April
Feis nan Oran	May
Lewis Half Marathon	May
Lewis Mod	June
Erisort Regatta	June
Hebridean Celtic Music Festival (01851 621234; www.hebceltfest.com)	July
Hebridean Maritime Festival	July
Lewis Highland Games (www.lewishighlandgames.co.uk)	July
West Side Agricultural Show	July
Feis Eilean an Fhraoich	July
Carloway Agricultural Show	August
Fish Festival	August

FURTHER READING

The Islands Book Trust (01851 810681;
www.theislandsbooktrust.com)
   Port of Ness; The trust aims to increase
   understanding and appreciation of the history
   of the Scottish islands in both Celtic and
   Scandinavian contexts, with a range of talks,
   visits, conferences, publications, research and
   education

Around the Peat-Fire (Smith, Calum)
   Birlinn, 2001
Children of the Black House (Ferguson, Calum)
   Birlinn, 2006
Discovering Lewis and Harris (Grant, James Shaw)
   John Donald, 1998
Historic Stornoway (Denison, Elizabeth Patricia)
   Historic Scotland/Scottish Cultural Press, 1997
The Lewis Chessmen (Taylor, Michael)
   British Museum Press, 1978
Lewis and Harris (Thompson, Francis)
   David and Charles (Pevensey), 1999
Lewis: a History of the Island (Macdonald, Donald)
   Steve Savage Publishers, 2004
Lewis: the Story of an Island (Macdonald, Christine)
   Acair, 1998
Rona: the Distant Island (Robson, Michael)
   Acair, 1990
The Soap Man: Lewis, Harris and Lord Leverhulme
   (Hutchinson, Roger)
   Birlinn, 2003
Tales and Traditions of the Lews
   (MacDonald of Gisla, Donald)
   Birlinn, 2000

GREAT BERNERA

('great Bjorn's island' from
Norse; Bearnaraigh)

**www.scotland-
inverness.co.uk/
bernera.htm
www.visithebrides.com
(Western Isles)**

Tourist Information Centre
Stornoway (01851 703088)
   Open Jan-Dec

Map Landranger sheet: 13

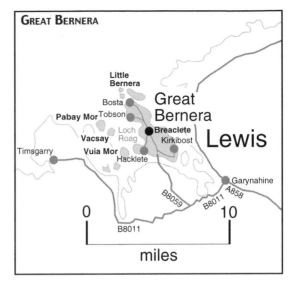

TRAVEL

Great Bernera is reached by road over the 'bridge over the Atlantic'. The turn-off is
from the A858 south of Callanish, on Lewis, onto the B8011, then B8059.

DESCRIPTION

Great Bernera is the largest of a group of islands in Loch Roag, which cuts into the
west coast of Lewis. The island is five miles long and up to three miles wide. The
land is rough in places, rises to eighty-seven metres to the north, and there are
many lochans. There is an excellent sandy beach at Bosta.

There are several settlements: Breaclete (Breacleit), in the middle of the island,
which has a post office, shop, community centre, cafe, museum and toilets, as well
as the school and churches; Kirkibost (Circebost) to the east, where the fishing
boats are based; Barraglom; Hacklete (Tacleit) to the west; Tobson to the northwest;
and Croir (Crothair) in the north.

To the north of the island is the small island of Little Bernera (Bearnaraigh Beag),
and other islands in Loch Roag include Pabay Mor (Pabaigh Mor), Vacsay (Bhacsaigh)
and Vuia Mor (Fuaidh Mor; which once had a population of forty-six before it was
cleared in 1841) to the west.

Bearasay (Beirisaidh) was the refuge of Neil MacLeod who tried to restore the
Island of Lewis to his own clan after it had been granted to the Mackenzies of
Kintail. He was eventually captured and taken to Edinburgh, where he was hanged
in 1613.

WILDLIFE

Many seabirds can be seen here, including eagles and gannets; and there are otters,
seals and dolphins.

HISTORY

The islanders 'rioted' here in 1874 after poor treatment, and eviction notices were
issued by Sir James Matheson's factor. They were involved in scuffles with local law
enforcement officers. There is a memorial at the Tobson crossroads to those who
took part. The bridge was built in 1953 at the demand of the islanders, who had
threatened to blow up the hillside by the sound to form a causeway. The population

has declined, as with many of the islands, and now stands at around 260 people. Many of the islanders are involved in lobster fishing, which has sustained the island for generations; there is a fish processing plant at Kirkibost.

Tours
GREAT BERNERA
Just north of the bridge, by the road at Barraglom, are the Tursachan standing stones [NB 164342], a group of three monoliths, the tallest of which is about three metres high. To the north by the east shore of Loch Baravat is Dun Bharavat [NB 156356], a dun or broch, which survives to a height of more than three metres.

The road runs north to Breaclete, where there is the Bernera Museum which houses the archive of the local history group (01851 612331; open May-Sep, Mon-Fri 11.00-16.00). The centre holds various exhibitions, such as on lobster fishing, and has a collection of photographs as well as an archive. Refreshments and lunches are available in the summer months.

There is a wonderful beach by the abandoned township at Bosta with a car park, and it was with the erosion of sand dunes that the prehistoric settlement [NB

Bosta

138401] was discovered. This consists of several Iron Age houses, and the site was occupied until Viking times. A reconstructed house stands nearby, showing how the dwellings would have looked.

There is also a restored horizontal grain mill [NB 167370].

Monuments on the island have been waymarked.

PLACES TO STAY

6 Kirkibost (01851 612341)
 B&B; evening meals available; open Feb-Nov
Bhalasay (01851 612288; www.hebridean-
 holidays.co.uk)
 Self-catering house, sleeps four; short breaks
 and offers sometimes available; open all year
1 Croir (01851 612285)
 Self-catering flat, sleeps four
Hacklete (01851 612269; www.hacklete.co.uk)
 Self-catering cottage, sleeps five; open all year
17 Tobson (01851 870706;
 www.tobsoncottage.co.uk)
 Self-cat ering cottage, sleeps six; open all year;
 short breaks sometimes available

PLACES TO EAT

Community Centre
 Breaclete; teas/coffee, snacks, lunches and
 carry-out meals available in summer months

FURTHER INFORMATION

There is a post office and shop at Breaclete

EVENTS

Ceilidhs and dances are held in the Community
 Centre throughout the year

WALKING

There is a walk along the west coast, and two of
 the historical sites have been way-marked

FISHING

Good trout fishing is available in many of the
 fresh-water lochs

ACKNOWLEDGMENTS

Thanks to Noreen Maciver for reading over the
text. Image courtesy Colin Palmer
(www.buyimage.co.uk)

Harris, Scalpay, Taransay, Scarp, the Shiant Isles and Nearby Islands

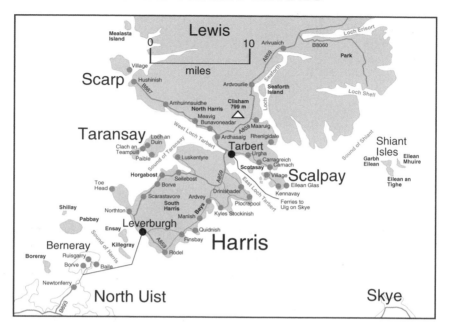

Harris

HARRIS

('high island' from Norse; Na Hearadh, 'the heights', in Gaelic)

www.explore-harris.com
www.north-harris.org
www.harristweed.com
www.harrisarts.net
www.leverburgh.co.uk
www.visithebrides.com (Western Isles)

Tourist Information Centres
Tarbert, Harris (01859 502011)
    Open Jan-Dec
Stornoway (01851 703088)
    Open Jan-Dec

Map Landranger sheets: 13, 14, 18 (HIH map page 216)

TRAVEL

The vehicle ferry (CalMac 01470 542219/01859 502444; www.calmac.co.uk) leaves Uig on Skye (A87) and arrives at Tarbert on Harris. There are sailings every day, including Sundays, and the crossing takes one hour and forty-five minutes.

By vehicle ferry (CalMac 01859 502444/01876 502444; www.calmac.co.uk) from Berneray on North Uist to Leverburgh on Harris; the journey take three quarters of an hour. There are up to four sailings each day, with a reduced service on a Sunday. Berneray is joined by a causeway to North Uist, and hence to Benbecula and South Uist and Eriskay with a ferry service to Barra and onwards to Vatersay.

Harris is not an individual island and can be reached by road (A859) from Lewis. This route is narrow in places, although there are spectacular (or perhaps hair-raising to some) views along the way.

A bridge crosses to the island of Scalpay, which is located in the mouth of East Loch Tarbert along an unlisted road from Tarbert.

There are also boat trips to Taransay (from Horgabost Beach: 07786540224; www.visit-taransay.com), and the islands in the Sound of Harris (Strond Wildlife Charters 01859 520204; www.erica.demon.co.uk/Strond.html).

DESCRIPTION

Harris is not actually a separate island, although it is divided from Lewis by the long sea lochs of Loch Seaforth and Loch Resort and the mountains of north Harris. It is also nearly cut in two at Tarbert, where there are only a few hundred metres between East and West Loch Tarbert. Harris is twenty-one miles long by eighteen wide, and covers some ninety square miles. The land is much more mountainous than its northern neighbour Lewis, and the highest hill is Clisham at 799 metres.

There are superb beaches on the west coast of Harris, including at Taobh Tuath (Northton), Traigh Scarasta, Luskentyre and Hushinish Bay (B887), where there are fine views to the neighbouring island of Scarp. The east side of Harris, the Bays, is much hillier and rougher, and there are many inlets, sea lochs and lochans; Loch Seaforth cuts deep into the land.

The population of Harris is about 2,200, many of whom are Gaelic speakers and devout Presbyterians. Although Lewis and Harris are one island, the folk of Harris speak a distinct dialect of Gaelic compared to their northern neighbours in Lewis.

Beach, Harris

The largest settlement is at Leverburgh (originally Obbe or An t-Ob, but renamed after Lord Leverhulme had purchased the South Harris estate) on the south coast; but the village of Tarbert (An Tairbeart) to the north and east of Harris is the administrative centre and terminal for the ferries from Uig on Skye and has a hotel, places to eat, general stores and craft shops, petrol, a leisure centre and a swimming pool, a bank, public toilets and a tourist information centre. There are also villages at Rodel (Roghadal) to the southeast, which was formerly the main settlement and has a hotel and the impressive St Clement's Church; Northton (Taobh Tuath) to the west; Ardhasaig (Aird Asaig) to the north-west of Tarbert, which has a shop, a post office and a petrol station; and a smattering of settlements up the rough east coast.

The A859 runs from north to south, meandering its way across Harris through Tarbert, Leverburgh and ending at Rodel. This is mostly a single-track road. There are branches running west to Hushinish (B887; Huisinis), and to Scalpay (unlisted from Tarbert), and a picturesque unlisted road running down the south-east coast with many twists and turns from Plocrapool (Plocrapol) in the north to Rodel. There are many townships along this route.

WILDLIFE

Wildlife on Harris includes deer, hare, and wild goats; and many species of birds including buzzards and eagles, gannets, divers, terns and gulls. There are many grey and common seals, otters (although more elusive) and dolphins, porpoises, basking sharks and minke, pilot and killer whales.

HISTORY

Harris was occupied from prehistoric times, and there are many ancient monuments, including standing stones and ruinous duns. After a period of Viking occupation, the lands were held by the MacDonald Lords of the Isles, and then the MacLeods of Dunvegan and Harris, their ownership being confirmed in 1498. Alasdair Crotach MacLeod of Dunvegan built himself a fine carved tomb in the impressive church at

Rodel, which was formerly the most important place on the island.

The lands were sold to the Murray earls of Dunmore in 1834, who built Amhuinnsuidhe Castle (Abhainn Suidhe; pronounced 'avuin-suey' and at which it is possible to stay) west and north of Tarbert . The population of Harris was large at this time, and many islanders were evicted from their crofts on the west coast of South Harris and replaced by sheep. The north part of Harris (North Harris estate) was sold to Sir Edward Scott in 1861, along with Scarp and Scalpay, while the soap magnate Lord Leverhulme purchased South Harris in 1918-1919. He tried to make this part of the island more prosperous by buying fishing boats and improving communications: Leverburgh is named after him. When he died in 1925 his schemes were abandoned by his executors.

The island was the centre of the Harris Tweed industry, which was popularised by the wife of the Earl of Dunmore, although more of the fabric is now produced on Lewis. The whaling industry was once important, employing many local people until the 1930s, and there are the remains of a Norwegian whaling station at Bunavoneadar (Bun Abhainn Eadarra). Lord Leverhulme bought the station in 1922, along with three ships, and over the next years the station processed some 6,000 tons of whale flesh. The station was closed in 1929 and, although it briefly opened again in the 1950s, it is now in ruins.

The North Harris estate, which includes Tarbert, was bought by the islanders in 2003, and is now managed by local people. The mainstays of Harris are fishing and fish farming, as well as crofting and tourism.

Tours
TARBERT TO ARIVRUAICH (A859)
Tarbert has a range of facilities, with places to eat (including a fish and chip shop), places to stay, shops including Harris Tweed outlets, a bank, a post office, a tourist information centre, petrol and a leisure centre with swimming pool, gymnasium and jacuzzi (01859 502944). The village was developed in the eighteenth century as a fishing port, and is where the main ferry lands.

From the village an unlisted road off the A868 runs along the north side of East Tarbert Bay, through Urgha Beag, Carragreich, Kyles Scalpay and Carnach, to the bridge across to the island of Scalpay.

In Tarbert the A859 goes south, while another branch goes north along the north side of West Loch Tarbert.

At West Loch Tarbert is Soay Studio (01859 502361), which has a range of jumpers, hats and other clothing made from Tweed using hand dyeing with natural substances such as nettles, brambles and dock leaves.

At Ardhasaig is a petrol station, as well as a post office and shop, and just north of here is the turn-off for Hushinish (B887). The main road then climbs into the picturesque and imposing hills of Harris on its way to Lewis, skirting the feet of Clisham, the highest hill on Harris.

There are excellent views from the road of East and West Loch Tarbert and the south part of Harris. The road runs along the west side of Loch Seaforth, and an unlisted road goes down the prettily sited settlement of Maaruig (Maraig) on the shore of the loch. A narrow route travels down to Rhenigidale (Reinigeadal), where there is a hostel. A rough track goes west from here and eventually arrives at Urgha, a mile or so east of Tarbert.

The main road runs up the west side of Loch Seaforth, passing the impressive Seaforth Island before arriving at Arivruaich on the way to Lewis and the north.

Bunavoneadar to Hushinish (B887)

This is a beautiful route, but the road is narrow and may be challenging for some. At Bunavoneadar are the remains of what was an extensive whaling station [NB 131039], which was built by Norwegians but stopped operation for the last time in the 1950s. Much of it is gone, but a brick chimney and the ramp for drawing up the whales survive.

Amhuinnsuidhe Castle [NB 049079] is an impressive castellated mansion (there are excellent views of it from the road which passes close by). It was built by the architect David Bryce for the earls of Dunmore in Victorian times, and was rented by J. M. Barrie, author of *Peter Pan*, in 1912. It is possible to stay at the castle (although it is expensive), and there is a post office here.

The road ends at Hushinish, where there are fine views across to the island of Scarp and up the coast, and a public telephone. A couple of miles to the north is a fine beach.

Tarbert to Leverburgh and Rodel (A859)

The A859 runs south of Tarbert and then turns west across the island; to the east is Plocrapool and several other settlements along the coast. There is a wonderful beach at Luskentyre, and at the village is Luskentyre Harris Tweed (01859 550261; www.luskentyreharristweed.co.uk; open all year except Oct, Mon-Fri).

On a headland north of Horgabost, which has fine beaches to the east and west, is Clach Mhic Leoid [NG 041973], 'MacLeod's Stone', an impressive three-metre high standing stone. There are excellent views from here.

There are boat trips to Taransay from Horgabost Beach (07786540224; www.visit-taransay.com), and it is possible to stay on the island. At Borve is Dun Borve [NG 032940], the ruins of a broch or dun on a rocky outcrop. The walls survive to a height of nearly two metres. Twenty-five metres to the east is a rock decorated with eighty or so cup marks, small carved depressions thought to date from the Bronze Age.

Just north of the road at Borvemor is another tall standing stone [NG 021930]; and Traigh Scarasta and Traigh an Taoibh Thuath is a stretch of fantastic sandy beach. The Isle of Harris Golf Club (www.harrisgolf.com) is at Scarista.

At Northton is Seallam! Visitor Centre (01859520258; www.seallam.com; open Mon-Sat) which has information about Harris life, wildlife and geology, and the neighbouring islands, and resources for genealogical research as well as a tea and coffee bar and small craft shop. The MacGillivray Centre has displays on the ornithologist W. MacGillivray; and there is a post office at Northton. There are some good walks along the Toe Head peninsula with the hill of Chaipaval at 339 metres, where there are the scant remains of an old chapel on the south side [NG 970914].

The road turns south to Leverburgh, or Obbe or An t-Ob, but renamed after Lord Leverhulme in 1919 when he developed the harbour for herring fishing. There are shops, a post office (The Cauldron) and places to eat, including An Clachan, public toilets and petrol; and the ferry for Berneray and North Uist departs from here. There are also boat trips to the islands in the Sound of Harris.

The impressive craggy mountain of Roneval, which rises to 460 metres, is to the east. There were plans to establish a 'super-quarry' here but, after a long fight by conservationists, these were abandoned in 2000.

A few miles beyond Leverburgh is Rodel on the south-eastern tip of Harris. The settlement is dominated by St Clement's Church [NG 047833], a substantial sixteenth-century building with an older parapeted tower. Several old carvings decorate the tower, one a Sheila na Gig, a suggestive female fertility symbol, also found on the nunnery on Iona. The church was dedicated to St Clement, a thirteenth-century bishop of Dunblane on the mainland, and was restored in 1787 and 1873.

This is the most impressive medieval church in the Western Isles, and inside is the splendid carved tomb and stone effigy of Alasdair Crotach MacLeod, who owned Harris and built the 'Fairy Tower' of Dunvegan Castle on Skye. The inscription reads 'the tomb was prepared by Lord Alexander, son of Willielmus MacLeod, lord of Dunvegan, in the year of Our Lord 1528' (twenty years before he died). Others

St Clement's Church, Rodel

of the family were interred here, and another stone effigy dates from 1539. There are also carved slabs and a ring-headed cross; and interesting memorials in the burial ground. In the church is also reputedly buried the bard Mairi nighean Alasdair Ruaidh, who was interred face-down, said to be the fate of all female bards.

Above the church are the scant remains of an old dun [NG 051832], and there is a hotel in the cluster of houses and a public toilet, as well as the small picturesque harbour, which was first built in the sixteenth century.

An unlisted road travels up the west side of the island and eventually rejoins the A859 some miles south of Tarbert.

TARBERT TO RODEL (EAST COAST ON UNLISTED ROAD)

Narrow and twisting roads go east from the A859 to the communities along the south and east coast, known as the Bays. The route down the coast is known as the Golden Road because it cost so much to build, and goes through a rocky but very picturesque area.

At Plocrapool is Tweeds and Knitwear (Tweeds and Knitwear (01859 511217; www.harristweedandknitwear.co.uk; toilets; open Mon-Sat). There are post offices at Drinishader and at Finsbay; a youth hostel at Kyles Stockinish; and there are excellent views all along the coast.

From Finsbay, where there is the Finsbay Gallery (01859 530244), there are roads to Leverburgh or Rodel, where it joins the A859. This route then goes up the north and west coast, and goes on to Tarbert.

SCARP

Scarp ('scarped or cliff island') is just off the coast of the north-west side of Harris at Hushinish (B887). It is some three miles long and a couple wide, and is rough and hilly, and covers some 2,500 acres. The highest point is 308 metres at Sron Romul.

Scarp

At one time more than 200 people lived here, but the island is now uninhabited, the last islanders leaving in 1971.

It was here that in the 1930s a German scientist, Gerhard Zucker, tried to use rockets to deliver the post, although it was soon decided that this was impractical when the first test blew up.

There are holiday cottages on the south-east coast of Scarp. Sea Trek (01851 672464; www.seatrek.co.uk; departures from Miavaig jetty (B8011) at Uig on Lewis) sometimes run boat trips to Scarp, as do Strond Wildlife Charters (01859 520204; www.erica.demon.co.uk/Strond.html), leaving from Leverburgh pier. Westernedge Charters Ltd (01506 824227/07811 387633; www.westernedge.co.uk) also have trips to Scarp.

PABBAY

Pabbay ('priest's island'; Pabaigh) is a picturesque island in the Sound of Harris, five miles west of Leverburgh and two miles north-west of Berneray. It is two and a half miles wide, and the north of the island rises to 196 metres, while there are sandy beaches to the south and east. It was a property of the MacLeods of Dunvegan and Harris, and they are said to have had a castle or seat here, possibly at Seana Chaisteal, although the remains appear to be from an older dun. The MacDonalds raided Pabbay in the fifteenth century, but their boats were cast adrift and when a strong force of MacLeods arrived the MacDonalds were slaughtered. The island was later held by the MacLeods of Pabbay, and a storm and sandstorm overwhelmed part of the island in 1697. Pabbay was known as the 'granary of Harris', and the island supported a substantial population (338 in 1841) in the nineteenth century. It was cleared for sheep by its landlord in 1846 and many of the people went to live on

Scalpay, near Tarbert on Harris. There are the remains of two chapels, one Teampull Mhoire [NF 890870], which was dedicated to St Mary, while the other was dedicated to St Moluag and lies close by.

Shillay ('seal island') is a mile or so to the north, and is well named: it has a large colony of grey seals and is managed by the Scottish Wildlife Trust (www.swt.org.uk).

Strond Wildlife Charters (01859 520204; www.erica.demon.co.uk/Strond.html) make trips to the Sound of Harris, leaving from Leverburgh pier.

BORERAY

Boreray ('borg or burgh island' from Norse; Boraraigh) is located three miles north of the north coast of North Uist in the Sound of Harris. It is about two miles west of Berneray (although administratively it is part of Harris). It is one and a half miles long and one wide, there is a beach and dunes down the east coast, and it rises to fifty-six metres at Mullach Mor. It had good fertile land supporting a population of more than 150 in 1891. It was held by the MacLeods of Boreray, who were buried at Aird a' Mhorain on North Uist, but has been uninhabited since the 1960s. There are the remains of a burial cairn [NF 857816], and an abandoned settlement.

Barnacle geese winter here, and common seals can be seen here in the summer.

Strond Wildlife Charters (01859 520204; www.erica.demon.co.uk/Strond.html) make trips to the Sound of Harris, leaving from Leverburgh pier.

ENSAY AND KILLIEGRAY

Ensay ('John's island' from Norse; Easaigh) is a small island, lying about two miles west of Harris at Leverburgh. It is about two miles long, rises to forty-nine metres, and there are sandy beaches along the north and east coasts. The island had sixteen inhabitants in 1841, but is not now permanently occupied. The chapel [NF 981866], beside Ensay House, was known as Christ Church and was restored from ruin about 1910. Pilgrims go to the island and worship at the chapel in June, although the building is usually closed. Martin Martin, author of the first detailed description of the Western Isles, set out for St Kilda from here in 1695.

Killiegray ('burial ground island'; Ceileagraigh) lies just to the south of Ensay, is about one and a half miles long, and rises to forty-five metres. There are dunes to the north. There were a small number of inhabitants, but no permanent residents since the 1940s. There are the remains of a small chapel Teampuill na h-Annait [NF 975831] to the north of the island.

Strond Wildlife Charters (01859 520204; www.erica.demon.co.uk/Strond.html) make trips to the Sound of Harris, leaving from Leverburgh pier.

HOTELS AND GUEST HOUSES

Ardhasaig House (01859 502066;
www.ardhasaig.co.uk;)
Ardrishaig, near Tarbert; hotel and restaurant;
open all year
Carminish House (01859 520400;
www.carminish.com)
Strond; guest house; evening meals and packed
lunches available; open Apr-Sep
Grimisdale Guest House (01859 520460;
www.grimisdale.co.uk)
Leverburgh; guest house; open Apr-Nov
Harris Hotel (01859 502154; www.harrishotel.com)
Tarbert; hotel, restaurant and bar; open all year

Leachin House (01859 502157; www.leachin-
house.com)
Tarbert; hotel; open Feb-Nov
Macleod Motel (01859 502364;
www.macleodmotel.com)
Tarbert; motel, restaurant and bar; open
May-Sep
Rodel Hotel (01859 520210; www.rodelhotel.co.uk)
Rodel, South Harris; accommodation and food
in eighteenth-century listed building; open
Apr-Dec
Scarista House (01859 550238;
www.scaristahouse.com)
Scarista; hotel and restaurant in eighteenth-
century building; also self-catering cottages;
open all year except Christmas and
occasionally in the winter

St Kilda Guest House (01859 520419)
Leverburgh; guest house

It is also possible to stay at Amhuinnsuidhe
Castle (01859 560200; www.amhuinnsuidhe-
castle.co.uk) – it is not cheap to do so

BED AND BREAKFAST

Avalon (01859 502334/07748 484398;
www.avalonguesthouse.org)
Tarbert; B&B; open all year
Beul-na-Mara (01859 550205;
www.beulnamara.co.uk)
12 Seilebost; B&B; open all year
Borrisdale House (01859 520201)
3 Borrisdale, Leverburgh; B&B; open Apr-Sep
Caberfeidh House (01859 520276)
Leverburgh; B&B; open all year
Carminish House (01859 520276;
www.carminish.com)
Strond; B&B; open most of the year
Ceol na Mara (01859 502464;
www.ceolnamara.com)
7 Direcleit; B&B; open all year
Dunard (01859 502340)
Tarbert; B&B; open all year
Dunvegan View (01859 530294;
www.dunveganview.co.uk)
Cluer; B&B; open all year
Garryknowe (01859 520246)
Leverburgh; B&B
Grimsdale (01859 520460; www.grimsdale.co.uk)
Leverburgh; B&B; open all year
Hillcrest (01859 502119)
Tarbert; B&B
Langracleit (01859 502413)
Kendibig, near Tarbert; B&B; open all year
Moravia (01859 550262; www.scotland-info.co.uk/
moravia/)
Luskentyre; B&B in traditional croft house,
Gaelic spoken; open Mar-Oct
Mount Cameron (01859 530356;
www.mountcameron.com)
2 Cluer; B&B
14 Seilebost (01859 550233; www.14seilebost.co.uk)
Seilebost; B&B
Skyeview (01859 502095)
Tarbert; B&B; open Apr-Oct
Sorrel Cottage (01859 520319)
2 Glen, Leverburgh; B&B; open all year
Tigh na Mara (01859 502270; www.tigh-na-
mara.co.uk)
Tarbert; B&B

SELF-CATERING PROPERTIES

Bayhead (01851 702436;
www.bayheadmeavaig.co.uk)
Bayhead; self-catering house, sleeps eight; open
all year
Beul na Mara (01859 550205)
Seilebost; two self-catering cottages, each sleep
six; open all year

Blue Reef Cottages (01859 550370; www.stay-
hebrides.com/bluereef.html)
Scarista; two self-catering cottage, sleep two
each; open all year
Borvemor Cottages (01859 550222/291;
www.borvemor.zetnet.co.uk)
Borve, near Scarista; two self-catering cottages,
each sleeps six
Cabhalan Cottage (01859 530255)
Quidinish; self-catering cottage
Clisham Cottage (01859 502066;
www.ardhasaig.co.uk)
Ardhasaig, near Tarbert; self-catering house,
sleeps six
Cnoc na Ba (01859 530232; www.cnocnaba.co.uk)
Finsbay; self-catering cottage, sleeps four; open
all year
Crowlin (01224 867392;
www.crowlinselfcatering.co.uk)
Leacklee; self-catering house, sleeps six; open
all year
Dun Corr (01463 231891; www.westernisles-
holiday.co.uk)
Tarbert; self-catering cottage, sleeps five.
Glen Carragrich (01224 584864;
www.harrisholidayhome.co.uk)
East Loch Tarbert, near Tarbert; self-catering
house, sleeps six
Hill Cottage (01859 502063;
www.cameronharrisltd.co.uk)
Tarbert; two self-catering semi-detached
houses, sleep two each; open all year
Kinnoull (01573 224751/07876 771647;
www.witb.co.uk/links/goodfellowsc.htm)
Tarbert; self-catering bungalow, sleeps seven-
eight
Kirklee Terrace (01859 502364;
www.macleodmotel.com)
Tarbert; four self-catering cottages, sleep four-
six each; open all year
Luskentyre (01859 550257)
Luskentyre; self-catering house, sleeps up
to eight
4 Maraig (Maaruig) (07811 399928;
www.urbanmesh.com/harris.htm)
Loch Seaforth; self-catering crofting cottage,
sleeps six
Monadh Liath (01540 673531; www.witb.co.uk/
links/monadhliath.htm)
Leverburgh; self-catering bungalow, sleeps five;
open all year
Rowan Cottage (01859 502204; www.rowan-
cottage.org)
Kyles; self-catering cottage, sleeps four; open
all year
Scarista House (01859 550238; www.scotland-
info.co.uk/scarista/)
Scarista; two self-catering apartments
Schoolhouse (01859 502177; www.schoolhouse-
rhenigidale.co.uk)
Rhenigidale, self-catering house, sleeps six;
open all year
Seaforth Cottage (01859 502447; www.witb.co.uk/
links/woodwardsc.htm)
Rhenigidale; self-catering cottage, sleeps six;
open all year

Sealladh na Mara (01859 502270; www.tigh-na-mara.co.uk)
Tarbert; self-catering apartment, sleeping five-seven

Seaside Cottage (01859 502157; www.seaside-cottage.com)
Ardhasaig; self-catering cottage, sleeps two; open all year

Seaview (01859 502033; www.witb.co.uk/links/seaviewsc.htm)
Ardhasaig; self-catering house, sleeps six; open all year

18 Seilebost (01859 550236)
Seilebost; self-catering cottage, sleeps five

Shore Cottage (01859 550219; www.scotland-info.co.uk/shore/)
Luskentyre; self-catering cottage, sleeps six

Taigh Iomhair (01859 502225; www.taighiomhair.co.uk)
Carragreich; self-catering cottage, sleeps three; open all year

Tigh na Seileach (01859 502411; www.tighnaseileach.co.uk)
Bowglass; self-catering restored thatched blackhouse, sleep two-four; open all year

Ullabhal and Cleiseabhal (01859 502063)
Tarbert; two self-catering houses, each sleep two-four

Urgha (01851 703744; www.urgha.co.uk)
Tarbert; self-catering house, sleeps four

Urgha Self Catering (01859 502114; www.urgha.com)
Urgha; self-catering bungalow, sleeps six

Vallay House (01859 550222/291; www.borvemor.zetnet.co.uk)
Scarista; self-catering house, sleeps four-six

West Ranah Cottage (01463 718024; www.scotland-info.co.uk/scarista/)
Scarista; self-catering cottage, sleeps four

White Cottage (01859 550324; www.thewhitecottage.co.uk)
Ardhasaig; self-catering traditional cottage, sleeps three-four

White Cottage (www.harriswhitecottage.com)
Rodel; self catering cottage, sleeps four

HOSTELS AND RETREATS

Am Bothan Bunkhouse (01859 520251; www.ambothan.com)
Leverburgh; self-catering accommodation, kitchen, communal room, kitchen and showers; camping available

Drinishader Bunkhouse (01859 511255)
Drinishader ; hostel, sleeping thirteen

Rhenigidale (www.gatliff.ic24.net/rhenigidale.htm)
Thirteen miles from Tarbert, including five mile walk; sleeps thirteen; bed linen not provided; open all year

Rockview Bunkhouse (01859 502211)
Tarbert; accommodation, kitchen, lounge and showers, sleeps thirty-two ; bike hire can be arranged; open all year

Scaladale Centre (01859 502502; www.scaladale.co.uk.)
Ardvourlie; self-catering accommodation, sleeps up to twenty-eight; open all year

CAMPING AND CARAVANS

No official campsite; Horgabost beach has public toilets and a water tap

Grosebay Caravans (www.grosebaycaravans.co.uk)
Grosebay; two caravans, each sleeping six in each; open all year

Am Bothan Bunkhouse (01859 520251; www.ambothan.com)
Leverburgh; self-catering accommodation, kitchen, communal room, kitchen and showers; camping available

PLACES TO EAT

Anchorage Restaurant (01859 520225)
Breakfast, lunch, evening meals, snacks and take-aways

An Clachan (01859 520370; www.witb.co.uk/links/anclachan.htm)
Leverburgh; tearoom, craftshop and St Kilda exhibition; groceries, newspapers and petrol/diesel

Ardhasaig House (01859 502066; www.ardhasaig.co.uk)
Ardrishaig, near Tarbert; hotel and restaurant; open all year

First Fruits Tearoom (01859 502439)
Pier Road Cottage, Tarbert; traditional tearoom; open Apr-Sep, Mon-Sat; evening meals Jun-Aug

Harris Hotel (01859 502154; www.harrishotel.com)
Tarbert; hotel; open all year

Isle of Harris Inn (01859 502566)
Tarbert; inn serving meals; open all year, Mon-Sat

Rodel Hotel (01859 520210; www.rodelhotel.co.uk)
Rodel, South Harris; accommodation and food; open Apr-Dec

Scarista House (01859 550238; www.scaristahouse.com)
Scarista; hotel and restaurant; also self-catering cottages; open all year

Further Information
TRANSPORT

BUSES
(see www.cne-siar.gov.uk/travel/)
Galson Motors (01851 840269)
Harris Coaches (01859 502441)
Leverburgh to Harris and Lewis
Hebridean Transport (01851 705050)

CYCLE HIRE
Blazing Saddles (Tarbert) (01859 502417)
Harris Cycle Hire (Leverburgh) (01859 520319)
Tarbert (01859 502271)

CAR HIRE

Gaeltech Car Hire (01859 520460;
www.grimisdale.co.uk)
Grimisdale
Harris Car Service (01859 502221)
Tarbert

ACTIVITIES AND SPORTS

BOAT TRIPS

Strond Wildlife Charters (01859 520204;
www.erica.demon.co.uk/Strond.html)
Depart Leverburgh; wildlife trips to the isles in
the Sound of Harris
Scenic Cruises (01859 530310/07788 500 302;
www.scenic-cruises.co.uk)
Flodabay; boat trips along the east coast of
Harris

FISHING AND ANGLING

Finsbay Fishing (01859 530318)
Access to more than 100 lochs
Harris Sea Angling Club (01859 530310)
Lacasdale Lochs (Harris Hotel: 01859 502154;
www.harrishotel.com)
Obbe Fishings (01993 830179;
www.obbefishings.co.uk)
Leverburgh; loch and sea fishing; no fishing on
Sundays
Rodel Fisheries (07789 584314;
www.rodelfishery.co.uk
Rodel; trout and salmon fishery on South
Harris; no fishing on Sundays

DIVING

Information can be obtained from the Am
Bothan Bunkhouse (01859 520251;
www.ambothan.com)

TENNIS

Tennis is available at Bunavoneadar (West Loch
Tarbert) (01859 502376): booking in advance
essential

GOLF

Isle of Harris Golf Club (01859 550226;
www.harrisgolf.com)
Scarista; nine-hole course; no golf on Sundays

WALKING AND CLIMBING

There are many good walks and climbs, some
challenging, some less so; there are a series of
paths and leaflets are available, describing the
routes

SWIMMING AND SPORTS

Harris Leisure Centre (01859 502944)
Near Tarbert; swimming pool, children's pool,
jacuzzi, sauna and fitness suite; open all year:
tel. to confirm times

ARTS AND CRAFTS

The Cloth Bag Company
(www.tweedswithstyle.com)
Tarbert; hand-made Harris Tweed clothing
Finsbay Gallery (01859 530244)
Finsbay, four miles north-east of Rodel; small
contemporary gallery; open Easter-Nov, Mon-
Sat; other times by appt only; closed Sun and
Feb

Harris Tweed Shop (01859 502493;
www.isleofharristweedshop.co.uk)
Tarbert; large stock of Tweed, knitwear and
gifts
Isle of Harris Knitwear (01859 511240;
www.isleofharrisknitwear.co.uk)
Grosebay; exclusive hand-made knitwear from
Harris
Luskentyre Harris Tweed (01859 550261;
www.luskentyreharristweed.co.uk)
6 Luskentyre; hand-woven Harris Tweeds and
tartans
Rose Cottage Industries (01859 502226;
www.rosechess.co.uk)
Tarbert; hand-crafted Lewis chessmen,
collectors chess men, and Celtic tile boards
Scarista Studio (01859 550224;
www.milespaintings.co.uk)
Scarista; paintings by David Miles
Soay Studio (01859 502361)
West Tarbert; traditional natural dying, using
plants and lichens.; gifts
Soay Studio (01859 502361)
West Loch Tarbert; traditional Harris tweed
weaver and dyer; open Tue-Thu
Tweeds and Knitwear (01859 511217;
www.harristweedandknitwear.co.uk)
4 Plocrapool, Drinishader; weaving
demonstrations and Harris Tweed, wool and
knitwear for sale; toilets; open Mon-Sat
Willie Fulton (01859 511218; www.williefulton.com)
3 Drinishader; painting and prints from the
Hebrides

VISITOR ATTRACTIONS AND MUSEUMS

Seallam! Visitor Centre (01859520258;
www.seallam.com; also see
www.billlawson.com)
Northton; exhibitions about Harris and the
surrounding area; genealogical research; books
and gifts; toilets; open Mon-Sat
MacGillivray Centre
Northton; display on the ornithologist W.
MacGillivray; toilets; open all year

ADDITIONAL INFORMATION

There is a bank in Tarbert, as well as a mobile
bank service; there is a cashline machine at the
Tourist Information Centre
Petrol is available at Tarbert and Ardhasaig
North Harris Estate (01876 500239)
North Harris Trust (01859 502222; www.north-
harris.org)
Publications and genealogical information about
Harris, Taransay, North Uist and the area are
available from Bill Lawson Publications at
Northton (01859 520488; www.billlawson.com)
(also see Seallam!)

EVENTS

Harris Mod   June
Harris Half Marathon   June
Harris Festival   July
South Harris Agricultural   July

FURTHER READING

Harris in History and Legend (Lawson, Bill)
   John Donald, 2002
Hebridean Island: Memories of Scarp (Duncan, Angus)
   Tuckwell Press, 1995
Place-names of Scarp (Maclennan, John)
   Stornoway Gazette, 2001
The Soap Man: Lewis, Harris and Lord Leverhulme
   (Hutchinson, Roger)
   Birlinn, 2003

ACKNOWLEDGMENTS

Thanks to Mary Macdonald for getting the text checked. Image (page 222) courtesy Colin Palmer (www.buyimage.co.uk)

SCALPAY

('ship river island' or 'scallop island'; Scalpaigh)

www.scalpay.com
www.visitthebrides.com (Western Isles)

Tourist Information Centres
Tarbert, Harris (01859 502011)
   Open Jan-Dec
Stornoway (01851 703088)
   Open Jan-Dec

Map Landranger sheet: 14 (HIH map page 216)

TRAVEL
Scalpay is reached by bridge from Harris, five miles east of Tarbert, on a minor road off the A868 at Tarbert.

DESCRIPTION
The island, also known as Scalpaigh and Scalpa, lies at the mouth of East Loch Tarbert, off the east coast of Harris. Scalpay is three miles long by two wide, and the highest point is Ben Scoravick at 104 metres, from where there are great views; there are many small islets on the west side.

The island has a relatively large population of around 320 people, many of them involved in fishing (for which they had become (and still are) renowned in the nineteenth century) and shipping, and who mostly live on the north and the west of the island. The Free Church of Scotland is strong on Scalpay, and Sunday is observed as a day of rest; there is also no alcohol for sale (Tarbert is a short drive away). The village has a shop, a post office and a community centre, and the harbour is a good anchorage for yachts.

The small island of Scotasay is about one mile west of Scalpay, also in East Loch Tarbert.

Lighthouse, Scalpay

HISTORY

Bonnie Prince Charlie was sheltered on the island in 1746. The lighthouse on the southern tip, Eilean Glas Lighthouse, was first erected in 1787, and was one of the first four lighthouses built by the Commissioners of Northern Lights. It was rebuilt in 1827 (the original light mechanism is in the Museum of Scotland in Edinburgh), and then given an incandescent light in 1907. There is a walk, boggy in places, to the lighthouse.

Places to Stay
BED AND BREAKFAST

Hirta House (01859 540394/07876 041369; www.hirtahouse.co.uk)
  B&B; open all year
New Haven (01859 540325 /07833 527630; www.scalpaigh.btinternet.co.uk/newhaven/)
  B&B; open all year
Seafield (01859 540250)
  B&B

SELF-CATERING PROPERTIES

Cuddy Point (01859 540282; www.cuddypoint.co.uk)
  Self-catering house, sleeps four
Hamarsay House (01463 236049; www.hamarsay-house.com)
  Self-catering bungalow, sleeps six
Highbury (01478 613489; www.highbury-scalpay.co.uk)
  Self-catering bungalow, sleeps up to seven
Stac Pollaidh (01859 540394/07766 398139 ; www.scalpaycottage.co.uk)
  Self-catering house, sleeps four; open all year

FURTHER INFORMATION

BUS
(see www.cne-siar.gov.uk/travel/)
Bus service from Tarbert to Scalpay runs Mon-Sat
YACHTING AND SAILING
Both the north and south harbours can be used by yachts, and there are facilities, including showers, in the community centre
DIVING
Scalpay Diving Centre (01859 540328; www.scalpay.com)
ARTS AND CRAFTS
Scalpay Linen (01859 540298/07867752448; www.scalpaylinen.com)
  Scalpay; linen maker; open Mon-Thu and Sat 14.00-18.00, Fri 14.00-22.00: tel. to confirm
Scalpay Island Teddies (01859 540222; www.scalpay.com)
  Teddy bear maker

ACKNOWLEDGMENT

Image courtesy Colin Palmer (www.buyimage.co.uk)

TARANSAY

('St Taran's Isle'; Tarasaigh)

www.visit-taransay.com
www.visithebrides.com (Western Isles)

Tourist Information Centres
Tarbert, Harris (01859 502011)
   Open Jan-Dec
Stornoway (01851 703088)
   Open Jan-Dec

Map Landranger sheet: 18 (HIH map page 216)

TRAVEL

Day trips available Mon-Fri (07867 968560; www.visit-taransay.com – weather permitting) from Horgabost Beach, leaving at 9.30 and arriving back at 17.00. Horgabost is on the A859 between Tarbert and Leverburgh on Harris. Holiday accommodation, with boat transfers, is available on the island.

   Westernedge Charters Ltd (01506 824227/07811 387633; www.westernedge.co.uk) on Berneray run trips to Taransay, the Flannan Isles, Scarp, the Monach Islands, Mingulay, Barra, and St Kilda.

DESCRIPTION

Taransay lies about one and a half miles off the west coast of Harris at the mouth of West Loch Tarbert. The island is some four and a half miles long and about three miles wide at most. It is nearly divided in two at Loch na h-Uidhe, and is hilly and rough, the highest point being at Ben Raah (267 metres). There are fine sandy beaches along the east coast, and there is a natural rock arch.

Taransay

WILDLIFE

Many birds visit the islands, including puffins and shelducks. There were mink on the island (which ate the eggs of ground-nesting birds) but these have been eradicated. There is a small herd of red deer.

HISTORY

Loch an Duin Dun [NB 022013] is a ruinous Iron Age stronghold with a causeway out to the island; and Clach an Teampull [NB 1300] is a two-metre-high standing stone, decorated with a cross. There are the remains of two chapels [NG 031991] in an old burial ground at Paible, one dedicated to St Taran (perhaps St Ternan, and after whom the island is named), the other to St Keith. Women were buried at the former, men at the latter.

A party of the Morrisons of Ness were slain by the MacLeods while on a raiding expedition on Taransay in 1544. The island had a population of eighty-eight people in 1841, but was abandoned by the remaining inhabitants in the 1970s, and the land is used for farming.

Taransay became famous in 2000 with the showing of the BBC production *Castaway 2000*. The schoolhouse and Mackay house, where the castaways stayed, have been upgraded to self-catering cottages.

PLACES TO STAY

The Mackay Farmhouse
    Self-catering; open Apr-Oct
Old School Chalet
    Self-catering; open Apr-Oct
Contact 07867 968560; www.visit-taransay.com

EVENTS

Taransay Fiddle Week   July

FURTHER READING

Isle of Taransay (Lawson, Bill)
    Bill Lawson Publications, 1997

ACKNOWLEDGMENTS

Thanks to Visit-Taransay.com for checking the text. Image courtesy Colin Palmer (www.buyimage.co.uk)

Shiant Isles

('sacred, enchanted or fairy isles' from Gaelic; pronounced 'Shant'; also Eileanan Mora)

www.shiantisles.net
www.visithebrides.com (Western Isles)

Tourist Information Centres
Stornoway (01851 703088)
  Open Jan-Dec
Tarbert, Harris (01859 502011)
  Open Jan-Dec

Map Landranger sheet: 14 (HIH map page 216)

Travel
Private arrangements from Stornoway or elsewhere: check locally (01851 703908 or 01859 540250).

Description
This group of beautiful small islands are some four miles south-east of the east coast of Lewis, across the Sound of Shiant. The largest island, consisting of Garbh Eilean and Eilean an Tighe, which are joined by a spit of land, is about two miles long. There is a smaller island, Eilean Mhuire, to the east. The islands are hilly and rise to 125 metres, and there are cliffs and impressive hexagonal columns similar to those found on Staffa and Ulva.

Wildlife
There are large colonies of breeding seabirds, some 250,000 in all, including guillemots, razorbills, fulmars, shags and great skuas. Common seals also breed here, and in the waters around the Shiants can be seen dolphins, porpoises, basking sharks and Minke whales. Black rats also live here, but are a protected species.

History
The isles were described as being the 'resort of fairies, elves and other supernatural beings'. There was a small chapel on Eilean Mhuire, dedicated to St Mary, hence the name of the island; a hermitage or early Christian monastery can be seen on Garbh Eilean.

The islands were part of the Park estate on Lewis. The Shiants are now uninhabited, except for sheep, although in the 1930s Compton Mackenzie spent some time on the Shiants to write.

Places to Stay
It is possible to stay on the islands, but there are no facilities: the house is described as sometimes being rat ridden. If planning a trip, the owner of the island must be contacted well in advance – see www.shiantisles.net for details

Further Reading
Sea Room (Nicolson, Adam)
  HarperCollins, 2002

North Uist, Berneray, Baleshare and Heisker

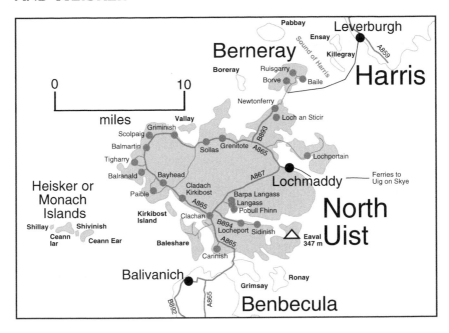

North Uist

NORTH UIST

('north abode'; Uist a' Tuath in Gaelic)

www.theuists.com
www.uistonline.com
www.virtualhebrides.com
www.visithebrides.com (Western Isles)

Tourist Information Centres
Lochmaddy (01876 500321)
    Open Apr-Oct
Stornoway (01851 703088)
    Open Jan-Dec

Map Landranger sheets: 18, 22 (HIH map page 233)

TRAVEL

A vehicle ferry (CalMac 01470 542219/01876 500337; www.calmac.co.uk) leaves from Uig on Skye (A856) and docks at Lochmaddy on North Uist. The crossing takes one hour and forty-five minutes, and there are up to two crossings a day on Friday to Monday and Wednesday, and one crossing on Tuesday and Thursday.

By vehicle ferry (CalMac 01876 502444/01859 502444; www.calmac.co.uk) from Leverburgh on Harris to the island of Berneray; the journey takes three quarters of an hour. There are up to four sailings each day, with a reduced service on a Sunday. North Uist is reached from Berneray by a causeway (B893).

North Uist can also be reached by causeway from Benbecula (which has an airport) and South Uist (A865). This means that facilities or amenities on these islands are also within easy reach.

DESCRIPTION

North Uist lies about twenty miles northwest of Skye, and is situated between Harris to the north and Benbecula and South Uist to the south. It covers an area of 115 square miles, and is eighteen miles long and fourteen or so at its widest. The east coast is very rugged; the highest point is the prominent hill of Eaval at 347 metres, and North Lee and South Lee are 262 metres and 231 metres respectively. Marrival, in the middle of the island, rises to 230 metres in height. There are hundreds of lochans on the east side of the island, with extensive areas of sand along the north and west coasts, including at Baleshare, Traigh nam Faoghailean, Vallay (Bha-

Beach, North Uist

laigh) Strand, and Traigh Iar and Traigh Ear. Many wild flowers grow on the machair in late spring, with different species on acid peaty soil.

North Uist has fertile stretches of land, especially to the south and west, and was once home to a population of more than 5,000 people: there are now around 1,300. Parts of the island were cleared in the nineteenth century. The population is largely Gaelic speaking and Presbyterian. A single-track road encircles the island (A867 and A865), with branches to Newtonferry and the causeway to Berneray (B893), and to Locheport (B894) and Sidinish. The Committee Road, which was built to give islanders work in the nineteenth century, runs across the island from east of Bayhead to east of Sollas.

The largest settlement is at Lochmaddy ('loch of the dogs'; Loch nam Madadh), where the ferry lands, to the east of the island. Lochmaddy has a bank, shops, hotels, petrol and an excellent museum, Taigh Chearsabhagh, which houses galleries, a museum, shop, cafe and post office.

There are villages at Lochportain north-west of Lochmaddy (on unlisted road); Newtonferry on the road to Berneray; Sollas (Solas) on the north coast, with a Co-op supermarket and post office; Bayhead (Ceann a Bhaigh) to the south-west, with a shop and petrol; Clachan, which has a post office and shop; Carinish (Cairinis) to the south with another hotel; and Locheport (Loch Euphort) (post office) and Sidinish (Saighdinis) to the south of Lochmaddy (B894). The North Ford causeway linked North Uist to Benbecula in 1960 and recently a causeway was built to Berneray, making travel between the islands much easier.

The mainstays of the island economy are crofting, fishing for lobsters and shellfish, and tourism.

WILDLIFE

Corncrakes are found on the island, and there are organised corncrake walks; there is an RSPB bird reserve and visitor centre at Balranald (www.rspb.org.uk/reserves/guide/b/balranald; guided tours in summer; open all year). Other birds include gannets, skuas, fulmars, petrels, manx shearwaters, herons and different types of gull, as well as dunlin, ringed plover, turnstone, redshank and eider duck. Raptors which can be seen include golden eagles, sea eagles, buzzards, merlins, hen-harriers and short-eared owls. Otters (which are most likely to be seen in the morning or evening, especially where there is a freshwater lochan near the coast: a leaflet is published by Comann na Mara (comann-na-mara.org), and seals can be spotted around the coasts, and dolphins and whales offshore.

HISTORY

North Uist has an excellent range of impressive prehistoric monuments, perhaps the most notable being the chambered cairn of Barpa Langass, the stone circle of Pobull Fhinn, and the fine ruinous duns of Dun an Sticer and Dun Torcuill. Indeed, many of the islands in the large number of lochans were once fortified. Although first built in the Iron Age, many of these were occupied or reoccupied in medieval and even early modern times.

North Uist was raided and then settled by the Vikings, although nothing survives of their occupation except place names such as Marrival and Eaval. The lands were held by the Lords of the Isles, then were given to the MacDonalds of Sleat (on Skye) in 1495, and they held them for 450 years until 1855. There were apparently no medieval castles on North Uist, but Dun an Sticer was used by the MacDonalds until at least the beginning of the seventeenth century.

Teampull na Trionaid ('church of the Trinity'), near Carinish, was an important religious and educational establishment. It may have been founded by Beathag, daughter of the famous Somerled, or Amy MacRuari, from whom Clanranald are descended. There is also an old cross at Kilphedder.

The tracts of good lands, and then the kelp industry, maintained a large and growing population at the beginning of the nineteenth century. But when the kelp industry failed in the first years of the 1820s, MacDonald of Sleat had many of the islanders cleared from their

Pobull Fhinn

land. The islanders resisted the evictions, and this came to a bloody confrontation with police from Skye at Sollas. The MacDonalds sold the property in 1855. Lochmaddy became a busy fishing port, and as many 400 vessels visited the place at one time.

Tours
LOCHMADDY TO CARINISH (A867 AND A865)

The ferry from Skye lands at Lochmaddy, which has many amenities, not least Taigh Chearsabhagh (01876 500293; www.taigh-chearsabhagh.org; open Mon-Sat 10.00-17.00), which is housed in a building which dates from the eighteenth century and has two galleries, a museum, arts workshop, shop, post office and cafe. There is also a general store, a bank, a seasonal tourist information centre and two hotels: the Lochmaddy Hotel (01876 500331; www.lochmaddyhotel.co.uk), which, along with its other attractions, can advise on fishing; and the Tigh Dearg Hotel (01876 500700; www.tighdearghotel.co.uk), which has a bar, a restaurant and a leisure club with sauna, gym and steam room. There are also public toilets, and the local sheriff court: it was to Lochmaddy that those accused of helping themselves to the cargo of the SS *Politician*, which had foundered off Eriskay (and featured in *Whisky Galore* by Compton Mackenzie), were brought for trial.

Nearby is the Uist Outdoor Centre (01876 500480; www.uistoutdoorcentre.co.uk), which offers a range of outdoor activities, including diving, kayaking, rock climbing, abseiling and even offshore island survival skills. Also at Lochmaddy, on the Sponish peninsula, is the Hut of the Shadows (Sea/Sky Chamber), which was built in 1997 and is a kind of camera obscura, housed in a small domed building with a curved passageway. Lochmaddy Bay is now a European Special Area of Conservation, and there are explanatory plaques outside Taigh Chearsabhagh and near the Hut of the Shadows. Comann na Mara (comann-na-mara.org) is a charitable organisation which plans to establish a marine education and research centre in Lochmaddy.

In a remote spot beneath South Lee is Loch Hunder Dun [NF 905652], an Iron Age stronghold on an island in the loch, linked to the mainland by two causeways. Dun Ban [NF 902653] is also on an island in the loch, and is protected by the remains of two walls.

On the north-western side of the hill of Ben Langass is one of the best and most

Barpa Langass

interesting prehistoric burial cairns on the islands. Barpa Langass [NF 837657] consists of a huge mound of stones, some four-metres high, covering a passageway and intact chamber. The chamber is accessible, but should not be entered for safety reasons. A waymarked walk from a parking place on the A867 leads to the cairn, and then to Pobull Fhinn Stone Circle [NF 843650]. This route can be marshy and it is possible to reach the circle by road (Langass). The circle originally consisted of some forty-eight stones, but only around thirty are in situ, and some of these have fallen. The tallest stone is more than two metres high, and there are fine views from the stones. The name Pobull Fhinn refers to the warriors who followed the ancient mythical hero Finn MacCool. There is also a fine hotel at Langass.

In a remote spot on an island in a lochan to the north of Loch Eport are the ruins of a dun called Dun Nighean Righ Lochlainn [NF 864460], 'dun of the daughter of the king of Norway'. Even more remote is the cairn at Tigh Cloiche [NF 833696], which is located on the south-east side of the hill of Marrogh. This is a round chambered cairn, twenty metres in diameter and four metres high, with some of the kerb stones in place. The passageway to the chamber is intact, but the central chamber has been disturbed.

The B894 and then an unlisted road heads east from the main road, going to Locheport and Sidinish, where there is a post office. South of the road a mile from the turn-off is Sornach a' Phobuill stone circle [NF 829630], oval in shape with fourteen stones remaining. To the south and east are several cairns.

Just beyond the turning, back on the A867, is the village of Clachan an Luib which has a post office and store, as well as public toilets. From here the A865 leads west to Bayhead or to Carinish and the south. A mile or so south on the A865 is the turn-off to the east across a causeway to the island of Baleshare.

Further south, at Carinish is a hotel, and the ruins of Teampull na Trionaid [NF 816602], the 'Church of The Trinity'. This building was one of the largest pre-Reformation churches in the Western Isles and was also a centre of learning. It

Teampull na Trionaid

dates from the thirteenth or fourteenth centuries, and is ruinous, although the smaller chapel of Clan MacIver is better preserved. A holy well was called Tobar na Trionaid [NF 814601].

There was a battle at Carinish in 1602 when the MacLeods of Dunvegan were defeated by the MacDonalds.

The A865 continues on to the causeway to Grimsay, Benbecula and the south.

East of Carinish is a stone circle [NF 832602], through which the A865 has been driven. Seven stones survive on one side; two more on the other. Caravat Barp [NF 837603] is another very large burial cairn, fifty metres long and up to two metres high. Several slabs from the chamber can be seen. On an island in Loch Caravat is Dun Ban [NF 843608], originally an Iron Age strongpoint but still in use in medieval times and later. A hall block stands opposite the entrance, which was apparently still roofed in 1850.

Much further away is Loch a' Gheadais [NF 914594], on an island in which is a ruinous dun, surviving to a height of two metres, linked to the shore by a causeway.

CLACHAN TO SOLLAS (A865)

There are fine beaches along the south-west, west and north-west coasts.

The Hebridean Smokehouse (01876 580209; www.hebrideansmokehouse.com; open Mon-Sat 9.00 -17.00) uses peat to smoke salmon, sea trout and scallops. The smoke house shop has a range of smoked fish, pates, and tableware and other gifts, and there is a viewing gallery to see the produce being made and information display.

A couple of miles along the road is the Claddach Kirkibost Centre (01876 580390; open seasonally) which has a conservatory cafe selling local produce such as preserves, chutneys and tablet (also see Hebridean Kitchen at www.hebrideankitchen.co.uk) and has public internet facilities and seasonal exhibitions.

On the southern side of Uneval are the remains of a chambered cairn [NF 800667] and an Iron Age house, which was later built into it. Near the shore, a mile west of Claddach Kirkibost, is a three-metre standing stone, known as Clach Mhor a' Che [NF 770662] and said to mark the site of a battle. Over the bay is the flat island of Kirkibost.

On the south-east side of the hill of Toroghas are two standing stones, thirty metres apart, known as Fir Bhriege [NF 770703] the 'false men'. The stones have sunk into the peat. Three miles north of Bayhead is Clettraval Chambered Cairn [NF 749713], on the south side of the hill. The slabs of the chamber and passageway can be seen: the site was reused in the Iron Age, and a wheelhouse was inserted into the cairn. There is a standing stone to the south-east and beyond that another chambered cairn [NF 752710].

At Balranald is an RSPB reserve and a visitor centre (01876 560287; www.rspb.org.uk/reserves/guide/b/balranald) with public toilets. There are guided walks but, although the reserve is open all year, the visitor centre is only open from April to August. There are long stretches of fine beaches; and on Aird an Runair, a mile and a half west of Hougharry and in the reserve, are the ruins of an Iron Age settlement [NF 697712], consisting of several round cells and extensive midden material. The ruins were not discovered until a storm exposed them from their covering of sand dunes. There is a post office at Hougharry and many of the island's more important folk are said to be buried in the burial ground [NF 708706]. On the coast at Tigharry is a natural rock arch and a spouting cave.

At Kilphedder, on the west side of the road, is stone round-headed cross [NF 726744] near the site of a chapel and burial ground dedicated to St Peter. Further north is Scolpaig Tower [NF 731750], a nineteenth-century folly and summerhouse, built in the remains of an ancient dun. It was constructed in 1830 to give work to local men.

Another prehistoric settlement has been discovered at Foshigarry [NF 742764] on the north coast. There are the slight remains of several roundhouses and a souterrain.

Across Vallay Strand, with its excellent sands, is the island of Vallay, a tidal island with a ford: driving there may be perilous and check tides if venturing across by vehicle or foot. Vallay is three miles long, and is flat and fertile. Along the south-east coast is a ruinous dun [NF 785763], the remains of chapel dedicated to St Mary [NF 786764], and two substantial standing stones [NF 791765], probably the remains of a chambered burial cairn. Another chapel [NF 773772], dedicated to St Oran, can be found on the north coast. The stark prominent ruin is that of Vallay House, which was the seat of the Beveridge-Erskine family.

SOLLAS TO LOCHMADDY (A865 AND B893)

At Sollas is a Co-op supermarket and post office. There is also a memorial to the people cleared from the area in the nineteenth century.

To the north are the beaches of Traigh Iar and Traigh Ear, with machair land between. The peninsula ends at Aird a' Mhorain, where there is the burial ground [NF 837787] for the MacLeans of Boreray. A rock is inscribed with a large cross.

Lying to the south-west side of the hill of Maari is another impressive burial cairn, Barpa nam Feannag [NF 857721], some fifty metres long and up to two metres high. The name means the 'cairn of the hooded crow'. On the eastern side of the hill is a two-metre-high standing stone [NF 864729], which leans at an angle. Much nearer the road is the ruinous dun in Loch Aonghais [NF 856738], which is named after is last owner century, Angus Fionn MacDonald, who held it in the sixteenth century.

Beyond this is the turn-off for Newtonferry and the causeway to the isle of Berneray (B893).

Back on the main road, Dun Torcuill [NF 888737] is a ruinous but very impressive dun or broch, which is connected to the mainland by a short causeway. The walls remain to a height of three metres, and the entrance, cells and gallery can be seen. The inside of the dun is filled with rubble, but access to the dun is not easy, even though it lies less than half a mile from the road.

A narrow unlisted road runs east to Lochportain, which is a picturesque route. There are the remains of a souterrain known as Tigh Talamhant [NF 949712] on the west side of Loch Hacklett. The name means 'house under the ground', and the passageway was one and a half metres high with three entrances.

Returning to the main road, on the north-west side of the hill of Blashaval is a setting of three standing stones known as Na Fir Bhriege [NF 888718] 'the false men'. The stones are not very tall, and may have sunk into the peat, but the story goes that they were three unfaithful husbands from Skye turned to stone by a witch.

NEWTONFERRY (B893)

A turn-off (B893) runs north to Newtonferry. Off an unlisted road is a souterrain, known as Druin na h'Uamha [NF 863753], by the shore of Vallaquie Strand. This was a curved underground passage, some six metres long, with a higher domed roof at one end. It was discovered in 1861, but since then many of the lintels have been removed.

Clach an t-Sagairt [NF 878761] is a massive standing stone, more than two metres high and three wide, with an inscribed cross. This may have been a sanctuary stone of the nearby St Columba's chapel, but there are also stories that it marks buried treasure.

Just south of Newtonferry is Loch an Sticir. On an island in the loch are the substantial remains of the Iron Age dun, Dun an Sticer [NF 898779], which survive to a height of three metres. The causeways which run from the mainland to another islet, and then to the site, are well preserved and of particular interest. The dun was

Loch an Sticir and Dun an Sticer

still in use in 1602, when Hugh MacDonald sheltered here from his kin, Donald Gorm, chief of the MacDonalds of Sleat. Hugh had planned to kill his kin, was pursued and eventually captured here, then taken back to Duntulm Castle on Trotternish in Skye, where he was reputedly starved to death in the dungeon there.

The road runs on to Newtonferry, a pleasant settlement, and the causeway across to Berneray.

COMMITTEE ROAD (UNLISTED)

The Committee Road runs through the middle of the island, passing to the west of Marrival, from the summit of which are fine views on a good day. On the south-western side, and about a mile from the road, is Airidhan an t-Sruthain Garbh Cairn [NF 796693]. This is the remains of a burial cairn, some twenty metres in diameter and more than two metres high. Nearer the road is An Carra [NF 786691], a tall standing stone, which leans at an angle.

HEISKER OR THE MONACH ISLANDS

Heisker ('bright skerry' from Norse) or the Monach Islands (from 'monk') are a group of islands which lie eight miles west off North Uist at Baleshare. The largest and most easterly of the islands is Ceann Ear ('east head') which is one and a half miles long and very flat and sandy. It is joined by tidal sands to its westerly neighbours Shivinish and Ceann Iar ('west head'). There is an old lighthouse on the most westerly isle, Shillay, which has not been used since the 1940s. It is thought that a light here was first maintained by monks in medieval times, and that there was also a nunnery.

There is a huge breeding colony of some 10,000 grey seals; one tenth of the world population can be found here every autumn. Birds which can be found here include barnacle geese, waders, shags, terns, eider ducks, shelducks, fulmars and black guillemots. The machair is particularly colourful in the late spring.

Heisker was apparently joined to North Uist by sands until these were washed away in a storm in the sixteenth or seventeenth century: the same event is said to have devastated part of Baleshare.

The islands were held by the MacDonalds but were sold in 1856; at one time Heisker supported a population 140 people(1891). This is believed to be one of the places where Rachel, Lady Grange, was held; and the islands were populated until the lighthouse keepers left in the 1940s. The islands are a National Nature Reserve, and are managed by Scottish Natural Heritage (01870 620238; www.snh.org.uk).

Northern Light Charters (01631 740595; www.northernlight-uk.com), Guideliner Hebridean Wildlife Cruises (01470 532393/07808 899356; www.guideliner.co.uk), Westernedge Charters Ltd (01506 824227/07811 387633; www.westernedge.co.uk) and Island Cruising (01851 672381; www.island-cruising.com) make trips to Heisker. Also see www.northuist.net/monach and www.nnr-scotland.org.uk. If landing on the islands is planned, it is recommended you contact Scottish Natural Heritage in advance (01870 620238; www.snh.org.uk).

HOTELS AND GUEST HOUSES

Carinish Inn (01876 580673;
  www.macinnesbros.co.uk)
  Carinish; hotel; open all year
Langass Lodge (01876 580285;
  www.langasslodge.co.uk)
  Locheport; hotel, sporting lodge, bar and fine dining; open all year

Lochmaddy Hotel(01876 500331;
  www.lochmaddyhotel.co.uk)
  Lochmaddy; hotel, bar and meals; open all year
Rushlee (018766 500274)
  Lochmaddy; guest house
Tigh Dearg Hotel (01876 500700;
  www.tighdearghotel.co.uk)
  Lochmaddy; luxury hotel, bar, restaurant with gym, sauna and steam room; open all year

Temple View Hotel (01876 580676;
www.templeviewhotel.co.uk)
Carinish; hotel and restaurant; open all year

BED AND BREAKFAST

Lapwings (01876 510736)
Bayhead; B&B
The Old Courthouse (01876 500358;
www.scotland-inverness.co.uk/johnson.htm)
Lochmaddy; B&B; open all year
Old Shop House (01876 510395)
Bayhead; B&B; open all year
Orisaigh (01876 560300; www.witb.co.uk/links/
orisaigh.htm)
Lochmaddy; B&B; open all year
Seallach Traigh (01876 580248)
Cladach Kirkibost; B&B; open all year
Sgeir Ruadh (01876 510312; www.sgeirruadh.co.uk)
Hougharry; B&B; open all year
Sheillaidh (01876 560332)
8 Sollas; B&B; open Apr-Oct
Struan House (01876 560282)
Sollas; B&B

SELF-CATERING PROPERTIES

Airigh an Obain (01876 580229;
www.northuistselfcatering.co.uk)
Near Clachan; self-catering cottage, sleeps four
Balard (01876 510379)
Paiblesgarry; self-catering cottage, sleeps four
Balemore (01795 439770; www.balemore.co.uk)
Balemore; sleeps five
Corncrake Cottage (01876 510353;
www.corncrakecottage.co.uk)
Knockintorran; self-catering cottage, sleeps
four; open all year
Grand View (0161 727 8647)
11 Cladach Kirkibost; self-catering cottage,
sleeps two; open all year
Larkfield House (01876 560238/01876 560271;
www.geocities.com/larkfield_house)
Middlequarter; self-catering house, sleeps six;
open all year
Loch Portain House (0131 447 9911;
www.trinityfactors.co.uk)
Lochportan; self-catering semi-detached
cottage, sleeps seven; open all year
Smithy Croft (01876 500391)
Lochmaddy; self-catering cottage, sleeps four-
six; open all year
Struan Cottage (www.northuist.net)
Sollas; self-catering croft house, sleeps seven,
open all year
Taigh Alasdair (01470 521404;
www.tighalasdair.co.uk)
Sidinish; self-catering cottage, sleeps four;
open all year
Tigh na Boireach (01876 500225;
www.tighnaboireach.co.uk)
Clachan Sands; self-catering thatched cottage,
sleeps two-four, open all year

Tigh na Mara (0871 910 6731; www.tigh-na-
mara.biz)
Claddach Kirkibost; self-catering bungalow,
sleeps eight; open all year
Mr William MacDonald (01876 580672;
www.northuistselfcatering.co.uk)
Clachan Locheport; self-catering flat, sleeps
five; open May-Sep

HOSTELS AND RETREATS

Taigh Mo Sheanair (01876 580246;
www.witb.co.uk/links/taighmosheanair.htm)
Claddach Baleshare; hostel, sleeps ten; open
all year
Uist Outdoor Centre (01876 500480;
www.uistoutdoorcentre.co.uk)
Cearn Dusgaidh, Lochmaddy; accommodation
for twenty people; full board or self catering
available; activities offered: rock climbing,
abseiling, overnight expeditions, offshore
island survival skills, diving, kayaking

CAMPING AND CARAVANS

Lots of fine sites: seek permission from the
nearest house
Caravan (01876 580608)
Knockqueen; caravan, sleeps four-six; open all
year
Caravan (01876 580635)
Knockqueen; caravan, sleeps four-six; open
Mar-Oct

PLACES TO EAT

Carinish Inn (01876 580673;
www.macinnesbros.co.uk)
Carinish; hotel; open all year
Claddach Kirkibost Centre (01876 580390)
Open seasonally; conservatory cafe, local
produce and home baking
Langass Lodge (01876 580285;
www.langasslodge.co.uk)
Locheport; guest house; open all year
Lochmaddy Hotel(01876 500331;
www.lochmaddyhotel.co.uk)
Lochmaddy; hotel; open all year
Taigh Chearsabhagh Art Centre and Museum
(01876 500293; www.taigh-chearsabhagh.org)
Lochmaddy; cafe in the art centre and museum
Tigh Dearg Hotel (01876 500700;
www.tighdearghotel.co.uk)
Lochmaddy; hotel, bar, restaurant; leisure club
with gym, sauna and steam room; open all year
Temple View Hotel (01876 580676;
www.templeviewhotel.co.uk)
Carinish; hotel; open all year

Further Information

TRANSPORT

BUS SERVICE
(see www.cne-siar.gov.uk/travel/)
Most services run Mon-Sat
Grenitote Travel (01876 560244)
Postbus (08457 740740; www.royalmail.com/
postbus)

TAXIS
Alda Taxis (01876 500215)
Lochmaddy

CYCLE HIRE
Tigh Dearg Hotel (01876 500700;
www.tighdearghotel.co.uk)
Lochmaddy

ACTIVITIES AND SPORTS

ANGLING AND FISHING
Clachan Stores (01876 580257)
Clachan; permits for Newton Estate
Lochmaddy Hotel(01876 500331;
www.lochmaddyhotel.co.uk)
Lochmaddy
North Uist Angling Club (01876 580341)
Fishing available on Newton and Balranald
Estates
North Uist Estate (01876 500239)
Fishing available
Uist Outdoor Centre (01876 500480;
www.uistoutdoorcentre.co.uk)
Cearn Dusgaidh, Lochmaddy; can arrange sea-
angling trips
No Sunday fishing

SHOOTING
North Uist Estate (01876 500239)

GOLF
Sollas Golf Club (www.sollasgolfcourse.co.uk)
Sollas; nine-hole golf course
Sports, Diving and Outdoor Activities
Uist Outdoor Centre (01876 500480;
www.uistoutdoorcentre.co.uk)
Cearn Dusgaidh, Lochmaddy; rock climbing,
abseiling, overnight expeditions, offshore
island survival skills, diving, kayaking;
accommodation for twenty people; full board
or self catering available

BIRD WATCHING
Balranald RSPB reserve (01876 560287;
www.rspb.org.uk/reserves/guide/b/balranald)
Balranald; visitor centre and toilets; visitor
centre open all year, 9.00- 18.00; reserve open
all year; guided tours in summer

WALKING
There are many fine, safe and easy walks on
moors and near beaches, as well as the
waymarked routes between Barpa Langass and
Pobull Fhinn, and a four-mile walk from Taigh
Chearsabhagh in Lochmaddy. There is a local
leaflet

SURFING
Good surfing can be found on the beaches to the
north-west of the island

SWIMMING
Many beaches are not safe to swim from because
of undertow: ask locally

BOAT HIRE
Calum Iain MacCorquodale (01876 510253)

SAILING AND YACHTING
Nine visitor moorings in Lochmaddy Bay, as well
as many secluded anchorage sites. For trailer/
sailors there are many slipways giving access to
the waters around the island: ask locally for
somewhere to park vehicles and trailers

LOCAL PRODUCE

Hebridean Smokehouse (01876 580209;
www.hebrideansmokehouse.com)
See Visitor Attractions, below
Hebridean Kitchen (01876 580390;
www.hebrideankitchen.co.uk)
Claddach Kirkibost Centre; conservatory cafe
selling local produce such as preserves,
chutneys and tablet; and has internet facilities
and seasonal exhibitions; open seasonally
Lobsters, langoustines and crabs are available
from Kallin pier on Grimsay or from a
weekly van

ARTS AND CRAFTS

Shoreline Ceramics (01876 580372)
Locheport
Ealain Ghaidhlig (01876 580611;
www.calanas.co.uk)
Uppertown, Carinish; residential or non-
residential craft courses

VISITOR ATTRACTIONS AND MUSEUMS

Taigh Chearsabhagh (01876 500293; www.taigh-
chearsabhagh.org)
Lochmaddy; two galleries, museum, arts
workshop, shop, post office and cafe; Internet
available; open Mon-Sat 10.00 -17.00
Hebridean Smokehouse (01876 580209;
www.hebrideansmokehouse.com)
Smokehouse using peat to smoke salmon, sea
trout and scallops; smoke house shop for
smoked fish, pates, and a range of tableware
and other gifts; viewing gallery to see the
produce being made and information display;
open Mon-Sat 9.00 -17.00

ADDITIONAL INFORMATION

Bank of Scotland (01876 500323)
Lochmaddy
NHS (01876 500333)
Lochmaddy; twenty-four hours
Police (01876 500328)
There are petrol stations at Lochmaddy and
Bayhead
Presbyterian services in all districts, morning and

evening on Sun: most have Gaelic Psalm
singing

Private flyers can land at Grenitote beach (tidal;
01851 830366); two 'fly ins' with BBQ each
summer

EVENTS

Lochmaddy Boat Festival	May-June
Feis Tir an Eorna	July
North Uist Highland Games	July
Sollas Weeks	end July
North Uist Agricultural Show	July/August
Twin Peaks Hill Race	August

FURTHER READING

North Uist in History and Legend (Lawson, Bill)
John Donald, 2004

Uists and Barra (Thompson, Francis)
David and Charles (Pevensey), 1999

ACKNOWLEDGMENTS

Thanks to Norman MacLeod at Taigh
Chearsabhagh, Dr John MacLeod, and Judith
Entwisle-Baker at the Hebridean Smokehouse

Beach, Baleshare (see page 248)

BERNERAY

(possibly 'Bjorn's island' from Norse; Bearnaraigh)

www.isleofberneray.com
www.visitthebrides.com (Western Isles)

Tourist Information Centres
Lochmaddy (01876 500321)
   Open Apr-Oct
Stornoway (01851 703088)
   Open Jan-Dec

Map Landranger sheet: 18 (HIH map page 233)

TRAVEL

The island can be reached by causeway from North Uist (A865, then B893, eight miles north of Lochmaddy).

By vehicle ferry (CalMac 01876 502444/01859 502444) from Leverburgh (A859) on Harris. The journey take threes quarters of an hour. There are up to four sailings each day, with three on Sundays.

DESCRIPTION

Berneray is located off the north coast of North Uist in the Sound of Harris. The island is three and a half miles long by about two wide, and covers 2,496 acres. The highest point is at Beinn Shleibhe at ninety-three metres, from which there are fine views. There is an excellent white sandy beach running along the west and north of the island, and another on the northeast. There are also small coves and beaches on the south coast.

There is a lot of fertile land, and the population was once more than 700: Berneray grew many of the potatoes that fed the people of Harris. Now about 120 people live

Berneray

on the island, mostly down the east coast in the settlements of Borve (Borgh) and Ruisgarry (Ruisigearraidh), making a living from fishing for lobsters, crabs and prawns, sheep farming and crofting. There is a shop and post office (01876 540249) and cafe on the island.

HISTORY

A souterrain, a subterranean walled passage, was found at Sgalabraig [NF 907815] and there is an old burial ground at Cladh Maolrithe [NF 912807] with a two-and-a-half metre standing stone known as Clach Mor. The site was dedicated to St Maelrubha. There was another chapel [NF 928826], dedicated to St Anselm, but it has gone.

The island was a held by the MacLeods of Berneray, who had a stronghold on the island known as the Gunnery [NF 933815], and was the birthplace of Sir Norman MacLeod, laird of the island, in 1614. He was a famous scholar and fought at the Battle of Worcester in 1651.

Berneray

A stone at Beinn a' Chlaidh [NF 912806] is said to have a footprint scooped out of it, and to have been a place of inauguration for the Lords of the Isles. The most famous example of this kind of 'footprint' is at Dunadd. In 1697 the settlement of Siabaidh was overwhelmed by sand during a fierce storm. At Borve [NF 909816] there is a stone shaped like a chair and said to have been a place of execution. Near this stone is a burial cairn and a standing stone.

Berneray was the birthplace of Angus 'Giant' MacAskill, who was more than two and a quarter metres tall and died in 1863 in Canada. There is a memorial to him at the south of the island; and a museum about him at Dunvegan on Skye.

Prince Charles (the current heir to the throne; not the Young Pretender) has been a regular visitor to Berneray.

PLACES TO STAY

Burnside Croft (01876 540235;
www.burnsidecroft.biz)
B&B; working croft (visited by Prince Charles);
cycle hire; open Feb-Nov
Tir nan Og (01876 540333;
www.isleofberneray.com)
B&B
Gatliff Hebridean Hostel (www.gatliff.org.uk)
Located in thatched black houses; sleeps
sixteen; camping also available; open all year
32 Backhill (01876 540249;
www.isleofberneray.com)
Backhill; self-catering house, sleeps four/five;
open all year
18 Borve (01876 540224)
Borve; self-catering house, sleeps seven
Wester Rhumhor (01876 540253;
www.westerrhumhor.co.uk)
Self-catering house, sleeps ten

PLACES TO EAT

Ardmaree Stores and Lobster Pot Cafe (01876
540288; www.isleofberneray.com)
Licensed cafe and grocery store; also sells
outdoor clothing, stained glass panels,
hardware and DIY; toilets for customers

Further Information

TRANSPORT

Bus

(see www.cne-siar.gov.uk/travel/)
There is a frequent bus service to Lochmaddy,
which does not run on a Sunday

Cycle Hire

Burnside Croft (01876 540235;
www.burnsidecroft.biz)

ACTIVITIES AND SPORTS

Boat Trips

Nighean Ghorm (01876 540289/07786 306745;
www.isleofberneray.com)
Berneray Boat Club (www.isleofberneray.com)
Westernedge Charters Ltd (01506 824227/07811
387633; www.westernedge.co.uk)
Berneray; trips to Taransay, Flannan Isles,
Scarp, Monach Islands, Mingulay, Barra, and
St Kilda

Fishing

Ardmaree Stores (01876 540288;
www.isleofberneray.com)
Fishing permits for Loch Bhruist

ARTS AND CRAFTS

Berneray Pottery (01876 540310;
www.isleofberneray.com)
Pottery also selling locally produced jewellery,
art and gifts; open daily, 14.00-17.00
Stained glass (01876 540279) is available to buy
from the Lobster Pot Tearoom

VISITOR ATTRACTIONS AND MUSEUMS

Berneray Information Centre
(www.isleofberneray.com)
One mile or so from causeway; history, pictures
and leaflets about the island; open Jun-Sep,
11.00-15.00

ADDITIONAL INFORMATION

There is a fine harbour at Bays Loch.
Post Office open Mon, Tue, Thu & Fri 9.30-13.00
No petrol on the island (Lochmaddy on North
Uist has petrol)
Berneray Historical Society (01876 540279;
www.isleofberneray.com)
A guide to the island is available to download
from the website
Ardmaree Stores and Lobster Pot Cafe (01876
540288; www.isleofberneray.com)
Licensed cafe and grocery store; also sells
outdoor clothing, stained glass panels,
hardware and DIY; toilets for customers; open
Mon-Sat, 9.00-17.30
Berneray Community Centre (01851 612331)
Exhibitions; showers and toilets; open in
summer

EVENTS

Berneray Week   July

ACKNOWLEDGMENTS

Thanks to John Kirriemuir for checking the text
and for the picture of the island (page 246).
Image (page 245) courtesy Colin Palmer
(www.buyimage.co.uk)

BALESHARE

('east township'; Baile Sear)

www.virtualhebrides.com
www.visithebrides.com (Western Isles)

Tourist Information Centres
Lochmaddy (01876 500321)
   Open Apr-Oct
Stornoway (01851 703088)
   Open Jan-Dec

Map Landranger sheets: 18, 22 (HIH map page 233)

TRAVEL

A causeway (unlisted road off A865, two miles north of Carinish) links Baleshare to North Uist.

DESCRIPTION, WILDLIFE AND HISTORY

Baleshare is a small flat island off the east coast of North Uist, and linked to it by a causeway from the A865 a mile or so south of Clachan on North Uist. The island is three miles long by under two miles across, and is very fertile. There are dunes around the coasts and beautiful stretches of white sand. Illeray lies to the north of Baleshare.

At the northern tip of Illeray is Carnan nan Long Cairn [NF 791637], the remains of a large prehistoric burial cairn. It is some thirty metres long and survives to a height of three metres.

The name Baleshare means 'east township'. There may have been a 'west township' but one story is that this was overwhelmed by sand or a tidal wave in the 1500s. The population is currently around fifty, although in 1891 ait was more than 300 people. The causeway was completed in 1962.

Kirkibost (Eilean Chircebost) lies just to the north of Baleshare, and is now uninhabited. It is about two miles long and half a mile wide; and is flat and also surrounded by sands.

PLACES TO STAY

Bonnieview (01876 580211)
   Baleshare; B&B; open all year
Taigh Mo Sheanair (01876 580246;
   www.witb.co.uk/links/taighmosheanair.htm)
   Claddach Baleshare (nearby on North Uist);
   hostel, sleeps ten; open all year

FURTHER INFORMATION

There is a phone box on Baleshare
Buses run to the island: see www.cne-siar.gov.uk/
   travel/)

Benbecula and Grimsay

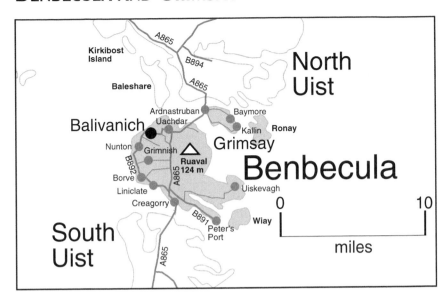

Benbecula

BENBECULA

('mountain (or hill) of the fords' – the emphasis in on the second syllable; Beinn na Faoghla in Gaelic; pronounced 'Ben-na-Voola' in Gaelic)

www.benbeculahistorysociety.co.uk
www.virtualhebrides.com
www.theuists.com
www.uistonline.com
www.southuist.com
www.visithebrides.com (Western Isles)

Tourist Information Centres
Lochmaddy (01876 500321)
   Open Apr-Oct
Lochboisdale (01878 700286)
   Open Apr-Oct
Stornoway (01851 703088)
   Open Jan-Dec

Map Landranger sheet: 22 (HIH map page 249)

TRAVEL

A bridge and causeways join Benbecula to North Uist via Grimsay and to South Uist (A865). These islands also have a range of amenities, places to stay and eat, and shops, which are mostly within easy reach.

Flights (British Airways 0345 222111; www.britishairways.com) from Glasgow, Stornoway and Barra land at Benbecula Airport (01870 602310; www.hial.co.uk/benbecula-airport.html), near Balivanich (B892). There are services daily except on Sundays.

Benbecula

DESCRIPTION

The island is sandwiched between North Uist and South Uist, and is eight miles long by around five wide at the most. The highest point on the island is at the prominent hill of Rueval at 124 metres, from where there are excellent views, although, apart from this hill, most of the land is flat. The west coast has fine stretches of sand and dunes, while the east coast has a profusion of inlets, sea lochs and lochans, islands, islets and skerries. The interior of the island is also peppered with freshwater lochs.

Most of the population live on the west side, and the main village is at Balivanich (Baile a' Mhanaich) on the north-west coast, which has shops including MacGillivrays (01870 602525) with crafts and souvenirs, hotels, a bank, places to eat, a post office and the island's airport. There are also settlements at Gramsdale (Gramasdail), Uachdar, Nunton (Baile nan Cailleach), Griminish (Griminis) with a craft shop (01870 602992), Torlum, Liniclate (Lionacleit) which has a sports centre, museum and cafe, and Creagorry (Creag Ghoraidh) with a post office (01870 602431) and Co-op (01870 602231).

The island is also on the boundary of religion, with Presbyterians to the north and Roman Catholics to the south. The population has been more stable than some of the islands: in 1841 it had a population of more than 2,100, although by 1891 this had declined to 1,659. Recently the number of inhabitants was given as around 1,800, although many of these were service personnel at Balivanich, and in 2001 the population had dropped to 1,249 with the closing of the base.

HISTORY

Benbecula has a peppering of prehistoric monuments, the most impressive of which is probably Airidh an h-Aon Oidhche, a chambered burial cairn south of the hill of Rueval. There are also the ruins of several fortified duns on islands in the many lochans, and the vestige of a stone circle at Gramsdale.

Benbecula was one of the islands to have evidence of Pictish occupation: a carved stone was found near the small island of Sunamul to the north of Benbecula. Further evidence includes aisled houses and a souterrain, which were found at the airport.

St Torannan is reputed to have brought Christianity here in the sixth century and he may have founded a monastery, the site of which is now occupied by Teampull Chaluim Chille, to the south of Balivanich, which itself means the 'township of monks'. There are two other ruined chapels, one at Nunton. There may have been a nunnery here, but it is more likely that the name comes from the fact that the lands were owned by the nunnery on Iona.

The island was one of the many possessions of the MacDonald Lords of the Isles, after coming to them by marriage of the heiress Amy MacRuari. She was divorced by her husband so that he could marry a daughter of the king of Scots, but it was though her that the Clanranald branch were descended. The chiefs stayed at Borve Castle, but later moved to Nunton. The clan did not fight for the Jacobites in the Rising of 1745-6, but after defeat at Culloden Bonnie Prince Charlie was sheltered on South Uist and then Benbecula, before being taken to Skye.

In 1839 the island was sold to the Gordons of Cluny, whose family held the island until 1942. The Gordons were responsible for driving many people from their homes and forcing them to emigrate or take land in poor areas.

One of the strangest stories is that the body of a mermaid, killed when boys threw stones at her, was found at Culla around 1825. The remains were reputedly buried after investigation at the bay, although recent investigations of the shore could find no evidence for her existence.

Benbecula was used by the armed forces, and there was a Royal Artillery base which had a missile range as well as the airfield at Balivanich. At one time there were 500 servicemen based here.

Tours
GRAMSDALE TO CREAGORRY (A865)

The causeway to Benbecula crosses Grimsay on its way to Benbecula. At Gramsdale is a standing stone [NF 825561], the last upright stone from a stone circle; there was another setting nearby [NF 824552].

A track runs to the east a mile or so south of Gramsdale towards Rueval: this is the route taken by Bonnie Prince Charlie and Flora MacDonald as he fled from the Uists across to Skye disguised as Flora's maid, Betty Burke. South-west of Rueval is Airidh an h-Aon Oidhche [NF 817525], an impressive chambered burial cairn, twenty metres in diameter and more than three metres high. Nearby is Striaval Cairn [NF 812526], less well preserved and with upright slabs from the chamber and passageway. There are fine views from the top of the hill, and the track leads around the south to Rossinish on the east coast, although it is a very long walk.

The A865 runs down the island's middle, passing Liniclate, until it reaches Creagorry, where there is a hotel, post office and shop, and the causeway to South Uist.

GRAMSDALE TO BALIVANICH AND LINICLATE (B892)

The B892 leaves the A865 at Gramsdale and runs to the east. In Loch Dun Mhurchaidh is Dun Buidhe [NF 794546], the ruins of a dun on an island which was reached by a causeway. A wall enclosing the island is more than two metres high in places, and the site may have been used by the Vikings. A mile to the west are the ruins of a rectangular chapel known as Teampull Chaluim Chille [NF 782549], the 'church of St Columba'. This may be an ancient Christian site, first founded by St Torannan in the sixth century. A well is surrounded by piles of stones, some 200 metres south of the chapel. These stones are said to have been left by pilgrims who came to drink some of the well water.

Balivanich is the main settlement on Benbecula, and there are shops (MacGillivrays 01870 602525) and places to eat (including the Stepping Stone Restaurant and Sinteag, a licensed restaurant), as well as a golf course, a riding school with pony trekking, a bank, petrol and an airport (with flights to Stornoway, Barra and Glasgow). The size of the village is directly attributable to the army base and airfield, but operations have been scaled down here over the years. The village is not perhaps the most beautiful part of the Western Isles with the many forces' buildings being at best functional.

There is a good sandy beach at Culla Bay, and at Nunton there is an old chapel and burial ground. The chapel [NF 766538] was dedicated to St Mary and dates from the fourteenth century. It is thought that there was a nunnery here before the Reformation (and even that the nuns were massacred at this time, although this would have been a very unusual event), but the name appears to refer to the fact that the lands were held by the nunnery on Iona. The chiefs of Clanranald moved to Nunton from Borve some time after 1625 (probably after Ormiclate Castle was burned down in 1715), and occupied Nunton House [NF 764535]. In 1746 the MacDonalds sheltered Bonnie Prince Charlie, before he was taken across the island to Rossinish and then by boat to Skye, dressed as Flora MacDonald's Irish maid. The clothes which made up his disguise were brought from Nunton House.

Nunton Steadings (01870 603774; www.nuntonsteadings.com) have been restored and house a tearoom, training facilities with broadband internet access, exhibition facilities and eight-eenth century stables

In a lochan to the south-west of Nunton is Dun Torcusay [NF 794546], the remains of a fortified dun on a small island.

There is another fine beach down the coast, although it is known as Stinky Bay, because of the sea-weed which can accu-mulate here and then rot.

Nunton

Craig Lea Crafts (01870 602992) is located at Griminish, on an unlisted road.

At Borve are the reduced ruins of Borve Castle [NF 774506], which had very thick walls and dates from the fourteenth century. This was a stronghold of the Clanranald branch of the MacDonalds, and the castle may have been built by Amy MacRuari. The clan moved to Nunton in about 1625 (as mentioned above), and Borve was destroyed by fire in the late eighteenth century. On the other side of the road is Teampull Bhuirgh [NF 769774], where there are some remains of an old chapel.

At Liniclate, and housed in the modern school, is the Museum nan Eilean (01870 602864; www.cne-siar.gov.uk/museum/sgoil/museum.htm), which features a library and photographic material on aspects of the history and culture of the Uists and Barra. In the complex are also a swimming pool, sports facilities and a cafe (01870 603526; www.cne-siar.gov.uk/lsc). There is also a hotel.

LINICLATE TO PETER'S PORT AND UISKEVAGH (B891)

The B891 goes east from the A865, through the township of Hacklet, across the islet of Grimsay and Eilean na Cille to Peter's Port, where the road runs out at the pier. This is not one of the best harbours, despite being specially built in 1896, and is hazardous to enter.

Offshore and to the east is the small but hilly island of Wiay ('temple island' or 'yellow or pleasant island'; Fuidhaigh in Gaelic), which is a couple of miles long and wide and covers some 920 acres. Wiay has been uninhabited since the 1900s, and is a bird sanctuary.

An unlisted road leads north from Hacklet, passing several townships, before eventually arriving at the east coast at Uiskevagh.

These are both pleasant walks, cycles or drives, but the roads are narrow and may be difficult in places.

Places to Stay
HOTELS AND GUEST HOUSES

Borve Guest House (01870 602 685)
  Torlum; guest house; open all year
Dark Island Hotel (01870 603030;
  www.isleshotelgroup.co.uk)
  Lionacleit; hotel and meals; open all year

Isle of Benbecula House Hotel (01870 602024;
  www.isleshotelgroup.co.uk)
  Creagorry; hotel, restaurant and bar; open
  all year
Lionacleit Guesthouse (01870 602176;
  www.lionacleit-guesthouse.com)
  27 Lionacleit; guest house, as well as self-
  catering property; open all year

BED AND BREAKFAST

Creag Liath (01870 602992; www.witb.co.uk/links/
creagliath.htm)
   15 Griminish; B&B; open all year
9 Lionacleit (01870 602532)
   Lionacleit; B&B; open Jan-Nov
Hestimul (01870 602033)
   Lionacleit; B&B; open Jan-Nov

SELF-CATERING PROPERTIES

Baile Sear View (07803 170039;
   www.bailesearview.freeserve.co.uk)
   Balivanich; self-catering house, sleeps six; open
   all year
Hillview Holiday Cottage (01878 700862;
   www.uistonline.com/hillviewcottage.htm)
   Balivanich; self-catering, sleeps four-six people
House (01870 602432)
   Balivanich; self-catering, sleeps seven; open
   all year
Tigh Curstaig (01870 602536;
   www.btinternet.com/-donald.macdonald5/)
   Kyles Flodda, Gramsdale; self-catering
   thatched croft cottage, sleeps two-four; open
   all year
Taigh Ailean (01870 602376; www.ceanngarbh.u-
net.com)
   Island Flodda; self-catering cottage, sleeps six

HOSTELS AND RETREATS

Taigh-na-Cille (01870 602522/07740 582778;
   www.uistonline.com/taighnacille/)
   Balivanich; bunkhouse, sleeps eight

CAMPING AND CARAVANS

Shellbay Caravan and Camping Park (01870
   602447; www.uistonline.com/shellbay.htm)
   Lionacleit; holiday caravans and camping; open
   Apr-Oct

PLACES TO EAT

Dark Island Hotel (01870 603030;
   www.isleshotelgroup.co.uk)
   Liniclate; hotel and restaurant; open all year
Isle of Benbecula House Hotel (01870 602024;
   www.isleshotelgroup.co.uk)
   Creagorry; hotel and restaurant; open all year
Low Flyer (01870 602426)
   Balivanich Development Centre
Lionacleit Sports Centre (01870 603526; www.cne-
siar.gov.uk/lsc)
   Lionacleit; there is a cafe in the complex
Nunton Steadings (01870 603774;
   www.nuntonsteadings.com)
   Nunton; tearoom, training facilities with
   broadband wireless internet access, exhibition
   facilities and a restored eighteenth-century
   stable block
Stepping Stone Restaurant (01870 603377)
   Balivanich, near Benbecula airport; restaurant,
   takeaway available; open all year

Further Information

TRANSPORT

BUS SERVICES
(see www.cne-siar.gov.uk/travel/)
Services (01851 701702)
   Buses for from Balivanich to both North and
   South Uist
Postbus (08457 740740; www.royalmail.com/
   postbus)

CAR HIRE
The Garage (01870 602818)
   Creagorry
Ask Car Hire (01870 602818)
   Lionacleit
MacLennan Brothers (01870 602191)
   Balivanich

TAXIS
Benbecula Taxis (01870 602464)
Buchanans (01870 602277)
Buster (01870 610374)
Donald John (01870 610374)
MacVicars Taxis (01870 603197)

ACTIVITIES AND SPORTS

GOLF
Benbecula Golf Course (www.golfhebrides.com/
   courses/benbecula/)
   Balivanich; nine holes with eighteen tees; no
   facilities at course

PONY TREKKING
Uist Community Riding School (UCRS) (01870
   604283/01870 602186;
   www.uistridingschool.homestead.com)
   Balivanich; pony rides, beach treks, picnic
   treks, lessons; classes for the disabled

SWIMMING AND SPORTS
Lionacleit Sports Centre (01870 603526; www.cne-
   siar.gov.uk/lsc)
   Lionacleit; twenty-five metre swimming pool,
   fitness suite, games hall, sauna and cafe

ARTS AND CRAFTS

MacGillivrays (01870 602525)
   Balivanich; shop selling a variety of Tweed,
   gifts, souvenirs, books and fishing tackle

VISITOR ATTRACTIONS AND MUSEUMS

Museum nan Eilean, Sgoil Lionacleit (01870
   602864; www.cne-siar.gov.uk/museum/sgoil/
   museum.htm)
   Lionacleit; museum with displays on the Uists,
   Benbecula and Barra

ADDITIONAL INFORMATION

Bank of Scotland (01870 602044)
  Balivanich
Petrol: MacLennan Brothers (01870 602191) at
  Balivanich
There are phone boxes in some of the more
  remote spots, including at Hacklet and Aird
  Cumhang and on Flodda

EVENTS

Benbecula Half Marathon   June
Feis Tir a' Mhurain   August

FURTHER READING

Uists and Barra (Thompson, Francis)
  David and Charles (Pevensey), 1999

ACKNOWLEDGMENTS

Thanks to Alasdair McKenzie for checking the
  text and providing two of the photographs

GRIMSAY

('Grim's island' from Norse; Griomasaigh)

www.virtualhebrides.com
www.visithebrides.com (Western Isles)

Tourist Information Centres
Lochmaddy (01876 500321)
  Open Apr-Oct
Lochboisdale (01878 700286)
  Open Apr-Oct
Stornoway (01851 703088)
  Open Jan-Dec

Map Landranger sheet: 22 (HIH map page 249)

TRAVEL

The causeway between Benbecula and North Uist (A865) crosses the western side of the island.

DESCRIPTION, WILDLIFE AND HISTORY

Grimsay nestles between North Uist and Benbecula, and is three miles long and up to one and a half miles wide. An unlisted road runs around the picturesque island. There are settlements at Balagas (Baile Glas), Baymore (Bagh Mor), Kallin (Na Ceallan) with its harbour and Ardnastruban (Aird nan Sruban). The population in 1861 was more than 300, although it has since declined. The causeway was built in 1960, and there is a post office at Ardnastruban. The mainstay of the island economy is fishing for lobsters and shellfish as well as fish farming: there is an information board at Kallin. There is a colony of grey seals.

On an island at the east end of Loch Hornary are the remains of Dun Ban [NF 870569], the walls of which survive to a height of two metres. There was a causeway out to the island. Near Kallin is St Michael's Chapel [NF 882548] on the eastern tip of Grimsay. The chapel is ruined and stands in an old cemetery which was used to bury the bodies of unknown seaman who were washed up on the island.

Ronay ('Ronan's Isle'; Ronaigh) lies to the east of Grimsay, and is more than two miles long and the same wide. It is rough and hilly, and rises to 115 metres at Beinn a' Charnain. The island once had a population of 180 people, but these were cleared to make way for sheep; and by the 1930s Ronay was abandoned. The uninhabited islands of Floddaymore and Floddaybeg lie to the north and east of Ronay.

PLACES TO STAY

Ardnastruban House (01870 602452;
  www.ardnastrubanhouse.co.uk)
  B&B; open all year
Glendale (01870 602029; sites.ecosse.net/glendale)
  B&B; open all year
Rona View (01606 44422; www.rona-view.com)
  Self-catering house, sleeps six; open all year

LOCAL PRODUCE

Lobsters, langoustines and crabs are available
  from Kallin pier

FURTHER INFORMATION

There is a post office at Ardnastruban (open
  Mon-Sat), and telephone boxes at
  Ardnastruban and at Kallin harbour

EVENTS

Grimsay Boat day   end May

ACKNOWLEDGMENTS

Thanks to Katie and Margaret Wiseman for
  checking over the entry

SOUTH UIST AND ERISKAY

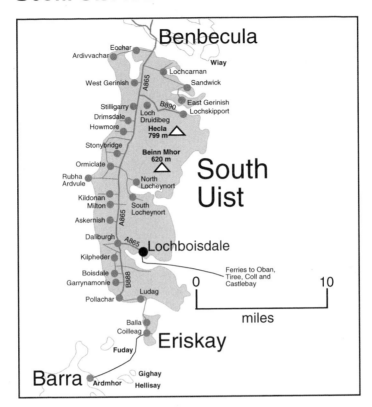

Benbecula

Eochar
Ardivvachar
Wiay
Lochcarnan
West Gerinish
A865
Sandwick
East Gerinish
Stilligarry
B890
Lochskipport
Drimsdale
Loch
Druidibeg
Howmore
Hecla
799 m
Stonybridge
Beinn Mhor
620 m
Ormiclate
**South
Uist**
Rubha
Ardvule
North
Locheynort
Kildonan
Milton
A865
South
Locheynort
Askernish
Daliburgh
A865
Lochboisdale
Kilpheder
Boisdale
B888
Ferries to Oban,
Tiree, Coll and
Castlebay
Garrynamonie
Pollachar
Ludag

0   10

miles

Balla
Coilleag
Eriskay
Fuday

Barra Ardmhor
Gighay
Hellisay

South Uist

257

SOUTH UIST

('south abode'; Uist a' Deas in Gaelic)

www.southuist.com
www.virtualhebrides.com
www.theuists.com
www.uistonline.com
www.visithebrides.com (Western Isles)

Tourist Information Centres
Lochboisdale (01878 700286)
    Open Apr-Oct
Stornoway (01851 703088)
    Open Jan-Dec

Map Landranger sheets: 22, 31 (HIH map page 257)

TRAVEL

A vehicle ferry (CalMac 01631 566688, 01871 810306 or 01878 700288; www.calmac.co.uk) leaves from Oban on the mainland and arrives at Lochboisdale on South Uist. There are trips on Tuesday, Thursday, Saturday and Sunday; and the journey takes five hours. There is also a service to Castlebay, on Barra, on a Monday, and arriving from Castlebay on a Sunday, taking one hour and thirty minutes.

A causeway links South Uist to Benbecula (which has an airport) and North Uist. Lochmaddy on North Uist has a shorter ferry crossing to Uig on Skye.

CalMac (01851701702; www.calmac.co.uk) also runs a vehicle service from Ardmhor on Barra to Eriskay, which is connected by a causeway to South Uist (B888 and unlisted road). This runs up to five times daily, and the crossing takes forty minutes. Ardmhor is seven miles north of Castlebay.

DESCRIPTION

South Uist lies between Benbecula and Barra, and is twenty-one miles long and up to six miles wide, occupying 141 square miles. To the north it is linked to Benbecula by a causeway, which was first built in 1943, making access between the islands much easier – the causeway was rebuilt in 1983. As Eriskay has been joined to South Uist, it means that there is a causeway, bridge or regular ferry between all the inhabited islands from Lewis to Vatersay.

The west coast of South Uist has a string of wonderful sandy beaches running virtually the length of the island, although some have warning signs. There is more sand along the south coast. There is a peppering of small lochans behind the beaches and machair land, and to the north of the island. Two of the largest lochs, Loch Bee and Loch Druidibeg, have many birds, and the latter is a national nature reserve. The east side of the island is much rougher and remoter, and is extremely hilly, with Hecla at 606 metres and Beinn Mhor at 620 metres; it is indented by sea lochs.

The largest villages are Lochboisdale (Loch Baghasdail), on the east coast to the south of the island, which has a post office, a shop, a bank, a hotel and a tourist information centre, and is where the ferry from Oban and from Barra lands; and Daliburgh (Dalabrog), a few miles inland, which has a Co-op supermarket, a post office and a hotel. There are villages and settlements all up the western side, including (from south to north) Pollachar (Pol a' Charra), which has a hotel; Kilpheder (Cille Pheadair); Milton, birthplace of Flora MacDonald; Kildonan (Cill Donnain), which

South Uist

has a museum, cafe and craft outlet; Howmore (Tobha Mor) with its chapels and a shop; West Gerinish (Geirinis); Eochar (Iochdar), where there is a shop and Hebridean Jewellery; and Carnan (Carnain). The main road, the A865, runs up the west side from Lochboisdale by the causeway to Benbecula: it is single track and narrow in places, so care should be taken. There are routes to the east to Loch Eynort (Loch Aineort; unlisted); Lochskipport (Loch Sgioport; B890), which has the oldest pier on the island; and on the north coast (unlisted) to Lochcarnan (Loch a' Charnain), where there is a smokery and a hotel, and Sandwick (Sanndabhaig).

The population of the island is around 1,800 people and, along with Barra, many islanders are Roman Catholic and speak Gaelic. Because of this, more things are open on a Sunday and attitudes to activities on the Sabbath are relaxed.

WILDLIFE

Many birds can be seen on the island, especially at Loch Skipport, Loch Bee and Loch Druidibeg, where there is a nature reserve (01870 620238; www.nnr-scotland.org.uk/reserve.asp). These include greylag geese, corncrakes, swans, ducks and other wild fowl. Otters can be seen along the coasts of the sea and lochs, especially on the east coast, and there are also seals and dolphins around the seashore.

One unwelcome introduction has been the hedgehog, introduced to control slugs in a garden but which have bred in great numbers and consume the eggs of ground-nesting birds. Steps have been taken to eradicate the prickly pest.

HISTORY

The island has a fine range of prehistoric monuments, including impressive burial cairns, standing stones and many ruinous duns on islands in lochans. Some of these duns were used into medieval times, and even into the sixteenth and seventeenth centuries. There are also several souterrains, mostly in inaccessible places on the east coast; as well as the imposing ruins of wheel or aisled houses, mostly found on the west coast. These may indicate a period of Pictish occupation.

South Uist was held by the Vikings, and excavations at Bornish revealed a large

259

Norse settlement. Finds included coins, pottery, soapstone weights, combs and bronze pins.

It was later one of the territories of the Lords of the Isles, and was a property of Clanranald, a branch of the MacDonalds (who were descended from Amy MacRuari and her husband John MacDonald, Lord of the Isles. He subsequently divorced her so that he could marry a daughter of Robert II, King of Scots). Many of the clan and their successors are buried at Howmore, where there was an important ecclesiastical complex. The south of the island was held by the MacNeils of Barra until 1621, when it passed to the Mackenzies of Kintail, although the MacNeils remained as tenants.

There were several strongholds around South Uist: Caisteal Calvay, on an island in the mouth of Loch Boisdale; Caisteal Bheagram on an island in a lochan at Drimsdale; and Ormiclate Castle, built in 1708 and burnt out seven years later.

One tradition is that there was a battle between the MacDonalds and a raiding part of MacLeods of Dunvegan; the latter were defeated near Snishival.

The chief of Clanranald was killed fighting for the Jacobites at the Battle of Sheriffmuir in 1715, and the clan did not support the Jacobites in the 1745-6 Rising. Nevertheless, Bonnie Prince Charlie was helped by the MacDonalds when he took refuge on South Uist after defeat at Culloden in 1746. He sheltered in Caisteal Calvay and in a small cave above the remote Corodale Bay, known as the Prince's Cave [NF 843313], before being taken to Benbecula, and from there over the sea to Skye. He was helped by Flora MacDonald, who was born at Milton; the prince was disguised as an Irish weaver and Flora's maid, Betty Burke.

In 1838 South Uist, along with Eriskay and Benbecula, were sold to Gordon of Cluny. They went on to clear much of the population and replaced them with sheep: at one time more than 7,000 people lived on South Uist, while now it is around 1,800. Crofting, farming and fishing for lobsters and shellfish help to support the population.

Tours
LOCHBOISDALE TO KILDONAN (A865)
Lochboisdale is where the ferries from Oban and Barra land, and it has a range of facilities, including a hotel, places to eat, crafts, a bank, a post office, public toilets, a tourist information centre and shops. The village was once a busy herring fishing port, and is now home to about 300 people. The A865 runs inland, and soon becomes single track.

At the mouth of the loch, on the islet of Calvay, is Caisteal Calvay [NF 817182], a ruinous stronghold of the MacNeils, used to shelter Bonnie Prince Charlie in 1746.

In a remote spot at Eligar [NF 813228] is a souterrain, consisting of a six-metre-long passageway and the ruin of two cells. By Loch a' Bharp [NF 777214], a mile north of the main road, is what has been a massive chambered burial cairn which, although partly robbed, is twenty-five metres in diameter and more than five in height.

At Daliburgh is a supermarket and hotel, and here the A865 heads north, while the B888 heads south for Pollachar and the causeway to Eriskay.

The local parish church [NF 754214], which was completed in 1880 and is Church of Scotland, is open to the public; as is the large Catholic church [NF 745211], dedicated to St Peter and dating from 1868. A fantastic sandy beach runs virtually up the whole of the west coast of South Uist. Danger Areas because of use by the military are marked on Ordnance Survey maps.

To the north is an original Tom Morris golf course at Askernish (www.askernishgolfclub.com) in a beautiful spot by the west coast, and there is a hotel nearby and a gallery (www.william-neill.co.uk) featuring landscape and wildlife pictures.

Off the unlisted road to Mingary is Barp Reineval [NF 755260], located on the north side of the small hill of Reineval. This is the remains of chambered burial cairn and the entrance passage can be traced. The cairn is twenty metres in diameter, and more than three metres high.

Flora MacDonald was born at Milton [NF 741269] in 1722, and a cairn marks her birthplace. She helped Bonnie Prince Charlie flee from the Uists to Skye, and was eventually caught and imprisoned. Released in a general amnesty, she married and lived on Skye.

Kildonan is home to the island's excellent museum, which has displays on island life, along with archives, a local information centre and Clanranald Stone (01878 710343; open Apr-Sep, Mon-Sat 10.00-17.00, Sun 14.00-17.00). The building also houses a cafe and shop with local crafts from Uist Craft Producers such as knitting, painting, woodwork and flower craft; there is also a public toilet. There are some remains of a church and other buildings, which were occupied from the Iron Age to the late medieval period.

KILDONAN TO CARNAN AND LOCHCARNAN (A865 AND UNLISTED ROAD)

North of Kildonan is an unlisted road which runs across the machair to the headland called Rubha Ardvule. On the south side of the headland is Dun Vulan [NF 713297], a broch or dun with walls surviving to more than four metres. There is a cell within a wall and a stairway to a first-floor gallery. The site was occupied from the Bronze Age until 300 AD. The headland is supposedly named after Vule, a Norse princess. Danger Areas because of use by the military are marked on Ordnance Survey maps.

Further north an unlisted road runs across to Loch Eynort. This is a picturesque route across to the east coast, flanked by the rising hills. The road branches, one route going north, the other south, but both running out after a couple of miles. To the north-east of North Locheynort is a burial cairn [NF 778297], some three metres high.

Probably the last castle built in Scotland, Ormiclate Castle was begun in 1708 by Allan, chief of Clan-ranald, and was only occupied for seven years before being accidentally burnt out, reputedly on the eve of the Battle of Sher-iffmuir. The chief was slain at the battle; although one story has the castle torched as a result of a drunken party. The MacDonalds of Clanranald moved to Nunton on Benbecula.

Ormiclate Castle

About quarter of a mile from the main road, on the western side of Beinn Charra is An Cara [NF 770321], an exceptionally tall standing stone at five metres high.

Howmore [NF 758365] was an important ecclesiastical centre in medieval times, and there is a ruinous complex of churches, chapels and burial grounds. The area was surrounded by a bank and this was probably an early Christian site. The largest of the surviving buildings is Teampull Mor, dedicated to St Mary and used as the parish church. There is also Dugall's Chapel, St Dermot's Chapel

Howmore

and Clanranald's Chapel; members of the family were buried here. Howmore is an interesting village, and some of the houses are thatched, including the youth hostel (www.gatliff.org.uk). The simple Church of Scotland parish church is whitewashed and used as a landmark by fisherman. It is open to the public.

To the east of Howmore and on the north-east side of Haarsal is Glac Hukarvat [NF 779362], a chambered burial cairn with a forecourt, three metres in height and more than fifteen metres in diameter. To the north of here are two further cairns, and on an island to the south of Loch Druidibeg is Dun Raouill [NF 778371]. This is the ruin of a dun or medieval fortification.

To the north of Howmore is Caisteal Bheagram [NF 761731], a small ruinous tower house on an islet in Loch an Eilean, a property of Clanranald.

The main road travels through the nature reserve at Loch Druidibeg.

On the slopes of Rueval Hill, the 'hill of miracles' is a statue of the Madonna and Child, which was carved in 1957 by Hew Lorimer. The statue is more than eight metres high, and the inscription reads Failte dhut a' Mhoire ('Hail Mary'). South Uist is, of course, predominantly Roman Catholic. There is a footpath to the statue; higher up on the side of the hill are buildings used by the military.

Just south of West Gerinish is Loch an Duin Mhor, and on an island are the ruins of Dun Mor [NF 776415], the walls of which survive to a height of three metres. There was a causeway out to the island.

Far more remote near the east coast is Uamh Iosal [NS 843333], the ruin of a wheel house and a souterrain. The house had cells within the walls, and the souterrain was entered from it, a covered passageway leading to a corbelled cell. There are more souterrains nearby, one known as Uamh Ghrantriach [NF 842334], which consists of two passageways and three round chambers, part of which is still roofed. To the north-west is the second highest point on South Uist at Hecla, while to the southwest is the mass of Beinn Mhor. Needless to say there are stunning views from the summits on a good day, but both hills are quite remote.

South of Eochar is another ruined dun known as Dun Uiselan [NF 778454] on an island in the lochan. The wall is more than two metres high, and there is a causeway. Further to the east are the remains of a wheelhouse [NF 756413], and there are two more [NF 758404 and NF 756413] west of Drimore.

At Eochar is the Hebridean Jewellery, which has a workshop, a shop and a cafe

(01870 610288; www.hebridean-jewellery.co.uk), and has a range of locally made jewellery and other crafts and gifts; while at Carnan is a shop and the causeway to Benbecula. At Lochcarnan is Salar Fish Farm Shop and Smokehouse (01870 610324; www.salar.co.uk), renowned for the award-winning Salar Flaky Smoked Salmon, as well as the Orasay Inn, a small hotel.

DALIBURGH TO POLLACHAR AND LUDAG (B888 AND UNLISTED ROAD)

At Kilpheder are the ruins of an aisled wheelhouse [NF 734202], a round house with cells arranged around the inside, which was finally abandoned around 200. The walls survive to more than two metres, and this was known as Bruthach a' Sithean ('brae of the fairy hill').

Our Lady of the Sorrows [NF 758165] at Garrynamonie was built in 1965 and is open every day.

At Pollachar are fine views of Eriskay and Barra on a clear day, and an impressive standing stone [NF 746145] which is two metres tall, and a hotel. The road runs on through Ludag to the causeway to Eriskay. There are regular ferries from Eriskay to Barra.

Places to Stay
HOTELS AND GUEST HOUSES

Borrodale Hotel (01878 700444;
   www.isleshotelgroup.co.uk)
   Daliburgh; hotel, bar and meals; open all year
Brae Lea House (01878 700497;
   www.braelea.co.uk)
   Lochboisdale; guest house; dinner available;
   open all year
Lochboisdale Hotel (01878 700332;
   www.lochboisdale.com)
   Lochboisdale; hotel and restaurant; open
   all year
Orasay Inn (01870 610298; www.witb.co.uk/links/
   orasayinn.htm)
   Lochcarnan; hotel; open all year except 25 Dec
Polochar Inn (01878 700215;
   www.polocharinn.co.uk)
   Pollachar; hotel, restaurant and bar; open
   all year

BED AND BREAKFAST

Anglers Retreat (01870 610325;
   www.anglersretreat.net)
   Iochdar; B&B; open Mar-Dec
Bulard Kilpheder (01878 700425)
   Kilpheder, near Lochboisdale; B&B; open
   all year
Clanranald (01878 700263; www.uistonline.com/
   clanranald.htm)
   247/8 Garryhallie; B&B; open Apr-Oct
Karingeidha (01878 700495)
   Daliburgh; B&B; open all year
Lochside Cottage (01878 700472;
   www.uistonline.com/lochside.htm)
   Lochboisdale; B&B; open all year
Joan MacDonald (01878 700517)
   Kilchoan Bay, Lochboisdale; B&B; open
   Apr-Sep

Isabel Mackenzie (01878 710371;
   www.uistaccommodation.co.uk)
   Bronish; B&B; two self-catering cottages
The Sheiling (01878 700504; www.witb.co.uk/
   links/peteranna.htm)
   238 Garryhallie; B&B; open Apr-Oct
363 Leth Meadhanach (01878 700586;
   www.macphee363.co.uk)
   South Boisdale; B&B; open all year

SELF-CATERING PROPERTIES

Kilpheder (01878 700491; www.uistonline.com/
   kilphedar.htm)
   310 Kilpheder; self-catering cottage, sleeps six
Loch Bee View (01870 620202;
   www.uistonline.com/lochbeeview.htm)
   Loch Bee; self-catering traditional croft house;
   sleeps five
Milton (01878 710371; www.croftingholidays.co.uk)
   Milton; self-catering cottage, sleeps eight
Ocean View (01878 700383/07900 082046;
   www.uistonline.com/oceanview.htm)
   Smerclate; two self-catering houses, each
   sleep six
South Boisdale (01878 700371; www.southuist-
   cottages.fsnet.co.uk)
   364 South Boisdale; two self-catering
   properties; open all year
Stoneybridge (01870 620322)
   209 Stoneybridge; self-catering, sleeps four;
   open all year

HOSTELS AND RETREATS

Howmore Youth Hostel (www.gatliff.org.uk)
   Howmore; hostel sleeping twenty; camping
   available

CAMPING AND CARAVANS

Camping is available: ask locally for permission

Howmore Youth Hostel (www.gatliff.org.uk)
Howmore; hostel sleeping twenty; camping
available
Caravan (01878 710363)
Bornish; caravan, sleeps four-six; open all year
Caravan (01870 610325)
Ardmore; caravan, sleeps four-seven; open
all year
Caravan (01878 700472)
Lochboisdale; caravan, sleeps four-six; open
all year
Ocean View Caravan (01878 700383;
www.witb.co.uk/links/caravan.htm)
Smerclate; caravan, sleeps eight

PLACES TO EAT

Borrodale Hotel (01878 700444;
www.isleshotelgroup.co.uk)
Daliburgh; hotel, bar and meals; open all year
Kildonan Museum Cafe (01878 710343)
Kildonan; open Apr-Sep, Mon-Sat 10.00-17.00,
Sun 14.00-17.00
Lochboisdale Hotel (01878 700332;
www.lochboisdale.com)
Lochboisdale; hotel
Orasay Inn (01870 610298; www.witb.co.uk/links/
orasayinn.htm)
Lochcarnan; hotel
Polochar Inn (01878 700215;
www.polocharinn.co.uk)
Pollachar; hotel

Further Information
TRANSPORT

BUSES
(see www.cne-siar.gov.uk/travel/)
Hebridean Coaches (01870 620345)
Lochboisdale; services along the main routes,
including to Ludag and Eriskay and Benbecula
TAXIS
Busters Private Hire (01870 610374)
Carnan Eochar
Aitken (01878 710333)
North Locheynort
CYCLE HIRE
Rothan Cycles (01870 620283; 07720 558064)
9 Howmore; cycle hire, sales, spares and repairs

ACTIVITIES AND SPORTS

BIRD WATCHING AND WILDLIFE
Loch Druidibeg (01870 620238; www.nnr-
scotland.org.uk/reserve.asp)
Best May-Jun for breeding wildfowl, waders
and corncrakes; walk: leaflet available from
SNH or tourist information centre

HILL WALKING AND CLIMBING
There are many excellent walks and climbs
varying in difficulty
FISHING AND ANGLING
South Uist Angling Club (01878 710336;
www.uistonline.com/suac.htm)
Fishing available on many lochs and rivers;
permits can be purchased from Campbell
Sports Shop, Benbecula; Caravan Park,
Liniclate, Benbecula; post office, Creagorry,
South Uist
South Uist Estate Fishings (01878 710 366/07833
357254)
Bornish Fish (01878 710366/07833 357254)
GOLF
Askernish Golf Course
(www.askernishgolfclub.com)
Askernish; nine-hole course; honesty box;
limited facilities but the Borrodale Hotel is
nearby; this will be a famous eighteen-hole
course by the summer of 2006

LOCAL PRODUCE

Salar Fish Farm Shop and Smokehouse (01870
610324; www.salar.co.uk)
The Pier, Loch Carnan; award-winning Salar
Flaky Smoked Salmon; available by mail order

ARTS AND CRAFTS

Ceolas Music Summer School (01878 700154;
www.ceolas.co.uk)
Festival with daytime tuition and evening
performances of dance, song, Gaelic culture,
fiddle and bagpipes. It is held in July
Hebridean Jewellery (01870 610288;
www.hebridean-jewellery.co.uk)
Eochar; range of locally made jewellery and
other crafts and gifts; cafe
Uist Craft Producers (01878 710258)
Kildonan Museum; local crafts available in the
shop; open Apr-Sep, Mon-Sat 10.00-17.00, Sun
14.00-17.00
William Neill Studio Gallery (www.william-
neill.co.uk)
Askernish; work by the artist William Neill,
featuring landscapes, wildlife; also other artists;
open Apr-Sep

VISITOR ATTRACTIONS AND MUSEUMS

Kildonan Museum (01878 710343)
Kildonan; displays on island life, cafe and shop
with craft outlet; open Apr-Sep, Mon-Sat
10.00-17.00, Sun 14.00-17.00

ADDITIONAL INFORMATION

Petrol is available at Lochboisdale, Daliburgh and
    Howmore
There is a Royal Bank of Scotland (01878 700399)
    branch in Lochboisdale

EVENTS

Uist Mod	May/June
South Uist Highland Games	July
South Uist Agricultural Show	July
Ceolas Music Summer School (01878 700154;	
www.ceolas.co.uk)	July

FURTHER READING

Folksongs and Folklore of South Uist
    (Shaw, Margaret Fay)
    Birlinn, 1999
A School in South Uist (Rea, Frederick)
    Birlinn, 1997
Stories from South Uist
    (MacLellan, Angus; translated by John Lorne
    Campbell)
    Birlinn, 1997
To the Edge of the Sea: Schooldays of a Crofter's Child
    (Hall, Christina)
    Birlinn, 1999
Uists and Barra (Thompson, Francis)
    David and Charles (Pevensey), 1999

ACKNOWLEDGMENTS

Thanks to Hebridean Jewellery (John Hart) and
    Karen MacAulay at the Lochboisdale Hotel for
    checking over the text. Image (page 259)
    courtesy Colin Palmer (www.buyimage.co.uk)

Eriskay

('goblin or water-sprite island' or 'Eric's island' from Norse; Eiriosgaigh; known in Gaelic as Eilean na h-Oige, 'island of youth')

www.ampolitician.co.uk
www.w-isles.gov.uk/eriskay/eriskay.htm
www.theuists.com
www.uistonline.com
www.visithebrides.com (Western Isles)

Tourist Information Centres
Lochboisdale (01878 700286)
    Open Apr-Oct
Castlebay (01871 810336)
    Open Apr-Oct
Stornoway (01851 703088)
    Open Jan-Dec

Map Landranger sheet: 31 (HIH map page 257)

Travel

The island is reached by causeway from Ludag on the south coast of South Uist, south of Lochboisdale (A865, then B888).

A vehicle ferry (CalMac 01878 708288/01871 810306; www.calmac.co.uk) sails from Ardmhor on the north-east side of Barra to the west side of Eriskay. There are up to five sailings a day, seven days a week, and the crossing takes forty minutes.

Description

Eriskay lies one mile off the south coast of South Uist and five miles north-east of Barra. It is three miles long and one and a half miles wide, and is hilly, the highest point being Ben Scrien at 185 metres, from where there are fantastic views. Excellent white sandy beaches can be found at Coilleag a' Phrionnsa (where Bonnie Prince Charlie landed) and on the north and east coasts.

Houses are scattered along the north and west coasts, including at Haun and Balla, and there is a post office and shop, the Am Politician pub, and a community centre which serves refreshments in the summer.

Wildlife

The island has its own breed of hardy ponies, no more than 12-13 hands high, which were used to carry peat and seaweed. Eriskay Pony (Mother Society) is based on the island and may be contacted at 01878 720224. There are many seabirds as well as seals around the coast.

History

The island was held by the MacNeils of Barra, and there was a small stronghold, Weaver's Castle [NF 787072], on an almost inaccessible rock stack on Eilean Lethan, one of the Stack Islands, to the south of the island. In 1758 Eriskay passed to the MacDonalds of Clanranald.

Bonnie Prince Charlie first landed on Eriskay on 23 July 1745 at the outset of the Jacobite Rising of 1745-46. Finding little support, he headed off for the mainland,

Eriskay

and raised his father's standard at Glenfinnan. During his time here, he is said to have dropped seeds of a pink flower, sea bindweed (a plant not native to the Hebrides) when he landed at Coilleag a' Phrionnsa. This, the Prince's Flower, then grew on the island, flowering in July – it does, however, also flower on Vatersay. In 1838 the island, along with Barra and South Uist, were sold to Gordon of Cluny, who cleared much of the population to make way for sheep.

Although the population of Eriskay had been small in the eighteenth century, by 1851 more than 400 people lived here. The land is not particularly good, and this increase in inhabitants was caused by people being evicted from more fertile areas. They were expected to survive mainly by fishing, which remains important to the economy of the island, although they now fish for scallops, prawns, crabs and lobsters. The population is now around 170, who live in the north and east of Eriskay. They are mostly Roman Catholic, and the church, dedicated to St Michael and built in a prominent position, dates from 1903. It was built by Father Allan MacDonald, who is renowned for making a collection of Gaelic songs and folklore. The church bell came from a German warship scuttled in Scapa Flow in 1919, and Father MacDonald is buried in the old cemetery.

In February 1941 during the Second World War the *SS Politician* ran aground near Calvay to the south of Eriskay, laden with a cargo of 20,000 cases of whisky bound for the Americas. The islanders salvaged much of the cargo for their own consumption, to the chagrin of Customs and Excise, and some of the islanders were sent to prison. Compton Mackenzie used this as the plot of his novel *Whisky Galore*, which was turned into an Ealing comedy in 1948 (although it was filmed on Barra and has an exclamation mark *Whisky Galore!*). The pub on the island is called Am Politician.

PLACES TO STAY

Aird na Haun (0141 339 2143;
www.visiteriskay.com)
1a Haun; self-catering
Cuan Siar, Baile (0141 586 8096/07776 144161;
www.cuansiar.com)
Self-catering
The Flat (01878 720274/01540 673060)
2 village; self-catering property, sleeps four;
open all year

PLACES TO EAT

Am Politician (01878 720246;
www.ampolitician.co.uk)
Public House (named after the SS Politician
which ran aground near here). Meals available;
functions, wedding receptions; the pub is open
from 11.00 from Jun-Sep (open all year) serving
food all day: pre-booking essential out of
season
Cafe, Community Centre
Refreshments and snacks

Further Information

TRANSPORT

BUS

(see www.cne-siar.gov.uk/travel/)
A community bus service links the island to South
Uist and Benbecula

ARTS AND CRAFTS

Eriskay jerseys are made on the island by the local
cooperative, produced in either traditional
navy blue, as well as now also in cream. They
are very warm, and have intricate patterns with
traditional motifs covering the jumper. Each
knitter has an individual pattern, and it takes
two weeks to complete each jumper. This
appears to be a dying art, done primarily by
older women, and exclusively on Eriskay. They
are available from the local shop

ADDITIONAL INFORMATION

There is a well-stocked shop and post office
(01878 720236), which also sells Eriskay
jumpers; and a community centre and cafe,
which holds regular events such as ceilidhs and
dances
There is a waymarked route around the island.
Polly by Roger Hutchinson (Mainstream, 1990)
tells the true story of the *SS Politician* and
Whisky Galore

FURTHER READING

Eriskay Where I Was Born
(MacInnes, Angus Edward)
Mercat Press, 1997
Polly (Hutchinson, Roger)
Mainstream, 1990
Whisky Galore (Mackenzie, Compton)
Vintage, 1947 (repr 1994)

ACKNOWLEDGMENTS

Thanks to Margaret at Am Politician for checking
the text. Image courtesy Colin Palmer
(www.buyimage.co.uk)

Barra, Vatersay, Mingulay and Neighbouring Islands

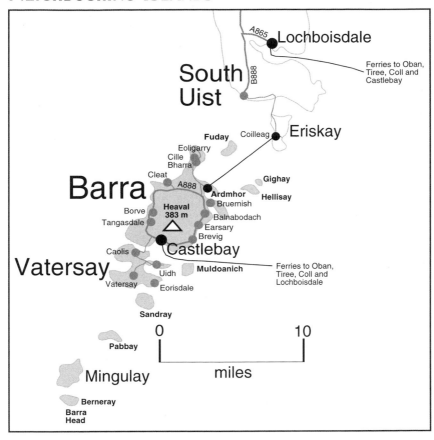

Lochboisdale

A865

South Uist

B888

Ferries to Oban, Tiree, Coll and Castlebay

Fuday   Coilleag   Eriskay

Eoligarry
Cille Bharra
Cleat

Barra

A888

Borve
Tangasdale

Caolis

Gighay

Ardmhor   Hellisay
Bruernish
Balnabodach
Earsary
Brevig

**Heaval
383 m**

Castlebay

Vatersay

Uidh   **Muldoanich**
Vatersay   Eorisdale

Ferries to Oban, Tiree, Coll and Lochboisdale

Sandray

0   10

Pabbay

Mingulay   miles

Berneray
Barra
Head

Traigh Mor, Barra

BARRA

(possibly 'island of Barr', from St Barr or Finnbarr, although this is disputed, and may be from barr for 'top' from Gaelic; Barraigh)

www.isleofbarra.com
www.visitthebrides.com (Western Isles)

Tourist Information Centres
Castlebay (01871 810336)
   Open Apr-Oct
Stornoway (01851 703088)
   Open Jan-Dec

Map Landranger sheet: 31 (HIH map page 269)

TRAVEL

CalMac runs vehicle ferries from Oban on the mainland, some via Coll or Tiree, and from Lochboisdale on South Uist (CalMac 01631 566688 (Oban), 01871 810306 (Castlebay), 01878 700288 (Lochboisdale); www.calmac.co.uk). The ferry sails to Castlebay on Barra, taking five hours from Oban. The ferry leaves Oban every day (times vary) in the summer, leaves Lochboisdale on Mondays and Wednesdays and stops at Tiree and Coll on Thursdays. There is a reduced service in winter.

CalMac (01851701702; www.calmac.co.uk) also runs a vehicle service from Eriskay (which is connected by a causeway to South Uist) to Ardmhor on Barra, which is to the north of the island. This runs up to five times daily. Ardmhor is some seven miles from Castlebay, and there is a cafe, which is open all year.

There is also an airstrip (01871 890212; www.hial.co.uk/barra-airport.html) at Traigh Mor, with flights (except Sunday) from Glasgow Airport (British Airways 0345 222111; www.britishairways.com). The airstrip is seven miles from Castlebay with a cafe which is open all year. There are also regular flights from Stornoway and Benbecula.

A causeway joins Barra to Vatersay.

Boat trips from Barra can be made to Mingulay and some of the southerly islands, also known as the Bishop's Isles.

DESCRIPTION

The island lies six miles south-west of the tip of South Uist, and is about eight miles long and some five wide, covering twenty square miles. Barra is hilly, particularly the middle where there is Heaval at 383 metres, and the southwest, where there is Ben Tangaval at 332 metres. There are fantastic views from both. Along with impressive cliffs, there are many good stretches of sand along the west and north coasts, and there are fine beaches at Halaman Bay, Allasdale, Traigh Eais, Traigh Scurrival, and Traigh Mhor, which is also used as an airstrip. Fertile land can also be found, especially along the coasts, and the island once supported a population of more than 2,600. Although there has been depopulation, there has been much less than elsewhere, and currently around 1,100 people live on Barra. Most of the inhabitants speak Gaelic; and many people believe that this is one of the friendliest and most laid-back of islands

The main village is Castlebay (Bagh a' Chaisteil), which has hotels, a cafe, shops, a post office, a heritage centre, petrol and a tourist information centre as well as other amenities. Numerous smaller settlements can be found around the coast, and there is a post office at Northbay (Bagh a' Tuath).

The island is circumnavigated by a single-track road (A888), and unlisted roads connect to Vatersay, to the airstrip near Eoligarry (Eolaigearraidh), and to the ferry to Eriskay at Ardmhor.

There are several small and uninhabited islands between Barra and South Uist, including Fiaray, Lingay, Fuday and Orosay; Gighay, Hellisay, Flodday and Fuaiy.

WILDLIFE

Seals and otters can be seen around the coasts, and some 150 species of birds have been recorded on Barra, including sea eagles, golden eagles, puffins, guillemots, kittiwakes, oystercatchers and plovers.

HISTORY

Several impressive or interesting prehistoric monuments survive on Barra, including the chambered cairn of Dun Bharpa and the duns of Dun Scurrival and Dun Cuier.

In the seventh century, St Barr or Finnbarr of Cork (or one of his followers) is reputed to have come to Barra. He is said to have converted the locals to Christianity, persuading them to give up their heathen ways, which apparently included cannibalism, the story going that they had eaten the previous missionary. There are three old chapels near Eoligarry, known as Cille Bharra. St Barr died in 623, although there is apparently no direct evidence that he ever came here, and the island has more associations with St Brendan.

Barra was raided by Vikings, and seized by the Norseman Onund Wooden Leg in 871. Later it was one of the extensive possessions of the Lords of the Isles, although the MacNeils of Barra were confirmed as lords in 1427. Their association with the island is reputed to have started long before this, and Kissimul Castle, their stronghold, is said to have been first built in the eleventh century. Although many sites in the Hebrides were occupied from early times, nothing of the present structure is likely to be as old as this. The MacNeils were accused of piracy against the ships of Elizabeth of England, and fought for the Jacobites at Killiecrankie in 1689, then in the 1715 Rising. They did not come out for Bonnie Prince Charlie in

Beach, Barra

the 1745-6 Rising, so they did not share the fate of many Jacobites and retained their lands until 1838. By then the MacNeil chief had got into serious debt, and he sold Barra and emigrated.

The island was purchased by Gordon of Cluny, who also owned South Uist, Benbecula and Eriskay and who offered Barra to the government to be used as a penal colony. He then brutally cleared many of the islanders.

Barra became a centre of the herring industry, and at one time vessels stretched right across Castlebay, some 400 boats working from here in 1886. Despite the clearing of people in the 1850s, then the failure of the fishing industry, the island still has a sizeable population compared to many of the other Hebrides. Much of the island was bought back in 1937 by the forty-fifth chief of the MacNeils.

Although many of the Outer Isles (with the exception of South Uist, Eriskay and parts of Benbecula) are mostly Protestant (and many devoutly Presbyterian), Barra's inhabitants are mostly Roman Catholic. Consequently, restrictions on what should be done on a Sunday are not relevant here.

Whisky Galore!, the Ealing comedy film based on Compton Mackenzie's book, was filmed on Barra, although the sinking of the *SS Politician* actually took place off nearby Eriskay. Compton Mackenzie lived for some time on Barra and was buried in Cille Bharra at Eoligarry.

Tours

EAST COAST: CASTLEBAY TO EOLIGARRY (A888 AND UNLISTED ROAD)

The ferry lands at Castlebay, passing the picturesque Kissimul Castle, which guards the approaches on a small island in Castle Bay, just to the south of the village. Castlebay itself has most of the island's amenities, including a post office, shops including the community shop (01871 810354), Co-op and Spar, hotels, a gallery and cafe, a heritage centre (also with a cafe), a library with internet access, the castle, petrol, and a swimming pool.

Kissimul Castle (01871 810313; open Apr-Sep, daily 9.00-18.00) was a stronghold of the MacNeils of Barra, and may date from as early as the eleventh century when

Kissimul Castle

Neil of the Castle built a fortress here, although the present building is believed to be considerably later. One of its most famous occupants was Marion of the Heads, second wife of MacNeil of Barra, who ensured her own son's succession by beheading her stepsons. The island was sold by the MacNeils in 1838, although the castle was already ruinous by 1795 after suffering a fire – the chiefs moved to Eoligarry House [NF 704076]. The castle was bought back and then restored, and is now in the care of Historic Scotland. Eoligarry House, which was an Adam-style mansion, was itself demolished in 1979.

Barra Heritage and Cultural Centre (01871 810413; centre open summer; tel. to confirm) has rotating displays on topics such as the prehistory and history of Barra and other isles, plus a large collection of old photographs. The centre has a cafe and shop.

Our Lady of the Sea is an attractive Roman Catholic church with a bell tower and chiming clock, which was finished in 1886, and is open all year.

The road leaves Castlebay and runs towards the east coast. Heaval, the highest hill on Barra, stands to the north-east of Castlebay. There are fine views from the top; and half-way up the mountain is a statue of Our Lady of the Sea [NL 679992], a Madonna and Child made from white marble. At Brevig, north of the A888, is an impressive standing stone [NL 689990], which stands on a ridge and is three metres high. A second standing stone nearby has fallen and is broken. Also here is the Kisimul Gallery (01871 810580) with a gift shop, music, crafts and cards, as well as a cafe.

There is a post office at Northbay, and the church [NF 707031], dedicated to St Barr and built in 1912, is open to the public. There is a statue of St Barr on the shore.

About six miles north of Castlebay is the turn-off for Ardmhor (where the ferry lands from South Uist and Eriskay), the airstrip and the north of the island. At Ardmhor is a cafe, which is open all year, and a twin otter sculpture, which was unveiled in 2006.

This unlisted road skirts the side of Traigh Mhor, a beautiful area of sand and dunes, which is used as the island's airport where there is a cafe.

Cille Bharra

273

At Eoligarry is Cille Bharra [NF 704077], an old ruinous church, dating from the twelfth century, and two chapels, one of which has been restored to house several impressive carved graveslabs with carvings of animals and foliage. There was a fourth chapel but this has gone. A tenth- or eleventh-century carved stone decorated with a cross and a runic inscription was located here. The original is now in the Museum of Scotland, while a cast of the stone was returned to the island. The inscription may read 'after Thorgerth, Steiner's daughter, the cross was raised'. This is an old site, and there was probably a cashel or monastery here in the sixth or seventh century. Many of the MacNeils of Barra are buried here, as is Compton Mackenzie, author of *Whisky Galore*, who lived on Barra. The parish church [NF 703076], a petite building, stands nearby. The MacNeils moved to Eoligarry in the eighteenth century, although Eoligarry House was demolished in 1979.

Nearby is Dun Scurrival [NF 695081], the remains of an old fort on a promontory above the sea. There are fine views from here.

The A888 runs across the north of the island, and then down the west coast and back to Castlebay.

WEST COAST: CASTLEBAY TO GREAN

Leaving Castlebay to the west there is a turn-off for the south of the island and the causeway to Vatersay. The main road crosses the island to the west coast, passing the hill Ben Tangaval and Loch Tangusdale. On an island in the loch is the ruinous Castle Sinclair [NL 648997], which is also known as Dun Mhic Leod or MacLeod's Tower. This is an old castle of the MacNeils, dating from the fifteenth century, which was reached via a submerged causeway.

To the north, at Borve, are two small standing stones [NF 653014], one of which has fallen. A Viking burial, probably that of a woman, was found here.

Not far away to the north is Dun Bharpa [NF 671019], a prehistoric chambered cairn, consisting of a huge mound of stones, five metres high and more than thirty metres in diameter. Tigh Talamhanta [NF 677023] is the overgrown remains of a wheel house and souterrain, and the name means 'house under the ground'.

On a crag above the road at Allasdale is Dun Cuier [NF 664034], a well-preserved dun or broch, which was occupied until the seventh or eighth century. There are good views from the site. Nearby at Grean is the island's golf course.

The A888 continues around the north of the island until it reaches the turn-off for Ardmhor and Eoligarry. It continues down the east coast back to Castlebay.

HOTELS AND GUEST HOUSES

Castlebay Hotel (01871 810223; www.castlebay-hotel.co.uk)
  Castlebay; hotel, bar and meals; closed Xmas and New Year
Craidard Hotel (01871 810200; www.isleofbarra.com)
  Castlebay; hotel and meals; open all year
Heathbank Hotel (01871 890266; www.barrahotel.co.uk)
  Bayherivagh, north of island; hotel and meals; open Easter-beg. Oct
Isle of Barra Hotel (01871 81038; www.isleofbarra.com)
  Tangasdale Beach, two miles west of Castlebay; hotel, restaurant and bar; open end Mar-beg. Oct

Tigh-na-Mara (01871 810304; www.isleofbarra.com)
  Castlebay; guest house; open all year

BED AND BREAKFAST

Aros Cottage (01871 890355)
  Balnabodach; B&B; open May-Sep
Barradale (01871 810601)
  Castlebay; B&B; open May-Sep
Faire Mhaoldonaich (www.fairemhaoldonaich.com)
  Nask, Castlebay; B&B; open Apr-Oct
Grianamul (01871 810416; members.aol.com/macneilronnie)
  Castlebay; B&B; open Mar-Oct

Northbay House (01871 890 255;
    www.barraholidays.co.uk)
    Balnabodach; B&B and self-catering
    accommodation
Ocean View (01871 810590;
    www.beatonbarra.co.uk)
    Borve; B&B; open Apr-Oct

SELF-CATERING PROPERTIES

Arnamul (01871 810376; www.isleofbarra.com/
    ARNAMUL.htm)
    Castlebay; self-catering cottage, sleeps four
Bogach (01871 890286)
    Northbay; self-catering, sleeps four; open
    all year
Brevig (01871 810580/645)
    Castlebay; self-catering, sleeps two; open
    May-Sep
Ceum a Bhealaich (01871 810 644;
    www.ceumabhealaich.co.uk)
    Castlebay; self-catering flat, sleeps two; open
    all year
Croft Cottage (01871 810590;
    www.beatonbarra.co.uk)
    Borve; sleeps seven; open Apr-Oct
Harbour Cottage (01871 810579;
    www.hebrideancottageholidays.co.uk)
    Earsary; self-catering cottage, sleeps six
Hebridean Highland Cottages (01871 810579;
    www.hebrideancottageholidays.co.uk)
    Three miles east of Castlebay; two cottages
Northbay House (01871 890255;
    www.isleofbarra.com/northbay-house.html)
    Balnabodach; self-catering, sleeps four; open
    Apr-Oct
Reaver's View (01851 706509; http://
    members.aol.com/user375951)
    Eoligarry; self-catering, sleeps six
Sandray (01871 810319; members.aol.com/
    macneilronnie/)
    Sandray; self-catering, open Apr-Oct
Sea Breezes (01871 890384; www.isleofbarra.com/
    seabreezes.html)
    Bruernish; two self-catering apartments,
    sleeping six and four

HOSTELS AND RETREATS

Dunard (Isle of Barra Hostel) (01871 810443;
    www.dunardhostel.co.uk)
    Castlebay; family-run hostel; sixteen beds;
    open all year

CAMPING AND CARAVANS

Barra Caravans (01871 810293;
    www.barracaravans.co.uk)
    Glen, near Castlebay; sleeps two-seven; open
    all year
Castle View Caravan (01871 810622)
    Glen (Castlebay); caravan, sleeps four
Caravan (01871 810363)
    Brevig; caravan, sleeps four; open Apr-Sep

There is no official camping site, but ask locally

PLACES TO EAT

Ardmhor
    Ferry terminal; cafe; open all year
Castlebay Hotel (01871 810223; www.castlebay-
    hotel.co.uk)
    Castlebay; closed Xmas and New Year
Craigard Hotel (01871 810200;
    www.isleofbarra.com)
    Castlebay; open all year
Heathbank Hotel (01871 890266)
    Bayherivagh
Heritage Cafe (at heritage centre) (01871 810354)
    Castlebay; open Apr-Sep
Isle of Barra Hotel (01871 810383;
    www.isleofbarra.com)
    Tangasdale Beach, two miles west of Castlebay;
    open end Mar-beg. Oct
Kisimul Cafe/Gallery
    Castlebay
Traigh Tearoom (Airport Cafe) (01871 810354)
    Open 9.30-16.30 peak season but varies with
    time of year

Further Information

TRANSPORT

BUSES
(see www.cne-siar.gov.uk/travel/)
Timetables from TIC and local outlets
Council/bus services (01851 703773)
Bus services (01851 701702)
Postbus (08457 740740; www.royalmail.com/
    postbus)

CYCLE HIRE
Barra Cycle Hire (01871 810284)
    Castlebay; available May-Sep, booking ahead
    recommended

TAXIS
01871 810001
01871 810216
01871 810590

CAR HIRE
Barra Car Hire (01871 890313)
    ، Castlebay; available all year
Macmilan Self Drive (01871 890366)
    Eoligarry
Bus and Minibus Hire
Hector MacNeil (01871 810262)

ACTIVITIES AND SPORTS

GOLF
Barra Golf Course (01871 810 240;
    www.isleofbarra.com)
    Grean Head; nine-hole course on west coast of
    island; day tickets from hotels, Community
    Shop in Castlebay (01871 810354) and the
    Tourist Information Centre

FISHING AND ANGLING
Fishing is available on all of the inland lochs:
    permits from the Community Shop in
    Castlebay (01871 810354)
Barra Angling Club (01871 810562)
    Castlebay; fishing permits and boat hire

Barra Fishing Charters (01871 890384;
www.barrafishingcharters.com)
Sea fishing

BOAT TRIPS

Barra Boat Trips (01878 720238/01878 720265)
Trips to Mingulay and some of the other
uninhabited islands

Barra Fishing Charters (01871 890384;
www.barrafishingcharters.com)
Trips to Mingulay and some of the other
uninhabited islands

SEA KAYAKING TRIPS

Dunard 'Isle of Barra Hostel' (01871 810443;
www.clearwaterpaddling.com)
Dunard

LOCAL PRODUCE

Hebridean Toffee (01871 810898;
www.hebrideantoffeecompany.com)
Castlebay; products can be bought on-line

ARTS AND CRAFTS

The Craft Shop Gallery
Skallary, three miles from Castlebay; pictures
of Barra and Vatersay and local crafts; open
Mon-Fri, Sat AM

Kisimul Gallery (01871 810580)
Brevig, Castlebay; gift shop, music, crafts and
cards; cafe

VISITOR ATTRACTIONS AND MUSEUMS

Kissimul Castle (01871 810313)
Castlebay; restored stronghold of the MacNeils
on an island; ferry to castle; open Apr-Sep,
daily 9.00-18.00

Barra Heritage and Cultural Centre (01871 810413)
Castlebay; museum, cultural centre, shop and
cafe; open summer: tel. to confirm

ADDITIONAL INFORMATION

There are post offices at Castlebay and Northbay

Public telephones can be found at Eoligarry, near
Ardmhor, Cleat, Bruernish, Tangasdale,
Balnabodach, Skallary and Castlebay

There is a branch of the Royal Bank of Scotland
in Castlebay

Petrol is only available in Castlebay

EVENTS

Feis Bharraigh (Barra Festival; 01871 810888)
end July

Barra Half Marathon (01871 810262)   early July

Highland Games   late July

FURTHER READING

Barra: Archaeological Research on Ben Tangaval
(Branigan, Keith and Patrick Foster)
Sheffield Academic Press, 2000

The Book of Barra
(Mackenzie, Compton, John Lorne Campbell and
Carl Borgstrom)
Acair, 1998

Cille Bharra (Macquarie, Alan)
Grant Books, 1989

From Barra to Berneray
(Branigan, Keith and Patrick Foster)
Sheffield Academic Press, 2000

Tales from Barra (The Coddy)
Birlinn, 2003

Times Subject to Tides (Calderwood, Roy)
Kea Publishing, 1999

Uists and Barra (Thompson, Francis)
David and Charles (Pevensey), 1999

ACKNOWLEDGMENTS

Thanks to Peter Brown at VABV for reading over
the entry. Images (pages 271, 272 and 273)
courtesy Colin Palmer (www.buyimage.co.uk)

VATERSAY

('glove island' or 'fathers' island' from Norse; Bhatarsaigh)

www.isleofbarra.com/vatersay.htm
www.visithebrides.com (Western Isles)

Tourist Information Centres
  Castlebay (01871 810336)
Open Apr-Oct
  Stornoway (01851 703088)
Open Jan-Dec

Map Landranger sheet: 31 (HIH map page 269)

TRAVEL

Vatersay is connected to Barra by a causeway, the turn-off for the island is on the west side of Castlebay and is along a narrow but passable single-track road.

DESCRIPTION

Vatersay is located just off the south coast of Barra, and is about three miles long and about two and a half miles wide at most. It is nearly cut in two at Vatersay Bay and Bagh Siar, the inlets cutting into the island. There are large expanses of sand here. Vatersay rises to 190 metres at Heishival Mor (from which there are fine views) and 169 metres at its twin summit, Heishival Beag.

Vatersay is now the most southerly inhabited island in the Outer Hebrides. The population is about 120 people, most of whom live at the village of Vatersay (Am Baile) to the south of the island, where there is a post office and a community centre, which has refreshments during the summer. At Uidh is the small church [NL 646961], which is open to the public. There is a fine walk around the south of Vatersay of about four miles, taking in many sites of interest.

Vatersay

277

WILDLIFE

Corncrakes can be found, and other birds that visit here include golden eagles, gulls, terns, guillemots and oystercatchers. Otters and seals have been seen around the coasts, including at Cornaig Bay.

HISTORY

The island was occupied from prehistoric times, and there are the remains of an interesting broch, Dun a' Chaolais [NL 628971] near Caolis. Also near here is the ruin of Vatersay House, which dates from the 1800s. At Vatersay are the scant remains of a dun [NL 627947] known as Dun Vatersay, and nearby is an arrangement of standing stones [NL 633942].

The island was held by the MacNeils of Barra. One of the most infamous characters was Marion of the Heads, wife of the twenty-ninth chief and who lived in the fifteenth century. She had her stepsons beheaded, traditionally at a spot on the shore of Cornaig Bay, so that her own son could inherit. Ghostly screams are said to be heard coming from here on New Year's Day. The story goes that she would also have islanders who were no longer able to work drowned at a spot on the coast and then buried at Uinessan, where there is a cemetery and the slight ruin of an old chapel [NL 664957]. The chapel was known as Cille Bhrianan or Caibeal Moire nan Ceann ('chapel of Mary of the Heads'). Marion is said to be buried here.

At the turn of the twentieth century Vatersay had been sold to Gordon of Cluny, and the island was owned as one farm. People desperately needed land, and the Vatersay Raiders, from Barra and Mingulay, set up crofts, using an ancient law which asserted that if they could built a dwelling and have a fire burning in the hearth in the same day they could claim the land on which it was built. This was not accepted by the authorities, and some of them were imprisoned. There was an outcry, and the island was eventually purchased by the government and divided into fifty-eight crofts. The village of Eorisdale (Eorasdail) [NL 645940], established by fishermen from Mingulay, was only abandoned in the 1970s, and can be reached by foot. The causeway linking the island to Barra was opened in 1991.

The *Annie Jane*, a ship which was carrying emigrants from Liverpool to the Americas, was shipwrecked off Bagh Siar (West Bay) in 1853. More than three hundred men, women and children were drowned and many were buried on Vatersay; only about a quarter of those aboard survived. There is a monument to the victims at Bagh Siar [NL 630953]. On the north side of Vatersay Bay are the scattered remains of a wartime Catalina flying boat, which crashed here with the loss of three lives.

SANDRAY

Sandray ('sand island'; Sanndarigh) lies one mile to the south of Vatersay, across the Sound of Sandray. Roughly round in shape, the island has a diameter of one and a half miles. The highest hill is Cairn Galtar at 207 metres, and much of the island is covered by shifting sand dunes, hence the name. One of the small islands to the west has a natural arch.

The ruins of a dun [NL 651919] with its defensive outworks survive on the southern slopes of Cairn Galtar, and a chapel [NL 651919] was dedicated to St Bride. The population was only ten in 1881, and Sandray was abandoned from 1911.

PABBAY

Pabbay ('priest's isle'; Pabaigh) is two miles south-west of Sandray, and lies equidistant between that island and Mingulay. It is some three miles long and two wide, rising to 171 metres at the Hoe. There is a small sandy beach on the east coast and impressive cliffs.

The remains of a dun, Dunan Ruadh [NL 613876], much of which has been lost to coastal erosion, survive to the east of the island. In the burial ground [NL 607875] are the remains of a small rectangular chapel and three cross-slabs, two of which are upright: this is thought to have been an early Christian site. There is a rare carved stone with Pictish symbols – a crescent and a v-rod and a flower – as well as a later cross, evidence that the Picts had a presence here.

The population was twenty-six in 1881, but Pabbay too was abandoned early in the twentieth century after many of the menfolk were drowned when their boat was lost in a storm in 1897.

PLACES TO STAY

Vatersay School (01871 810283;
  www.vatersayschool.co.uk)
  Five miles from Castlebay; self-catering
  accommodation in converted school, sleeps six;
  open Easter-Oct
Cottage (02083 486770)
  Vatersay; self-catering cottage, sleep five; open
  all year
Cottage (01871 810467)
  Vatersay; self-catering cottage

Camping is available on the island: ask locally
(honesty box at the community hall)

PLACES TO EAT

The Community Centre is open for teas and
  coffee in the summer

FURTHER INFORMATION

Post Office at Vatersay village
A bus service runs from Vatersay to Castlebay: ask
  locally for a timetable; also see www.cne-
  siar.gov.uk/travel/
Vatersay Walk of four miles, which takes in many
  of the points of interest on the island: details
  from the TIC in Castlebay. It starts from a
  small car park at the village on the south of the
  island
Castlebay on Barra has a wide range of facilities,
  including hotels, shops, a cafe, petrol, etc – see
  section on Barra for more details

ACKNOWLEDGMENTS

Thanks to Judy Rapoport and to Peter Brown at
  VABV for reading over the text. Image
  courtesy Colin Palmer (www.buyimage.co.uk)

MINGULAY

('big island' from Norse; Miughlaigh)

www.nts.org.uk
www.visitthebrides.com (Western Isles)

Tourist Information Centres
Castlebay (01871 810336)
  Open Apr-Oct
Stornoway (01851 703088)
  Open Jan-Dec

Map Landranger sheet: 31 (HIH map page 269)

TRAVEL

Boat trips to Mingulay and some of the other uninhabited neighbouring islands can be made from Barra, including with Barra Boat Trips (01878 720238/01878 720265) and Barra Fishing Charters (01871 890 384; www.barra fishingcharters.com). Trips can also be arranged through John Allan MacNeil (01871 810449) and George McLeod (01871 810223).

Westernedge Charters Ltd (01506 824227/07811 387633; www.westernedge.co.uk) also make trips to Mingulay and are based on Berneray.

DESCRIPTION

The island lies some ten miles south of Barra, and two miles south-west of the nearby island of Sanday. It is three miles long and some two wide, and is extremely hilly, rising to 273 metres at Carnan, 219 metres at Hecla and 224 metres at Macphee's Hill. Around the coast are dramatic cliffs (150 metres high), an impressive natural arch and a fine sandy beach with dunes at Mingulay Bay.

Mingulay

WILDLIFE

The island is home to many breeding colonies of seabirds, including kittiwakes, razorbills, puffins, gulls and guillemots. Mingulay was made a Site of Special Scientific Interest in 1993 and is a European bird protection area.

HISTORY

Mingulay was occupied from prehistoric times, and there are the remains of a fort, Dun Mingulay [NL 548823], on a promontory. The island was a property of the MacNeils of Barra, although it and those to the south were formerly known as the Bishop's Isles. The islanders exploited the many seabirds.

It was occupied until 1911, indeed there were some 150 inhabitants in 1881. But life here was tough and many of the inhabitants then went to Vatersay and Barra. Mingulay was abandoned, except for a flock of sheep, and it has been in the care of the National Trust for Scotland since 2000 (01463 232034; www.nts.org.uk).

BERNERAY

Berneray ('Bjorn's island' from Norse and sometime also known as Barra Head; Bearnaraigh) is just to the south of Mingulay, across the Sound of Berneray, and is some one and a half miles long and about one wide. It rises to more than 190 metres, and there are impressive cliffs.

The island is visited by many seabirds and there are breeding colonies of kittiwakes, auks, guillemots and puffins. The islanders survived by exploiting the birds, which involved great feats of daring and bravery to harvest eggs and young birds from the cliffs. The island once had a population of more than fifty, but this dwindled and the last people left when the lighthouse was automated in the 1970s. There are also grey seals.

The island was inhabited from the Bronze Age or earlier, and there are ruins of two forts. Dun Briste [NL 548806], at the north-western tip, has an impressive wall. Sron an Duin Dun [NL 548802] is on the south-western tip by the white stone Barra Head lighthouse, part of it being demolished when the lighthouse was built. The wall survives to a height of three metres, and the entrance passage has three lintels still in place.

The island has been owned by the National Trust for Scotland since 2000 (01463 232034; www.nts.org.uk).

FURTHER READING

Mingulay: An Island and its People (Buxton, Ben)
Birlinn, 1995

ACKNOWLEDGMENTS

Thanks to Isla Robertson and the National Trust for Scotland for the permission to use the photo

St Kilda or Hirta

('western isle' or 'shield shaped' from Norse; also known as Hirta or Hiort from 'deer' or possibly 'dangerous' in Norse; there is no St Kilda)

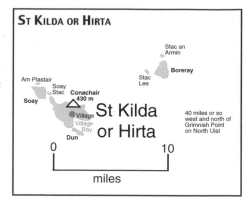

www.kilda.org.uk
www.visithebrides.com
(Western Isles)

Tourist Information Centre
Stornoway (01851 703088)
  Open Jan-Dec

Map Landranger sheet: 18

Travel

There is no regular service available, but the following operators have trips or cruises to St Kilda (consult websites first if possible and also see www.kilda.org.uk for full regulations for a visit)

Operators include:

National Trust for Scotland (0131 243 9334; www.nts.org.uk)
  Cruises to St Kilda
Adventure Hebrides (01851 820726; www.canoehebrides.com)
  Sea-kayaking trips to St Kilda and other isles
Ardnamurchan Charters (01972 500208/07799 608199; www.west-scotland-tourism.com/ardnamurchan-charters)
  Acharacle, Ardnamurchan; excursions to St Kilda
Guideliner Hebridean Wildlife Cruises (01631 720610/07808 899356; www.guideliner.co.uk)
  Dunstaffnage Marina, Argyll mainland; cruises to St Kilda; open May-Sep
Hebridean Island Cruises (01756 704704)
  Cruises to St Kilda
Island Cruising (01851 672381; www.island-cruising.com)
  Uig, Lewis; cruises to the Western Isles
Kilda Cruises (01859 502241; www.kildacruises.co.uk)
  Fasgadh, Tarbert
Northern Light Charters (01680 814260; www.northernlight-uk.com)
  Lochbuie, Mull; cruises to St Kilda
Sea Trek (01851 672464; www.seatrek.co.uk)
  Trips to St Kilda
Westernedge Charters Ltd (01506 824227/07811 387633; www.westernedge.co.uk)
  Berneray; trips to many islands including St Kilda
Wilderness Scotland (0131 625 6635; www.wildernessscotland.com)
  Trips to remote parts of Scotland including St Kilda

Description

St Kilda is the most remote 'inhabited' part of Scotland, and lies forty-one miles west northwest of Grimnish Point on North Uist. The group consists of three islands and a number of stacks, the result of volcanic eruptions some sixty million years ago. St Kilda or Hirta is the largest island and is three miles long and about the same wide at its most. It is extremely hilly, and the highest points are Conachair at 430 metres and Mullach Mor at 361 metres; views from the summits are stunning on a clear day. There are spectacular towering sea cliffs, which drop more than 400 metres from nearly the highest part of the island at Conachair down to the water. The small island of Dun is just offshore to the southeast.

Soay ('sheep island' from Norse; Soaigh), a small island about half a mile across, lies just to the west of St Kilda, along with Soay Stac, Stac Dona and Am Plastair.

Four miles to the north-east is the dramatic island of Boreray (Boraraigh), which is a mile long, near which are the impressive rock stacks Stac an Armin at 196 metres and Stac Lee at 172 metres.

WILDLIFE

A vast number of seabirds breed on the islands and their stacs. There is the largest gannetry in the world with 60,000 pairs on Boreray and the stacs, and large populations of fulmars (62,000 pairs puffins (140,000 pairs), guillemots (20,000 pairs), kittiwakes (10,000 pairs), gannets (60,000 pairs) as well as razorbills, manx shearwaters, storm petrels, Leach's petrels and great skuas. The St Kildan Wren is a subspecies unique to the islands and is larger than its mainland relatives and paler in colour. Dolphins, minke whales and killer whales may be seen in the waters around the group; and seals by the shores.

An early breed of sheep which has its origins in the Bronze Age are known as Soay Sheep (it has four horns) and originated on the St Kildan isle of Soay. There is also the St Kildan fieldmouse, a larger wood mouse; although the St Kildan house mouse died out when the islanders left in the 1930s.

HISTORY

St Kilda or Hirta was home to a community for many years, and stone tools found here indicate that Bronze Age people at least visited. An impressive souterrain and

Street, St Kilda

Boreraig

the scant remains of a wheelhouse were known as Taigh an t-Sithiche [NF 100994] ('house of the fairies') – evidence that the Picts probably had a presence here.

Viking burials have been found on St Kilda, and place names such as Oiseval and Ruaival are Norse in origin. The islands were part of the territories of the Lords of the Isles in the medieval period, before coming to the MacLeods of Dunvegan from 1498 until 1930. Evidence for three chapels exists, dedicated to St Brendan, St Columba and Christ. Little now survives except the enclosure of a burial ground and some remains of the chapel dedicated to St Brendan [NF 098984]; nearby was a well, the water of which was believed to help secure a favourable wind back to Harris. There is also the 'Amazon's House', a beehive cell.

In 1726 most of the population died of smallpox, except for some of the men who were out collecting birds, and the island had to be repopulated with people from Harris. Rachel, Lady Grange (also see Trumpan on Skye) was imprisoned on St Kilda after learning of her husband's Jacobite sympathies. She was held in various places around the Hebrides and was eventually taken to Skye, where she died in 1742 and is thought to be buried in the cemetery at Trumpan.

The islanders always had very difficult lives and survived by exploiting the thousands of seabirds: for food, feathers and oil for lamps. Puffins were used as snacks and each islander is estimated to have eaten 115 fulmars a year. Collecting the birds and eggs was extremely hazardous, involving climbing the dizzying and dangerous cliffs. Soay sheep and a few cattle were kept, there being decent grazing in Gleann Mor. There were more than 1,400 cleits, stone-built huts used for storing dried seabirds, eggs, fish, hay and turf, and for protecting lambs from the weather. St Kilda had a very democratic system of government, which consisted of an island council made up of all the menfolk. The island had a population of 78 in 1861, although it was put at 180 in 1697, but infant mortality was very high (as many as four-fifths of babies are believed to have died), possibly because of toxins from the diet of seabirds or from tetanus.

The present row of houses above village bay was built in the 1830s, although in the 1880s many of the islanders left for a better life in Australia. The last inhabitants left in the 1930s, partly because of storms that had cut off the community for weeks, partly because life was so hard.

The group of islands were given to the National Trust of Scotland in 1957 and they were made Scotland's first world heritage site in 1987; in 2004 this was extended to include the marine environment. There is a Ministry of Defence establishment on St Kilda. Although it is possible to visit the islands as part of a work party, an organised cruise or by private charter or yacht, the National Trust for Scotland should be advised in advance and their rules followed.

PLACES TO STAY

Further information can be obtained from www.kilda.org.uk or Scottish Natural Heritage, 135 Stilligarry, South Uist HS8 5RS (01870 620238; www.snh.org.uk)
There are six two-week work parties of eleven are available on St Kilda, leaving from Oban and running from mid-May to August; accommodation is provided (St Kilda Work Parties 01463 232034). Camping is also available, but only for a maximum of six people

FURTHER INFORMATION

There is a museum and a shop which opens by arrangement, but there are no public toilets on St Kilda
The diving around St Kilda is exceptional
No pets or animals should be taken onto the islands; nor should boats use the pier as mice or rats might get ashore: dinghies should be used for ferrying – a full list of regulations is posted on the website
The anchorage at Village Bay is not sheltered from winds from the east

FURTHER READING

An Isle Called Hirte: A History and Culture of the St Kildans to 1930 (Harman, Mary)
Maclean Press, 1997
The Decline and Fall of St Kilda
Islands Book Trust, 2006
Island on the Edge of the World: the Story of St Kilda (Mclean, Charles)
Canongate, 2006
Life and Death of St Kilda (Steel, Tom)
HarperCollins, 1988
St Kilda Island Guide (Quine, David and Colin Baxter)
Colin Baxter Photography, 2000
St Kilda and the Wider World (Fleming, Andrew)
Windgather Press, 2005
St Kilda: a Journey to the End of the World (McCutcheon, Campbell)
Tempus, 2002
St Kilda: an Island on the Edge of the World (Maclean, Charles)
Canongate, 1996

ACKNOWLEDGMENTS

Thanks to Isla Robertson and the National Trust for Scotland for the permission to use the photos

INDEX

Acairseid Mhor 42, 43
Achadun Castle 111
Achamore 155, 156
Achmore 199
Achnacloich 14
Achnacroish 108, 110
Aiginis 198, 204
Ailsa Craig 191
Aird of Sleat 13
Alexander II 114
Alexander III 7
Allasdale 274
Am Baile (Vatersay) 277
Am Fraoch Eilean 143, 144
Amhuinnsuidhe Castle 219, 220
Annait 21
Ardalanish 80
Ardbeg 132
Ardfin 144
Ardhasaig 218, 219
Ardmhor 258, 266, 270, 273
Ardminish 155
Ardnastruban 256
Ardtreck Point 24
Ardvasar 7, 13
Arinagour 61, 62
Arivruaich 204, 219
Armadale 7, 13, 14
Armadale Castle 13, 14, 36
Arnol 201
Aros Castle (Jura) 143, 145
Aros Castle (Mull) 77, 81
Arran 173-186
Ascog 162
Ascog House 160
Askernish 260

Bac Mor 105
Bachuil 111
Back 198
Bagh na h-Uamha 49
Baile Mor 95, 96
Balagas 256
Balallan 203

Balamory 76, 82
Balemartine 69
Balephetrish 70
Balephuil 69
Baleshare 237, 241, 248
Balgown 17
Balivanich 251, 252
Ballachuan 116, 118
Ballantrushal 202
Balliemore 113
Ballikillet 169, 170
Ballygown 84
Ballygrant 133
Balranald 239
Balvicar 116, 117, 118, 124, 125
Bannatyne family 160, 164
Barnhill 143
Barpa Langass 237
Barr, St 271
Barra 277, 278, 280, 281
Barra Head 281
Barraglom 213, 214
Barrapol 69
Barrie, J. M. 220
Barvas 201, 202
Bayhead 235, 239
Baymore 256
Bearasay 213
Beaton clan 79
Belnahua 124, 125
Benbecula 250-255, 260
Bernera (Lismore) 111
Berneray 20, 220, 234, 240, 245-247, 280
Berneray (Mingulay) 281
Bishop's Isles 281
Black Cuillin see Cuillin hills
Blackwaterfoot 178
Blaise, St 178
Blane, St 160, 163, 188
Bloody Bay, battle of 77, 82

Bonnie Prince Charlie 8, 10, 11, 13, 16, 18, 19, 39, 229, 251, 252, 260, 266, 271
Book of Kells 95
Boreray (Harris) 223
Boreray (St Kilda) 283
Borline 24
Borreraig 23
Borve (Barra) 274
Borve (Berneray) 246
Borve (Harris) 220
Borve (Skye) 16
Borve Castle 251, 252, 253
Bosta 214
Boswell, James 10, 39, 41, 62, 63, 86, 102
Bousd 62
Bowmore 133
Boyd earls of Kilmarnock 175
Boyle earls of Glasgow 169
Bracadale 6, 23
Braes 12
Braes, battle of the 10, 12
Bragar 201
Breachacha Castle 62, 63
Breaclete 213, 214
Breasclete 200
Brendan, St 124, 271
Brevig 273
Bridge across the Atlantic (Great Bernera) 205
Bridge over the Atlantic (Seil) 116, 117
bridge to nowhere 196, 198, 203
Bridgend 133
Broadford 6, 11
Brochel Castle 39, 40
Brodick 175, 177

Brodick Castle 175, 176, 186
Brolass 79
Brue 201
Bruichladdich 134
Bullough family 50
Bunavoneadar 219, 220
Bunessan 79
Bunnahabhain 134
Burg 85
Burke, Betty see Bonnie Prince Charlie
Bute 159-167, 188
Butt of Lewis 195, 203

Cairn na Burg Beg 105
Cairn na Burg Mor 105
Caisteal Bheagram 262
Caisteal Calvay 260
Caisteal Chamuis 8, 14
Caisteal Coeffin 110
Caisteal Maol 8, 10, 15
Caisteal Uisdein 8, 16, 17
Calgary 83, 84
Callanish 199, 200
Campbell clan 68, 78, 81, 96, 109, 110, 115, 123, 130, 131, 135, 143, 145, 149
Campbell, John Lorne 59
Canna 57-59
Caol Isla 134
Caolas (Tiree) 70
Caolis (Vatersay) 278
Cara 154, 156, 157
Carbost (Loch Harport) 6, 24
Carbost (Portree) 19
Carinish 235, 237, 238
Carloway 201
Carnan 263
Carsaig 79, 86

Castle Loch Heylipol 68
Castle Sinclair 274
Castlebay 66, 258, 270, 272
Catacol 180
Ceann Ear 241
Ceann Iar 241
Charles Edward Stewart see Bonnie Prince Charlie
Cille Bharra 271, 272, 274
Clachan (Lismore) 108, 110
Clachan (North Uist) 235, 237
Clachan (Raasay) 38, 40
Clachan (Seil) 116, 117
Claddach Kirkibost 239
Claig Castle 143, 144
Clanranald 49, 53, 56, 59, 131, 252, 253, 260, 261, 262, 266
Claonaig 173, 180
Cleadale 53
Clearances and land raids 10, 39, 43, 68, 77, 109, 131, 213, 236, 251, 260, 267, 272, 278
Cliad 62
Coilleag a' Phrionnsa 267
Colbost 6, 23
Colintraive 159
Coll 60-65
Coll (Lewis) 203
Colonsay 148-153
Colonsay House 149, 150, 153
Columba, St 7, 14, 17, 58, 95, 96, 97, 98, 109, 149
Committee Road 241
Congan, St 14
Cormac, St 145
Coroghon Castle 58
Corrie (Arran) 181

Corriecravie 178
Corryvreckan 118, 125, 143, 144
Craighouse (Jura) 143, 144
Craigmore 162
Craignure 75, 77, 78
Creagorry 251, 252
Croig 83, 103, 105
Croir 213
Crossapol (Tiree) 69
Crowlin Islands 25
Crowlista 205
Cuillin hills 5, 6, 12, 14, 15, 24
Cullipool 117, 122, 123
Culnaknock 19
Cultoon 135
Cumbrae 168-171

Dalbeg 201
Daliburgh 258, 260
Dervaig 83
Donan, St 53
Drambuie 9
Drinishader 221
Drumadoon 178
Drynoch 23
Duart Castle 77, 78, 92
Duich Moss 133
Duisdale 15
Dun 283
Dun an Sticer 17, 235, 240
Dun Ara 82
Dun Ban 102
Dun Beag 22
Dun Bharpa 274
Dun Carloway 200
Dun Channa 58
Dun Mhic Leod 274
Dun Mor 67, 70
Dun Sgathaich 8
Dunagoil 163
Dunakin see Caisteal Maol
Duncan, King of Scots 96
Duntulm Castle 8, 17, 18, 241
Dunvegan 6, 8, 20, 218, 246, 284

Dunvegan Castle 8, 20, 21, 37, 221
Dunyvaig Castle 131
Dutchman's Cap 105

Easdale 117, 118, 120-121
Edinbane 6, 19, 20
Eigg 52-54
Eileach an Naoimh 124
Eilean Iarmain See Isleornsay
Eilean More 145
Elgol 7, 16
Elishader 19
Ellanabeich 116, 117, 118, 120, 125
Ensay 223
Eochar 259, 262
Eoligarry 271, 272, 274
Eoligarry House 273, 274
Eorisdale 278
Eoropie 202
Eorsa 84
Eriskay 263, 266-268, 270, 272
Erraid 100
Ettrick Bay 163
Eye Peninsula 195, 196, 204
Eynort 24
Eyre 16

Fairlie family 160
Fairy Bridge 20
Fairy Flag 8, 20, 21
Feolin Ferry 142, 144
Fiaray 271
Fife Adventurers 197
Fingal's Cave 103
Finlaggan 130, 134, 140
Finsbay 221
Fintray Bay 169
Fionnphort 80, 94, 103, 105
Fishnish 74, 80
Fladda (Luing) 125
Fladda (Treshnish) 105

Flannan Isles 206
Flodday (Barra) 271
Floddaybeg 256
Floddaymore 256
Flodigarry 9, 18
Fuaiy 271
Fuday 271

Gallanach (Kerrera ferry) 113
Gallanach (Muck) 55
Galmisdale 53
Galson 202
Garbh Eileach 124
Garenin 201
Garrynamonie 263
Garvellach Isles 124
Garynahine 199, 205
Giants Causeway 103
Gigha 154-157
Gighay (Barra) 271
Girvan 191
Gisla 205
Glackindaline Castle 102
Glaid Stone 170
Glasnakille 16
Glass family 160
Glen Brittle 6, 8, 24
Glen Garrisdale 143, 145
Glen More 75, 76, 79
Glendale 6, 10, 23
Glenegedale 133
Glengorm Castle 82
Goatfell 174, 176
Golden Road 221
Gometra 101, 102
Gordons of Cluny 251, 260, 267, 272, 278
Gorm Castle 135
Gott 70
Graham family 160
Gramsdale 252
Grange, Rachel Lady 22, 241, 284
Gravir 204
Great Bernera 197, 205, 213-215
Great Cumbrae 168
Gribun 84
Griminish 251, 253

Grimsay 256
Grishipoll 62
Gruline 84
Gunna 64
Gunnery of MacLeod 246
Gylen Castle 114, 115

Hacklet (Benbecula) 253
Hacklete (Great Bernera) 213
Hakon, King of Norway 7, 10, 114, 155, 161, 169, 175, 188
Hallaig 39, 40
Hallin 21
Hamilton earls of Arran 175, 176, 177, 178
Harrapool 11
Harris 8, 217-227
Heisker 241
Hellisay 271
Heylipol 69
Hirta 282-285
Holm Point 198, 204
Holy Island 177, 187-188
Horgabost 220, 230
Hough 69
Hougharry 239
Howmore 259, 260, 261, 262
Hunter family 170
Hushinish 220, 222
Hynish 68, 69

Idrigill Point 22
Ile 129, 132
Illeray 248
Inch Kenneth 84, 86
Inchmarnock 164
Insh Island 121
Inverarish 38, 39, 40
Iona 76, 94-99
Iona Abbey 55, 59, 95, 96, 97, 99, 102
Islay 128-140
Islay House 133
Isle Martin 44
Isle Ristol 45
Isleornsay 7, 15

James IV 130, 180
James V 12, 18, 161
Jamieson family 160
Johnson, Dr Samuel 10, 39, 56, 62, 63, 85, 86, 102
Jura 142-147

Kallin 256
Kames Castle 160, 164
Keills 134
Kelspoke 162
Kennacraig 128, 148
Kennedy family 191
Kenovay 70
Kensaleyre 16
Kerrera 113-115
Kerrycroy 162
Kershader 204
Kidnapped 100
Kilbrandon 116, 118
Kilbride (Arran) 177
Kilbride (Islay) 131
Kilbride (Skye) 15
Kilchattan (Gigha) 155
Kilchattan (Luing) 124
Kilchattan (Oronsay) 150
Kilchattan Bay 162
Kilcheran 108, 109
Kilchiaran 135
Kilchoan 74, 82
Kilchoman 136
Kildalton Cross 132
Kildonan (Arran) 175, 178
Kildonan (South Uist) 258, 261
Kildonnan (Eigg) 53
Kilearnadil 144
Kilkenneth 69
Killiegray 223
Killunaig 62
Kilmaluag 39, 40
Kilmarie (Skye) 15
Kilmore (Skye) 14
Kilmory (Arran) 178
Kilmory (Rum) 49
Kilmuir (Skye) 9, 10, 17, 18
Kilnave 135

Kilninian 84
Kiloran 149, 150, 151
Kilphedder (North Uist) 239
Kilpheder (South Uist) 263
Kiltragleann see Portree
Kingarth 162
Kingsburgh 9, 16, 18
Kingscross Point 177
Kinloch (Rum) 49
Kinloch (Sleat) 15
Kinloch Castle 50, 51
Kirkapol (Tiree) 67, 70
Kirkibost (Great Bernera) 213
Kirkibost (island, North Uist) 248
Kissimul Castle 271, 272
Kneep 205
Kyle of Lochalsh 7
Kyleakin 7, 10
Kylerhea 7, 13

Lady's Rock 78
Lagavulin 131
Lamlash 175, 177, 187
Laphroaig 131
Largs 168
Laxay 203
Lealt 19
Lesser Cumbrae see Little Cumbrae
Leurbost 203
Leverburgh 218, 220, 234, 245
Leverhulme, Lord 198, 218, 219
Lewis 194-212
Lews Castle 197, 199
Lingay 271
Liniclate 251, 253
Linicro 17, 18
Lismore 108-112
Little Bernera 213
Little Colonsay 102
Little Cumbrae 168, 170
Livingstone, David 104

Loch an Sgoltaire 151
Loch Bee 258
Loch Bhasapoll 67, 69
Loch Druidibeg 258, 262
Loch Fad 163
Loch Frisa 76
Loch Gruinart 129, 135
Loch Roag 213
Loch Skipport 259
Loch Spelve 79
Lochaline 74, 80
Lochboisdale 258, 260, 270
Lochbuie 85
Lochcarnan 263
Lochdon 79
Locheport 235, 237
Lochmaddy 235, 236
Lochportain 235
Lochranza 180
Lochranza Castle 175, 180
Longay 24-25
Lords of the Isles 14, 62, 67, 76, 81, 96, 123, 130, 134, 152, 155, 157, 196, 218, 235, 246, 260, 271
Lower Gylen 114, 115
Luing 122-125
Lunga (Luing) 125
Lunga (Treshnish) 105
Luskentyre 220

Maaruig 219
MacArthur clan 18, 102
MacAskill, Angus 20, 37, 246
MacAskill clan 14

MacAulays of Uig 197, 200, 202, 205
Macbeth 96
MacCrimmon clan 20, 21, 23
MacDonald clan 8, 13, 14, 16, 18, 21, 49, 53, 56, 58, 59, 62, 67, 81, 96, 102, 105, 123, 130, 131, 132, 133, 134, 135, 143, 144, 149, 151, 152, 155, 157, 178, 190, 196, 218, 235, 236, 238, 241, 251, 252, 253, 260, 266
MacDonald, Flora 8, 9, 10, 13, 15, 16, 18, 252, 258, 260, 261
MacDougall clan 62, 81, 105, 109, 110, 114, 115, 117, 123, 124, 130
MacDuffie clan 149, 151
MacEwen family 56
MacGregor, James Dean of Lismore 110
Machrie Moor 179
MacIan clan 131
Mackenzie, Compton 232, 272, 274
Mackenzies of Kintail 197, 213, 260, 267
MacKinlay clan 160, 164
MacKinnon clan 8, 9, 10, 15, 24, 25, 82
Mackinnon's Cave (Mull) 84
MacLaine clan 77, 79, 85, 86, 105
MacLean clan 18, 49, 55, 59, 62, 63, 68, 77, 78, 79, 81, 85, 86, 96, 105, 123, 124, 126, 130, 135, 143, 145, 155, 239
MacLean, Sorley 39
MacLeod clan 8, 14, 18, 20, 21, 22, 25, 39, 40, 43, 53, 54, 196, 197, 204, 213, 218,

221, 222, 223, 231, 238, 246, 260, 284
MacLeod's Maidens 22
MacLeod's Tables 6, 22
MacNeil clan 149, 152, 155, 156, 260, 266, 271, 272, 273, 274, 278, 281
MacNicol clan 19, 196, 197
MacPhee clan 149
Macquarie, Lachlan 84, 101
Macquarie Mausoleum 84
MacQuarrie clan 101, 102, 104
Maelrubha, St 7, 11
Magnus Barelegs 67, 76, 175, 190
Malcolm IV 130
Mallaig 48, 52, 55, 57
Margaret, St 96
Marion of the Heads 273, 278
Marnock, St 164
Martin, Martin 223
Matheson, Sir James 197, 198
Maxwell, Gavin 11, 25
Meikle Kilmory 160, 163
Melbost 204
Mendelssohn, Felix 104
Miavaig 205
Millport 168, 169
Milton 258, 261
Mingulay 278, 280-281
Molaise, St 188
Moluag, St 7, 109
Monach Islands see Heisker
Monkstadt 9, 18
Montgomery family 169, 170, 180
Morrisons of Ness 197, 200, 202, 231
Mount Stuart House 162, 166
Moy Castle 77, 85

Muck 55-56
Mull 74-93
Murray earls of Dunmore 219, 220

Nerabus 135
Ness 196, 202, 203
Newtonferry 240, 241
Nicolson see MacNicol
North Cuan 116, 118, 122
North Harris 219
North Tolsta 203
North Uist 220-227
Northbay 270, 273
Northton 218, 220
Nunton 251, 252, 261

Oa, The 132, 133
Oban 60, 66, 74, 108, 148, 258
Old Man of Storr 5, 19
Oran, St 97, 149, 151, 152
Orbost 22
Ormiclate Castle 252, 261
Oronsay 148-153
Oronsay Priory 152
Orosay (Barra) 271
Orsay (Islay) 131
Orwell, George 125, 143
Oskaig 38, 40

Pabay (Skye) 25
Pabbay (Harris) 222-223
Pabbay (Vatersay) 278
Paps of Jura 142
Park 195, 197, 204
Park Deer Raid 198
Peinduin 16
Pennycross 79
Pennyghael 79
Pennygown 80
Peter's Port 253
Picts 7, 19, 21, 40, 251, 259, 279
Pladda 178
Plocrapool 220, 221

Pobull Fhinn 237
Point 195, 196
Pollachar 258, 263
Port Appin 108
Port Askaig 134, 142, 148
Port Bannatyne 164
Port Charlotte 135
Port Ellen 131
Port Mor 55
Port of Ness 202
Port Ramsay 108, 109, 111
Port Wemyss 135
Portnahaven 135
Portnalong 24
Portree 6, 12, 13, 42
Prince's Cave 260

Quiraing 5, 17, 18

Raasay 8, 38-41
Raasay House 39, 40, 41
Red Cuillin see Cuillin hills
Rhenigidale 219
Rhinns of Islay 130
Rhubodach 164
Roag 2
Robert I see Robert the Bruce
Robert II 161
Robert III 161, 170
Robert the Bruce 175, 176, 177, 179, 180, 190
Rodel 21, 218, 219, 220
Rona 42-43
Rona (North Rona) 206
Ronan, St 203, 206
Ronay 256
Ross of Mull 79
Ross Road 174, 181
Rothesay 159, 160, 161, 162
Rothesay Castle 160, 161, 167
Rubh' an Dunain 24
Ruisgarry 246
Rum 8, 48-51

Salen 80
Sanda 189-190
Sandaig 69
Sandavore 53
Sanday (Canna) 57-59
Sandray (Vatersay) 278
Sandwick 204
Sannox 180
Saucy Mary 10, 12, 15
Scalasaig 149, 150
Scalpay 219, 228-229
Scalpay (Skye) 8, 12, 24
Scarba 125
Scarinish 67, 68
Scarista 220
Scarp 219, 220, 222
Sconser 6, 12, 38
Scotasay 228
Scott, Sir Walter 102, 104
Seil 116-119, 122
Shader 202
Shawbost 201
Sheriffmuir, Battle of 260, 261
Shiant Isles 232
Shillay 223
Shiskine 178, 181, 188
Shivinish 241
Shuna 124, 126
Sidinish 237
Skeabost 19
Skerryvore Lighthouse 68, 69
Skye 2, 3, 4-37
Slate Islands 116, 117, 120, 123
Sleat 5, 13
Sligachan 12, 23
Snizort 19
Soay (Skye) 25
Soay (St Kilda) 283
Sollas 235, 236, 239
Somerled 96, 130, 143, 175
Sorisdale 62
Sorobaidh 69
South Harris 219
South Uist 258-265
Spence family 160, 164
Sponish 236

SS Politician 267, 272
St Blane's Church (Bute) 162, 163
St Clement's Church, Rodel 220
St Kilda 8, 282-285
St Moluag's Church, Eoropie 202
Stack Islands 266
Staffa 103-104
Staffin 19
Stein 21
Stevenson, Robert Louis 100, 104
Stewart, Charles Edward see Bonnie Prince Charlie
Stewarts of Appin 109, 110
Stewarts of Glenbuchie 63
Stewarts of Glenbuckie 62
Stewarts of Menteith 175
Stinky Bay 253
Stornoway 195, 196, 197, 198, 199
Storr 5
Strathaird 9, 15
Strathcona, Lords 150
String Road 174, 181
Stronach 176
Struan 6, 23
Stuarts of Bute 160, 161, 162, 169
Suisnish 38, 39
Sula Sgeir 206
Suladale 19
Summer Isles 45-46

Talisker Bay 24
Tanera Beag 45
Tanera Mor 45, 46
Taransay 220, 230-231
Tarbert (Gigha) 156, 157
Tarbert (Harris) 218, 219
Tarbert (Jura) 145
Tarskavaig 14
Taylinloan 154

Teampull na Trionaid 235, 237
Teangue 14
Texa 131
Tigh Iseabel Dhaidh 110
Timsgarry 205
Tiree 66-72
Tirefour Castle 111
Tiumpan Head 195
Tobermory 74, 75, 76, 82
Toberonochy 117, 122, 124
Tobson 213
Tokavaig 14
Tormont End 169
Tormore 179
Torosay Castle 78, 93
Torran (Raasay) 41
Torrin (Skye) 15
Torrylinn 178
Torsa 124
Totronald 61, 63, 64
Townhead 162
Traigh Gruinart, Battle of 79, 130, 131, 135
Traigh Mhor (Barra) 273
Treaty of Westminster-Ardtornish, 1461 130
Treshnish Isles 86, 105-106
Trotternish 5, 8, 16, 17
Trumpan 8, 21, 22, 54, 284
Tunga 203

Uidh 277
Uig (Lewis) 205
Uig (Skye) 6, 17, 217, 234
Uinessan 278
Uisken 80
Uiskevagh 253
Ullapool 194, 195
Ullinish 22
Ulva 101-102
Ulva Ferry 84, 101, 103, 105
Upper Killeyan Farm 129, 132

Urgha 219

Vallay 239
Valtos 205
Vatersay 267, 271, 274, 277-279, 279, 281
Vey, St 170

Waterloo 11
Waternish 6, 21
Waterstein 6, 23
Weaver's Castle 266
Wee Cumbrae see Little Cumbrae
Wemyss Bay 159
West Loch Tarbert 219
Wester Kames Castle 160, 164
Whisky Galore 267, 274
Whisky Galore! 267, 272
Whiting Bay 177
Wiay (Benbecula) 253
Wiay (Skye) 22